ENGLISH FUNDAMENTALS

Why Do You Need This New Edition?

If you're wondering why you should buy this new edition of *English Fundamentals*, here are 10 good reasons!

❶ **A proven history** - After more than eight decades of offering strong, lucid explanations, the newest edition of *English Fundamentals* has truly reinvented itself to provide you with the skills necessary to master the principles of quality writing.

❷ **Over 100 pages of new material** moves the learning from passive recognition to active production, enabling you to enhance your writing skills in a proactive way.

❸ **A new Lesson 28** provides step-by-step instruction and extensive practice in changing sentence structures to provide variety in recognizing and correcting errors.

❹ **A combined Lesson 26** deals with puzzling word choices and homonyms, emphasizing the importance of precise word choices so that you can make your writing more effective.

❺ **Twenty-one new paragraph writing assignments** close lessons with active composition assignments that have you creating your own paragraph structures as a review of the lesson itself.

❻ **A new emphasis** on careers and getting the most out of your writing skills to gain a better footing in the workplace is included in the introduction.

❼ **New** material on noun and adjective phrases has been included, enabling you to gain a better understanding of these topics that students typically struggle with.

❽ **New** Practice Sheets, Exercises, Diagnostic Tests, and Progress Tests offer ample opportunities for practice and review.

❾ **New** material on quotations and inserting quotations into a paper is included so you can use sources properly and avoid plagiarising.

❿ And now—use *English Fundamentals* alongside Pearson's unique **MyWritingLab** (www.mywritinglab.com) and find a world of resources developed specifically with you in mind!

English Fundamentals

Fifteenth Edition

Donald W. Emery
Late of The University of Washington

John M. Kierzek
Late of Oregon State University

Peter Lindblom
Miami-Dade College

New York San Francisco Boston
London Toronto Sydney Tokyo Singapore Madrid
Mexico City Munich Paris Cape Town Hong Kong Montreal

Acquisitions Editor: Matthew Wright
Senior Marketing Manager: Thomas DeMarco
Senior Supplements Editor: Donna Campion
Production Manager: Ellen MacElree
Project Coordination, Text Design, and Electronic Page Makeup: Electronic Publishing Services
Inc., NYC
Cover Designer/Manager: John Callahan
Cover image courtesy of iStock Photo
Senior Manufacturing Buyer: Dennis J. Para
Printer and Binder: Courier/Stoughton
Cover Printer: Courier/Stoughton

Library of Congress Cataloging-in-Publication Data

Emery, Donald W. (Donald William), 1906–
    English fundamentals / Donald W. Emery, John M. Kierzek, Peter Lindblom.—15th ed.
        p. cm
    Includes index.
    ISBN 978-0-205-61781-4
    0-205-61781-6
    1. English language—Grammar—Problems, exercises, etc. 2. English language—Rhetoric—
Problems, exercises, etc. 3. Report writing—Problems, exercises, etc. I. Kierzek, John M.,
1891– II. Lindblom, Peter D., 1938– III. Title.

PE1112.E47 2008
428.2—dc22

2008019454

Please visit us at http://www.ablongman.com

ISBN 13: 978-0-205-61781-4
ISBN 10:   0-205-61781-6

2 3 4 5 6 7 8 9 10—10 09 08 07

Contents

Preface

English Fundamentals, appearing now in its fifteenth edition, marks the eighth decade of the book's service to students and teachers of English, particularly students and teachers who focus their efforts on improving writing skills.

Because the book has been around for several decades, there naturally arises a slightly skeptical question:

Should we, in this age of electronic communication, when we reach out to other people by text-messaging and e-mail as our primary methods of written communication, study a traditional and rather technical analysis of the English language?

The answer to that question depends on the definition of the words "other people." If by "other people" we mean friends and acquaintances, if by "other people" we mean family—parents, brothers, sisters, and assorted relatives—the answer to the question "should we?" is probably simple: There really isn't much of a justification for learning so technical a subject as is taken up in *English Fundamentals*.

We get along just fine with smiley-face emoticons and abbreviations such as *LOL*. We have developed a separate, shorthand version of English for use with these devices. And for those devices and the "other people" we connect with by using them, that new version of the language seems to work rather well.

If, on the other hand, the "other people" are college professors, if the "other people" are law and medical school professors, if the "other people" are managers and executives in that first job after finishing that final degree, the answer to that question, "Should we?" is a straightforward, unequivocal

YES, NOW, MORE THAN EVER

Smiley faces and other emoticons, shorthand abbreviations, and all the other tricks we employ in e-communication are simply not suited for, and simply not effective enough for, formal written communication in colleges, professional schools, and the businesses and professions we hope to enter.

Communicating effectively, forcefully, and convincingly in such contexts requires a thorough knowledge, a mastery, a mental embedding, of all the aspects of that wonderful communication tool we call the English language.

Effective use of this tool requires mastery of everything necessary to put together a successful written communication:

- Sentence skills
- Process skills
- Essay skills
- Paragraph skills
- Correction skills

These skills, defined below, serve as the vital core of written communication:

- *Sentence Skills*   Mastering the wide array of sentence structures available in the language gives the writer the power to make a point in exactly the right way, a way that provides both precision and variety in the written piece. Mastery of this wide repertoire of structures allows the writer to avoid confusing or questionable structures that might be considered incorrect by a reader. Mastering the enormously rich vocabulary of English allows the writer to be explicit and precise in the presentation of ideas.

- *Process Skills*   Embedding the steps of the writing process provides the writer with the confidence that no writing assignment is too big a challenge, that every kind of written work can be done efficiently and without hesitation. Knowing the first step, the second, and all the rest to the completion of a project is the ultimate productivity enhancer.

- *Essay Skills*   Organizing and reorganizing a piece so that it goes together and flows in the best possible way is part of learning the writing process. The writer's ability, and willingness, to try different arrangements, to rework until the pattern of the essay produces the most effective and precise presentation, and creating successful introductions and conclusions is all part of what it takes to become a successful writer.

- *Paragraph Skills*   Recognizing and using the wide array of rhetorical forms of paragraphs, instructional process and comparison/contrast, for example, gives the writer an opportunity to fill out, to amplify, the presentation of each point by providing the reader with a wealth of detail and example. Recognizing paragraph forms, seeing that a paragraph is starting out to be, or should be developed as, for example, a comparison/contrast, offers the writer a chance to check the form of such a paragraph to be sure that every possible avenue for development has been explored.

- *Correction Skills*   Proofreading and correcting are the finishing touches of the writing process, the last step before the final draft is printed for submission. These final steps come easily to those who have diligently studied the materials in *English Fundamentals* because they have learned to construct essays, paragraphs, and sentences that are both effective and correct.

Some would say, "But I intend to be an engineer or an accountant; I will not need to use the language as much as I will need to use numbers." The heads of major accounting and engineering firms respond this way:

Yes, you need the accounting or the engineering skills, but you must be able to communicate to your client what the numbers tell you, or you will remain forever in the rear ranks of your profession.

So to those who wonder whether the materials taught here, the fundamentals of the English language, are vital survival skills, the answer rings loud and clear:

NOW, MORE THAN EVER

The irreplaceable foundations of the textbook are still present in the 15th edition of *English Fundamentals*.

- Step-by-step presentation of the structure and organization of the language.
- A continuum, a set of building blocks for the language that takes the student from the simplest, most basic concepts of subject–verb combinations to the production of entire essays.
- Two levels of drill work: Practice Sheets offer simple versions of the concepts taught in each lesson; these are keyed at the back of the book and can be used independently

by the students. Exercises offer more advanced, sophisticated work on the concepts to guarantee mastery of each element of the language.

- Practice Sheets and Exercises make references to science, business, history, and other fields so that every student can find some connection to the subject matter in the lessons.

- Check Sheets at the end of each group of lessons provide a concise overview of the principles taught in the section. Students may use these for review and for reference during writing assignments.

- A Test Bank of 30 additional exercises is available to teachers for use in the classroom; these exercises are keyed so that students can take a copy for independent review.

- Sentence-combining drills offer a different approach to the development of sentence skills and review the structures taught in the lessons. They may be used with the lessons or toward the end of the course to polish the skills of the students.

- Sequences and connections are a vital part of the presentation of the fundamentals of the language. The earliest lessons show how one word can change its form from adjective to adverb to noun. *Immediate* becomes *immediately* and becomes *immediacy*, illustrating the ways in which basic forms can change so that the words can be used for different purposes. In later lessons, compound sentences become complex sentences made up of a main clause and an adverbial clause, an illustration of the wide variety of sentence strategies available in the language.

New approaches and materials enhance the solid presentations that have always been present in the book.

- One entirely new lesson, Lesson 28, deals directly with proofreading and correcting. This chapter provides step-by-step instructions and extensive practice in the changing sentence structures to provide variety, in recognizing errors, and in correcting those errors. An intense focus on finding and correcting errors rounds out this new chapter.

- A combined lesson, Lesson 26, deals with Puzzling Word Choices and Homonyms, with emphasis on the importance of precise word choices as a necessity for effective writing.

- Newly constructed Practice Sheets, Exercises, Diagnostic Tests, and Progress Tests, 190 pages of material, offer ample opportunities for practice and review.

- One hundred and two pages of this new material move the students from passive recognition, a choice between two items, to active production, asking students to write correct forms, insert words, transform sentences from one structure into another, write entire sentences, and compose short paragraphs.

- Twenty-two one-paragraph writing assignments close out each lesson, beginning with Lesson 7, with an active composition assignment. These assignments ask the student to create short paragraphs, usually five or six sentences long, and they specify sentence structures taught in that lesson. These short assignments offer one more opportunity for students to create their own structures as a review of the lesson.

- Direct references follow each lesson to pertinent sections of MyWritingLab, Pearson Longman's newly designed Web site for online review and practice of the principles taught in the lessons of *English Fundamentals* (**www.MyWritingLab.com**).

THE TEACHING AND LEARNING PACKAGE
FOR *ENGLISH FUNDAMENTALS*

An Answer Key and Test Bank are available to adopters of English Fundamentals Fifteenth Edition. These components have been crafted to ensure that the course is a rewarding experience for both instructors and students. The Answer Key (0-205-61786-7) contains answers to all in-text questions. The Test Bank (0-205-61788-3) contains a wealth of additional quizzes, tests, and exercises—keyed to each lesson in the student text.

THE PEARSON DEVELOPMENTAL WRITING ANCILLARY PACKAGE

In addition to the book-specific supplements discussed above, Pearson offers a wealth of instructor and student ancillaries to complement *English Fundamentals*. Please visit our online catalog at www.pearsonhighered.com/devenglish or consult your local Pearson arts and sciences representative for options that best suit your interests.

Multimedia Offerings

Q: Do your students have trouble transferring skill and drill lessons into their own writing or seeing errors in others' writing? • Would you like constant awareness of your students' progress and work in an easy-to-use tracking system? • Would a mastery results reporter help you to plan your lectures according to your class' weaknesses? • Do you want to save time by having work automatically graded and feedback supplied?

MyWritingLab [www.mywritinglab.com] A prompt to use MyWritingLab is integrated into each lesson of *English Fundamentals*. MyWritingLab is a complete online learning system with *better* practice exercises to make students better writers. The exercises in MyWritingLab are progressive, which means within each skill module students move from literal comprehension to critical application to demonstrating their skills in their own writing. The 9,000-plus exercises in the system do rehearse grammar, but they also extend into the writing process, paragraph development, essay development, and research. A thorough diagnostic test outlines where students have not yet mastered the skill, and an easy-to-use tracking systems enables students and instructors to monitor all work in MyWritingLab. Visit www.mywritinglab.com for more details.

ACKNOWLEDGMENTS

Our thanks go to all those who offered advice and suggestions for improving this and previous editions: Edwin J. Blesch, Jr., Nassau Community College; Ladson W. Bright, Cape Fear Community College; James Vanden Bosch, Calvin College; Bernadine Brown, Nassau Community College; Alma G. Bryant, University of South Florida; Kitty Chen Dean, Nassau Community College; Patricia Derby, Chabot College; Robert DiChiara, Nassau Community College; Neil G. Dodd, East Los Angeles College; Loris D. Galford, McNeese State University; Gary Graupman, Taft College; Harold J. Herman, University of Maryland; William T. Hope, Jefferson Technical College; Sue D. Hopke, Broward Community College; Clifford J. Houston, East Los Angeles College; George L. Ives, North Idaho College; Edward F. James, University of Maryland; Thomas Mast, Montgomery College; Walter Mullen, Mississippi Gulf Coast Community College; Mary E. Owens, Montgomery College; Optimism One, Modesto Junior College; Jill Peacock, Santa Monica College; Deborah Pounders, Ouachita Baptist University; Dr. Jessica Rabin, Anne Arundel Community College; Crystal Reynolds, Indiana State University; Bill Sartoris, Camden College; Albert Schoenberg, East Los Angeles Community College; Ines Shaw, North Dakota State Unviersity; Holly Shi, Winona University; Barbara Stout, Montgomery College; Robert S. Sweazy, Vincennes University Junior College; Barbara Van Voorden, University of Missouri, St. Louis; and Larry Weirather, Clark College; Jay Curlin and the English faculty at Ouachita Baptist University.

Donald W. Emery

John M. Kierzek

Peter Lindblom

Basic Sentence Patterns

Lessons, Practice Sheets, and Exercises

Lesson 1 — *The Simple Sentence; Subjects and Verbs*

While you might find it difficult to produce a satisfying definition, you probably know that the sentence is a basic unit of written or oral expression. Thus, if you were asked, you might define a sentence as "an orderly arrangement of words that makes sense." If you wished to be more specific and more formal, you might say a sentence is "a self-contained grammatical unit, usually containing a subject and a verb, that conveys a meaningful statement, question, command, or exclamation."

You need to understand the basic construction of the sentence in order to write and speak effectively and correctly. In the first few lessons of this book, you'll examine the parts that make up a sentence and the distinctive characteristics of a few types of sentences that serve as the basic structures of more complicated units.

To begin, be sure you can recognize the two indispensable parts of a sentence:

1. The **subject**: the unit about which something is said.

2. The **predicate**: the unit that says something about the subject.

Although the predicate usually includes other modifying words and phrases, the indispensable part of a predicate is the verb, the word (or words) that says what the subject does or is. Here are a few things to remember about the subject-verb relationship:

1. In a sentence that reports a specific action, the verb is easily recognized. For instance, to find the subject and verb in *The rusty bumper on the front of my truck rattles noisily*, ask the question "What happens?" The answer, *rattles*, gives the verb. Then, by asking the question, "Who or what rattles?", you will find the subject, *bumper*. Notice that neither "front rattles" nor "truck rattles" makes the basic statement of the sentence.

2. Some sentences do not report an action. Instead, the sentence says something about the *condition* of the subject. It points out a descriptive quality of the subject or says that something else resembles or is the same thing as the subject. In this kind of sentence, you must look for verbs like *is, are, was, were, seem,* and *become*. Such verbs are often called *describing (linking) verbs*. These verbs serve as connectors; they join the subject to something that is said about the subject. They are words that are almost impossible to define because they lack the concrete exactness and action of verbs like *rattle, throw, smash,* and *explode*.

In a sentence using a describing verb, the subject usually reveals itself easily. For example, in the sentence "The long first chapter seemed particularly difficult," the verb is

1

seemed. The question "Who or what seemed?" provides the subject, *chapter*. The other possible choices—*long, first, particularly,* and *difficult*—do not make sense as answers to the question "Who or what seemed?"

3. Very often, the subject of a sentence has material between it and its verb:

> The *price* of potatoes *is* high. [The subject is *price,* not *potatoes.*]
> *Each* of my sisters *is* tall. [The subject is *each,* not *sisters.*]
> Only *one* of these watches *works.* [The subject is *one,* not *watches.*]

4. Most modern English sentences place the subject before the verb, but in some sentences, the verb precedes the subject:

> Behind the house *stood* [verb] an old *mill* [subject].
> Under the table *sat* [verb] a large *cat* [subject].

A very common type of sentence with the verb–subject arrangement uses *here* or *there* preceding the verb:

> There *are* [verb] three willow *trees* [subject] in our yard.
> Here *is* [verb] the *list* [subject] of candidates.

5. Casual, informal language often combines short verbs and subjects with apostrophes representing the omitted letters:

> I'm (I am)   It's (It is)   You've (You have)   They're (They are)

For your first practice work, you'll be using only a single subject for each sentence. Within this limitation, the subject is always a noun or a pronoun. Before the first practice, it would be wise to review a few facts about nouns, pronouns, and verbs so that you can recognize them easily.

NOUNS

A **noun** is a word that names something, such as a person, place, thing, quality, or idea. If the noun names just any member of a group or class, it is called a *common noun* and is not capitalized:

man, city, school, relative

A noun is a *proper noun* and is capitalized if it refers to a particular individual in a group or class:

Albert Lawson, Toledo, Horace Mann Junior High School, Aunt Louise

Most nouns have two forms; they show whether the noun is naming one thing (singular number) or more than one thing (plural number, which adds *s* or *es* to the singular): one *coat,* two *coats;* a *lunch,* several *lunches.* Proper nouns are rarely pluralized, and some common nouns have no plural form—for example, *honesty, courage, ease,* and *hardness.* (Lesson 27 examines in detail the special spelling problems of plural nouns.)

Nouns often follow *the*, *a*, or *an*, words that are called **articles**. A descriptive word (an adjective) may come between the article and the noun, but the word that answers the question "What?" after an article is a noun:

Article	$\left(\begin{array}{c}\textit{optional}\\\textit{adjective}\end{array}\right)$	noun
A (or The)	happy	girl.

Another way to identify nouns is to recognize certain suffixes. A **suffix** is a unit added to the end of a word or to the base of a word (see Supplement 1).* Here are some of the common suffixes found in hundreds of nouns:

age [break*age*]; ance, ence [resist*ance*, insist*ence*]; dom [king*dom*]; hood [child*hood*]; ion [prevent*ion*]; ism [national*ism*]; ment [move*ment*]; ness [firm*ness*]; or, er [invest*or*, los*er*]; ure [expos*ure*]

PRONOUNS

A **pronoun** is a word that substitutes for a noun. There are several classes of pronouns. (See Supplement 2.) The following classes can function as subjects in the basic sentences that you will examine in these early lessons:

Personal pronouns substitute for definite persons or things: *I, you, he, she, it, we, they.*

Demonstrative pronouns substitute for things being pointed out: *this, that, these, those.*

Indefinite pronouns substitute for unknown or unspecified things: *each, either, neither, one, anyone, somebody, everything, all, few, many,* and so on.

Possessive pronouns substitute for things that are possessed: *mine, yours, his, hers, its, ours, theirs.*

VERBS

A **verb** is a word that expresses action, existence, or occurrence by combining with a subject to make a statement, to ask a question, or to give a command. One easy way to identify a word as a verb is to use the following test:

Let's _____
      (action word)

Any word that will complete the command is a verb: "Let's *leave*." "Let's *buy* some popcorn." "Let's *be* quiet." This test works only with the basic present form of the verb, not with forms that have endings added to them or that show action taking place in the past: "Let's *paint* the car" (not "Let's *painted* the car").

*In some lessons of this book, you will find notations referring you to a supplement that appears at the end of the lesson. Read the supplement *after* you have thoroughly studied the lesson. The lesson contains the essential information that is vital to your understanding of subsequent lessons and exercises. The supplement presents material that has relevance to some points of the lesson. The supplements at the end of this lesson are found on page 4.

SUPPLEMENT 1

Hundreds of nouns have distinctive suffix endings. The definitions of some of these suffixes are rather difficult to formulate, but you can quite readily figure out the meanings of most of them: *ness*, for instance, means "quality or state of" (thus *firmness* means "the state or quality of being firm"); *or* and *er* show the agent or doer of something (an *investor* is "one who invests").

A unit added to the beginning of a word is called a **prefix**. Thus, to the adjective *kind*, we add a prefix to derive another adjective, *unkind*, and a suffix to derive the nouns *kindness* and *unkindness*. An awareness of how prefixes and suffixes are used will do far more than aid you in your ability to recognize parts of speech: Your spelling will improve and your vocabulary will expand.

SUPPLEMENT 2

Two classes of pronouns, the **interrogative** and the **relative**, are not listed here. Because they are used in questions and subordinate clauses but not in simple basic sentences, they will not be discussed until later lessons.

Another type of pronoun that you use regularly (but not as a true subject) is the **intensive** or **reflexive** pronoun, the "self" words used to add emphasis:

You *yourself* made the decision.

These pronouns also name the receiver of an action when the doer is the same as the receiver:

The boy fell and hurt *himself.*

The first example is the intensive use; the second is the reflexive. Pronouns used this way are *myself, yourself, himself* (not *hisself*), *herself, itself, ourselves, yourselves,* and *themselves* (not *themself, theirself,* or *theirselves*).

The "self" pronouns are properly used for these two purposes only. They should not be substituted for regular personal pronouns:

Mary and I [not *myself*] were invited to the dance.
Tom visited Eric and me [not *myself*] at our ranch.

A fourth type of pronoun is the **reciprocal pronoun**, which denotes a mutual relationship—for example, *one another, each other:*

We try to help *each other* with our homework.

English Fundamentals Online

After you have completed Practice Sheets and Exercises in this lesson, you can find additional help and drill work at **MyWritingLab.com**, in the section on Subjects and Verbs.

Subjects and Verbs

NAME _____   SCORE _____

Directions: In the space at the left, copy the word that is the verb of the italicized subject.

_____ 1. The *woman* drove her car into the lot.

_____ 2. *She* parked the car in the last space in the last row.

_____ 3. The *car* was a beautiful silver color.

_____ 4. The *color* of the car matched the color of the clouds.

_____ 5. The *clouds* filled the sky in the west late in the afternoon.

_____ 6. Two *people* were late for class yesterday.

_____ 7. The *instructor* arrived a little late also.

_____ 8. The *arrival* of that package created great excitement at home.

_____ 9. The *package* came late yesterday afternoon.

_____ 10. The *company* packaged the CDs in jewel cases.

_____ 11. Inside the package lay an *invoice* for the CDs.

_____ 12. *Sam* opened the package with the CDs inside.

_____ 13. The *CDs* featured two new singers.

_____ 14. *Sam* played the CDs in his car that afternoon.

_____ 15. The *CD player* in Sam's car is part of a very powerful stereo
system.

_____ 16. Later, *Sam* ripped the CDs into his computer.

_____ 17. Then *he* made copies of the CDs for his friends.

_____ 18. Last, *he* copied the CDs to his iPod.

_____ 19. Thus, the *music* became available to Sam all the time.

_____ 20. *Sam* thoroughly enjoys the music on the new CDs.

5

Directions: In the space at the left, copy the word that is the subject of the italicized verb.

_____ 1. One of the people in the office *lives* in a nearby apartment.

_____ 2. The lives of those birds *interest* certain scientists.

_____ 3. Some of those birds *have* nests near the office.

_____ 4. Some books on that shelf *deal* with the study of birds.

_____ 5. A deal for the purchase of that company *happened* today.

_____ 6. Two wealthy people from Texas *purchased* that company.

_____ 7. The wealth of those two people *is* immense.

_____ 8. Two of the women in that room *are* owners of new cars.

_____ 9. Those women *own* two beautiful new cars.

_____ 10. I *purchased* my own car three years ago.

_____ 11. All of us students *studied* hard for the final exam.

_____ 12. The detectives *examined* the evidence very thoroughly.

_____ 13. No one *detected* the loss of that painting until yesterday.

_____ 14. The painter often *works* in watercolors.

_____ 15. The maintenance crew *painted* the hallway last night.

_____ 16. The team *maintained* its confidence in spite of those early losses.

_____ 17. Maintenance work *occurs* every night in this building.

_____ 18. The occurrence of snowstorms *is* highest in these mountains in February.

_____ 19. The man *stormed* from the room at the end of the speech.

_____ 20. The speaker *ended* his speech with a very bad joke.

NAME _____ SCORE _____

Directions: In the first space at the left, copy the subject of the sentence. In the second space, copy the verb.

_____   1. Years ago, the site of that football field served as a landfill.

_____

_____   2. At the edge of the park sits a small picnic table.

_____

_____   3. Families often picnic there before football games.

_____

_____   4. The President fielded several difficult questions at the press
conference.

_____   5. We conferred with a group of experts on that subject.

_____

_____   6. Our managers wanted all the available information on that
problem.

_____   7. The people in our management group discovered several possible
solutions to that problem.

_____   8. Apparently, there are several possibilities open to us at this time.

_____

_____   9. The experts opened the meeting with a short slide presentation.

_____

_____   10. The quarterback slid to a stop at the end of his run.

_____

_____   11. The cross-country team members often run down to the river
and back during their workout.

_____   12. Marge often remembers the discovery of the raccoon in the attic of
their house.

_____   13. The raccoon frightened everyone in the family by making loud
noises in the middle of the night.

_____   14. That fright kept everyone on edge for several nights.

_____   15. Finally, the animal moved out of the attic into the woods near
the house.

_____   16. The final inspection of our new house occurred yesterday.

_____   17. The inspector made a thorough examination of the house.

_____

_____   18. She examined the roof and the basement with special care.

_____

_____ 19. My father especially appreciated the careful work of the inspector.

_____
_____ 20. The appreciation in the value of the house last year was about
_____   10 percent.

_____ 21. At the edge of the crowd in the back of the room sat a young
_____   woman with a guitar in her hands.

_____ 22. She picked the guitar with her left hand.

_____
_____ 23. The postal carrier handed a fat envelope to the secretary at the
_____   front desk.

_____ 24. A cloud of fog enveloped the road and the nearby fields down
_____   in the valley.

_____ 25. The driver backed the truck down the driveway and into
_____   the backyard.

_____ 26. The two men carried the lumber from the truck to the back of
_____   the yard, near the fence.

_____ 27. The two farmers trucked the vegetables to the market early
_____   Saturday morning.

_____ 28. The company hired a marketing firm as support for its sales
_____   campaign.

_____ 29. Those two beams support the roof of the living room and the
_____   adjacent porch.

_____ 30. Last week the carpenters replaced the supports of the deck down
_____   by the creek.

_____ 31. The huge waves washed over the deck of the pontoon boat
_____   out in the middle of the bay.

_____ 32. The celebrities in the limousines waved at the people in the crowd
_____   along the side of the street.

_____ 33. Alexandra recently celebrated her 25th birthday with a huge party
_____   at a local hotel.

_____ 34. Everyone at the party enjoyed the celebration of Alexandra's 25th
_____   birthday.

_____ 35. A majority of the people at the family reunion traveled more than
_____   100 miles from their homes.

_____ 36. The President's motorcade drove down a major highway through
_____   the city.

_____ 37. The drive down that valley through the forest offers some very
_____   beautiful views to the travelers.

_____ 38. Yesterday, the coaches previewed the films of last year's victory
_____   at the homecoming game.

_____ 39. The camera operator also filmed the halftime show with the
_____   marching band and flag corps.

_____ 40. The soldiers on the parade ground marched up to the platform
_____   in front of all the generals and other officers.

In Lesson 1 you learned how to recognize a verb. Every verb has a **base** or **infinitive**. This form of the verb "names" the verb. But verbs change their form according to various conditions, three of which are person, number, and tense. You should learn these forms because they occur in nearly every sentence that you speak or write.

> **Person** specifies the person(s) speaking (first person: *I, we*); the person(s) spoken *to* (second person: *you*); and the person(s) or thing(s) spoken *about* (third person: *he, she, it, they*).
>
> **Number** shows whether the reference is to *one* thing (*singular* number) or to more than one thing (*plural* number).
>
> **Tense** refers to the time represented in the sentence, whether it applies to the present moment (I *believe* him) or to some other time (I *believed* him, I will *believe* him).

To demonstrate these changes in form, you can use a chart or arrangement called a *conjugation*. In the partial conjugation that follows, three verbs are used: *earn, grow,* and *be.* The personal pronoun subjects are included to show how the person and number of the subject affect the form of the verb.

Indicative Mood
Active Voice*

Present Tense

	Singular	*Plural*
1st person	I earn, grow, am	We earn, grow, are
2nd person	You earn, grow, are	You earn, grow, are
3rd person	He earns, grows, is†	They earn, grow, are

Past Tense

1st person	I earned, grew, was	We earned, grew, were
2nd person	You earned, grew, were	You earned, grew, were
3rd person	He earned, grew, was	They earned, grew, were

continued on next page

---

*Indicative mood indicates that the verb expresses a fact as opposed to a wish, command, or possibility. *Active voice* indicates that the subject of the verb is the *doer,* rather than the receiver, of the action of the verb.

†The pronoun *he* is arbitrarily used here to represent the third-person singular subject, which may be any singular pronoun (*she, it, who, nobody*); singular noun (*girl, neighbor, elephant, misunderstanding, Alice, Christopher Robert Klein III*); or word groups constituting certain types of phrases or clauses that will be studied in later lessons.

Future Tense

1st person I will earn, grow, be*	We will earn, grow, be
2nd person You will earn, grow, be	You will earn, grow, be
3rd person He will earn, grow, be	They will earn, grow, be

Present Perfect Tense

1st person I have earned, grown, been	We have earned, grown, been
2nd person You have earned, grown, been	You have earned, grown, been
3rd person He has earned, grown, been	They have earned, grown, been

Past Perfect Tense

1st person I had earned, grown, been	We had earned, grown, been
2nd person You had earned, grown, been	You had earned, grown, been
3rd person He had earned, grown, been	They had earned, grown, been

Future Perfect Tense

1st person I will have earned, grown, been	We will have earned, grown, been
2nd person You will have earned, grown, been	You will have earned, grown, been
3rd person He will have earned, grown, been	They will have earned, grown, been

Notice that in the past tense, *earn* adds an *ed* ending, but *grow* changes to *grew*. This difference illustrates **regular** and **irregular verbs**, the two groups into which all English verbs are classified. *Earn* is a regular verb; *grow* is an irregular verb. (Lesson 21 discusses irregular verbs in more detail.)

Notice also that some verb forms consist of more than one word (*will earn, have grown, had earned, will have been*). In such uses, *will*, *had*, and *have* are called **auxiliary verbs**. More auxiliary verbs are examined in Lesson 5.

With the "naming" words (nouns and pronouns) and the "action" words (verbs), you can construct true sentences:

Janice arrived.

He laughed.

Power corrupts.

But to make sentences more varied and complete, you need modifiers or "describing" words (adjectives and adverbs) and prepositional phrases.

ADJECTIVES

An **adjective** is a word that describes or limits—that is, gives qualities to—a noun. Adjectives are found in three positions in a sentence:

---

*Earlier, some writers made distinctions in the use of *shall* and *will* in the future and future perfect tenses. *Shall* was always used with the first person singular and *will* was used in the second and third person plural. In addition, there was an emphatic mood created by reversing *shall* and *will*. So in the emphatic mood, people employed *I will* and *you* or *he shall*. In recent years, those distinctions have been lost, and we now employ *will* for all three persons in both tenses.

1. Preceding a noun that is in any of the noun positions within the sentence

    The *small* child left. He is a *small* child. I saw the *small* child. I gave it to the *small* child.

2. Following a describing (linking) verb and modifying the subject

    The child is *small*. Mary looked *unhappy*. We became *upset*.

3. Directly following the noun (less common than the two positions described above)

    He provided the money *necessary* for the trip. The hostess, *calm and serene*, entered the hall.

Certain characteristics of form and function help you recognize adjectives. There are several suffixes that, when added to other words or roots of other words, form adjectives. Here again, an understanding of the meaning of a suffix can save trips to the dictionary. For instance, in the hundreds of adjectives ending in *able* (*ible*), the suffix means "capable of" or "tending to"; thus, *usable* means "capable of being used" and *changeable* means "tending to change."

able, ible [read*able*, irresist*ible*]; al [internation*al*]; ant, ent [resist*ant*, diverg*ent*]; ar [lun*ar*]; ary [budget*ary*]; ful [meaning*ful*]; ic, ical [cosm*ic*, hyster*ical*]; ish [fool*ish*]; ive [invent*ive*]; less [blame*less*]; ous [glamor*ous*]; y [greas*y*]

One note of warning: Many other words in English end with these letters, but you can easily see that they are not employing a suffix. T*able*, ferm*ent*, arr*ive*, d*ish*, and pon*y*, for instance, are not adjectives. (See Supplement 1 for more information on adjectives.)

ADJECTIVES USED IN COMPARISONS

Nearly all adjectives, when they are used in comparisons, can be strengthened or can show degree by changing form or by using *more* and *most*:

great trust, *greater* trust, *greatest* trust
sensible answer, *more sensible* answer, *most sensible* answer

The base form (*great* trust, *sensible* answer) is the **positive degree**. The second form (*greater* trust, *more sensible* answer) is the **comparative degree**: it compares two things. The third form (*greatest* trust, *most sensible* answer) is the **superlative degree** and distinguishes among three or more things. (See Supplement 2.)

ADVERBS

Another modifier is the **adverb**, a word that modifies anything except a noun or a pronoun. Most adverbs modify verbs (She walked *quickly*). Some adverbs modify adjectives and other adverbs (The *very* old man walked *quite slowly*). Some adverbs modify whole sentences (*Consequently*, we refused the offer).

Adverbs tell certain things about the verb, the most common being:

1. **Manner:** John performed *well*. We worked *hard*. The child laughed *happily*. I would *gladly* change places with you.

2. **Time:** I must leave *now*. I'll see you *later*. *Soon* we shall meet *again*.

3. **Frequency:** We *often* go on picnics, *sometimes* at the lake but *usually* in the city park.

4. **Place:** *There* he sat, alone and silent. *Somewhere* we shall find peace and quiet.

5. **Direction:** The police officer turned *away*. I moved *forward* in the bus.

6. **Degree:** I could *barely* hear the speaker. I *absolutely* refuse to believe that story.

The most frequently used adverbs answer such questions as "How?" (manner or degree), "When?" (time or frequency), and "Where?" (place or direction).

Adverbs of a subclass called **intensifiers** modify adjectives or adverbs but not verbs—for example, a *very* good meal, his *quite* surprising reply, *too* often, *somewhat* reluctantly.

Many adverbs change form the way adjectives do, to show degree:

to drive *fast*, to drive *faster*, to drive *fastest*

to perform *satisfactorily*, to perform *more satisfactorily*, to perform *most satisfactorily*

See Supplement 2 for details on some common irregular intensifiers.

PREPOSITIONS

A **preposition** is a word that introduces a phrase and shows the relationship between the object of the phrase and some other word in the sentence. Notice that many prepositions show a relationship of space or time. Here are some common prepositions; those in the last column are called *group prepositions*:

about	beside	inside	through	according to
above	besides	into	throughout	because of
across	between	like	till	by way of
after	beyond	near	to	in addition to
against	by	of	toward	in front of
around	down	off	under	in place of
at	during	on	until	in regard to
before	except	out	up	in spite of
behind	for	outside	upon	instead of
below	from	over	with	on account of
beneath	in	since	without	out of

A preposition always has an object; with its object and any modifiers, the preposition makes a **prepositional phrase**. You can easily illustrate the function of prepositions by constructing sentences like the following:

After breakfast I walked *to* town *without* my friend. [Objects: *breakfast, town, friend.*]

On account of the rain, I canceled my plans *for* a game *of* tennis *at* the park *with* John. [Objects: *rain, game, tennis, park, John.*]

The trees *outside* the window *of* the kitchen are full *of* blossoms *during* the spring. [Objects: *window, kitchen, blossoms, spring.*]

SUPPLEMENT 1

Besides what could be called true adjectives are other classes of words that modify nouns. If you concentrate on the *functions* of the various kinds of words, however, you can safely classify as adjectives all words that precede nouns and limit their meaning. Such adjectives include articles, numerals, and possessives (*an* apple, *the* weather, *my three* roommates); modifiers that can be used also as pronouns (*these* people, *some* friends, *all* workers); and nouns that modify other nouns (*basketball* players, *summer* days, *crop* failures).

Many words can be used as adjectives or as pronouns; the position of a word within the sentence determines which part of speech it is:

Several [*adj.*] classmates of mine [*pron.*] read this [*adj.*] report.

Several [*pron.*] of my [*adj.*] classmates read this [*pron.*].

SUPPLEMENT 2

A few commonly used modifiers form their comparative and superlative degrees irregularly:

good (*adj.*)	better	best
well (*adv.*)	better	best
bad (*adj.*)	worse	worst

English Fundamentals Online

After you have completed Practice Sheets and Exercises in this lesson, you can find additional help and drill work at **MyWritingLab.Com**, in the section on Adjectives; Adverbs.

NAME _____   SCORE _____

Directions: Identify the part of speech of each italicized word by writing one of the following numbers in each space at the left.

| 1. noun | 3. verb | 5. adverb |
| 2. Pronoun | 4. adjective | 6. preposition |

_____   1. The people in the room *have worked* there *for* the past six hours.

_____

_____   2. *Their* work has almost exhausted *them*.

_____

_____   3. The *exhaust* system of my car needs a new *muffler*.

_____

_____   4. *Perhaps* the *car* needs an entirely new exhaust system.

_____

_____   5. Those *acoustic* materials *will muffle* the sounds of the machinery in this

_____   room.

_____   6. *Acoustics* is the *study* of various aspects of sound.

_____

_____   7. My friend Art has studied architecture for the past *two years*.

_____

_____   8. *Previously* his studies took him *to* Europe for one year.

_____

_____   9. *In* the semester *previous* to this one, Marta worked in construction.

_____

_____   10. The workers *from* the *construction* company have built a new dormitory for

_____   the college.

_____   11. *Because of* the very bad weather over the past three months, completion of

_____   the dormitory will be several months *late*.

_____   12. *Lately*, the weather has improved *considerably*.

_____

_____   13. Any *improvements* in my grades *are* a product of my serious efforts in my

_____   studies.

_____   14. My efforts this semester have been *much better* than last semester's.

_____

_____   15. Ellen's studies seem *almost effortless* in comparison to my hard work.

_____

_____   16. Ellen *has* always *been* a *very* good student.

_____

_____   17. Yesterday Walt *spent* the *whole* day in the library.

_____

_____ 18. The *rest* of *us* have not spent even an hour in the library this week.

_____ 19. *Few* of the people in our classes have spent *much* time in the library.

_____ 20. The *only* person in the computer lab *tonight* is Mr. Harrison, the technician.

_____ 21. *Technically*, that sewing machine has one of the most *sophisticated* designs in our factory.

_____ 22. *Sophistication in* management techniques is also a characteristic of our company.

_____ 23. The main *character* in that movie resembles *certain* politicians in our state.

_____ 24. The physical *resemblance* between the movie actor and those politicians *is* quite striking.

_____ 25. "Please *strike* that comment from the record," said the judge *angrily*.

_____ 26. The role of *that* actor in the movie will probably win an Oscar *nomination*.

_____ 27. The team *has nominated* Webster and Andrews as captains *for* the next game.

_____ 28. The coaches will certainly approve of the *selection of* Webster and Andrews.

_____ 29. Have *you* selected your courses for the *next* term?

_____ 30. My *most* difficult course will be a *course* in advanced calculus.

_____ 31. *Without* calculus, I *won't make* any further advances in my major, engineering.

_____ 32. The members of the marching band *advanced* across the field in *evenly* matched, parallel lines.

_____ 33. The more *advanced* players on the *soccer* team will probably play on the All-Star Team.

_____ 34. *Soccer* is the *most* popular sport in the world.

_____ 35. The sport is played *by* people in *almost* every country in the world.

_____ 36. *According to* sports historians, soccer is also one of the *oldest* sports.

_____ 37. Worldwide, there is *no* sport *equal* to soccer in popularity.

_____ 38. The World Cup, *like* baseball's World Series, produces the champion of the *entire* world in soccer.

_____ 39. Children begin *their* soccer *careers* at the age of five or six.

_____ 40. My little sister *continued* her *participation* in soccer until after her high school graduation.

Exercise 2 *Parts of Speech*

NAME _____ SCORE _____

Directions: Identify the part of speech of each italicized word by writing one of the following numbers in each space at the left.

1. noun	3. verb	5. adverb
2. pronoun	4. adjective	6. preposition

_____ 1. This office *reported* an *increase* in profits for the last quarter of the year.

_____

_____ 2. Our profits increased *significantly* in the last quarter *of* the year.

_____

_____ 3. This *significant* increase made *us* the top office in our company.

_____

_____ 4. The officers of the company are *very pleased* with our performance.

_____

_____ 5. Our office *performed* well above their *expectations*.

_____

_____ 6. The members of the staff of this office *expect* a raise in the *near* future.

_____

_____ 7. All of us are waiting *expectantly* for a notice *about* our raise.

_____

_____ 8. The *wait* for our increase in pay *will* probably *be* about two weeks long.

_____

_____ 9. *We will wait* patiently for our raise.

_____

_____ 10. The company will reward *our* performance and our *patience* very soon.

_____

_____ 11. The players on our baseball team met *their* new coach *yesterday*.

_____

_____ 12. The college president introduced *him to* the members of the team.

_____

_____ 13. The president's *introductory* remarks were *very* brief.

_____

_____ 14. The coach gave a talk about *himself* and *his* hopes for the players.

_____

_____ 15. *They* were very impressed *by* his introductory speech.

_____

_____ 16. First *impressions* are always *very* important.

_____

_____ 17. The players *applauded* him *with* great enthusiasm.

_____

_____ 18. The *baseball* players were quite *enthusiastic* about the arrival of the new coach.

_____ 19. People of all ages play *baseball enthusiastically.*

_____ 20. The college baseball team started the season *with* a very *impressive* victory.

_____ 21. The *four* of us spent the *entire* day yesterday in the library.

_____ 22. In my opinion, that was *entirely too* much time inside a stuffy old building.

_____ 23. The *outside* of the library building is exceedingly *attractive.*

_____ 24. *Across* the front of the building stand six *ornate* white columns.

_____ 25. *These* columns *frame* a pair of beautiful oak doors.

_____ 26. *Unfortunately,* the *inside* of the library building is dark and depressing.

_____ 27. *Inside* the library, the walls *are* a very dark wood.

_____ 28. A huge desk *walls* the books off *from* the students.

_____ 29. *We* studied very *thoroughly* for tomorrow's history test.

_____ 30. *Thorough* preparation for a test usually *produces* good grades.

_____ 31. A test in *any* subject always makes *my* brother nervous.

_____ 32. *Any* of his friends *will testify* to that fact.

_____ 33. *Interestingly* enough, my brother's grades are *quite* good.

_____ 34. *Perhaps* his *nervousness* motivates him to harder work.

_____ 35. *For* most people, *nerves* are not a great motivator.

_____ 36. The sales *manager at* our company gives great motivational speeches.

_____ 37. *She* always *manages* our sales meetings very skillfully.

_____ 38. Her skills are always clearly *evident* in our *sales* meetings.

_____ 39. Her *techniques* have produced outstanding results *in* our department.

_____ 40. *Those* sales figures *have resulted* in high salaries for all of us in the
_____   department.

Directions: Each of the following words is labeled as a noun, a verb, an adjective, or an adverb. In the spaces following each word, write related words of the parts of speech indicated. (Do not use adjectives ending in *ing* or *ed*.) Use a dictionary when necessary.

1. abundance (n.) _____ (adj.) _____ (adv.)

2. alternate (v.) _____ (n.) _____ (adj.)

3. bear (v.) _____ (adj.) _____ (adv.)

4. capable (adj.) _____ (n.) _____ (adv.)

5. charge (n.) _____ (v.) _____ (adj.)

6. differ (v.) _____ (adj.) _____ (n.)

7. durably (adv.) _____ (adj.) _____ (n.)

8. essential (adj.) _____ (n.) _____ (adv.)

9. expect (v.) _____ (adj.) _____ (adv.)

10. final (adj.) _____ (v.) _____ (adv.)

11. frisky (adj.) _____ (v.) _____ (n.)

12. happiness (n.) _____ (adj.) _____ (adv.)

13. ideal (adj.) _____ (adv.) _____ (v.)

14. inspect (v.) _____ (n.) _____ (n.)

15. kindly (adv.) _____ (adj.) _____ (n.)

16. magnet (n.) _____ (v.) _____ (adj.)

17. militate (v.) _____ (adj.) _____ (adv.)

18. obscurity (n.) _____ (v.) _____ (adj.)

19. poetic (adj.) _____ (adv.) _____ (n.)

20. react (v.) _____ (n.) _____ (adj.)

Subjects and Verbs

NAME _____ SCORE _____

Directions: In the first space at the left, copy the subject of the sentence. In the second space, copy the verb. Some of the verbs consist of more than one word.

_____ 1. Many of the fans cheered her for that brilliant play in last night's
_____   game.
_____ 2. Many people have called the television station about the strange
_____   object in the western sky.
_____ 3. Some longtime residents object to the changes in the parking
_____   arrangements for the downtown area.
_____ 4. We will arrange a meeting with all of you in the very near future.

_____ 5. In a closet in the basement of his house, my grandfather once
_____   discovered a secret compartment.
_____ 6. According to many local residents, the discovery of gold in the near-
_____   by mountains has changed the economic status of this small town.
_____ 7. During the second half of the football game, the athletic trainer
_____   stood on the sideline near the coaches.
_____ 8. In this college, athletics of all kinds are very important to students
_____   and faculty alike.
_____ 9. James Jackson is a very capable administrator and an exceptionally
_____   gifted teacher.
_____ 10. The doctor will probably administer a mild anaesthetic before the
_____   removal of that tiny mole.
_____ 11. A cute little mole has dug an easily visible tunnel across our front
_____   yard.
_____ 12. At the front of the classroom stands a wooden flagpole with a flag
_____   of the United States at its top.
_____ 13. By the end of the day we will have climbed these stairs at least
_____   ten times.
_____ 14. Few members of that particular generation avoided military
_____   service of some kind.
_____ 15. Few of the houses in this county have a coal-burning furnace.

_____ 16. We counted the number of people in the library on Saturday
_____   afternoon on the fingers of one hand.
_____ 17. Those of us at the stadium that afternoon, however, numbered
_____   in the thousands.
_____ 18. The number of students at the stadium far exceeded the number
_____   of students in the library.

_____ 19. In addition to that important football game, the campus hosted
_____ a number of other interesting events last weekend.
_____ 20. Our hosts for that visit to the local museum provided us with a
_____ fascinating presentation about the geology of this area.
_____ 21. In addition to great performances by the drummer and the bass player,
_____ that band performed marvelous vocal renditions of two of the songs.
_____ 22. A great performance by the college's drama department occurred
_____ last week in the presentation of that Shakespearean tragedy.
_____ 23. Those of us in the audience during that production will never
_____ forget its beauty and majesty.
_____ 24. Besides Alice and Mario, several other people from my hometown
_____ came to the state capital for the inauguration of the governor.
_____ 25. On that last night in the mountains, beside a noisy stream under
_____ a canopy of oak trees, the hikers pitched their tents.
_____ 26. For most of us on that committee, the selection of Alicia for the
_____ role of treasurer had been the easiest choice of all.
_____ 27. The stone building, tall and majestic, houses all the branches of
_____ the local government except the fire and police departments.
_____ 28. Many of the people in my architecture class will build beautiful
_____ scale models of houses for their semester projects.
_____ 29. Sadly, we barely heard the speaker from our seats in the back row
_____ of the auditorium.
_____ 30. Amazingly, your brother, over the past year, has grown at least
_____ 4 inches taller.
_____ 31. By the end of this semester, I will have earned 24 semester hours
_____ of credit toward my degree.
_____ 32. Difficult budgetary considerations have taken the first two hours
_____ of the commission's meeting today.
_____ 33. The clumsy work of that carpenter has turned a beautiful, artistically
_____ elegant room into an eyesore badly in need of repair and restoration.
_____ 34. My experiences in last week's exams have taught me the importance
_____ of regular, dedicated work on the materials in each of my classes.
_____ 35. There on the stage sat several baseball players from the
_____ championship team of ten years ago.
_____ 36. The children in the front rows of the audience laughed happily at
_____ the performances of the clowns in the center ring of the circus.
_____ 37. The firefighters had never seen a fire more fierce and awe-inspiring
_____ than the one in that valley last week.
_____ 38. We will always return to our grandmother's farm during the
_____ summers in the years ahead.
_____ 39. During the summer, I worked very hard in preparation for
_____ football season.
_____ 40. On the end of the dock sat a slightly older man with a fishing
_____ pole in his hands.

As you know from Lesson 1, the sentence, which is a subject and predicate arranged to make a statement, is the basic unit of written and oral communication. There are just five sentence types or patterns, and learning to recognize those five patterns can help you become a more effective communicator. In this lesson and the following lesson, we look at the five patterns so that you can learn to use them in your writing.

The nature of the verb is the key to recognizing sentence patterns. There are two types of verbs, **transitive** and **intransitive**. The prefix *trans* means "across," and the letters *it* come from the Latin word meaning "to go," so *transit* means "to go across." The additional prefix *in* means "not," so *intransit* means "not to go across." (Don't confuse the Latin word with the colloquial *in transit*, which means in the act of going somewhere.)

When an **intransitive verb** is used, the verb does not transfer its action to an object. In the sentence "John spoke softly," the action is *spoke* and the actor is *John*. The action does not "go across" to a noun that receives that action. The verb is intransitive. Some intransitive verbs do not express an action; they simply connect or link the subject to a noun that renames the subject or to an adjective that modifies the subject. These types of intransitive verbs are called **linking verbs**. In the following sentences there is no action:

John *is* a genius.
John *is* brilliant.

The subject *John* is simply linked by the verb to a word that identifies or modifies it.

Sentence Patterns 1 and 2 use intransitive verbs. Sentence Patterns 3, 4, and 5 use transitive verbs and are addressed in Lesson 4.

SENTENCE PATTERN 1

Sentence Pattern 1 contains an intransitive verb and is the only sentence pattern that does not require a word to complete the sense of the action. Some activity takes place in each of these sentences, but no completer is needed because the action of the verb is not transferred to anything.

The child *runs*.
The tree *fell*.
The customer *complained* loudly.
The professor *walked* into the room unexpectedly.

The action of the verb is complete within itself. Pattern 1 sentences nearly always contain modifiers that tell how, when, and where the action occurred:

Yesterday the neighborhood children played noisily in the vacant lot.

Notice that the material associated with the verb is all adverbial: "When?" *Yesterday.* "How?" *Noisily.* "Where?" *In the vacant lot.* The important characteristic of a Pattern 1 sentence is that there is no noun answering the question "What?" after the verb. The best way to recognize an intransitive verb is to spot the lack of a noun answering the question "What?" after the verb.

In some Pattern 1 sentences, the purpose of the statement is simply to say that the subject exists. Usually some adverbial material is added to show the place or the time of the existence:

> The glasses *are* in the cabinet.
> Flash floods often *occur* in the spring.
> There *were* several birds around the feeder.

COMPLEMENTS

Now we need to define a term that identifies an important part of the sentences in the four remaining patterns. As you know, the two parts of any sentence are the subject and the predicate. The core of the predicate is the verb, but the predicate also often includes words that complete the thought of the sentence. Words that follow the verb and complete the thought of the sentence are called **complements**. Complements can be nouns, pronouns, or adjectives, but all serve the same purpose in the sentence: They complete the idea or sense of the sentence.

SENTENCE PATTERN 2

Pattern 2 includes two closely related kinds of sentences. The purpose of the first type of Pattern 2 sentence is to rename the subject, to say that the subject is the same as something else. In the sentence "John is a genius," the noun *genius* is called a **subjective complement** because it completes the verb and renames the subject. (See Supplement.) The intransitive linking verb used in Pattern 2 sentences is often a form of *be.*

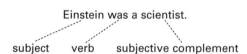

> Einstein was a scientist.
>
> subject   verb   subjective complement

Note that both words, *Einstein* and *scientist,* refer to the same thing. There is no action; rather, a connection is established between the subject and the verb.

In the second type of Pattern 2 sentence, the subjective complement is an adjective, a word that describes rather than renames the subject. For example, in the sentence "The child is clever," the subject is joined by the verb to an adjective, again called a subjective complement. Comparatively few verbs serve the linking function. For convenience, you can think of them in three closely related groups:

1. *Be,* the most commonly used linking verb and a few others meaning essentially the same thing (*seem, appear, prove, remain, continue,* and so forth):

   > John *is* a talented musician.
   > The performer *seemed* nervous.
   > He *remained* calm.
   > His words *proved* meaningless.

2. *Become*, and a few others like it (*turn, grow, work, get, wear,* and so forth):

> Later she *became* an accountant.
> Soon he *grew* tired of the game.
> Billy *turned* red from embarrassment.

3. A few verbs referring to the senses (*look, smell, taste, feel, sound*), which can be followed by adjective subjective complements that describe the condition of the subject:

> The roses *look* beautiful in that vase.
> This milk *tastes* sour.

The ability to recognize Pattern 2 sentences will help you understand a few troublesome usage problems that are examined in a later lesson—to understand why, for instance, careful writers use "feel bad" rather than "feel badly": "I *feel* bad about the election results."

SUPPLEMENT

A note about grammatical terminology is needed here. A noun following a linking verb and renaming the subject is sometimes called a *predicate noun* or a *predicate nominative*; an adjective following a linking verb and describing the subject is sometimes called a *predicate adjective*.

> subjective complement (n.) = predicate noun
> predicate nominative
> subjective complement (adj.) = predicate adjective

English Fundamentals Online

> After you have completed Practice Sheets and Exercises in this lesson, you can find additional help and drill work at **MyWritingLab.com**, in the section on Basic Sentence Patterns.

NAME _____ SCORE _____

Directions: Each of the following sentences is either a Pattern 1 or a Pattern 2 sentence with a noun (or pronoun) subjective complement. If the sentence is a Pattern 1 sentence, write the numeral 1 in the space at the left. If the sentence is a Pattern 2 sentence, write the subjective complement in the space at the left.

_____ 1. Into the room walked a woman in an elegant blue suit.

_____ 2. The boys in the backyard ran quickly to the side of the house.

_____ 3. The two men in the gray coveralls are the technicians for the stage show.

_____ 4. Jim's little brother has become a very skilled guitar player.

_____ 5. His older brother will become a certified EMT this June.

_____ 6. The last members of the group arrived about fifteen minutes ago.

_____ 7. The meeting, however, had already started before their arrival.

_____ 8. All the men in that group are supporters of the current plan.

_____ 9. The current plan is the product of many hours of work.

_____ 10. After graduation from college, June will become a law student.

_____ 11. Alec has remained a good friend to all three of us for many years.

_____ 12. His friendship has always been a strong support for all of us.

_____ 13. That one pine tree stands out very clearly among those smaller oaks.

_____ 14. Everyone in the office waited impatiently for the arrival of the morning mail.

_____ 15. Janice limped noticeably for several days after the injury to her ankle.

_____ 16. Over the summer, Andrea somehow became a much better hitter.

_____ 17. In June we will have been members of this club for more than three years.

_____ 18. Jim has become a licensed pilot after four years of work.

_____ 19. The rest of the glasses are behind that stack of plates in the corner cabinet.

_____ 20. Together, the members of the debate team will be impressive representatives of the college.

Directions: Most of the following sentences are Pattern 2 sentences with a noun or an adjective subjective complement. If the sentence is a Pattern 1 sentence, write the numeral 1 in the space at the left. If the sentence is a Pattern 2 sentence, write the subjective complement in the space at the left.

_____ 1. Julie remained quite calm through the entire test.

_____ 2. The two children grew restless during that long car ride.

_____ 3. The students felt sad about the team's loss in the conference championship.

_____ 4. At the end of that long exam, we were all mentally exhausted.

_____ 5. In spite of the negative commentary in the press, the politician remained firm in his position.

_____ 6. My mother's eggplant parmigiana always tastes delicious.

_____ 7. After that work in the garden, all of us looked tired and dirty.

_____ 8. That tall old sycamore tree fell across the road during the windstorm last night.

_____ 9. Thomas Edison remained a prolific inventor for almost his entire life.

_____ 10. In spite of my failure on that test, I felt good about my work in preparation for it.

_____ 11. The two men stopped beside the beautifully restored old car.

_____ 12. In my opinion, Barbara's apple pie tastes a little too sweet.

_____ 13. All the grass in the field turned brown because of the lack of water during the drought.

_____ 14. The only green grass stands near the spring at the lower end of the meadow.

_____ 15. That stand of oak trees is certainly a welcome sight to us tired hikers.

_____ 16. We had hiked for almost three hours across a broad, grassy field.

_____ 17. After a short rest and a snack, we all appeared rested enough for the rest of the hike.

_____ 18. The bright colors of the autumn leaves are very cheerful.

_____ 19. By this time next year, Marcie will have been a student here for five years.

_____ 20. She has always been a big fan of the college's football team.

Subjects, Verbs, and Complements

NAME _____ SCORE _____

Directions: These sentences are either Pattern 1 or Pattern 2 sentences. In the first space at the left, write the subject of the sentence. Write the verb of the sentence in the second space. Many of the verbs consist of more than one word. If the sentence is a Pattern 2 sentence, circle the subjective complement.

_____ 1. The exhausted players sat quietly on the bench after the game.

_____
_____ 2. They seemed especially tired because of the heat and the
intensity of the game.
_____ 3. Two of them sobbed quietly because of their loss.

_____ 4. Suddenly, a third player ran quickly away from the group.

_____ 5. She appeared amused by the tears of her fellow players.

_____ 6. The loss was apparently not particularly important to her.

_____ 7. The other members of the team remained inconsolable because
of the loss.
_____ 8. The coaches walked quickly to their cars after the last out.

_____ 9. The umpires had become annoyed by the sobs of the players.

_____ 10. They hurriedly left for the exit in their cars.

_____ 11. Yesterday the weather turned very stormy about sundown.

_____ 12. In the late afternoon the sky in the west looked very ominous.

_____ 13. Lightning crackled ominously everywhere around us.

_____ 14. The air smelled very fresh because of the electricity in the air.

_____ 15. Hail the size of golf balls fell all around us.

_____ 16. The fallen hail felt very cold to the touch.

_____ 17. Far into the night the cloud cover over the area remained
extremely heavy.

_____ 18. By the next morning, however, the sky had become clear
_____   and bright.
_____ 19. In the bright morning sunshine there were several options for
_____   outdoor recreation.
_____ 20. So the three of us drove happily to a nearby golf course.

_____ 21. The last of the late arrivals walked slowly into the classroom.

_____ 22. Almost everyone else had arrived on time.

_____ 23. This student was almost always a late arrival.

_____ 24. The lecturer in the class did not seem amused by the student's
_____   late arrival.
_____ 25. The student's late arrivals had become a source of great
_____   annoyance to the lecturer.
_____ 26. The lecturer looked unhappy because of the interruptions to the
_____   class.
_____ 27. He had been working very hard on the explanation of a very
_____   important concept.
_____ 28. The concept was a key point in the development of the lecture.

_____ 29. The lecturer stopped in the middle of his presentation.

_____ 30. The class grew very quiet until the end of the interruption by
_____   the student's late arrival.
_____ 31. Yesterday my little brother suddenly appeared in the doorway
_____   of my bedroom.
_____ 32. He appeared happy about something.

_____ 33. His new model train had come in the mail sometime during
_____   the morning.
_____ 34. The "model train" was actually a collection of 2,500 tiny pieces
_____   in four or five plastic bags.
_____ 35. My brother is very enthusiastic about the construction of models
_____   from these tiny pieces.
_____ 36. The pieces of the model are actually small squares with small
_____   round pegs in them.
_____ 37. The instructions for the model are probably too difficult for most
_____   adults.
_____ 38. Most twelve-year-olds seem capable of grasping the instructions
_____   easily.
_____ 39. My little brother works happily for hours on each new model.

_____ 40. Fifteen or twenty models stand on the shelves of my little
_____   brother's bedroom.

In Sentence Pattern 2 the intransitive verb links the subject to a noun or adjective that completes the idea of the sentence: "Maria is our pitcher"; "Maria is brilliant." When a **transitive verb** is used, the action expressed by the verb "goes across" to some noun that receives the action. That noun is called the **direct object** and is the receiver of the action expressed in the verb. In the sentence "John watched a movie," the action (the verb) is *watched*, and the actor (the subject) is *John*; the receiver of the action (the direct object) is *movie*. The direct object can be found by asking the question "What?" after the subject and verb have been found. "John watched what? John watched a movie."

SENTENCE PATTERN 3

In Pattern 3 sentences the verb is a transitive verb. It does not link or connect; instead, it identifies an action and transfers that action to a receiver or object of the action (the direct object). The subject-verb combination of the sentence does not complete a thought unless there is an object to receive the action named in the verb. For example, in the sentence "The child hits the ball," the subject-verb combination (*child hits*) does not make a complete statement. A complete statement requires that the child hit *something*.

The direct object is always a noun or a noun equivalent, such as a pronoun:

I broke my glasses. What names the activity? *Broke* is the verb. Who broke? *I* is the subject. I broke what? *Glasses.* Thus, *glasses* is the direct object.
Someone saw us. What names the activity? *Saw.* Who saw? *Someone* saw. Someone saw what? *Us* is the direct object.

We need to draw a contrast between a Pattern 2 sentence and a Pattern 3 sentence. Although both patterns require a complement, in a Pattern 2 sentence such as "The child is a genius," the subject is either renamed or modified by the subjective complement. In the sentence "Someone saw us," it is clear that *someone* and *us* are not the same. *Us* is the receiver of the action *saw* and simply cannot be taken to be the same as the *someone* who saw. In both Pattern 2 and Pattern 3 sentences, the thought of the sentence is not complete without a complement, but in Pattern 3 the subject acts upon the complement, the direct object.

SENTENCE PATTERN 4

Pattern 4 sentences also contain a direct object. But because Pattern 4 sentences use verbs such as *give* or *show*, the sentences need a **second** complement to complete their thought. After a transitive verb such as *shows*, *gives*, or *tells*, the direct object (the receiver of the action) answers the question "What?" and an **indirect object** answers the question "To whom?" or "For whom?" Thus, "She sang a lullaby" is a Pattern 3 sentence, but "She gave the children a gift" is a Pattern 4 sentence.

In the sentence "The parents give the child a present," you can easily see that two complements are used. The sentence mentions the thing that is given (*present*, the direct object) and the person to whom the direct object is given (*child*, the indirect object). Although the indirect object usually names a person, it can name a nonhuman thing, as in "We gave your *application* a careful reading."

Other verbs that are commonly used this way and therefore produce a Pattern 4 structure are *allow, assign, ask, tell, write, send, pay, grant*, and so on. Nearly all sentences using such verbs can make essentially the same statement by using a prepositional phrase, usually beginning with the preposition *to* or *for*. When the prepositional phrase is present in the sentence, it is a Pattern 3 sentence.

> The postman brought me a letter. [Pattern 4; *me* is an indirect object.]
> The postman brought a letter to me. [Pattern 3; *me* is the object of a preposition.]
> Mother bought us some candy. [Pattern 4]
> Mother bought some candy for us. [Pattern 3]

SENTENCE PATTERN 5

Pattern 5 sentences regularly use verbs such as *consider, call, think, find, make, elect, appoint*, and *name*. There are two closely related types of Pattern 5 sentences. Each type begins like a Pattern 3 sentence:

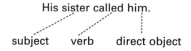

But the nature of the verb *called* allows the use of a second complement answering the question "What?" after *called him*. His sister called him what?

> His sister called him a genius.

The reference of the two nouns following the verb is a key to the difference between this type of sentence and a Pattern 4 sentence. In a Pattern 4 sentence the two noun complements refer to different things, but in a Pattern 5 sentence they refer to the same thing.

> Mother made us some fudge. [Pattern 4: *us* and *fudge* refer to different things.]
> This experience made John an activist. [Pattern 5: *John* and *activist* are the same thing.]

Thus, there are two complements in Pattern 5 sentences. The one closer to the verb is the direct object. The second complement is called the **objective complement**. In the first type of Pattern 5 sentence, the objective complement is a noun that *renames* the direct object. In the second type of Pattern 5 sentence, the objective complement is an adjective that *describes* the direct object.

> His sister called him a genius.
> His sister called him brilliant.

Because the objective complement renames or describes the direct object, we can use a handy test to help us recognize Pattern 5: The insertion of *to be* between the complements will give us an acceptable English wording.

We appointed Jones [to be] our representative.
I thought this action [to be] unnecessary.

Sometimes the word *as* is used between the direct object and the objective complement in Pattern 5 sentences:

We appointed Jones as our representative.

Some adjective objective complements are very important to the meaning of the verb. Thus, it is sometimes effective to place these objective complements immediately after the verb and before the direct object:

Usual order: He set the caged animals [D.O.] free [O.C.].
Variation: He set free [O.C.] the caged animals [D.O.].

SUPPLEMENT

One special kind of verb makes it difficult to distinguish between a direct object and the object of a preposition. Here are two examples:

Harry jumped off the box.
Harry took off his raincoat.

The first sentence is Pattern 1. *Off* is a preposition, *box* is the object of the preposition, and the prepositional phrase is used as an adverbial modifier because it tells *where* Harry jumped. The second sentence is Pattern 3. The verb, with its adverbial modifier *off*, is the equivalent of the transitive verb *remove*. *Raincoat* is the direct object.

There is another way to distinguish between the adverbial use and the prepositional use of such a word as *off* in the preceding examples. When the word is a vital adverbial modifier of the verb, it can be used in either of two positions: following the verb or following the direct object.

Harry took off his raincoat.
Harry took his raincoat off.

When the word is a preposition, the alternate position is not possible: "Harry jumped the box off" is not an English sentence. Here are some other examples of verbs with adverbial modifiers. Notice that in each case you can easily find a transitive verb synonym for the combination:

Give up [*relinquish*] her rights.
Leave out [*omit*] the second chapter.
Put out [*extinguish*] the fire.
Make over [*alter*] an old dress.
Make up [*invent*] an excuse.

SUMMARY OF VERBS USED IN DIFFERENT SENTENCE PATTERNS

1. **Verbs that serve a linking function and commonly form Pattern 2 sentences:**
   be, seem, appear, prove, remain, continue, become, turn, grow, work, get, wear, look, smell, taste, feel, sound

2. **Verbs that commonly produce Pattern 4 sentences:**
   allow, assign, ask, tell, write, send, pay, grant

3. **Verbs that commonly produce Pattern 5 sentences:**
   consider, call, think, find, make, elect, appoint, name

English Fundamentals **Online**

After you have completed Practice Sheets and Exercises in this lesson, you can find additional help and drill work at **MyWritingLab.com**, in the section on Basic Sentence Patterns; Varying Sentence Structure.

Complements of Transitive Verbs

NAME: _____   SCORE _____

Directions: Each of these sentences is a Pattern 3 sentence. Circle the subject and under-line the verb in each sentence. In the space at the left, copy the word that is the direct object of the verb.

_____ 1. At the table in the library, the five students opened their books.

_____ 2. The senators tabled that motion until a later date.

_____ 3. That movie dates itself quite clearly because of the age of the cars.

_____ 4. The boss has cleared her schedule for our meeting tomorrow.

_____ 5. I scheduled almost all my classes next term for early afternoon.

_____ 6. I will meet only one class in the morning.

_____ 7. Biologists have always classified plants and animals by genus and species.

_____ 8. My uncle Johnny owns two classic cars.

_____ 9. By the end of the year, he will have sold one of them.

_____ 10. Ownership of two classic cars creates too much maintenance work for one person.

_____ 11. John maintains both cars by himself without help from anyone else.

_____ 12. Yolanda often helps her roommate with math problems.

_____ 13. Without help from Yolanda, her roommate made several low grades on math tests.

_____ 14. Last week county workers graded the roads in our end of the county.

_____ 15. Next week they will pave several gravel roads near our house.

_____ 16. The workers also graveled several driveways as a favor to the homeowners.

_____ 17. The costs of home ownership often exceed the financial capabili-ties of elderly people.

_____ 18. Johann will probably finance his new car through a local credit union.

_____ 19. The credit card company has not credited the amount of that returned item to my account.

_____ 20. The company provides an itemized statement at the end of each billing period.

Directions: The following are Pattern 3, 4, or 5 sentences. Identify the italicized complement by writing one of the following abbreviations in the space at the left:

D.O. [direct object]   I.O. [indirect object]   O.C. [objective complement]

_____ 1. Our manager called Melanie the best *technician* in our office.

_____ 2. All of us supported the manager's *observation*.

_____ 3. Even the technicians in our other offices gave the *manager* their support.

_____ 4. Please give me a new *report* on the status of the repairs to the system.

_____ 5. The technicians in the field reported good *news* to the home office.

_____ 6. We have already sent *Mike* his invitation to the next seminar.

_____ 7. We have also invited *Adam* to that same meeting.

_____ 8. Last year's seminar made us all more *knowledgeable* about our work.

_____ 9. No one thought the meeting a *waste* of time.

_____ 10. The warnings about the blizzard made us all *wary* about our trip home.

_____ 11. The forecasting office sent *us* a bulletin around three o'clock.

_____ 12. This morning no one believed the *weather* a threat to any of our travel plans.

_____ 13. Now we will give our departure *time* careful attention.

_____ 14. Several people have selected new *routes* to their homes because of the blizzard.

_____ 15. The weather forecasters supplied *them* information on a regular basis.

_____ 16. Unfortunately, the travelers found the information *outdated*.

_____ 17. The snowstorm made exceedingly fast *progress* across the state.

_____ 18. The snow had blocked *some* of the roads before the end of the meeting.

_____ 19. Several of the people at the meeting delayed their *departures*.

_____ 20. By morning the snowplows had cleared the *roads* enough for safe travel.

Exercise 4

Complements of Transitive Verbs

NAME: _____   SCORE _____

Directions: Circle the subject and underline the verb in each of the following sentences. Identify the italicized complement by writing one of the following abbreviations in the space at the left:

S.C. [subjective complement]	D.O. [direct object]
I.O. [indirect object]	O.C. [objective complement]

_____ 1. All of us in the class considered Melanie's work on that experiment *brilliant*.

_____ 2. Even our usually skeptical instructor gave *it* her highest praise.

_____ 3. Even the skeptics in the class praised her *work* enthusiastically.

_____ 4. Melanie's work was easily the *best* in the class.

_____ 5. After the class, the instructor printed the *results* of the experiment for everyone's benefit.

_____ 6. The new construction in the heart of downtown has made travel into the heart of town extremely *difficult*.

_____ 7. Before the tourist season, no one gave the *problem* any serious attention.

_____ 8. A huge influx of tourists into our small town has jammed the *roads* from one end of town to the other.

_____ 9. The troubles with congestion on the downtown streets have made the business owners quite *angry*.

_____ 10. Traffic congestion is a serious *problem* in most cities in this country.

_____ 11. Just before the beginning of the season, the coach sent all the team *members* a copy of the practice schedule for the first week.

_____ 12. The new members of the team, recruits and walk-ons, will have *practice* early in the afternoon.

_____ 13. Returning players will join the *newcomers* at three o'clock every day.

_____ 14. The emphasis in the first week's practices will be an *improvement* in everyone's strength and agility.

_____ 15. The coaches consider increased strength and agility *vital* to good performance by any player.

_____ 16. The hard work on strength and agility will also discourage unmotivated *players*.

_____ 17. By the end of the first week, several players will have found the workouts too *hard* for them.

_____ 18. These people will seek out less-demanding recreational *opportunities*.

_____ 19. Those still around at the end of the week will become the genuine *prospects* for the team.

_____ 20. Unfortunately, however, not all of these prospects will actually make the *team*.

Directions: Using appropriate forms of the verbs indicated, write 20 original sentences illustrating the following sentence patterns:

Sentences 1–5	Pattern 2
Sentences 6–10	Pattern 3
Sentences 11–15	Pattern 4
Sentences 16–20	Pattern 5

1. be _____

2. seem _____

3. become _____

4. look _____

5. grow _____

6. grow _____

7. throw _____

8. see _____

9. choose _____

10. tell _____

11. tell _____

12. allow _____

13. bring _____

14. assign _____

15. make _____

16. make _____

17. call _____

18. color _____

19. name _____

20. select _____

Lesson 5 — Forms of the Verb; Auxiliary Verbs

In this lesson you will examine a few more forms and uses of verbs, including some additional auxiliary verbs. With these forms and those that you have already examined, you will be acquainted with nearly all of the verb forms that the average speaker and writer will ever use.

In Lesson 2 you examined the partial conjugation of three verbs: *earn*, *grow*, and *be*. You may want to refer to that conjugation (pages 9–10) as we discuss a few more points about changes in verb form.

Third-person singular verbs in the present tense end in *s* (or *es*): *earns*, *teaches*, *is*, *has*. Notice that on nouns the *s* (*es*) ending shows a plural form; whereas on verbs it shows a singular form:

dogs, peaches	(plural nouns)
wags, sniffs	(singular verbs)

If you review the conjugation of the verb *be* in Lesson 2, you will notice the verb is completely irregular. Unlike any other verb in the language, it has three forms (*am*, *is*, and *are*) in the present tense and two forms (*was* and *were*) in the past tense.

In general, the tenses are used as follows:

Present:	Action occurring at the present moment. He *earns* a good salary.
Past:	Action occurring at a definite time before the present moment. Last year he *earned* a good salary.
Future:	Action occurring at some time beyond the present moment. Next year he *will earn* a good salary.
Present perfect:	Action continuing up to the present moment. So far this year he *has earned* $10,000.
Past perfect:	Action continuing to a fixed moment in the past. Before leaving for college, he *had earned* $10,000.
Future perfect:	Action continuing to a fixed moment in the future. By next Christmas he *will have earned* $10,000.

In Lesson 21 you will be reminded of a few usage problems involving tenses.

PRINCIPAL PARTS

We noted in Lesson 2 that *earn* is a regular verb and *grow* is an irregular verb. We customarily make use of three distinctive forms, called the **principal parts** of the verb, to show the difference between regular and irregular verbs. The following are the principal parts:

- *Base* or *infinitive*, the "name" of the verb, used in the present tense with *s* (*es*) added in the third-person singular

- *Past*, the form used in the simple past tense
- *Past participle*, the form used in the three perfect tenses

In all regular verbs, the past and the past participle are alike, formed simply by the addition of *ed* to the base form (or only *d* if the base word ends in *e*). Thus, *earn* becomes *earned*. Irregular verbs are more complicated because, for nearly all of them, the past tense and the past participle are not spelled alike. Thus, the past tense of *grow* is *grew*, and the past participle of *grow* is *grown*. Following are the three forms of some irregular verbs illustrating spelling changes and endings:

Base	Past	Past Participle
be	was, were	been
become	became	become
bite	bit	bitten
break	broke	broken
catch	caught	caught
do	did	done
eat	ate	eaten
put	put	put
ring	rang	rung
run	ran	run
see	saw	seen

(You will study more principal parts of verbs and the usage problems associated with them in Lesson 21.) Both regular and irregular verbs add *ing* to their base form to produce the **present participle**. The present participle is often used with auxiliary verbs.

AUXILIARY VERBS

In the sample conjugation in Lesson 2, you observed the use of *will* and *have* as auxiliary verbs in the future tense and the perfect tenses. Another important auxiliary is *be*, used with the present participle (the *ing* form of the main verb) to produce what is called the **progressive form**. As an example of its use, suppose someone asks you what you are doing in your English class. You probably would not reply, "Right now, we *review* parts of speech." Instead, you probably would say, "Right now, we *are reviewing* parts of speech," to show that the action is not fixed in an exact moment of time but is a continuing activity. This very useful type of verb occurs in all six tenses:

We are reviewing.
We were reviewing.
We will be reviewing.
We have been reviewing.
We had been reviewing.
We will have been reviewing.

Another type of auxiliary verb includes *may, might, must, can, could, would,* and *should. May, can,* and *might* are used to suggest possibility. *Can* sometimes also suggests capability.

I may go to town tomorrow.   (If certain conditions exist.)
I might go to town tomorrow.   (If certain conditions exist.)
I can go to town tomorrow.   (I am able to go.)

Must indicates an obligation:

I must go to town.

Could is used to indicate ability, possibility, or permission in the past tense:

I could have gone to town.   (If I had wanted to go.)

These words are called **modal auxiliaries**, and they are used the way *will* is used:

I *should study* this weekend.
I *should have studied* last weekend.

Occasionally, *do* acts as a modal auxiliary and combines with the base form of a main verb to make an "emphatic" form: "But I *did* pay that bill last month." In Lesson 6 you will examine the much more common use of the *do* auxiliary in questions and negatives.

Note that each of these modals attaches a slightly different meaning to the verb. A careful writer will study the dictionary for precise meanings and distinctions.

Other variations of some modals and time auxiliaries make use of *to* in the verb phrase:

Mr. Nelson *has to retire* [must retire] early.
You *ought to eat* [should eat] more vegetables.
I *used to be* a secretary.
Jim *was supposed to be* here at 10 o'clock.
I *am to depart* for Miami early in the morning.
I *am going to depart* for Miami early in the morning.
We *meant to leave* much earlier today.

Here are a few other points to remember about auxiliary verbs:

1. *Have*, *be*, and *do* are not used exclusively as auxiliaries; they are three of the most commonly used main verbs:

   I *have* a brown pen. [Main verb]
   I *have* lost my brown pen. [Auxiliary]
   He *is* a good speaker. [Main verb]
   He *is* becoming a good speaker. [Auxiliary]
   He *did* a good job for us. [Main verb]
   Yes, I *did* embellish the story somewhat. [Auxiliary]

2. When the verb unit contains auxiliaries, short adverbial modifiers may separate parts of the whole verb phrase:

   We *have* occasionally *been* sailing.
   He *has*, of course, *been telling* the truth.

3. In a few set expressions following introductory adverbs (usually adverbs of time), the subject is placed within the verb phrase between an auxiliary and the main verb:

Only lately *have* I *learned* to drive.

Rarely *do* we *turn on* the television set.

English Fundamentals Online

After you have completed Practice Sheets and Exercises in this lesson, you can find additional help and drill work at **MyWritingLab.Com,** in the section on Varying Sentence Structure.

Auxiliary Verbs; Basic Sentence Patterns

NAME _____ SCORE _____

Directions: Most of these sentences contain at least one auxiliary verb. (Some have two; some have three.) Copy the auxiliary verbs in the first space at the left. In the second space, write **1**, **2**, **3**, **4**, or **5** to identify the sentence pattern. If the sentence does not have an auxiliary verb, write the base form of the verb in the first space.

_____
_____
1. By the end of this work day, we will have worked on this report for almost fifteen hours.

_____
_____
2. By the end of this work day, we will have been working on this report for almost fifteen hours.

_____
_____
3. I have not seen my uncle for several weeks.

_____
_____
4. More than likely I will be seeing him at his house this weekend.

_____
_____
5. I will have sent you that information by e-mail tomorrow morning.

_____
_____
6. You should find the information very interesting.

_____
_____
7. Jane did catch the early train to the city this morning.

_____
_____
8. She should have been happy about her early arrival at work.

_____
_____
9. Last week she caught the later train on Thursday and Friday.

_____
_____
10. The later train made her late for work both days.

_____
_____
11. The memo should have told us about the change in the schedule for the meeting.

_____
_____
12. The speaker did become quite angry at the sarcastic remarks from members of the audience.

_____
_____
13. The speaker probably considered the sarcastic remarks from the audience inconsiderate.

_____
_____
14. The fire alarm has been ringing for almost five minutes now.

_____
_____
15. In fact, it has rung several times across the course of the morning.

_____
_____
16. The repeated sounding of the alarm has been extraordinarily disruptive.

_____
_____
17. Disruptions to the peace and quiet of the office have always been a welcome diversion from work.

_____ 18. The alarm gives us an opportunity for a short break and a pleasant
_____ walk outside the building.
_____ 19. The office staff has given that project a much attention as possible
_____ under the circumstances.
_____ 20. The interruptions by the fire alarm made that task very difficult
_____ for everyone in the office.
_____ 21. Except for that error, the team might have won the game.

_____
_____ 22. Because of heavy traffic, we should leave fairly early on Friday
_____ afternoon.
_____ 23. All of us need to study for several hours before that exam
_____ tomorrow.
_____ 24. That success in yesterday's sales presentation might make
_____ Al more confident in the future.
_____ 25. That successful presentation should give Al more confidence in
_____ future presentations.
_____ 26. My brother and I have been sailing on this lake for the past ten
_____ years.
_____ 27. Only recently has my grandmother learned the use of e-mail as a
_____ tool for communicating with her grandchildren.
_____ 28. She was extremely proud of herself for that accomplishment.

_____
_____ 29. Now she is thinking of the purchase of a digital camera.

_____
_____ 30. With such a camera, she could send pictures to all the
_____ grandchildren.
_____ 31. With such a camera, she might send her grandchildren pictures at
_____ any time.
_____ 32. Perhaps she ought to consider the purchase of a webcam for
_____ real-time conversations.
_____ 33. With a webcam, however, she would no longer write her
_____ grandchildren those wonderfully funny letters.
_____ 34. In fact, she should probably stick to letters and e-mails for
_____ communication with us.
_____ 35. Letters by "snail mail" are gradually becoming a thing of the past.

_____
_____ 36. In earlier days, people used to write each other long, graceful,
_____ news-filled letters.
_____ 37. Now short, pithy notes are constantly flying back and forth across
_____ the Internet.
_____ 38. The Internet is also making written communication short and
_____ choppy.
_____ 39. For several years, my brother has been using the Internet search
_____ engines in his search for parts for his old Ford.
_____ 40. Before the development of the Internet, he had to use the
_____ telephone in his search for parts.

NAME _____ SCORE _____

Directions: In the first space at the left of the sentence, write the form of the base of the verb. In the second space, write any auxiliary verbs. Some sentences may not have auxiliary verbs.

_____ 1. Surely, you have been reading the assignments on a regular basis.
_____

_____ 2. That studying, especially the group discussions, made us all ready
_____ for that final exam.

_____ 3. I have always thought that long hill beside the river the most
_____ difficult part of the cross-country course.

_____ 4. That idea in the professor's lecture does not connect with anything
_____ in the reading assignment.

_____ 5. Perhaps she has not shown us the connection yet.
_____

_____ 6. By later this afternoon, I will have broken down that long
_____ assignment into manageable parts.

_____ 7. Most assignments appear too long and too unmanageable at first
_____ glance.

_____ 8. I have to find a small, easily finished part of an assignment at the
_____ beginning of my work.

_____ 9. Yesterday Anne and I should have known the answers to the last
_____ two questions on that quiz.

_____ 10. Unfortunately, we had flown across that section of the review
_____ sheet without any real concentration on the details.

_____ 11. Late that night the review sheet had probably become a blur in
_____ front of our eyes.

_____ 12. We will have gone over that section two or three times before the
_____ next test.

_____ 13. Anne and I will have found a third person as a study partner
_____ before the next test.

_____ 14. Surely, three great minds can get control of all the information
_____ pertinent to the test.

_____ 15. By the time of the test, we will have done several comprehensive
_____ reviews of the important material.

45

Directions: In the space at the left, write one of the following to identify the function of the italicized words:

S.C. [subjective complement]   I.O. [indirect object]

D.O. [direct object]   O.C. [objective complement]

If the italicized word is not a complement, leave the space blank. Circle every auxiliary verb.

_____ 1. The little children on the tour have always considered the gorilla their favorite *animal*.

_____ 2. During their tour of the zoo, the children will see five *gorillas* in a specialized habitat.

_____ 3. The gorillas have always appeared *amused* at the appearance of the children.

_____ 4. The sight of the gorillas has always offered the *children* a chance for some hearty laughter.

_____ 5. By the end of their tour, the children will have walked near *elephants*, giraffes, and many other animals.

_____ 6. By the end of my elementary school experience, I had accompanied my *classmates* on trips to the zoo at least a dozen times.

_____ 7. Recently, several large cities have built huge *aquariums* as both attractions for tourists and research facilities for scientists.

_____ 8. These facilities are not a *collection* of many small tanks of water, fish, and plants.

_____ 9. Instead, the aquarium, a large building, will have inside it several huge *tanks* 50 to 75 feet long and 20 to 30 feet deep.

_____ 10.We could probably consider each huge tank a *sample* of a particular water habitat.

_____ 11. The tanks might contain *inhabitants* of the ocean, or a lake, or a mountain stream.

_____ 12. Each tank is a complete *environment* with everything necessary for the life of the inhabitants inside it.

_____ 13. In one aquarium, visitors can walk down a long, sloping *ramp* past every level of a model river.

_____ 14. At the top of the ramp, a typical river bank opens *itself* before the eyes of visitors.

_____ 15. By the end of the walk visitors will have been *witnesses* to every level of the river's life.

Any long piece of writing made up exclusively of basic sentences would be too monotonous to read. You should think of the basic sentences not as models for your writing but as elementary units, important because they are the structures from which more effective sentences develop. In this lesson, we look at two alterations of basic sentence patterns:

1. Sentences that use passive verbs
2. Sentences in the form of a question

Lessons 7 through 11 then show how basic sentences can be combined and certain elements can be reduced to subordinate clauses and phrases to produce varied, well-developed sentences.

PASSIVE VOICE

In Lesson 2 you examined a partial conjugation of the verb *earn*. The forms listed there are in the active voice, which means that the subject is the doer of the action. A more complete conjugation would include the passive voice. In the passive voice, the subject is not the doer of the action; it is the receiver of the action. Thus, the verb is always transitive. Passive verb forms make use of the auxiliary verb *be* combined with the past participle of the verb, as shown in the following illustration of the third-person singular in the six tenses:

This amount is earned.
This amount was earned.
This amount will be earned.
This amount has been earned.
This amount had been earned.
This amount will have been earned.

The present and past tenses of progressive verbs can also be shifted to the passive voice, giving us forms in which *be* is used in two auxiliary capacities in the same verb form:

These cars *are being sold* at a loss.
These cars *were being sold* at a loss.

Because only transitive verbs have passive forms, only sentence patterns 3, 4, and 5 can be altered to the passive voice. When the idea of a Pattern 3 sentence in the active voice is expressed with a passive verb, there is no direct object (complement) in the sentence:

| **Active voice**: | Children play games. |
| **Passive voice**: | Games are played [by children]. |

If the doer of the verb's action is expressed in a sentence using a passive verb, the doer must occur as the object of the preposition *by*. When a Pattern 4 sentence is altered to form a passive construction, the indirect object that follows the active verb sometimes becomes the subject of the passive verb:

Active voice: John gave Allen a model plane.

Passive voice: Allen was given a model plane [by John].

Here the passive verb is followed by a complement, plane, which we continue to call a direct object in spite of the fact that it follows a passive verb. It is also possible, in a Pattern 4 sentence, to make the direct object the subject of a passive verb, making the sentence read thus:

The model plane was given to Allen (by John).

Notice also how a Pattern 5 sentence can be given a different kind of expression by means of a passive verb:

Active voice: The parents consider the child a genius.

The parents consider the child clever.

Passive voice: The child is considered a genius [by the parents].

The child is considered clever [by the parents].

In these sentences the direct object becomes the subject, but the passive verb requires a complement (*genius*, *clever*). Because the complement renames or describes the subject, it is called a subjective complement.

The passive voice serves a real purpose in effective communication: It should be used when the *doer* of the action is unknown or is of secondary interest in the statement. In such a situation, the writer, wishing to focus attention on the *receiver* of the action, places that unit in the emphatic subject position. The passive verb form makes this arrangement possible. Thus, instead of some vague expression, such as "Somebody should wash these windows," we can say, "These windows *should be washed*."

Sometimes the passive voice is described as "weak." Admittedly, some writers do get into the habit of using the passive form when there is little justification for it. In most narrative writing, the doer of the action is logically the subject of the verb. "The fullback crossed the goal line" would certainly be preferred to "The goal line was crossed by the fullback," a version that gives the same information but tends to stop any action suggested by the sentence. The passive voice also lends itself to a kind of muddied, heavy-footed writing that produces prose like this:

It *is* now *rumored* that the secretary of defense *has been informed* that contingent plans *have been made* to. . . .

The writer of such a sentence, however, probably finds the passive voice effectively hides the identity of the person who is spreading the rumor, who has informed the secretary of defense, or who has made the plans. This use of the passive voice creates an impersonal, bureaucratic language popular in many institutions.

You should practice using passive constructions so you can use this important device when it is called for. Equally important, if a criticism of your writing mentions doubtful uses of the passive voice, you need to be able to recognize passive verbs in order to change them when necessary.

QUESTIONS

In the sentence types you examined in earlier lessons, you noted the normal positioning of the main sentence parts: the subject first, followed by the verb, followed by the complement, if any. In questions, however, other arrangements are possible. As we study these new structures, we must first recognize the fact that there are two kinds of questions:

1. Questions answered by *yes* or *no*
2. Questions answered by information

QUESTIONS ANSWERED BY *YES* OR *NO*

In the following paired sentences, the first sentence is a statement and the second sentence a related question. These sentences demonstrate how the structure of a yes/no question differs from that of a statement.

1. Beth is happy.   Is Beth happy?

2. You were there.   Were you there?

3. You see Ms. Locke often.   Do you see Ms. Locke often?

4. You heard the announcement.   Did you hear the announcement?

Notice from these examples that if the verb is *be* in the present or past tense, the subject and the *be* form (*am*, *are*, *is*, *was*, or *were*) reverse positions. With other one-word verbs in the present or past tense, the proper form of the auxiliary *do* is used, followed by the subject and the base form of the main verb.

If the verb already has an auxiliary, the subject follows the auxiliary verb. If there are two or more auxiliaries, the subject follows the first one.

5. You have seen the movie.   Have you seen the movie?

6. They will arrive later.   Will they arrive later?

7. The house is being painted.   Is the house being painted?

8. He should have been told.   Should he have been told?

When the verb is *have* in the present tense, two versions of the question are possible: the subject-verb reversal and the *do* auxiliary. (See Supplement 1.)

9. You have enough money.   Have you enough money?

10. You have enough money.   Do you have enough money?

QUESTIONS ANSWERED BY INFORMATION

Some questions ask for information rather than for a *yes* or *no* response. These questions make use of words called **interrogatives**, words that stand for unknown persons, things, or descriptive qualities. The most commonly used interrogatives are these:

Pronouns:	*who (whom), which, what*
Adjectives:	*whose, which, what*
Adverbs:	*when, where, why, how*

The interrogative pronoun *who*, which stands for an unknown person or persons, has three forms:

1. *Who*, when it is used as a subject or a subjective complement
2. *Whose*, when it is used as a possessive modifier of a noun
3. *Whom*, when it is used as an object

(In a later lesson you will learn that these three forms of *who* have another important use in subordinate clauses; the choice between *who* and *whom* as a problem of usage is discussed more extensively in Lesson 24.)

In questions using these interrogatives, the normal arrangement of the main sentence parts is retained only when the interrogative is the subject or a modifier of the subject. Here again we use paired statements and related questions to demonstrate these structures:

1. *My brother* [S.] paid the bill. *Who* [S.] paid the bill?

2. *Five cars* [S.] were damaged. *How* many cars [S.] were damaged?

In all other situations the subject-verb position is altered as it is with yes/no questions. The interrogative word, or the unit containing the interrogative word, stands at the beginning of the sentence to signal that a question, not a statement, is forthcoming:

I studied *geometry* [D.O.] last night.
What [D.O.] did you study last night?

You saw *Jim* [D.O.] at the party.
Whom [D.O.] did you see at the party?

She is Mother's *cousin* [S.C.].
Who [S.C.] is she?

We can use Bill's *car* [D.O.].
Whose car [D.O.] can we use?

You spent 15 *dollars* [D.O.].
How much money [D.O.] did you spend?

You [S.] called *Bob* [D.O.] a *thief* [O.C.].
Who [S.] called Bob a thief?

Whom [D.O.] did you call a thief?
What [O.C.] did you call Bob?

When the interrogative unit is the object of a preposition, two arrangements of the question are often possible:

1. The entire prepositional phrase may stand at the beginning.
2. The interrogative may stand at the beginning with the preposition in its usual position.

The speaker was referring *to the mayor.*
To whom was the speaker referring?
Whom was the speaker referring to?

(See Supplement 2.)

SUPPLEMENT 1

The type of verb also determines the structuring of sentences that are negative rather than positive. The positioning of the negator *not* (or its contraction, *n't*) depends on the presence or absence of an auxiliary verb. Sentences using *be* or *have* must be considered special cases.

1. If the verb is *be* in the present tense or in the past tense, used either as the main verb or as an auxiliary verb, the *not* follows the *be* form:

    I *am not* pleased with the report.
    He *was not* [wasn't] available.
    They *were not* [weren't] invited.

2. With other one-word verbs in the present or past tense, the proper form of the auxiliary *do* is used followed by the negator and the base form of the main verb:

    I *do not* [don't] expect a reward.
    He *does not* [doesn't] attend regularly.
    We *did not* [didn't] respond.

3. If the verb already has an auxiliary, the negator follows the auxiliary. When there are two or more auxiliaries, the *not* follows the first one:

    We *could not* [couldn't] see very well.
    I *may not* have understood him.
    They *will not* [won't] refund my money.
    This cake *ought not* to have been baked so long.

4. When *have* in the present tense is the main verb, two negative forms are possible:

    I *have not* [haven't] enough time to play.
    I *do not* [don't] have enough time to play.

SUPPLEMENT 2

At the informal language level, another version—"*Who* was the speaker referring to?"—is often found, despite the traditional demand for the objective case for the object of a preposition. The formal level of both spoken and written English calls for "*To whom* was the speaker referring?"

English Fundamentals Online

> After you have completed Practice Sheets and Exercises in this lesson, you can find additional help and drill work at **MyWritingLab.com**, in the section on Consistent Verb Tense and Active Voice.

Alterations of Basic Sentence Patterns:
Passive Verbs; Questions

NAME _____ SCORE _____

Directions: These sentences follow patterns 3, 4, or 5. In the first space at the left, write the pattern number. In the second space, write the verb form used when the italicized word in the sentence becomes the subject.

_____4_____

will be sent   Tomorrow Jim will send you a copy of that letter.

_____   1. The manager named *John Douglas* chair of that new committee.

_____

_____   2. Jack told *us* the story of his misadventures on his vacation.

_____

_____   3. Will should have started *work* on that paper last week.

_____

_____   4. You must file a change of address *form* with the Postal Service.

_____

_____   5. The company keeps its *costs* for that item a secret from its
_____   competitors.

_____   6. The children colored their *pictures* of the pasture a peaceful green.

_____

_____   7. After a long search, Alice has discovered that *picture* of her
_____   grandparents.

_____   8. The company will give *Brian* the award for community service
_____   or this year.

_____   9. The company president has called *Brian* a genuine public servant.

_____

_____   10. By noon the teacher had already read the class two *chapters* of
_____   that novel.

Directions: This exercise contrasts the structure of a question with the structure of a statement. In the space at the left, copy the word from the question that serves the function indicated in the parentheses in the statement:

S. [subject]   O.C. [objective complement]

D.O. [direct object]   O.P. [object of preposition]

S.C. [subjective complement]

_____ 1. Will the new dive instructor be John Jenkins?
(S.C.)   The new dive instructor will be John Jenkins (S.C.).

_____ 2. What will I find on the bill?
(D.O.)   I will find the charges (D.O.) for that installation on the bill.

_____ 3. Which applicant is best qualified for that job?
(S.C.)   The last applicant is best qualified (S.C.) for that job.

_____ 4. What did you encounter in your preparations for that report?
(D.O.)   I encountered several problems (D.O.) in my preparations for that report.

_____ 5. How many people did you invite to the party?
(S.)   I (S.) invited twenty people to the party.

_____ 6. To whom did you give a copy of that report?
(O.P.)   I gave a copy of that report to all the managers (O.P.).

_____ 7. Who will be the director of that new movie?
(S.)   Jose Blanco (S.) will be the director of that new movie.

_____ 8. Will the studio name Jose Blanco the director of that new movie?
(O.C.)   The studio will name Jose Blanco the director (O.C.) of that new movie.

_____ 9. What did Barbara Phillips apply for?
(O.P.)   Barbara Phillips applied for the comptroller's job (O.P.).

_____ 10. Has the executive committee chosen Barbara Phillips as
(O.C.)   comptroller?
                       The executive committee has chosen Barbara Phillips as comptroller (O.C.).

_____ 11. Who is the captain of the varsity soccer team?
(S.C.)   The captain of the varsity soccer team is Georgina Olson (S.C.)

_____ 12. Who will the captain of the varsity soccer team?
(S.)   Georgina Olson (S.) will be the captain of the varsity soccer team.

_____ 13. What are those people on the boat concerned about?
(O.P.)   Those people on the boat are concerned about that nearby storm (O.P.).

_____ 14. How many people came to last night's meeting?
(S.)   Ten people (S.) came to last night's meeting.

_____ 15. What color will you paint that newly restored car?
(O.C.)   I will paint that newly restored car a bright yellow (O.C.).

Alterations of Basic Sentence Patterns: Passive Verbs; Questions

NAME _____ SCORE _____

Directions: Each of the following sentences contains a verb in the passive voice. Underline the verb. Rewrite each sentence using an active-voice form of that verb. (You will need to supply a logical subject if the passive verb does not do so.) If your rewrites are done correctly, your first four sentences will follow Pattern 3, your next three will follow Pattern 4, and the last three will follow Pattern 5.

1. By late afternoon, all the tickets to the big football game had been bought by fans.

   _____

2. That strange story will be examined from all angles by the television reporters.

   _____

3. That series of children's stories was written by a man with no special fondness for children.

   _____

4. The football games on Monday night are watched by millions in the United States and overseas.

   _____

5. All the students should have been shown the changes in the registration schedule.

   _____

6. Many more students could have been allowed the opportunity to attend that lecture.

   _____

7. A very difficult paper has been assigned us by our history teacher.

   _____

8. Within a few moments all our computers had been rendered inoperable by the computer virus.

   _____

9. By tomorrow at noon, all of that furniture will have been painted a glossy black.

   _____

10. At the team meeting last night, Josh Hawkins was chosen captain by the players.

    _____

Directions: The italicized word in each of the following sentences is a complement or the object of a preposition. In the space at the left, write one of the following abbreviations to identify the function of the italicized word.

D.O. [direct object]   O.C. [objective complement]
S.C. [subjective complement]   O.P. [object of preposition]
I.O. [indirect object]

_____ 1. Shall we declare this long, drawn-out game a *tie*?

_____ 2. *Which* of those three apartments are you moving to next semester?

_____ 3. Did Jennie consider herself *successful* in that sales job?

_____ 4. *Whom* should we choose as the treasurer for this next year?

_____ 5. Which of those two books shall we give *Margaret?*

_____ 6. Which of those two books shall we give to *Margaret?*

_____ 7. How *much* of that report did you show the managers yesterday?

_____ 8. Where in the backyard shall we plant that *dogwood tree*?

_____ 9. What *color* will you paint the outside of the house?

_____ 10. *What* is your sister's batting average for this season?

_____ 11. In what *condition* did you find those old documents in the attic?

_____ 12. Did you find those old documents still *readable*?

_____ 13. Why did no one tell *us* about that other road across the mountain?

_____ 14. How *close* is the deadline for submission of this report?

_____ 15. How much *time* do we have for the submission of this report?

_____ 16. Who set *free* all those pigeons in the cages at the zoo?

_____ 17. *What* was the cost of that new computer on your desk?

_____ 18. To which *teachers* did you send the copies of that report?

_____ 19. What *condition* was the car in after the accident?

_____ 20. Did you think that presentation Mary Sue's best *work*?

Check Sheet

You can use Check Sheets in three ways. You can use them as a quick review at the end of each unit; you can use them as another, shorter presentation of the materials in the unit; or you can use them as a quick reference guide to refresh your understanding of a principle as you write papers for English or other classes.

PARTS OF SPEECH

☐ **Nouns**

☐ Common nouns are the names of persons, places, things, qualities, or ideas.

☐ Proper nouns are the names of specific individuals in a class.

Common	Proper
girl	Maria
city	Minneapolis
bat	Omaha Classic
honesty	(no proper form)
economic theory	Marxism

☐ Common nouns are not capitalized, but proper nouns are.

☐ Nouns are singular if they indicate one in a class, plural if they indicate two or more.

☐ **Pronouns**

☐ Pronouns take the place of nouns when reusing the noun would be repetitive.
- *Personal pronouns*: I, you, he, she, it, we, they
- *Demonstrative pronouns*: this, that, these, those
- *Indefinite pronouns*: each, either, neither, one, anyone, and other examples
- *Possessive pronouns*: mine, yours, his, hers, its, ours, theirs

☐ Nouns and pronouns answer the question Who? or What?

☐ **Verbs**

☐ Verbs express action, existence, or condition, and they combine with nouns or pronouns used as subjects to make a statement.

Maria is tired.
Tom runs.
Tyrone sees the dog.

☐ Verbs answer the question What happens? or What is?

☐ Verbs change form to indicate
- *Person*: first—I, we; second—you; third—she, they
- *Number*: singular indicates one thing, plural indicates two or more

- *Tense*: time of the action or existence
  Present: I run
  Past: I ran
  Future: I will run
  Present perfect: I have run
  Past perfect: I had run
  Future perfect: I shall have run

☐ Verb forms for the various tenses are developed from the principal parts of the verb: base, past, and past participle.

☐ The sense of verbs may be changed by adding forms of *to be* and an *-ing* ending to the verb to create progressive tenses.

☐ The sense of verbs can be changed to indicate condition and possibility by adding modal auxiliaries such as *may, might, would, could,* and *should.*

☐ Transitive verbs change voice from active (*The boy saw the dog.*) to passive (*The dog was seen by the boy.*).

☐ Adjectives

☐ Adjectives modify nouns—that is, adjectives change our sense of the noun by adding a limit, description, or quality to the noun. Adjectives occur in three positions:

Preceding the noun	The tall girl ran.
Following a linking verb	The tall girl is happy.
Directly after the noun	The girl, happy. . . .

☐ Adjectives can show degree or strength by changing their form:
  The girl is happy.
  She is happier than I am.
  She is the happiest girl in our class.

☐ Adjectives answer questions such as How big? What shape? What color?

☐ Adverbs

☐ Adverbs change our sense of—modify—verbs, adjectives, other adverbs, or whole sentences:
  The girl walked quickly.
  She walked quite slowly.
  The very young girl walked out of the room.
  Certainly, we'll be there on time.

☐ Adverbs most frequently answer the question How? When? or Where?

☐ Prepositions

☐ Prepositions establish relationships between a noun (the object of the preposition) and another word in a sentence.
  The plane flew into the cloud, under the cloud, behind the cloud.

☐ **Sentence Patterns**

☐ The parts of speech are combined into sentences that follow five specific patterns.

The first two patterns employ intransitive verbs—that is, verbs that transfer no action to an object.
- Pattern 1 (intransitive verb with no complement needed to complete action)
    The bird flies.
- Pattern 2 (intransitive linking verb with subjective complement, either a noun or adjective)
    The man is a scientist.
    The man is brilliant.

The next three patterns employ transitive verbs—that is, verbs that transfer action from the subject to object.
- Pattern 3 (transitive verb with a direct object receiving the action)
    The pilot flies the plane.

Note that some verbs—for example the verb *to fly*—can be intransitive or transitive.
- Pattern 4 (transitive verbs such as *give* and *show*, with a direct object and an indirect object)
    The woman showed us two coats.
- Pattern 5 (transitive verb such as *call*, *think*, *find*, and *elect*, with a direct object and an objective complement, either a noun or an adjective)
    The teacher called her a genius.
    The teacher called her brilliant.

☐ All of these sentence patterns can be enriched with the use of adjective and adverb modifiers and prepositions.

☐ **Questions**

- Questions answered by *yes* or *no* employ a change in order to indicate the question:
    Maria is happy.
    Is Maria happy?
- Questions employ interrogatives to request information:
    Pronouns: who, whom, which, that
    Adjectives: whose, which, what
    Adverbs: when, where, why, how

Clauses and Phrases

Lessons, Practice Sheets, and Exercises

Lesson 7 · *Coordination: Compound Sentences*

To begin to study sentences that build on the simple patterns discussed in the previous lessons, let's examine a student writer's description of a snowstorm. Each sentence is numbered for later reference.

(1) The first really serious snowfall began at dusk and had already spread a treacherous powdering over the roads by the time the homeward-bound crowds reached their peak. (2) As the evening deepened, porch and street lights glowed in tight circles through semi-solid air. (3) The snow did not fall in a mass of fat, jovial flakes; it squatted in a writhing mist of tiny particles and seemed less snow than a dense, animated fog. (4) Through the night the wind rose, worrying the trees as a puppy shakes a slipper. (5) It rushed round the corners of buildings and tumbled over roofs, from which it snatched armfuls of snow to scatter in the streets. (6) Save for the occasional grumble of a sanitation truck sullenly pushing its plow, all sound stopped. (7) Even the wind was more felt than heard. (8) Day did not dawn. (9) The world changed from charcoal gray to lead between six and seven, but the change was one from night to lesser night. (10) The snow still whirled. (11) Drifts had altered the neat symmetry of peaked roofs into irregular mountain ranges ending in sheer cliffs four or five feet above the lesward eaves. (12) The downwind side of every solid object cast a snow shadow that tapered away from a sharp hump until it merged into the surrounding flat pallor. (13) Along the street, windshield wipers, odd bits of chrome, startling blanks of black glass, and isolated headlights decorated large white mounds. (14) Men and women shut off their alarm clocks, stretched, yawned, looked out of their windows, paused in a moment of guilt, and went back to bed. (15) Snow had taken the day for its own, and there was no point in arguing with it.

The 15 sentences of this paragraph are all made up of groups of related words called clauses. A **clause** is a group of words that always contains a subject and a verb in combination. Recalling the scenes, actions, and responses associated with the event, the author has created a series of clauses (subject-verb combinations): the snowfall began, the snowfall had spread a powdering, the homeward-bound crowds reached their peak, the evening deepened, lights glowed, and so on.

Although it may not be apparent when you first read the paragraph, the entire passage is based on short, simple sentences of the patterns studied in the preceding lessons. The writer's problem was to combine or alter these short statements in order to put them into their most pleasing and effective form. Presenting all of them as basic sentences would communicate the author's ideas but in a form that, in addition to being monotonous, would not give proper emphasis to the most important ideas. Only two sentences (8 and 10) are retained as one-subject, one-verb basic sentences. Some of the sentences (3, 9, and 15) combine two basic sentences, giving each clause equal force. Two sentences (1 and 5) join more than one verb to the same subject. Sentence 13 joins four subjects to the same verb, and Sentence 14 has two subjects joined to six verbs.

In the next several lessons, we examine the word groups—independent clauses, subordinate clauses, and phrases—that are the language tools allowing a writer to apply various strategies to produce effective sentences.

COMPOUNDING SENTENCES

A sentence, as you learned in Lesson 1, is a word group containing a subject and a verb. From this definition, and from the one already given for a clause, it would seem that a sentence and a clause are identical. And this is true for one kind of clause, the **independent clause** (also called the *main clause* or *principal clause*). The independent clause can stand by itself as a sentence. Every example sentence and every exercise sentence that you have worked with thus far in this book has been made up of one independent clause. We call a sentence consisting of one independent clause a **simple sentence**.

One means of combining or altering short, simple sentences is called *compounding*, joining grammatically equal parts so they function together. We can join two or more subjects, verbs, complements, or modifiers by using a **coordinating conjunction**. (**Conjunctions** are words that join words, phrases, or clauses; conjunctions that join grammatically equal units are called *coordinating*.) The three common coordinating conjunctions are *and*, *but*, and *or*; other coordinators are *nor*, *for*, *yet*, and *so*. With the use of a coordinating conjunction, we can join two very short sentences and create a longer, more readable sentence.

Dad read the notice. I read the notice.
Dad *and* I read the notice. [Compound subjects]

Margo enjoys golf. Margo enjoys tennis.
She enjoys golf *and* tennis. [Compound direct objects]

I studied very hard. I failed the test.
I studied very hard *but* failed the test. [Compound verbs]

I found the lecture interesting. I found the lecture instructive.
I found the lecture interesting *and* instructive. [Compound objective complements]

I can see you during your lunch hour. I can see you after 5 o'clock.
I can see you during your lunch hour *or* after 5 o'clock. [Compound prepositional phrases]

COMPOUND SENTENCES

Compounding is often used with two (sometimes more than two) independent clauses; the result is a common type of sentence called the **compound sentence**. We can create compound sentences in two ways.

CLAUSES JOINED BY A COORDINATING CONJUNCTION

Any of the coordinating conjunctions already mentioned can be used to join two independent clauses. The normal punctuation is a comma before the conjunction:

I had reviewed the material, and I did well on the test.

It is important to distinguish this sentence from a nearly identical version using a compound verb:

I had reviewed the material and did well on the test.

In this version, the sentence is not a compound sentence because there is no separate subject for the second verb. It is a simple sentence with a compound verb and should be written without a comma.

CLAUSES JOINED BY A SEMICOLON

Sometimes the two independent clauses stand side by side with no word tying them together:

No one was in sight; I was alone in the huge auditorium.

Often, the second of the two clauses joined by a semicolon begins with an adverbial unit that serves as a kind of tie between the clauses. This adverbial unit may be:

1. A simple adverb

Currently, we are renting an apartment; *later*, we hope to buy a house.
These were last year's highlights; *now* we must look at plans for next year.

2. A short phrase

I cannot comment on the whole concert; *in fact*, I slept through the last part of it.

3. A conjunctive adverb

Your arguments were well presented; *however*, we feel that the plan is too expensive.

The most common conjunctive adverbs are *therefore, however, nevertheless, consequently, moreover, otherwise, besides, furthermore*, and *accordingly*. These words, often followed by a comma, should be used cautiously; they usually contribute to a heavy, formal tone. To lessen this effect, writers often place them, set off by commas, within the second clause:

Your arguments were well presented; we feel, *however*, that the plan is too expensive.

Because adverbial units like *later* and *therefore* are *not* coordinating conjunctions, the use of a comma to join the two clauses is inappropriate. This error is often called a *comma splice* or a *comma fault*. The important thing to remember is that when independent clauses are joined by a coordinating conjunction, the use of a comma is the custom. When there is no coordinating conjunction, the comma will not suffice; the customary mark is the semicolon. Joining two independent clauses by using only a coordinating conjunction without a comma or by using only a conjunctive adverb with no punctuation creates a problem called a *run-on sentence*. Such sentences are awkward and can create confusion. Following the rules for joining independent clauses will help you to avoid these two problems. We study these punctuation rules thoroughly in Lesson 17.

English Fundamentals Online

After you have completed Practice Sheets and Exercises in this lesson, you can find additional help and drill work at **MyWritingLab.com**, in the section on Basic Sentence Patterns; Combining Sentences; Varying Sentence Structure.

NAME _____   SCORE _____

Directions: The following 25 sentences illustrate three types of sentences:

Type 1. The sentence is a simple sentence with a subject and a compound verb, i.e., two verbs joined by a coordinating conjunction. Normal punctuation: none

> *The men finished the work and left for home.*

Type 2. The sentence is a compound sentence, i.e., two independent clauses joined by a coordinating conjunction (*and, but, or, nor, for, yet,* or *so*). Normal punctuation: comma before the conjunction

> *The men finished the work, and they left for home.*

Type 3. The sentence is a compound sentence with no coordinating conjunction joining the independent clauses. (The second clause often contains an adverbial unit such as *now, thus,* or *therefore.*) Normal punctuation: semicolon

> *The men finished the work early; thus, they started the weekend at noon.*

In each of the following sentences, a ^ marks a point of punctuation. If the sentence is Type 1, write **0** in the space at the left. If it is Type 2, write **C** (for comma) in the space. If the sentence is Type 3, write **S** (for semicolon) in the space.

_____ 1. The girl in the back of the library opened her book ^ and started to read.

_____ 2. The girl in the back of the library opened her book ^ then she started to read.

_____ 3. The girl in the back of the library closed her book ^ and then she walked out with some of her friends.

_____ 4. The two men planned a round of golf ^ however, a heavy rain set in and kept them indoors all day.

_____ 5. The two stayed indoors all day ^ for it rained heavily from morning till late afternoon.

_____ 6. The heavy rain annoyed the two men ^ for other people, the rain brought a much needed rest.

_____ 7. The two women worked all day on that computer problem ^ yet by the end of the day they still had not solved it.

_____ 8. The two women worked all day on that computer problem ^ yet by the end of the day still had not solved it.

_____ 9. By the end of the day, the women had not solved the problem ^ so they called in a person from technical support.

_____ 10. That story is quite funny ^ but the students seem totally uninterested.

_____ 11. The students lacked interest in the story ^ for it was almost time for the football game.

_____ 12. Most of the students left for the game ^ a few, however, stayed for the end of the story.

_____ 13. Sam stayed for the end of the story ^ but did not find it very funny.

_____ 14. The football game provided an exciting end to the day ^ for the team won the game by one point.

_____ 15. Until the last few minutes of the game, the score was tied ^ finally, at the last minute, our team scored and won the game.

_____ 16. Our group printed the final version of our report ^ and then left the office for lunch.

_____ 17. Our manager did not pick up our report immediately ^ nor did she read it until the next day.

_____ 18. Finally, the manager read the report ^ and seemed pleased by the presentation.

_____ 19. One page of the report was missing ^ but apparently the manager did not notice that fact.

_____ 20. In our reading of the report, we noted the missing page ^ so we printed a new, complete copy of the report.

_____ 21. The weather is bright and clear this morning ^ so I will take the dog for a long walk.

_____ 22. The dog has a heavy winter coat ^ thus he is never bothered by cold weather.

_____ 23. I, however, must wear a heavy winter coat ^ or I will suffer from the cold.

_____ 24. My new jacket is made from recycled Styrofoam cups ^ therefore, the discarded cups are put to good use.

_____ 25. My new jacket is both light and warm ^ so I prefer it over my old jacket.

Coordination: Compound Sentences

NAME _____ SCORE _____

Directions: The following 25 sentences illustrate three types of sentences:

Type 1. The sentence is a simple sentence with a subject and a compound verb, i.e., two verbs joined by a coordinating conjunction. Normal punctuation: none

The men finished the work and left for home.

Type 2. The sentence is a compound sentence, i.e., two independent clauses joined by a coordinating conjunction (*and, but, or, nor, for, yet,* or *so*). Normal punctuation: comma before the conjunction

The men finished the work, and they left for home.

Type 3. The sentence is a compound sentence with no coordinating conjunction joining the independent clauses. (The second clause often contains an adverbial unit such as *now, thus,* or *therefore.*) Normal punctuation: semicolon

The men finished the work early; thus, they started the weekend at noon.

It is important to establish the relationship between the two clauses of a compound sentence by choosing an appropriate conjunction. In each of the following sentences, a blank space appears where a conjunction might appear. In the blank, write in the conjunction needed in that sentence. For Type 3 sentences, leave the space blank to indicate that there is no conjunction needed. In each sentences, a ^ marks a point of punctuation. If the sentence is Type 1, write **0** in the space at the left. If it is Type 2, write **C** (for comma) in the space. If the sentence is Type 3, write **S** (for semicolon) in the space.

_____ 1. That girl is one of my sister's best friends ^ _____ I have not seen her for several months.

_____ 2. Two of her friends recently moved to Seattle ^ _____ my sister will visit them this summer.

_____ 3. The visit will probably occur in June ^ _____ might be postponed until August.

_____ 4. In the middle of July, my sister will attend a conference in Aspen ^ _____ two prominent architects will make a presentation at the conference.

_____ 5. At this time my sister's major is architecture ^ _____ she might change her major to interior design.

_____ 6. Knowledge of architecture is useful for interior designers ^ _____ they must often supervise major renovation projects.

_____ 7. One of my friends is an engineering major ^ _____ she enjoys math and science courses.

_____ 8. She also has great skill in art ^ _____ wants a secure position with a steady salary.

_____ 9. Work as an artist cannot provide much security ^ _____ thus, she will pursue her art work only as a hobby.

_____ 10. My hobby is fishing in isolated places ^ _____ I find isolation in the wilderness a very calming influence.

_____ 11. I often go to a mountain stream near my grandfather's farm ^ _____ the stream provides a home for both rainbow and native brown trout.

_____ 12. I fish that stream during the summer and fall ^ _____ for the rest of the year, I fish off the coast in the Gulf of Mexico.

_____ 13. Some find the open waters of the Gulf a disturbing sight ^ _____ those waters always seem tranquil to me.

_____ 14. Usually the waters are quite calm ^ _____ occasionally, however, a passing squall makes the waters quite rough.

_____ 15. On those occasions I run my boat to the lee side of an island ^ _____ wait there for the winds to quiet down.

_____ 16. My sister does not like boats or fishing ^ _____ instead, she prefers soccer and volleyball.

_____ 17. My sister does not like boats or fishing ^ _____ prefers soccer and volleyball.

_____ 18. Soccer is wildly popular in many areas of this country ^ _____ hundreds of thousands of elementary and middle school kids play soccer every weekend.

_____ 19. Youth soccer is available for kids as young as 4 or 5 years of age ^ _____ is also available for 18- and 19-year-olds.

_____ 20. Soccer for boys and young men is quite popular ^ _____ the programs for girls and young women are even more popular.

_____ 21. Volleyball is an exciting sport ^ _____ its popularity is growing in many parts of the country.

_____ 22. High schools now offer varsity volleyball for boys ^ _____ many colleges now have both men's and women's volleyball teams.

_____ 23. My sister and her friends often play beach volleyball ^ _____ this game is played with two people on a team.

_____ 24. An actual beach is not required for the sport ^ _____ does the court need to be near an ocean or a lake.

_____ 25. A beach volleyball court can be anywhere ^ _____ only a sand-filled box, a net, and a ball are required for play.

Directions: Combine the short sentences in each numbered item into one longer compound sentence. Use coordinating conjunctions or conjunctive adverbs that clearly establish the relationship between the two clauses in the new sentence. Add punctuation where it is needed.

1. John has broken two strings on his guitar. He will need to go to the store for replacements.

   _____

2. A few people arrived on time for class. Most, however, were more than five minutes late.

   _____

3. Barbara has an A average in all her classes. She never seems to study very much for them.

   _____

4. Carl finished his work on the biology paper. Then, he studied for two hours for a history test.

   _____

5. Denice should buy a new car. Perhaps she should sell the old car and ride the bus to her classes.

   _____

6. I need to work in the library until late Friday afternoon. At that time I will meet heavy traffic on my way out of town.

   _____

7. Harry and Joe plan a trip to the West Coast this summer. From there they might go on to Alaska.

   _____

8. Margaret is falling behind in chemistry class. She might be able to pass with a great deal of extra study.

   _____

9. Alexis can take a job in Seattle after graduation. She might move back to her hometown.

   _____

10. The economy is improving slowly at this time. Consequently, more jobs might be available after graduation.

    _____

Brief Writing Assignment: Write a paragraph of five or six sentences describing the desk or table where you do your college assignments. Use one compound verb and two compound sentences.

To this point you have had practice with the simple sentence (one independent clause) and the compound sentence (two or more independent clauses). Basic as these sentences are to your thinking and writing, you need to move beyond these structures in order to make your writing flexible and effective. Often you can improve the precision of your statements if you use slightly more complex structures.

"Rain began to fall, and we stopped our ball game" is a perfectly correct sentence. But notice these slightly altered versions of that sentence:

> When rain began to fall, we stopped our ball game.
> After rain began to fall, we stopped our ball game.
> Because rain began to fall, we stopped our ball game.

These three, in addition to lessening the singsong tone of the compound sentence, are more informative. The first two tell the time at which the game was stopped—and notice that *when* and *after* point out slightly different time frames. The third version gives a different relation between the two statements; it tells not the time of, but the reason for, stopping the game.

If, instead of writing the compound sentence "Rain was falling, and we continued our ball game," you write "Although rain was falling, we continued our ball game," you have refined your thinking and your expression. Your readers now interpret the sentence exactly as you want them to; they now know that the ball game was continued in spite of the fact that rain was falling.

The process by which a statement is reduced to a secondary form to show its relation to the main idea is called subordination. The grammatical unit that expresses a secondary idea as it affects a main idea is the subordinate, or dependent, clause, which we define as a sub-ject-verb combination that cannot stand alone as a sentence. A subordinate clause works in a sentence in the same way that a single part of speech—an adverb, an adjective, or a noun—works. Instead of a single word—*quickly*, *quick*, *quickness*—used as an adverb, an adjec-tive, or a noun, a group of words is used. A sentence made up of one independent clause and at least one dependent clause is a **complex sentence**.

ADVERB CLAUSE

The **adverb clause** works in exactly the same way a one-word adverb works: It provides infor-mation by modifying a verb, an adjective, or another adverb. The most common types of adverb clauses modify verbs. In fact, they answer direct questions about the action: When? (time); Where? (place); Why? (cause); and How? (manner). The role of the adverb clause is shown by the conjunction that introduces the adverb clause. The conjunction—the structural signal of subordination—is not an isolated word standing between the two clauses; it is part of the subordinate clause. In such a sentence as "We left the house after the rain stopped," the unit "the rain stopped" could stand alone as an independent clause. But the clause is made depen-dent by the inclusion of the conjunction *after*. The dependent clause "after the rain stopped" establishes the time when "we left the house." Thus, the clause works as an adverb of time in the same way that the one-word adverbs work in the following sentences:

We left the house *early.*
We left the house *late.*
We left the house *yesterday.*

Various types of adverb clauses and their most common conjunctions are listed here with examples.

Time (*when, whenever, before, after, since, while, until, as, as soon as*):

The baby cried *when the telephone rang.*
The cat ran out *before Lou could shut the door.*
After the bell rings, no one can enter.
I've known Palmer *since he was in high school.*
You should not whisper *while Dr. Fuller is lecturing.*
You may leave *as soon as your replacement arrives.*

Place (*where, wherever*):

We parted *where the paths separated.*
I will meet you *wherever you want me to.*

Cause [or Reason] (*because, since, as*):

I walk to work every day *because I need the exercise.*
Since she could not pay the fine, she could not drive the car.
As you are the senior member, you should lead the procession.

Purpose (*so that, in order that*):

We left early *so that we could catch the last bus.*
They died *that their nation might live.*
They came to America *in order that they might find freedom.*

Manner (*as, as if, as though*):

Raphael acted *as if the party bored him.*
Please do the work *as you have been instructed.*

Result (*so . . . that, such . . . that*):

Derek arrived so late *that he missed the concert.*
The workmen made such a racket *that I got a headache.*

Condition (*if, unless, provided that, on condition that*). This kind of adverb clause gives a condition under which the main clause is true:

Sit down and chat *if you are not in a hurry.*
He will not give his talk *unless we pay his expenses.*
She will sign the contract *provided that we pay her a bonus.*
If I were you, I would accept the offer.
If you had told me earlier, I could have helped.

There is an alternate arrangement for certain kinds of conditional clauses. In this arrangement, *if* is not used; instead, a subject-verb inversion signals the subordination. Sentences like the last two preceding examples sometimes take this form:

Were I you, I would accept the offer.
Had you told me earlier, I could have helped.

Concession (*although, though, even if, even though, since*). This clause states a fact in spite of which the main idea is true:

Although she is only nine years old, she plays chess.
Our car is dependable *even though it is old.*

Comparison (*than, as*). Two distinctive characteristics of the adverb clause of comparison should be noted. First, part or all of the verb, although it is needed grammatically, is usually not expressed. Second, when an action verb is not expressed in the subordinate clause, the appropriate form of the auxiliary *do* is often used even though the *do* does not occur in the main clause:

Gold is heavier *than iron* [is].
Your computer is not as new *as mine* [is].
Her theme was better *than any other student's in the class* [was].
Ellen earned more bonus points *than her brother* [did].

Modification of Verbs, Adjectives, and Adverbs

Adverb clauses may also modify verbs, adjectives and adverbs. In this type of clause, the conjunction *that* is sometimes unexpressed.

Jim slept as late *as possible*. [Modifies the adverb *late*]
We are sorry *that you must leave early*. [Modifies the adjective *sorry*]
I am sure *(that) he meant no harm*. [Modifies the adjective *sure*]
The car is running better *than it did last week*. [Modifies the adverb *better*]

ELLIPTICAL CLAUSE

Ellipsis means *omission*, to *leave something out*. A clause that leaves some parts implicitly understood or unexpressed is called an **elliptical clause**. There are many types of elliptical clauses. You should be aware of them because they can lend variety to your writing. In the following examples, brackets enclose the parts of the clauses that may be unexpressed. (See Supplement.) Note that all the types of adverb phrases (time, place, cause, purpose, manner, result, condition, concession, and comparison) may be elliptical.

While [I was] *walking home*, I met Mr. Rodriguez.

When [he is] *in Cleveland*, he stays with us.

Call your office *as soon as* [it is] *possible*.

Adjustments will be made *whenever* [they are] *necessary*.

Mary, *although* [she is] *a talented girl*, is quite lazy.

If [you are] *delayed*, call my secretary.

Your ticket, *unless* [it is] *stamped*, is invalid.

A NOTE ON SENTENCE VARIETY

Although some adverb clauses—those of comparison, for instance—have a fixed position within the sentence, many adverb clauses may be placed before, inside, or following the main clause:

When they deal with the unknown, Greek myths are usually somber.

Greek myths, *when they deal with the unknown*, are usually somber.

Greek myths are usually somber *when they deal with the unknown*.

Notice that no comma is used in the third example above. Usually a comma is not needed when the adverbial clause is the final element of the sentence, as the third example below also illustrates:

Although he did not have authority from Congress, President Theodore Roosevelt ordered construction of the Panama Canal.

President Theodore Roosevelt, *although he did not have authority from Congress*, ordered construction of the Panama Canal.

President Theodore Roosevelt ordered construction of the Panama Canal *although he did not have authority from Congress*.

You should practice various arrangements to relieve the monotony that comes from reliance on too many main-subject-plus-main-verb sentences.

SUPPLEMENT

Occasionally, an elliptical adverb clause of comparison must be recast because the exact meaning is unclear when parts of the clause are unexpressed. Here are two sentences that are ambiguous in the shortened forms of the clauses:

Mr. Alton will pay you more *than Stan*.

Probable meaning: Mr. Alton will pay you more than [he will pay] Stan.

Possible meaning: Mr. Alton will pay you more than Stan [will pay you].

Parents dislike homework as much *as their offspring*.

Probable meaning: Parents dislike homework as much as their offspring [dislike homework].

Possible meaning: Parents dislike homework as much as [they dislike] their offspring.

SUMMARY OF ADVERB CLAUSES

1. *Function*: to modify a verb, an adjective, or an adverb

2. *Position*: fixed for some types (She sold more tickets *than I did*); others may be at the beginning, in the interior, or at the end of main clause

3. *Subordinators*: conjunctions, most of which show adverbial relationships such as time (*when, since, while*), cause (*because, as*), and so on

4. *Special structures*:
   a. An adverb clause modifying an adjective subjective complement and subordinated by *that* sometimes has the subordinator that unexpressed:

   I'm sure *(that) you are wrong.*

   b. Elliptical clauses:
   Mary is older *than I (am).*
   If (you are) unable to attend, call me.
   While (she was) preparing lunch, Mary cut her finger.

English Fundamentals Online

After you have completed Practice Sheets and Exercises in this lesson, you can find additional help and drill work at **MyWritingLab.com**, in the section on Combining Sentences; Varying Sentence Structure.

Adverb Clauses

NAME _____ SCORE _____

Directions: Identify each of the italicized adverb clauses by writing one of the following numbers in the space at the left:

1. Time	4. Purpose	7. Condition	10. Modification of
2. Place	5. Manner	8. Concession	an adjective or adverb
3. Cause	6. Result	9. Comparison	

_____ 1. We waited at the airport *until the last plane from Indianapolis had arrived.*

_____ 2. John waited as long *as he possibly could.*

_____ 3. I will wait for you *where the trail forks above the waterfall.*

_____ 4. Her time in the 100 meters was better *than anyone else's time in that meet.*

_____ 5. *Because we encountered two major traffic tie-ups*, we arrived shortly after the kickoff.

_____ 6. *Although I had studied very hard*, I did not make a good grade on that test.

_____ 7. We left part of the job unfinished *so that we could go to dinner at a decent hour.*

_____ 8. *If we had been given more time*, we could have done a better job on the repairs.

_____ 9. The center is limping *as though her knee is giving her a problem.*

_____ 10. The concert sold out so early *that none of us could buy tickets.*

_____ 11. We are delighted *that you will be able to visit us next weekend.*

_____ 12. My work on that paper is progressing more rapidly *than it did yesterday.*

_____ 13. Your paper was much more interesting *than anyone else's in the class.*

_____ 14. Your work out in the field is harder *than any I've ever done.*

_____ 15. *Even though we wanted to go to the game*, we had already agreed to work for Tom that afternoon.

_____ 16. We could not have broken our agreement with Tom *even if we had wanted to do so.*

_____ 17. *If you have a little time*, sit down and tell me about your day.

_____ 18. *Had I known of your plans in advance*, I could have gone along on that trip with you.

_____ 19. My little brother was so frightened by that storm *that he has never gone out in bad weather again.*

_____ 20. The men mowing the grass outside the classroom made so much noise *that we could not hear the lecturer.*

_____ 21. Olivia reacted to the sight of my grandmother *as though she had seen a ghost.*

_____ 22. During the lecture, try not to act *as if you are incredibly bored.*

_____ 23. *In order that we might save some money,* we should bring our own lunches to the office.

_____ 24. I worked very late last night *so that I could finish my paper well in advance of the due date.*

_____ 25. Jim lay down for a short nap *because he could not keep his eyes open any longer.*

_____ 26. *Since my connection to the Internet was down,* I decided to go for a long run.

_____ 27. Just stack those books *wherever you can find an empty spot.*

_____ 28. I will wait for you *where Mulberry Street crosses Miller Avenue.*

_____ 29. We should get to work *as soon as you get your computer set up.*

_____ 30. *Whenever you can find time,* please read through my paper and make any necessary corrections.

_____ 31. *While waiting for that bus,* I planned my entire week's work.

_____ 32. The bus was so late *that I had time to plan my entire week's work.*

_____ 33. I caught the bus *where it usually stops in my neighborhood.*

_____ 34. I was quite late for work *because the bus was very late this morning.*

_____ 35. Tomorrow I will catch an earlier bus *so that I won't be late for work.*

_____ 36. I walked into the office *as though I were right on time.*

_____ 37. *If the bus is late again tomorrow,* I will simply stay home from work.

_____ 38. *Because I have no car,* I must use the bus for transportation.

_____ 39. *Although the bus system is highly unreliable,* I must continue to rely on it for transportation.

_____ 40. *After I have been working for a few months,* I will have enough money saved to buy a car.

Exercise 8 — *Adverb Clauses*

NAME _____ SCORE_____

Directions: Each sentence contains one adverb clause. Underline each adverb clause. In the space at the left, write one of the following number to identify the type clause:

1. Time	4. Purpose	7. Condition	10. Modification of an
2. Place	5. Manner	8. Concession	adjective or adverb
3. Cause	6. Result	9. Comparison	

_____ 1. The children go to the zoo quite often because they love animals.

_____ 2. After I took a thirty-minute nap, I felt full of energy again.

_____ 3. Even though they were somewhat frightened by the darkness, the girls ventured into the cave.

_____ 4. I will sit here and read this novel until the rain passes over.

_____ 5. The A grade on my term paper made me so happy that I almost cried.

_____ 6. Mrs. Johnson's 1987 Dodge runs as well as any late model.

_____ 7. Unless Charlie calls us, we won't know the exact time of his arrival.

_____ 8. The timid poet hid her work where no one else could find it.

_____ 9. Because I had always enjoyed his music, I bought a ticket to the Alan Jackson concert.

_____ 10. As I was walking down the street, I saw an old man in a leather coat.

_____ 11. The weather was so cold and rainy that I decided to stay home all day.

_____ 12. You probably lost your glasses when you opened your purse for your wallet.

_____ 13. If you can't assemble the new cabinet, read the directions again.

_____ 14. Few bank robbers were more skillful than Willy Sutton.

_____ 15. Many of my fellow students can't study unless they are listening to loud music.

_____ 16. I'll meet you wherever it will be convenient for you.

_____ 17. I have more work now than I can manage.

_____ 18. The witness fidgeted nervously and acted as if he might faint at any moment.

_____ 19. Although she is very beautiful, I am not interested in dating her.

_____ 20. Edward R. Murrow had more impact on television newscasting than any other early newsman.

_____ 21. Unless we hear otherwise, we shall expect you the day after tomorrow.

_____ 22. Surprisingly, some very old cars are worth more than new ones.

_____ 23. In these days of inflation, we must look for bargains wherever we shop.

_____ 24. We are saving money so that we can take a long vacation trip.

_____ 25. The beauty of that mountain takes my breath away whenever I see it.

_____ 26. We made little headway through the pile of books even though we worked all day.

_____ 27. Our manager, Ms. Jordan, smiled broadly because she was very pleased with the report.

_____ 28. Since the children are quite young, they must be accompanied by adults on the field trip.

_____ 29. All the people in the class used the cameras as they had been taught.

_____ 30. Because they expected a hard freeze during the night, the men checked the antifreeze in all the cars.

_____ 31. Since the new manager took over the job, the morale of the office has improved greatly.

_____ 32. I finished the dishes and made the beds while you were at the grocery store.

_____ 33. All the others in the camp slept later than Marilyn.

_____ 34. Although the managers usually work very long hours, last Friday they left at noon.

_____ 35. Please notify the Coast Guard if we have not returned by sundown.

_____ 36. After Marie had sanded the car, she painted it a glossy black.

_____ 37. The boys stood in line for five hours so that they could buy tickets for tomorrow's game.

_____ 38. If you can register early, you will have a better selection of courses.

_____ 39. Breathing is more difficult at very high elevations than at sea level.

_____ 40. The plants blossomed perfectly because the nurseryman had given them special fertilizer.

Directions: In the first space at the left, write a subordinating conjunction that logically connects the two clauses. In the second space at the left, write one of the following numbers to identify the clause:

1. Time	4. Purpose	7. Condition	10. Modification of an
2. Place	5. Manner	8. Concession	adjective or adverb
3. Cause	6. Result	9. Comparison	

_____
_____
1. _____ there is a full moon, crime and strange events increase.

_____
_____
2. You will very likely get good seats for the concert _____ you are in line very early.

_____
_____
3. Jed and Tim got very good seats for the concert _____ they were in line very early.

_____
_____
4. This year's county fair did not draw as many people _____ last year's.

_____
_____
5. _____ we were exhausted from the long climb, we felt very proud of ourselves for reaching the top.

_____
_____
6. The second baseman is limping _____ she might have re-injured her ankle on that last play.

_____
_____
7. In her new job Rachel earned more in six months _____ she had in a full year at her old job.

_____
_____
8. The gate will open _____ you slide the gate card into the slot.

_____
_____
9. We stayed at the airport about an hour _____ Marie's plane had left.

_____
_____
10. _____you have a chance, check in with the office to keep us up-to-date on your progress.

_____
_____
11. _____our flight was delayed, we arrived in Tucson almost two hours behind schedule.

_____
_____
12. _____there is a change in schedule, you'll make your presentation Wednesday morning.

_____
_____
13. Our productivity has increased by almost 10 percent _____ the new machines were installed two months ago.

_____
_____
14. I certainly would take that job offer _____ I were you.

_____
_____
15. Marge stared at her test paper _____ she had never seen that type of problem before.

Directions: Rewrite the word groups (phrases, clauses, or sentences) in each item using an adverbial clause; use the subordinating conjunction that properly establishes the relationship between the word groups.

1. We hurried home from the park, for a thunderstorm was building up in the west. (Cause)

   _____

2. We had already sold all of the tickets for opening night of the show; therefore, we were unable to supply tickets for the people in the president's party. (Cause)

   _____

3. We had already sold all of the tickets for the opening night of the show, but we were able to find a few individual seats for the president's party. (Concession)

   _____

4. You need to find two more sources for your paper or you will not have enough material to develop your thesis. (Condition)

   _____

5. The workmen made a terrific racket with the circular saw, and I got a terrible headache. (Result)

   _____

6. Mike looked at the instructor (in a certain way). He did not understand the question. (Manner)

   _____

7. We found a nice place to pitch our tent. The ground is high and dry, and there is a nice view of the lake. (Place)

   _____

8. On Monday, we got up very early and went to the ticket office to be sure to get tickets for the playoff game. (Purpose)

   _____

9. All the people in the building were leaving for lunch. At that time the fire alarm sounded in the building. (Time)

   _____

10. The people in the stands stood and sang the national anthem, and then the umpire called out, "Play ball." (Time)

    _____

Brief Writing Assignment: Using the brief paragraph from Lesson 7 as a base, rewrite the paragraph to include two sentences with adverb clauses in them.

Lesson 9 — Subordination: Adjective Clauses

Just as a single-word adjective modifies a noun or pronoun, clauses that begin with *who*, *whom*, *whose*, *which*, or *that* can modify nouns or pronouns. A clause that modifies a noun or pronoun is called an **adjective** or **relative clause**. An adjective clause gives information about the noun in the same way that the one-word adjectives do. Both one-word adjectives and adjective clauses can be seen as basic sentences that have been worked into a main clause.

I looked into the sky. The sky was blue.
I looked into the blue sky.

I looked into the sky. The sky was filled with towering cumulus clouds.
I looked into the sky, which was filled with towering cumulus clouds.

In Item 1 the sentence "The sky was blue" becomes the one-word adjective *blue* and modifies the noun *sky*. In Item 2 the sentence "The sky was filled with towering cumulus clouds" cannot become a one-word adjective; therefore, the sentence becomes an adjective or relative clause opened by the word *which*. The clause modifies the word *sky* in the sense that it provides us with information about the sky.

ADJECTIVE CLAUSES

Nearly all of the adjective clauses you read, write, or speak use *who*, *whose*, *whom*, *which*, or *that* to tie the adjective clause to the noun it modifies. These words, in spite of the fact that they join one clause to a word in another clause, are not conjunctions. They are pronouns that have a connective or *relating* function; thus they are called **relative pronouns**. (See Supplement.) Relatives can function *within* the adjective clause as subjects, direct objects, or objects of prepositions.

It is helpful to think of an adjective clause as a simple sentence that is incorporated within another sentence. The relative pronoun, by substituting for a noun, refers ("relates") the clause directly to the word being modified. Because the relative pronoun is the word signaling the subordination, the pronoun, sometimes preceded by a preposition, always begins the adjective clause.

Examine the following paired units. Every A unit has two simple sentences; the second repeats a noun from the first sentence. The B sentence shows how the second idea has been reduced to an adjective clause and has become part of the first sentence. Notice that the normal position of an adjective clause is immediately following the noun or the pronoun it modifies.

A. This is a well-built truck. *The truck* will save you money.
B. This is a well-built truck *that* will save you money.
[The clause modifies *truck*. *That* is the subject in the adjective clause.]

A. Alice has a new boyfriend. *The new boyfriend* [*or He*] sings in a rock group.
B. Alice has a new boyfriend *who* sings in a rock group.
   [*Who* is the subject in the clause that modifies *boyfriend.*]

A. Here is the book. I borrowed the book [*or it*] yesterday.
B. Here is the book *that* I borrowed yesterday.
   [*That* is the direct object in the adjective clause.]

A. The firm hired Chet Brown. The boss had known *Chet Brown* [*or him*] in Omaha.
B. The firm hired Chet Brown, *whom* the boss had known in Omaha.
   [*Whom* is the direct object in the adjective clause.]

A. May I introduce Dick Hart? I went to college *with Dick Hart* [*or him*].
B. May I introduce Dick Hart, with *whom* I went to college?
   [The clause modifies *Dick Hart.* Notice that the preposition *with* stands at the beginning of the clause with its object *whom.* At the informal level of language usage, the preposition in this structure is sometimes found at the end of the clause. See Supplement 2 of Lesson 6 on page 52.]

A. She is a young artist. I admire the young *artist* [*or her*] work.
B. She is a young artist *whose* work I admire.
   [*Work* is in this position because, although it is the direct object of *admire*, it cannot be separated from its modifier, the relative adjective *whose*, which must be placed at the beginning of the adjective clause.]

We also use the adverbs *when* and *where* as relatives. *When* and *where* introduce adjective clauses in combinations meaning "time when" and "place where." The following examples show that the subordinator is really the equivalent of an adverbial prepositional phrase. (The B sentences are complex sentences combining the material of the two A sentences.)

A. Beth and I recalled the time. We considered ourselves rebels *at that time.*
B. Beth and I recalled the time *when* we considered ourselves rebels.

A. This is the spot. The explorers came ashore at this spot.
B. This is the spot *where* the explorers came ashore.

These clauses are logically considered adjective clauses because they immediately follow nouns that require identification, and the clauses give the identifying material. If you remember "time-when" and "place-where," you will not confuse this type of adjective clause with other subordinate clauses that may use the same subordinators.

Note: In certain adjective clauses, the relative word is unexpressed; the meaning is instantly clear without it: the food *(that) we eat*, the house *(that) he lived in*, the man *(whom) you saw*, the time *(when) you fell down*, and so on.

RESTRICTIVE AND NONRESTRICTIVE
ADJECTIVE CLAUSES

Depending on their role in a sentence, adjective clauses are restrictive or nonrestrictive. A **restrictive clause** provides identification of the noun it modifies. A **nonrestrictive clause** provides information that is not essential for identification. Thus, in the sentence "The man who owns that car just walked up," the man is identified by the clause *who owns that car*. But in the sentence "John Williams, who owns that car, just walked up," the clause *who owns that car* does not identify John Williams (he is identified by his name). The clause tells us something additional; it adds information about John Williams.

Restrictive Clauses

The restrictive adjective clause is not set off by commas because it is essential to the identification of the word being modified.

> The grade *that I received on my report* pleased me.
> Anyone *who saw the accident* should call the police.

Without the modifying clauses (*that I received on my report*; *who saw the accident*), the nouns are not identified. What grade and what anyone are we talking about? But when we add the modifiers, we identify the *particular* grade and the *particular* anyone. In other words, this kind of clause restricts the meaning of a general noun to one specific member of its class.

Nonrestrictive Adjective Clauses

The nonrestrictive adjective clause does require commas. Although the clause supplies additional or incidental information about the word that it modifies, the information is not needed for identifying the noun. (Don't, however, get into the habit of thinking that a nonrestrictive clause is unimportant; unless it has some importance to the meaning of the sentence, it has no right to be in the sentence.) Nonrestrictive modifiers are usually found following proper nouns (*Mount Everest, Philadelphia, Mr. Frank Smith*); nouns already identified (the oldest *boy* in her class, her only *grandchild*); and one-of-a-kind nouns (Alice's *mother*, the *provost* of the college, the *writer* of the editorial).

The following examples contrast restrictive and nonrestrictive adjective clauses. (See Supplement.)

> I visited an old friend *who is retiring soon*. [Restrictive]
> I visited my oldest and closest friend, *who is retiring soon*. [Nonrestrictive]

> The man *whose car had been wrecked* asked us for a ride. [Restrictive]
> Mr. Ash, *whose car had been wrecked*, asked us for a ride. [Nonrestrictive]

> A small stream *that flows through the property* supplies an occasional trout. [Restrictive]
> Caldwell Creek, *which flows through the property*, supplies an occasional trout. [Nonrestrictive]

> She wants to retire to a place *where freezing weather is unknown*. [Restrictive]
> She wants to retire to Panama City, *where freezing weather is unknown*. [Nonrestrictive]

SUPPLEMENT

A few distinctions in the use of *who, which,* and *that* in adjective clauses are generally observed. *Which* refers only to things; *who* refers to people; and *that* refers to things or people. *That* is used only in restrictive clauses; in other words, a "that" adjective clause is not set off by commas. Because *which* is the relative pronoun that must be used in a nonrestrictive clause modifying a thing, there is a convention that *which* should not introduce a restrictive adjective clause. This convention is generally, but by no means always, observed. People tend to use *which* in their writing when *that* would be better.

Certain problems associated with the loose or faulty use of relative pronouns and adjective clauses are discussed in Lesson 23.

SUMMARY OF ADJECTIVE CLAUSES

1. *Function*: to modify a noun or a pronoun

2. *Position*: follows the noun or pronoun that it modifies

3. *Subordinators*:
   a. relative pronouns (*who, whom, which, that*), which function within the adjective clause as subjects, direct objects, or objects of prepositions
   b. relative adjectives (*whose, which*)
   c. relative adverbs (*when, where*)

4. *Special problem*: Adjective clauses vital to the identification of the nouns being modified are restrictive and do not require commas. Clauses not necessary for identification are nonrestrictive and are set off by commas.

English Fundamentals Online

After you have completed Practice Sheets and Exercises in this lesson, you can find additional help and drill work at **MyWritingLab.com**.

NAME _____ SCORE _____

Directions: Each italicized unit is a relative clause. In the space at the left, copy the word that is the antecedent of the relative pronoun in the clause. Note that some of the adjective clauses occur within an adverbial unit and others have adverbial clauses within them. Note carefully the occasions when the clause is set off by commas.

_____ 1. Yesterday I saw for the first time in years a man *whom I had known when we were in high school.*

_____ 2. After the storm *that blew down that old tree* had subsided, we all went to work to remove the debris.

_____ 3. Jim Roberts, *who was a great athlete in high school*, has become the local high school's history teacher.

_____ 4. Mary Allen, *whose brother is a judge*, has begun to work as a graphic artist.

_____ 5. The math teachers are trying to find a textbook *that more students will enjoy using.*

_____ 6. Have you seen Joanna's new puppy, *which is a Shetland sheepdog?*

_____ 7. I need to find the person *whose book I picked up by mistake when I left class today.*

_____ 8. That person will need to study that book, *which is the main textbook for the class.*

_____ 9. When I find the person *whose book I took*, I will apologize for my mistake.

_____ 10. We have not found a place *where we can get our car serviced cheaply.*

_____ 11. Perhaps we should go to Gray's Repair Shop, *which has a good reputation here in town.*

_____ 12. Then we should select a time *when it is convenient for us to drop off the car.*

_____ 13. The man *who is standing over by the book table* is Senator Schmidt.

_____ 14. Senator Schmidt, *who is standing over by the book table*, is a strong supporter of the college.

_____ 15. Last year Senator Schmidt gave his support to a bill *that funded two special programs here at the college.*

_____ 16. That bill, *which was sponsored by Senator Schmidt*, provides funds for two community outreach programs.

_____ 17. Do you know anyone *who can tutor me in calculus?*

_____ 18. Yes, Jill Crockett, *who is a math major*, sometimes tutors people in calculus.

_____ 19. I need someone to *whom I can go for help.*

_____ 20. If I don't find someone *who can explain the subject to me*, I will probably withdraw from the course.

Directions: Each sentence contains one adjective clause. Underline the adjective clause and write the word it modifies (the antecedent) in the space at the left.

_____ 1. Although Marcie is someone we can usually depend on for a ride, we probably need to have an alternative plan for Monday's field trip.

_____ 2. The weather forecasters that I listen to have not been very accurate lately.

_____ 3. Weather forecasters have a good job because they can give information that is inaccurate and still not lose their jobs.

_____ 4. Baseball is a sport in which failure is fairly common.

_____ 5. A batter who is successful gets a hit only once in every three tries.

_____ 6. Everyone needs a job in which several mistakes are allowed without any penalty.

_____ 7. Accountants are people for whom accuracy is very important.

_____ 8. Accounting, which is not the same as bookkeeping, requires great attention to detail.

_____ 9. Accounting is a job that requires great attention to detail.

_____ 10. "Close enough" is not an expression that successful accountants can use.

_____ 11. My friends and I are usually satisfied when our checkbooks show a balance that is reasonably close to correct.

_____ 12. Jim's uncle, who is quite wealthy, keeps an extra $2,000 in his checking account.

_____ 13. His balance is usually so high that it will cover any mistakes that he makes.

_____ 14. People who don't have an extra large balance must be more careful in balancing their checkbooks.

_____ 15. Whenever I have money that seems to be extra, I find a way to spend it almost immediately.

_____ 16. All the people with whom I graduated from high school have moved out of town.

_____ 17. The people who have left town are living in a wide variety of places.

_____ 18. Most of the people are living in places where they can find interesting activities for recreation.

_____ 19. Some of the people have moved to Hawaii, where they can pursue surfing as a hobby.

_____ 20. Others have moved to Colorado because they love skiing, which is an exciting sport.

NAME _____   SCORE _____

Directions: Each of the following sentences contains an adjective clause, but appropriate commas are omitted. Underline each adjective clause. In the first space at the left, write the antecedent of the relative pronoun in the clause. In the second space, write **N** if the clause is nonrestrictive or **R** if the clause is restrictive. Add needed commas around nonrestrictive clauses.

_____   1. Bob is working on a deck that was designed by his uncle.

_____
_____   2. Bob's Uncle Mike who is an accomplished architect designed the deck for a client's lake house.

_____
_____   3. The deck is designed to take advantage of the view from the house which sits on a hill above the lakeshore.

_____
_____   4. For the deck, Bob carefully selected lumber that is straight and free of knots.

_____
_____   5. If the deck is going to please his uncle's client who has very high expectations it must be nearly perfect.

_____
_____   6. The deck looks out over a lake that has mountains behind it.

_____
_____   7. Around the edge of the deck there will be benches on which the client's guests can sit and watch the sunset.

_____
_____   8. The guests whom the client invites almost every weekend will appreciate the workmanship and the view from the deck.

_____
_____   9. The lake is a favorite spot for people who enjoy wakeboarding and waterskiing.

_____
_____   10. The lake also has many quiet coves where anglers can fish for bass.

_____
_____   11. The bass fishermen go out in bass boats some of which can go 70 or 80 miles an hour.

_____
_____   12. The anglers set out at a time when the sun is just about to rise.

_____
_____   13. The anglers need a fast boat because they want to get to as many places as possible where they can fish in one morning.

_____
_____   14. When they get to the cove in which they intend to fish, the anglers turn off the boat's powerful outboard motor.

_____
_____   15. Then they cruise slowly around the cove with the use of a trolling motor which is electric and runs very quietly.

_____
_____   16. The trolling motor pulls the boat along near the shore through the lily pads and other plants that grow in the shallow water.

_____
_____   17. There is usually a professional guide in the boat who selects the locations for fishing.

_____ 18. After the anglers have fished for a few minutes and caught all the
_____   fish they think are in that spot, they run quickly to another cove.
_____ 19. There are some anglers that fish as professionals and earn prize
_____   money for catching the most fish at a tournament.
_____ 20. These professionals fish at a variety of lakes around the country, a
_____   circuit that works much the way the professional golf tour works.
_____ 21. Meanwhile, Bob who has hired a crew to help him is working
_____   hard to finish the deck.
_____ 22. Bob believes that he can meet the deadline which is just in time
_____   for the fall "leaf season."
_____ 23. Leaf season is that time in autumn when the leaves change their
_____   colors from green to bright reds, yellows, and oranges.
_____ 24. At that time of year, the client's friends will gather on the deck to
_____   look at the bright colors that cover the hills around the lake.
_____ 25. Bob, although he built the deck from which the people will view
_____   the colors, will probably not be invited to the party.
_____ 26. Leaves on trees that grow in the Eastern United States offer a
_____   brilliant display of colors in the fall.
_____ 27. Leaves are the part of the tree that manufactures food to sustain
_____   the tree and causes it to grow.
_____ 28. The tree takes water from the ground and takes a gas which is
_____   called carbon dioxide from the air.
_____ 29. The leaves convert the water and carbon dioxide into glucose, the
_____   substance the tree uses for energy and growth.
_____ 30. The process the leaves use to create glucose is called photosynthesis.

_____ 31. "Photosynthesis" is a combination of two words which come from
_____   the Latin language of ancient Rome.
_____ 32. The combination of words creates a new word that means "putting
_____   together with light."
_____ 33. Another chemical which is called chlorophyll causes photosynthesis
_____   to occur.
_____ 34. Chlorophyll is the chemical that gives leaves their green color.

_____ 35. In summer the leaves produce more glucose than the tree can use
_____   and this excess which is turned into starch is stored until needed.
_____ 36. In autumn the supply of light and water that produces
_____   photosynthesis begins to diminish.
_____ 37. Without a sufficient supply of water, the green color of the leaves
_____   which is called chlorophyll begins to disappear.
_____ 38. When the leaves lose the green color that is produced by
_____   chlorophyll other colors begin to appear.
_____ 39. The brightest colors in the leaves are produced in a year when late
_____   summer is dry and autumn is rather cool.
_____ 40. It is those colors that Bob enjoys when he sits on his own deck
_____   beside the lake.

Directions: The two sentences in each item can be combined into one sentence by changing the second sentence into a relative clause. Write the new sentence in the blank.

1. Yesterday we visited John Yancey. He once was a librarian at the college.

   _____

2. He had recently been on a trip to a national forest. Trees more than 100 years old grow abundantly in that forest.

   _____

3. He camped in a forest glen. The trees there were well over 150 feet tall.

   _____

4. John writes regularly to the senator from his state. He asks the senator to support funding for national forests.

   _____

5. The senator has served in the Senate for many years. His record as a conservationist is not very good.

   _____

6. John has actually talked with the senator in a nearby town. The senator has a local office there.

   _____

7. John also works with local and national conservation organizations. Members of these organizations often volunteer to maintain trails in the national forest.

   _____

8. John was encouraged to become a conservationist by his grandmother. He often hiked in the forests with her.

   _____

9. John's grandmother is still active in causes related to conservation. She is 87 years old.

   _____

10. John maintains a long list of people. He sends e-mails and letters to them about issues related to the national forests.

    _____

Brief Writing Assignment: Write a paragraph of five or six sentences describing your actions as you prepare to work on a college assignment. Write two sentences containing adjective clauses.

Lesson 10 — Subordination: Noun Clauses

An adverbial clause such as *after the rain stopped* can work to set the time of the main verb just as the single-word adverb *yesterday* does. The adjective clause *whom I knew well* can modify our understanding of a noun in the same way the single-word adjective *tall* does. A noun clause works in a similar way: It does the work of a regular noun.

NOUN CLAUSES

A **noun clause** is a group of words containing a subject-verb combination and a subordinating word. The subordinating words that serve to introduce noun clauses are conjunctions (*that, if, whether*); pronouns (*who, whom, what, which, whoever, whatever, whichever*); adjectives (*whose, which, what*); and adverbs (*when, where, why, how*). Remember that the subordinating word is part of the clause and always stands at or near the beginning of the clause. As an example, consider the following similar sentences:

Marge now understands the answer.

The subject (Marge) acts (understands) on a direct object (the answer). In the same way a noun clause can replace a single word serving as a direct object:

Marge now understands why we were late.

The formula for the sentence is the same:

Marge (subject) understands (verb) why we were late (direct object).

The only grammatical difference between the two sentences is that the direct object in the second sentence is a clause (a group of words with a subject and a verb) instead of a single word.

Jill now wonders *if her answer was the correct one.*
[Noun clause subordinated by the conjunction *if* and used as a direct object.]

All of us hope *that you'll return soon.*
[Noun clause subordinated by the conjunction *that* and used as a direct object.]

I do not know *who he is.*
[Noun clause subordinated by the pronoun *who* used as the subjective complement within the clause.]

I know *what I would do with the extra money.*
[Noun clause subordinated by the pronoun *what* used as the direct object within the clause.]

Tell me *whom Mary is feuding with now.*
[Noun clause subordinated by the pronoun *whom* used as the object of the preposition *with.*]

You must decide *which car you will use today.*
[Noun clause subordinated by the adjective *which* modifying the direct object *car.*]

Why Morton left school still puzzles his friends.
[Noun clause subordinated by the adverb *why* serving as subject of *puzzles.*]

As you can see from these examples, a noun clause, like a noun, can be a subject, direct object, subjective complement, object of a preposition, or appositive (see page 95). You can understand the uses of the noun clause if you think of it as a clause equivalent to a "something" or a "someone" in one of these noun slots.

Subject (S)

The girl opened the window. [Single-word noun as S.]
Whoever came in first opened the window. [Noun clause as S.]
His *story* is very convincing. [Noun as S.]
What he told us is very convincing. [Noun clause as S.]

Subjective Complement (S.C.)

This is his *story.* [Single-word as S.C.]
This is *what he told us.* [Noun clause as S.C.]

Direct Object (D.O.)

Mr. Allen announced *his resignation.* [Single-word as D.O.]
Mr. Allen announced *that he would resign.* [Noun clause as D.O]
Can you tell me your *time* of arrival? [Single-word as D.O.]
Can you tell me *when you will arrive*? [Noun clause as D.O.]

Object of a Preposition (O.P.)

Give the package to the *man.* [Single-word as O.P.]
Give the package to *whoever opens the door.* [Noun clause as O.P.]

Note that the choice between *who/whoever* and *whom/whomever* depends on its use in the clause. This rule creates apparently awkward and sometimes tricky choices:

Give the book to whomever you see first. [*whomever* is the object of the verb *see*]
Give the book to whoever answers the door. [*whoever* is the subject of the verb *answers*]

(See Supplement 1.)

In noun clauses used as direct objects, the conjunction *that* is often unexpressed because the meaning is usually clear without it.

I know *that you will be happy here.*
[Noun clause subordinated by the conjunction *that.*]

I know *you will be happy here.*
[Noun clause with subordinating word omitted.]

This omission of the subordinating word creates an ellipsis, a construction similar to an elliptical adverbial clause. In adverbial clauses, the subject and part of the verb (the auxiliaries) are omitted. In this construction, only the subordinating word is omitted.

Most of the noun clauses that you read and write will be used as subjects, direct objects (the most common use), subjective complements, or objects of prepositions. However, two rather special uses should be noted, the *delayed* noun clause and the *appositive* noun clause.

DELAYED NOUN CLAUSE

One common use of a noun clause is as a delayed subject. The signal for this construction is the word *it* standing in the subject position, with the meaningful subject being a noun clause following the verb.

It is unfortunate *that you were delayed.*

Although the sentence begins with *It* and the clause follows the verb, the clause is the real subject. The meaning of the sentence is "That you were delayed is unfortunate."

A related noun clause use puts the word *it* in the direct object slot with a noun clause following an objective complement. This use, which is encountered less frequently than the delayed subject, gives us a clause that we can call a delayed direct object.

We think it unlikely *that Jones will be reelected.*

APPOSITIVE NOUN CLAUSE

To understand the other special noun clause, you must know what an appositive is. An **appositive** is a noun unit inserted into a sentence to rename another noun that usually immediately precedes the appositive. A simple example occurs in the following sentence:

Senator Jackson, a dedicated environmentalist, objected.

Because any noun unit can be used as an appositive, noun clauses sometimes function in this position. Some noun clause appositives are separated from the noun they are renaming by at least a comma, sometimes by a heavier mark.

There still remains one mystery: *how the thief knew your name.* [The noun clause renames the preceding noun, *mystery.*]

A rather special type of appositive noun clause, subordinated by *that* and following such nouns as *fact, belief, hope, statement, news,* and *argument,* is usually not set off by any mark of punctuation.

You cannot deny the fact *that you lied under oath.*
Your statement *that the boss is stupid* was undiplomatic.

(See Supplement 2.)

SUPPLEMENT 1

You have probably already noticed that the pronouns, adjectives, and adverbs that subordinate noun clauses are essentially the same words that are used in questions (Lesson 6).

The two uses are alike in the important fact that they always stand at the beginning of the clause. The two uses differ in that, as interrogatives, the words bring about the subject-verb inversion, whereas in noun clauses the subject-verb position is the normal one.

> *Whom* will the mayor appoint?
> [This sentence is a direct question; it calls for an answer. *Whom* is the D.O. of the main verb.]

> *I* wonder *whom the mayor will appoint.*
> [This sentence is a statement, not a direct question. Notice that a question mark is not required. *Whom* is the D.O. within the noun clause.]

SUPPLEMENT 2

Because an appositive is a renamer, it represents a reduced form of a Pattern 2 sentence in which the subject and a noun subjective complement are joined by a form of *be*. The writer of the sentence "Senator Jackson, a dedicated environmentalist, objected" could have written two simple sentences, the second one repeating a noun used in the first:

> Senator Jackson objected.
> Senator Jackson [or He] is a dedicated environmentalist.

The adjective clause offers the writer one device for compressing this information into one sentence.

> Senator Jackson, who is a dedicated environmentalist, objected.

The appositive represents a further compression.

> Senator Jackson, a dedicated environmentalist, objected.

If you think of the appositive as a renamer of the preceding noun (the two nouns could be joined by a form of *be*), you have a handy test to help you recognize any noun clause appositive use.

> There still remains one mystery: *how the thief knew your name.*
> [Test: The mystery *is* how the thief knew your name.]

> You can't deny the fact *that she has real talent.*
> [Test: The fact *is* that she has real talent.]

> Your contention *that the witness lied* has some merit.
> [Test: The contention *is* that the witness lied.]

If you remember a few points about the form, function, and positioning of adjective and noun clauses, you should have little difficulty in distinguishing between them. Although certain kinds of noun clauses in apposition may, at first glance, look like adjective clauses, a few simple tests clearly show the difference.

> The news *that you brought us* is welcome. [Adjective clause]
> The news *that Bob has recovered* is welcome. [Noun clause]

If you remember that an adjective clause is a describer and that an appositive noun clause is a renamer, you can see that in the first sentence the clause describes—in fact, identifies—the noun *news*, but it does not tell us what the news is. In the second sentence the clause does more: It tells us what the news is. Remember the *be* test. "The news is *that you brought us . . .*" does not make sense, but "The news is *that Bob has recovered . . .*" does; therefore, the second clause is a noun clause in apposition.

Another test that can be applied to these two types of sentences is based on the fact that in adjective clauses, but not in noun clauses, *which* can be substituted for *that*. "The news *which* you brought us . . ." is acceptable English; the clause, in this case, is an adjective clause. But because we can't say "The news *which* Bob has recovered . . ." the clause is a noun clause; it cannot be an adjective clause.

SUMMARY OF NOUN CLAUSES

1. *Function*: to work as a noun within a clause

2. *Positions*: subject (or delayed subject), renaming subjective complement, direct object (or delayed direct object), object of preposition, or appositive

3. *Subordinators*:
   a. conjunctions: *that, if, whether*
   b. pronouns: *who, whom, which, what,* and . . . *ever* forms, standing for unknown persons or things
   c. adjectives: *whose, which, what*
   d. adverbs: *when, where, why, how*

4. *Special problem*: Some noun appositive clauses closely resemble adjective clauses. They differ in that, in addition to describing the noun, the appositive clause renames the noun:

   The remark *that Jim made* (adjective clause) was unwise.

   The remark *that Mr. Smith cannot be trusted* (appositive noun clause) was unwise.

English Fundamentals Online

After you have completed Practice Sheets and Exercises in this lesson, you can find additional help and drill work at **MyWritingLab.com**.

Subordination: Noun Clauses

NAME _____ SCORE _____

Directions: Identify the function of each italicized noun clause by writing one of the following abbreviations in the space at the left:

S. [subject or delayed subject]   S.C. [subjective complement]

D.O. [direct object or   O.P. [object of preposition]
     delayed direct object]   Ap. [appositive]

_____ 1. The fact *that you were late for class* caused you to miss the announcement of the test.

_____ 2. It was unfortunate *that you missed the announcement of the test.*

_____ 3. *What I told you about the schedule for the test* is very important.

_____ 4. The important announcement was *that there will be a test next Friday.*

_____ 5. The instructor told us *that there will be a test next Friday.*

_____ 6. Please give this message to *whomever you see at the gym.*

_____ 7. We thought it unlikely *that your plane would land on time.*

_____ 8. *That your plane would land on time* seemed very unlikely.

_____ 9. A call to the airline verified the fact *that your plane would be an hour late.*

_____ 10. *Whoever is willing to take on that burdensome job* will surely be acceptable to all of us.

_____ 11. We should be happy with *whoever volunteers to do that hard work.*

_____ 12. It is wonderful *that Melanie has volunteered to do that work for this committee.*

_____ 13. I actually doubted *that anyone would be willing to take on that job.*

_____ 14. *That anyone would be willing to take on that job* came as a surprise to all of us.

_____ 15. The boss should probably give a raise to *whoever is willing to take on that job.*

_____ 16. Can you tell me *who called me earlier today*?

_____ 17. It is quite clear *that Mike is the best chess player in the school.*

_____ 18. Most of us believe *that Mike is the best chess player in the school.*

_____ 19. The news *that a blizzard is expected later today* caused the dean to cancel classes for the rest of the day.

_____ 20. The weather forecasters predict *that a blizzard will blanket this area with several inches of snow.*

Directions: Each of the following sentences contains a noun clause. Put brackets around the noun clause and identify its function in the sentence by writing one of the following abbreviations in the space at the left of the sentence:

S. [subject or delayed subject]   S.C. [subjective complement]

D.O. [direct object or   O.P. [object of preposition]
          delayed direct object]   Ap. [appositive]

_____ 1. The fact that she had studied accounting in college made Alexis a natural choice for that job.

_____ 2. Not many people knew that Alexis had studied accounting in college.

_____ 3. One requirement for that position is that the candidate hold a degree in accounting.

_____ 4. Does anyone know whose dog is sleeping in my driveway?

_____ 5. Can you tell me when that new movie will open in town?

_____ 6. It seems unlikely that this movie will open before the end of the month.

_____ 7. In fact, we don't know whether it will play in our small town or not.

_____ 8. Please tell the hostess if you will be joining us for dinner.

_____ 9. The crowd was surprised by what the speaker said in his opening remarks.

_____ 10. I think it possible that he was misunderstood.

_____ 11. Tell me who the woman in the blue suit over by that table is.

_____ 12. Most of the people in this room do not know why they were asked to attend this meeting.

_____ 13. Perhaps someone could explain what we are expected to do at this meeting.

_____ 14. That there is a representative here from each of our branch offices ought to be a clue.

_____ 15. Let me know if you see anyone here from the main office.

_____ 16. There is one question left unanswered: who actually called this meeting in the first place?

_____ 17. Can you remember who holds the record for the most home runs in a single season?

_____ 18. I would like to know where you found the recipe for this delicious chocolate cake.

_____ 19. It is well known that such recipes usually are passed down from grandmother to mother to daughter.

_____ 20. It came as a total surprise to me that your brother found the recipe and baked the cake.

NAME _____　SCORE _____

Directions: Each of the following sentences contains a noun clause. Some noun clauses occur within adverbial or adjective clauses. Others have such clauses within them. Put brackets around each noun clause and identify its function by writing one of the following abbreviations in the space at the left of the sentence:

S. [subject or delayed subject]　　　S.C. [subjective complement]

D.O. [direct object or　　　　　　　O.P. [object of preposition]
　　　delayed direct object]　　　　Ap. [appositive]

_____　1. When Mark told me that he had taken a job in another state, I was surprised.

_____　2. Mark announced that he had taken a job in another state because he dislikes the winters in his present location.

_____　3. No one knows where Mark will be living when he moves.

_____　4. The person who gave us the information that the exam had been cancelled was wrong.

_____　5. Joan believes that the incorrect information came from someone in another class.

_____　6. Joan does not know why anyone would give out such mistaken information.

_____　7. It is possible that the person who gave out the information made an honest mistake.

_____　8. We thought that the person who gave out that information made an honest mistake.

_____　9. We thought it possible that the person who gave out that information made an honest mistake.

_____　10. The problem with that assumption is that no one knows the source of the rumor.

_____　11. We should find out what the weather will be on the ski slopes next weekend.

_____　12. If we find that there will be no snow, we might postpone out trip.

_____　13. Perhaps, in that case, we could locate where snow had fallen recently and go there.

_____　14. The fact that we own a four-wheel drive vehicle will allow us to go almost anywhere.

_____　15. Fortunately, the weather reports suggest that there will be deep snow in several places this weekend.

_____　16. We are all skilled skiers, so we will be ready for whatever conditions face us on the slopes.

_____　17. We are convinced that anyone who goes with us will be able to handle every kind of condition on the slopes.

_____ 18. We are all aware of the possibility that a blizzard might set in while we are skiing.

_____ 19. At this time of year, it is always possible that severe weather might occur and keep us off the slopes.

_____ 20. The worst possibility is that conditions might be right for an avalanche, in which case we would stay in the ski lodge.

_____ 21. Once Maria has decided where she wants to live, she can begin to look for an apartment.

_____ 22. Our manager is considering several candidates for that job; whomever he hires will be better than the last person who held the position.

_____ 23. It is clear that some movies appeal to people with a juvenile sense of humor.

_____ 24. That some movies depend entirely on computer-generated special effects for their impact is also a well-known fact.

_____ 25. It is a well-known fact that some movies depend on computer-generated special effects for their impact.

_____ 26. The fact that some movies depend on computer-generated special effects does not lessen their entertainment value.

_____ 27. Such movies provide great entertainment for whoever pays the price of admission to the theater.

_____ 28. A box of good popcorn and whatever else we buy at the concession stand also makes the experience at the theater more enjoyable.

_____ 29. My brother says that he much prefers to watch movies on DVDs in the comfort of his living room.

_____ 30. Most of my friends think it impossible that people could enjoy a movie without an audience around them in a theater.

_____ 31. One question still lingers in everyone's mind: exactly how big was that fish Manny caught last Saturday?

_____ 32. Exactly how big the fish was that Manny caught last weekend is the question that is on everyone's mind.

_____ 33. Manny claims that he caught a fish bigger than any ever caught in that lake.

_____ 34. The problem with Manny's story is that he released the fish and did not take any pictures.

_____ 35. That Manny released the fish and did not take any pictures has caused some doubt among his friends.

_____ 36. Many of Manny's friends feel that he made up the story about the fish.

_____ 37. Many of his friends think it significant that Manny cannot tell the fish story with a straight face.

_____ 38. The fact that Manny cannot recount his fish story with a straight face raises doubts in the minds of his friends.

_____ 39. Anyone who has ever fished realizes that a fish often grows in size between the time it is caught and the time the story reaches the dock.

_____ 40. Since I am an avid angler, I think that I'll believe Manny's story so that he will later believe my stories.

Directions: Combine the following pairs of word groups into a single sentence by joining the second to the first as a noun clause.

1. (Something) was very funny. The president dropped the notes for his speech as he walked to the stage.

   _____

2. Please give those instructions to (someone). Whoever answers the phone in the office.

   _____

3. (Something) was not made clear in your note. Whether you are coming to town on Monday or Tuesday.

   _____

4. The suggestion caught everyone by surprise. (The suggestion was) that we should move our offices to a building out in the suburbs.

   _____

5. Neither John nor Janice knew (something). Why you left work early yesterday.

   _____

6. There seems to be only one possible solution to that problem. We need to increase our income and cut our expenditures.

   _____

7. My dad thought it strange. We left your car in the driveway and took the bus to town.

   _____

8. The coach has not announced (something) yet. Where the next round of the playoffs will be played.

   _____

9. The computer technician explained (something) to Jack. How he had deleted that entire file from his computer by mistake.

   _____

10. Representative Lopez told the committee (something). He had voted for tax reductions several times in the past.

    _____

Brief Writing Assignment: Write a paragraph of five or six sentences, two of which contain noun clauses, discussing your thoughts and attitudes before beginning a writing assignment.

NAME _____   SCORE _____

Directions: The italicized material in each of these sentences is a subordinate clause. In the space at the left, write one of the following to identify the clause:

Adv. [adverb clause]

Adj. [adjective clause]

N [noun clause]

In the second space, write one of the following to identify the use within the clause of the word printed in bold-face type:

S. [subject]   I.O. [indirect object]   O.C. [objective complement]

D.O. [direct object]   S.C. [subjective complement]

_____
_____ 1. The park ranger warned the group *that he would not be **responsible** for their safety if they continued the climb.*

_____
_____ 2. Ms. Strom explained to the children that the birds *that they had spotted in the fir tree were **robins**.*

_____
_____ 3. *If you can tell **us** the name of the capital of Zimbabwe,* you'll win a year's supply of detergent.

_____
_____ 4. Andy's poor grades in mathematics partially explain *why he never earned an engineering **degree**.*

_____
_____ 5. The car was registered in the name of a local entrepreneur *whom the **FBI** had been seeking.*

_____
_____ 6. The evening celebration was not entirely successful *because the noisy fireworks made a few of the children **hysterical**.*

_____
_____ 7. The advertisement reported that a handsome reward would go to ***whoever** finds the missing briefcase.*

_____
_____ 8. Our governor is a forgiving man; he recently appointed to the Board of Regents a woman *who once called him **incompetent**.*

_____
_____ 9. Mr. Benson beamed when the photographer told him *that he looked quite **youthful** for a man of sixty-five.*

_____
_____ 10. Time relationships sometimes become confused for people *as they grow **older**.*

_____
_____ 11. *As his hostess told **Tim** the Latin names for the flowers,* he busily wrote them in his notebook.

_____
_____ 12. "Anyone can see *why experts call this painting a **masterpiece**,*" said the pompous guide.

_____ 13. The food was greasy and overcooked, *although the half-starved hikers*
_____ *considered it very tasty.*

_____ 14. The carpet *that your store sent me* is not what I ordered.
_____

_____ 15. The story *she told us* left us speechless.
_____

_____ 16. During "show-and-tell" time in the lower grades, children sometimes report
_____ on family events *that should be kept secret.*

_____ 17. After the trial period the boss and her three assistants will decide *what your*
_____ *salary will be.*

_____ 18. "I think your concluding paragraph will be more effective *if you make it shorter*
_____ *by about half,*" said the teacher.

_____ 19. Official announcements from the White House have been enthusiastic,
_____ *although a few of the spokespersons remain cautious.*

_____ 20. Home owners in the Mud Lake area worry about what could happen if fire
_____ breaks out *while the water pressure is low.*

_____ 21. The three children were discussing an important matter: *what kind of dessert*
_____ *their mother should serve them.*

_____ 22. At a press conference tomorrow a representative of the search committee will
_____ announce *who the five finalists are.*

_____ 23. A recently hired night watchman is apparently the person *who had turned*
_____ *the burglar alarm off.*

_____ 24. An accountant *whom Peter knew only casually* came forth with the bail money.
_____

_____ 25. We finally found a place *where we could store our goods.*
_____

_____ 26. We are looking for a whitewater river *where we can do some exciting kayaking.*
_____

_____ 27. My son will drive you *wherever you need to go this afternoon.*
_____

_____ 28. *After turning my white shirt a bright red in the wash,* I finally found one like
_____ it in that store right down the street from my office.

_____ 29. *If you don't send your mother that card today,* it will not arrive in time for
_____ her birthday.

_____ 30. Pamela doesn't know *if she will be able to hand the teacher that paper by*
_____ *tomorrow morning.*

Directions: In each pair of word groups, use the first clause as a main clause and join the second to it as an adjective, adverb, or noun clause. Write the new sentence in the space below. Identify the subordinate clause you have created by writing one of the following in the space at the left:

Adv. (adverb clause)   Adj. (adjective clause)   N. (noun clause)

In some sentences the suggested subordinating word is included in brackets with the item.

_____ 1. We might need to take the car for a new paint job. [since, because]
The hailstorm last night damaged it severely.

_____

_____ 2. That woman can give you directions to the cafeteria. [who]
She is sitting at the desk in the front of the office.

_____

_____ 3. *Something* is not clear to any of us.
Why we didn't catch those errors before the catalog went to the printer.

_____

_____ 4. Do you know *something*?
Where I can buy a new table for my office.

_____

_____ 5. Julie needs to buy a new computer. [that]
She can carry it to classes.

_____

_____ 6. The rain on the metal roof was so loud. [that]
We could not hear the television.

_____

_____ 7. Please hand this package to *someone*.
Whoever meets you at the door of the office.

_____

_____ 8. Please hand this package to the person. [who]
The person meets you at the door of the office.

_____

_____ 9. You will have no trouble finding my house. [if]
You follow the map exactly turn by turn.

_____

_____ 10. You must follow the map exactly.
Exactly as I have drawn it.

_____

_____ 11. Maria knows *something*.
What needs to be done to achieve those goals.

_____

_____ 12. Maria knows the things. [that]
The things need to be done to achieve those goals.

_____

_____ 13. Yesterday I learned *something*. [how]
The way to connect to the Internet with my new cell phone.

_____

_____ 14. *Someone* should have told us about the change in the time for the meeting.
Whoever made the decision.

_____

_____ 15. The person should have told us about the change in the time for the meeting.
[who]
The person made the decision.

_____

_____ 16. We should all go to dinner. [after]
We have finished the final version of the report.

_____

_____ 17. We should all go to dinner. [because]
We have finished the final version of the report.

_____

_____ 18. The fact made us very happy.
The fact was that we have finished the final version of the report.

_____

_____ 19. The four umpires stood together on the third base line. [who]
They were not sure of the correct call on a foul ball.

_____

_____ 20. Have you decided *something*? [where]
The place you will live after graduation.

_____

Lesson 11 — *Subordination: Gerund and Infinitive Phrases*

A **phrase** is a group of related words that does *not* contain a subject and a verb in combination. Like the subordinate clause, the phrase is used in a sentence as a single part of speech. Many of the sentences that you have studied so far have contained a prepositional phrase, which consists of a preposition, a noun or a pronoun used as its object, and any modifiers of the object. Most prepositional phrases are used as adjectives or adverbs:

> Most *of my friends* live *in the East*.
> [The first phrase is used as an adjective to modify the pronoun *most*; the second is used as an adverb to modify the verb *live*.]

Much less commonly, a prepositional phrase is used as a noun:

> *Before lunch* is the best time for the meeting.
> [The phrase is the subject of the verb *is*.]

> She waved to us from *inside the phone booth*.
> [The phrase is the object of the preposition *from*.]

Another important kind of phrase makes use of a verbal. A **verbal** is a word formed from a verb but used as a different part of speech. There are three kinds of verbals: the gerund, the infinitive, and the participle.

GERUNDS

A **gerund** is a noun formed by adding *-ing* either to the base of the verb (*studying*) or to an auxiliary (*having studied, being studied, having been studied*). You might think of the gerund phrase as the equivalent of a noun. It can appear in any place in a sentence where a noun might appear: subject, direct object, renaming subjective complement, object of preposition, or (rarely) appositive.

> *Studying* demands most of my time. [Subject]
> I usually enjoy *studying*. [Direct object]
> My main activity is *studying*. [Renaming subjective complement]
> You won't pass the course without *studying*. [Object of preposition]
> Might I suggest to you another activity: *studying*? [Appositive]

These single-word gerund uses are uncomplicated. "He enjoys *studying*" and "He enjoys football" are alike in their structure; the only difference is that in one the direct object is a word formed from a verb and in the other it is a regular noun. Because they are formed from verbs and are thus "verbal nouns," gerunds can have a direct object or a subjective complement. The following examples will help clarify this important point.

> He enjoys *walking in the snow*.
> [The gerund has no complement. Compare "He walks in the snow."]

She enjoys building model airplanes.

[*Airplanes* is the direct object of the gerund *building*. Compare "She builds model airplanes."]

He enjoys *being helpful*. He enjoyed *being elected treasurer*.

[*Helpful* is the subjective complement of the gerund *being*; *treasurer* is the subjective complement of the passive gerund *being elected*. Compare "He is helpful" and "He was elected treasurer."]

She enjoyed *telling us the good news*.

[*Us* is the indirect object and *news* is the direct object of the gerund *telling*. Compare "She told us the good news."]

He enjoyed *making our vacation pleasant*.

[*Vacation* is the direct object of the gerund *making*, and *pleasant* is the objective complement of *vacation*. Compare "He made our vacation pleasant."]

A gerund phrase may contain a noun or pronoun that precedes the gerund to show the actor performing the action named by the gerund.

The group considered **your** *making those comments* a helpful addition to the discussion.

The group considered **Bob's** *making those comments* a helpful addition to the discussion.

Because *making those comments* is a gerund or verbal noun, the noun or pronoun showing who made the comments is in the possessive case. Contrast the use of a simple noun in these sentences:

The group considered her comments a helpful addition to the discussion.

The group considered Bob's comments a useful addition to the discussion.

In other words, the subject of a gerund phrase should be in the possessive case.

INFINITIVES

An **infinitive** is a verbal consisting of the base of the verb, usually preceded by *to* (*to* is called the sign of the infinitive). The infinitive uses auxiliaries to show tense and voice: *to study*, *to have studied*, *to be studying*, *to have been studying*, *to be studied*, *to have been studied*. An **infinitive phrase** consists of an infinitive plus its modifiers and/or complements. Infinitive units are used as nouns, as adjectives, and as adverbs:

To attend the party without an invitation would be tactless.

[The infinitive phrase is used as the subject of the sentence. Within the phrase, *party* is the direct object.]

It would be tactless *to attend the party without an invitation*.

[In this pattern, the infinitive phrase is called a delayed subject; hence it serves a noun use. The signal word is *it*; although *it* stands in subject position, the infinitive phrase is the meaningful subject. Sometimes the *it* is in the direct object slot with the delayed infinitive phrase following an objective complement: I would consider it tactless *to attend the party without an invitation*. Compare a similar noun clause use in Lesson 10.]

I wanted *to give Charles another chance*.

[The infinitive phrase is the direct object of *wanted*. Within the phrase, *Charles* is the indirect object and *chance* the direct object of the infinitive. Compare "I gave Charles another chance."]

My plan is *to become an active precinct worker*.

[The infinitive phrase is used as a noun; it is a subjective complement that renames the subject *plan*. Within the phrase, *worker* is the subjective complement of the infinitive. Compare "I became an active precinct worker."]

The test *to be taken next Friday* is an important one.
[The infinitive phrase is used as an adjective modifying *test*.]

I am happy *to meet you*.
[The infinitive phrase is used as an adverb modifying the adjective *happy*.]

To be sure of a good seat, you should arrive early.
[The infinitive phrase is used as an adverb modifying *should arrive*.]

Infinitive phrases sometimes include their own subjects. Notice that when a pronoun is used as the subject of an infinitive, the pronoun is in the objective case (see Lesson 24).

We wanted *her to resign*.
We know *him to be a good referee*.

In a rather common sentence type, the subject of an infinitive is preceded by *for*, which in this case is considered part of the phrase.

For us to leave now would be impolite.
It's silly *for you to feel neglected*.

The infinitive without *to* may form a phrase that is used as the direct object of such verbs as *let*, *help*, *make*, *see*, *hear*, and *watch*:

The teacher let *us leave early*.
Martha watched *her son score the winning touchdown*.

The infinitive without *to* is also sometimes used as the object of a preposition, such as *except*, *but*, and *besides*:

He could do nothing except *resign gracefully*.
He did everything but *write the paper for me*.

SUPPLEMENT 1

In Lesson 6, you learned that an interrogative unit in a direct question stands at the beginning of the sentence. Notice how this positioning can affect the internal makeup of a gerund phrase or an infinitive phrase:

How many natives did the missionaries succeed in *converting*?
[*Converting* is the gerund form of a transitive verb and therefore requires a direct object—in this case, *natives*.]

Which car did you finally decide *to buy*?
[*Car* is the direct object of the infinitive *to buy*.]

SUPPLEMENT 2

When the gerund is preceded by a pronoun, the pronoun should be in the possessive case.

The audience *enjoyed her dancing in the first act.*
[Compare "The audience enjoyed her dance in the first act."]

We appreciated *your helping the class with that project.*
[Compare "We appreciated your help with that project."]

SUMMARY OF GERUND AND INFINITIVE PHRASES

Gerund Phrases

1. Forms: *studying, having studied, being studied, having been studied*

2. Function: as a noun within the larger unit

3. Positions: subject, renaming subjective complement, direct object, object of preposition, and (rarely) appositive

Infinitive Phrases

1. Forms: *to study, to have studied, to be studying, to have been studying, to be studied, to have been studied.* Some infinitive phrases have subjects (We wanted her to run for office) in the objective case.

2. Function: as adjective (Here are the letters *to be mailed today*), as adverb (I am happy *to meet you*), or as noun (*To leave* now would be unwise)

3. Positions: subject (or delayed subject), direct object (or delayed direct object), renaming subjective complement, and (rarely) object of preposition.

4. Special structures:
   a. *For* sometimes introduces an infinitive phrase that has a subject.

   For you to criticize his work would be presumptuous.

   b. A phrase with a subject but without the marker *to* is often used as a direct object following one of these verbs: *let, help, make, see, hear, watch.*

   Mother let *us mix the cookie dough.*
   Ms. Jones heard *the man threaten the cashier.*

   c. The infinitive without *to* is used as object of prepositions *except, but, besides.*

   He could do nothing but *leave quietly.*

English Fundamentals Online

After you have completed Practice Sheets and Exercises in this lesson, you can find additional help and drill work at **MyWriting Lab.com**, in the section on Gerund and Infinitive Phrases.

NAME _____ SCORE _____

Directions: In the space at the left, copy the abbreviation that identifies the use of the italicized gerund phrase

S. [subject]   S.C. [subjective complement]
D.O. [direct object]   O.P. [object of preposition]

_____ 1. *Changing my major in college* crosses my mind occasionally.

_____ 2. Once in a while I think about *changing my major to some other field*.

_____ 3. Most students, at some point in college, consider *changing majors*.

_____ 4. For some students the most difficult decision in their first year of college is *selecting a major*.

_____ 5. For my uncle Harry, *finding a major* was a two-year project.

_____ 6. By *consulting an advisor*, Harry found a major suited to his skills.

_____ 7. The first step in the selection of a major should be *taking some aptitude tests*.

_____ 8. *Taking aptitude tests* is something that rarely occurs to most people.

_____ 9. Aptitude tests help us by *pointing out our strengths*.

_____ 10. Such tests also direct us in *avoiding weak spots in our skills*.

_____ 11. My cousin John never needed help in *choosing an occupation*.

_____ 12. From the time he was twelve, John considered *working on cars his future occupation*.

_____ 13. *Entertaining any other ideas* never crossed John's mind.

_____ 14. John's idea of wonderful fun was *tearing an engine apart and rebuilding it*.

_____ 15. When he was fifteen, John began *working for an auto racing team*.

_____ 16. *Cleaning wheels* was John's first job with the team.

_____ 17. Soon, however, his work involved *removing and replacing worn parts*.

_____ 18. As his skills grew, John became an expert at *fabricating small parts out of metal*.

_____ 19. Now, *studying automotive engineering* is John's passion.

_____ 20. He never considered *studying anything else*.

Directions: Each sentence contains one italicized infinitive phrase. Some phrases contain subjects. In the space at the left, write the abbreviation that identifies the use of the phrase in the sentence.

N. [noun]   Adj. [adjective]   Adv. [adverb]

_____ 1. A break in our schedule let *us attend last nights baseball game.*

_____ 2. We were happy *to watch such an exciting game.*

_____ 3. *To lose in the bottom of the ninth inning* was certainly disappointing.

_____ 4. The game *to be played later this week* will also be exciting.

_____ 5. We all want *to leave class a little early on the day of the game.*

_____ 6. I have been able *to attend almost every game this season.*

_____ 7. *To go to all the out-of-town games* is almost impossible for me.

_____ 8. *To attend all the home games* is difficult enough.

_____ 9. Most people consider it hard *to attend even five or six games.*

_____ 10. We all want *the team to do well this season.*

_____ 11. A good record will let *the team go to the playoffs at the end of the season.*

_____ 12. *To go to the playoffs* would make this season a success.

_____ 13. It would be wonderful *to win the conference championship.*

_____ 14. A conference championship would let *the team enter the College World Series.*

_____ 15. The first step toward the finals of the CWS is *to win a regional playoff.*

_____ 16. *To win a regional playoff* would be a major accomplishment for our team.

_____ 17. Any coach would be delighted *to win a regional playoff.*

_____ 18. *To have played in the College World Series* would be a source of pride for any player.

_____ 19. Our team, unfortunately, was unable *to advance past the conference playoffs.*

_____ 20. So we can do nothing but *fall back on that famous expression,* "Wait till next year."

Gerund and Infinitive Phrases

NAME _____ SCORE _____

Directions: Each sentence contains one gerund phrase. Underline the gerund phrase and identify its use by writing one of the following abbreviations in the space at the left of the sentence:

S. [subject]   S.C. [subjective complement]
D.O. [direct object]   O.P. [object of preposition]

_____ 1. Going to the library for an evening's work is always hard for me.

_____ 2. The most difficult part of my day is going to the library for an evening's work.

_____ 3. I have always admired your going to the library every evening.

_____ 4. I have always enjoyed reading books on technical subjects.

_____ 5. I would not know so much about technology without reading all those articles in the library.

_____ 6. Keeping track of so many books and magazines must be a very complicated task.

_____ 7. The job of keeping track of all the books in the library must be very difficult.

_____ 8. Checking out books before the use of computerized inventory systems was done with a card system.

_____ 9. Students once located books by using either the Dewey Decimal System or the Library of Congress System.

_____ 10. Using these systems, which are based on combinations of numbers and letters, allows librarians to position books in certain categories.

_____ 11. Books were placed on the shelves in the library by grouping them into these categories.

_____ 12. Locating a book required that students look in a huge set of trays called a card catalog.

_____ 13. Each book in the card catalog was found by looking at one of three cards.

_____ 14. Most students found looking through the cards very tedious.

_____ 15. Locating a book sometimes required a search through more than one tray of cards.

_____ 16. Students who were looking for a book sometimes found it by searching a subject index catalog.

_____ 17. Looking through all books that dealt with a certain subject was a very difficult job.

_____ 18. Students usually find looking for a book by computer an easy task.

_____ 19. Locating a book by computer, however, is not possible when the computer system goes down.

_____ 20. At such times the only option for students is going down to the local coffee shop and waiting for the technicians to fix the system.

Directions: In the space at the left, underline the infinitive phrase. In the space at the left, write the abbreviation that identifies the use of the infinitive phrase within the sentence.

N/s [subject or delayed subject]   Adj. [adjective]

N/sc [subjective complement]   Adv. [adverb]

N/d [direct object]

N/op [object of preposition]

_____   1. Most people I know would be delighted by an opportunity to go skiing for a week in Colorado.

_____   2. Jan's hope is to finish that paper early tomorrow morning.

_____   3. Ramona changed her job recently to get a higher salary and better working conditions.

_____   4. The changes in the market have given the company a chance to make huge profits over the next two years.

_____   5. The coach wants us to do our very best in these next three crucial games.

_____   6. To find that product for your shop, look in the *Thomas Register*.

_____   7. Surely, it will be possible for you to get here earlier next time.

_____   8. "We should be able to leave for home before 10 o'clock," said Jessie.

_____   9. Would someone please show me how to open this CD package without cutting myself?

_____ 10. Andy Lopez and Jim Thompson have been selected to be the captains for tomorrow's game.

_____ 11. Are you sufficiently interested in that ski trip to put down a deposit on the plane ticket now?

_____ 12. That brief delay will let us catch up with our work on that project.

_____ 13. It will be good to take a few days off after finishing our exams.

_____ 14. To take a few days off after finishing our exams will certainly be a great thing.

_____ 15. For you to drop that class this early in the term would probably be a big mistake.

_____ 16. Marcia stopped by the house earlier today to pick up her biology textbook.

_____ 17. This a good time to find out what kind of physical condition you're in.

_____ 18. The opportunity to meet such an important person doesn't come along very often.

_____ 19. You should be grateful to receive even a small raise in economic conditions such as these.

_____ 20. Your only hope at this point is to make a very high grade on the final exam.

Directions: Combine the two sentences in each item into one sentence by resolving one sentence into a gerund phrase or an infinitive phrase to replace the italicized word(s) in the other sentence.

1. Jim is painting the outside of his house.
   He does not enjoy *doing that job*.

   _____

2. Richard did not even stop to pick up his check.
   Without *doing something*, Richard left work to go home for the weekend.

   _____

3. When I first came to the campus, I needed to find an apartment.
   Doing something was my first priority.

   _____

4. Years ago Jorge learned to play the guitar.
   Doing something gave Jorge an appreciation for the work of great guitar players.

   _____

5. Janice wants to take a canoe trip through Minnesota's Boundary Canoe Waters.
   Janice's plan for her next vacation is *doing something*.

   _____

6. Taking that exam was easy.
   It was easy *to do something* once I organized my notes.

   _____

7. My plan at this time is *something*.
   I will reorganize my notes and study for two hours tonight.

   _____

8. In many theaters it is now possible *to do something*.
   You can buy tickets at a machine that accepts credit cards.

   _____

9. My highest priority for this last month of school is *to do something*.
   Finding a job for this summer is my highest priority for this last month of school.

   _____

10. Staying awake during that boring movie was very hard for me.
    It was hard for me *to do something*.

    _____

Brief Writing Assignment: In a paragraph of six or seven sentences, tell how you wrote your most successful writing assignment. Use two gerund phrases and two infinitive phrases.

A participle is an adjective formed from a verb by adding *-ing* or *-ed* to the base form of the verb (*studying, studied*) or to an auxiliary (*having studied, being studied, having been studied*). (Note that many verbs have irregular past participles. See pages 224–226 for lists of such verbs.) By itself, a participle works exactly as any one-word adjective works:

> The *injured* bird clung to the *swaying* branch.
>
> [The past participle *injured* modifies the noun *bird*; the present participle *swaying* modifies the noun *branch*.]

Often, however, the participle is combined with other words to form a **participial phrase** that modifies a noun.

> The taxi driver, *being a war veteran*, signed the petition.
>
> [The participial phrase modifies the noun *taxi driver*. Within the phrase, *veteran* is a subjective complement.]
>
> *Calling the man a hero*, the mayor gave him an award.
>
> [The participial phrase modifies the noun *mayor*. Within the phrase, *man* is a direct object and *hero* is an objective complement.]

PARTICIPIAL PHRASES

The similarity between an adjective clause and a participial phrase is obvious:

1. A man grabbed the microphone. The man [*or* He] was wearing a painted mask.
   [Two independent clauses.]

   a. A clown *who was wearing a painted mask* grabbed the microphone.
      [Adjective clause. *Mask* is a direct object of the verb.]
   b. A clown *wearing a painted mask* grabbed the microphone.
      [Participial phrase. *Mask* is a direct object of the participle.]

2. Jo's parents left the concert early. They found the music uncomfortably loud.
   [Two independent clauses.]

   a. Jo's parents, *who found the music uncomfortably loud*, left the concert early.
      [Adjective clause. *Music* is a direct object and *loud* an objective complement.]
   b. Jo's parents, *finding the music uncomfortably loud*, left the concert early.
      [Participial phrase. *Music* is a direct object and *loud* an objective complement.]

These two examples point out another similarity: Like the adjective clause, the participial phrase can be either restrictive or nonrestrictive. The phrase in the first example identifies the clown; it is restrictive and is not set off by commas. The phrase in the second example is not needed to identify parents; it requires commas because it is nonrestrictive.

Like adjective clauses, participial phrases must be very close to the noun they modify. An adjective clause must follow the noun it modifies. A restrictive (identifying) participial phrase normally follows the noun it modifies, as in the example, "A man wearing a black mask. . . ." Unlike a nonrestrictive adjective clause, however, a nonrestrictive participial phrase can move into another position in the sentence. Observe the positions of the participial phrase in the following sentences:

> Steve, having passed the test with flying colors, decided to celebrate.
>
> Having passed the test with flying colors, Steve decided to celebrate.

Occasionally, the participial phrase can be moved to the end of the clause:

> Steve decided to celebrate, having passed the test with flying colors.

Because a participle is an adjective formed from a verb and thus suggests an action, the participial phrase can be used to relieve the monotony of a series of short, independent clauses:

> Pam wanted desperately to hear the rock concert, but she was temporarily short of funds, and she knew that her cousin Alice had an extra ticket, and so she decided to call her. [Four independent clauses]
>
> Wanting desperately to hear the rock concert but being temporarily short of funds, Pam decided to call her cousin Alice, knowing that she had an extra ticket. [One independent clause and three participial phrases]
>
> Jensen stood at home plate. He waggled his bat. He eyed the pitcher coldly. He took a mighty swing at the first pitch. He hit the ball out of the park. [Five independent clauses]
>
> Standing at home plate, waggling his bat, and eyeing the pitcher coldly, Jensen took a mighty swing at the first pitch, hitting the ball out of the park. [One independent clause and four participial phrases]

ABSOLUTE PHRASES

The **absolute phrase** is a special kind of phrase using a participle, but it is unlike a standard participial phrase in two important ways:

1. The absolute phrase contains both a noun (or a pronoun) and a participle, which almost always follows the noun.
2. The absolute phrase does not directly modify a noun or pronoun in the main clause; rather, the absolute phrase modifies the entire main clause.

The absolute phrase is a versatile structure capable of many variations and widely used in modern writing to point out subtle relationships underlying the ideas within a sentence:

> *All things being equal*, Mary should easily win the race.
>
> *The storm having passed*, the ball game resumed.
>
> The police recovered eight of the paintings, *three of them badly damaged*.
>
> The mob reached the palace gates, *the leader (being) a burly, red-haired sailor*.
>
> [Occasionally an absolute phrase having a noun and a complement appears with the participle unexpressed.]

A special kind of phrase using *with* to introduce the absolute phrase can add subtle modifying and narrative coloring to a sentence:

With the band playing and the crowd applauding furiously, Jim Kinman was obviously uncomfortable as he stood on the stage.

They held the funeral on the second day, *with the town coming to look at Miss Emily beneath a mass of bought flowers, with the crayon face of her father musing profoundly above the bier.* . . . (William Faulkner)

But we can't possibly have a garden party *with a dead man just outside the front gate*. (Katherine Mansfield)

The face was a curious mixture of sensibility, *with some elements very hard and others very pretty*—perhaps it was in the mouth. (Katherine Anne Porter)

Notice that the *with* in this construction is quite unlike *with* in its common prepositional use:

The acquitted woman left the courtroom *with her* lawyer.
[*with* used as a preposition]

The acquitted woman left the courtroom *with her head held high*.
[*with* used to introduce the absolute phrase]

SUMMARY OF PARTICIPIAL AND ABSOLUTE PHRASES

Participial Phrases

1. Forms: *studying, studied, having studied, being studied, having been studied, having been studying*

2. Function: to modify a noun or pronoun. Those that identify the noun or pronoun are restrictive and require no punctuation; others are nonrestrictive and are set off by commas.

3. Position: if restrictive, always following the word it modifies. Nonrestrictive phrases may stand after the noun, at the beginning of the sentence, and occasionally at the end of the sentence.

Absolute Phrases

1. Form: a noun or pronoun followed by a participle

   The crops having failed, Grandfather sold the farm.

2. Function: adds to the meaning of the entire sentence but does not modify a word or fill a noun slot

3. Position: at the beginning, in the interior, or at the end of the larger unit; usually set off by commas

4. Special structures:
   a. The participle *being* is sometimes unexpressed.

      Its chairman [being] a retired military person, the committee is well disciplined.

   b. The phrase sometimes begins with the word *with*.

      With its supply of ammunition exhausted, the garrison surrendered.

English Fundamentals **Online**

After you have completed Practice Sheets and Exercises in this lesson, you can find additional help and drill work at **MyWritingLab.com.**

Participial and Absolute Phrases

NAME _____ SCORE _____

Directions: The italicized unit in each sentence is either a participial or an absolute phrase. If the unit is a participial phrase, write in the space at the left the noun or pronoun the phrase it modifies. If the unit is an absolute phrase, leave the space at the left blank.

_____ 1. At last, *with everyone almost exhausted*, the end of the work week was at hand.

_____ 2. *Almost worn out from the long week's hard work*, the people on that project completed their assignment.

_____ 3. The three people, *the completed project printed and ready for distribution*, walked happily to the manager's office.

_____ 4. *Laughing happily as they walked down the hall*, the three people entered the manager's office.

_____ 5. *The manager's office being dark and empty*, the three put a copy of the project on his desk.

_____ 6. *Closing the door quietly behind them*, the happy people walked down the hall to the exit.

_____ 7. The three workers, *quietly celebrating the successful completion of the project*, hurried into the parking lot.

_____ 8. The three people climbed into a car *parked at the far end of the lot*.

_____ 9. The car, *carrying the three people*, moved slowly down the street.

_____ 10. Then, the driver of the car turned the car onto a ramp *leading to a freeway*.

_____ 11. *The freeway being almost clear of any traffic*, the three people raced out of town.

_____ 12. *With no work required until Monday*, the people had a weekend for rest and relaxation.

_____ 13. The driver dropped one person, *airline tickets clutched tightly in her hand*, at the local airport.

_____ 14. The woman, *carrying a small suitcase and a plane ticket*, disappeared into the terminal.

_____ 15. She intended, *everything working as she planned*, to visit her brother's family in another city.

_____ 16. The second person, *prepared to meet his family for a weekend at the shore*, was dropped off at a train station.

_____ 17. His family met him at the train station, *their luggage already checked in for the trip*.

_____ 18. *Greeting the man with hugs and kisses*, the family led him to the train.

_____ 19. The driver headed out of town to his farm, *his two passengers having been taken care of.*

_____ 20. The next morning the man watched the sunrise from his front porch, *a cup of coffee steaming in his hand.*

_____ 21. Jorge's car, *having been parked outside in the cold weather,* was covered with ice and snow.

_____ 22. *The car having been parked outside in the rain and snow,* Jorge had to scrape off the ice from the windshield.

_____ 23. *With the snow falling all around him,* Jorge scraped the ice from the windshield of his car.

_____ 24. Jorge, *his hands almost frozen from scraping ice,* climbed into his car.

_____ 25. Unfortunately, the car, *having sat outside in subfreezing temperatures,* had a dead battery.

_____ 26. *Sitting in a car with a dead battery,* Jorge considered his options.

_____ 27. Jorge, *smiling grimly at his predicament,* reached into his jacket pocket for his cell phone.

_____ 28. The cell phone, unfortunately, sat *waiting for him on his desk back in the office.*

_____ 29. *Having no other available options,* Jorge pushed open the car door and walked back into the snow.

_____ 30. *Grumbling a little at his own carelessness,* Jorge walked back into his office.

_____ 31. Jorge called a tow truck and walked back to his car, *taking care to pocket his cell phone as he left the office.*

_____ 32. *With his car finally started,* Jorge drove carefully to his first appointment.

_____ 33. At this point Jorge was running very much behind schedule, *his first appointment located on the far side of town.*

_____ 34. *Stopped at a traffic light,* Jorge put the phone's hands-free device to his ear.

_____ 35. Then, *using a voice command,* he directed the phone to dial his client.

_____ 36. Jorge spoke briefly with his client, *hoping that she still had time to meet with him.*

_____ 37. *Arriving almost an hour late,* Jorge hurried into the client's office.

_____ 38. The client understood his problem completely, *her own car having failed to start a few mornings before.*

_____ 39. *Laughing at their mutual car troubles,* the client offered Jorge a seat in her office.

_____ 40. Once again, the cell phone, *having come into widespread use only a few years before,* saved the day for a harried businessman.

NAME _____   SCORE _____

Directions: Each of the following sentences contains one participial phrase or one absolute phrase. Put brackets around the phrase. If the phrase is a participial phrase, copy in the space at the left the noun or pronoun the phrase modifies. If the phrase is an absolute phrase, leave the space blank.

_____ 1. With no one being available to run the store while we are gone, we cannot possibly go out for lunch.

_____ 2. Having no one here to run the store while we are gone, we cannot possibly go out for lunch.

_____ 3. Going out to lunch with no one being available to run the store does not seem like a good idea.

_____ 4. Today is not a good day for going out to lunch, there being no one available to replace us while we are gone.

_____ 5. Choosing not to close the store while we went to lunch, we ordered a sandwich from a nearby deli.

_____ 6. Offering to run the store while we went out to lunch, my father walked in the door just as the sandwiches from the deli arrived.

_____ 7. My father, offering to run the store while we went out, walked in the door just as the sandwiches from the deli arrived.

_____ 8. My father arriving in time to run the store, we put the sandwiches in the refrigerator and went out to lunch.

_____ 9. Storing tomorrow's lunch in the refrigerator, we walked down the street to a small restaurant.

_____ 10. Refreshed by a break from running the store, we went back to work after an hour had passed.

_____ 11. Reading steadily for almost two hours, Cathy finished only two chapters of the five that she must read for tomorrow's class.

_____ 12. Of the five chapters assigned for tomorrow's class, Cathy had read only two by the end of the afternoon.

_____ 13. By the end of the afternoon, Cathy had read only 75 of the 150 pages assigned for tomorrow's class.

_____ 14. Cathy, facing a long night of reading, settled in at her dining room table with a cup of coffee and a slice of pizza.

_____ 15. Sitting at the table and holding her book, Cathy took careful notes from each page she read.

_____ 16. A hard night of work stretching out before her, Cathy called in two friends to help her study.

_____ 17. Walking in the door with fresh coffee and all their notes, the two friends began to help Cathy with her assignment.

_____ 18. Working on their computers, Cathy and her friends were able to find notes that helped with their studying.

_____ 19. Their work in the textbook finally completed, the three were able to get a short nap before class started.

_____ 20. The three friends went home immediately after class, having successfully passed the test on the five chapters.

_____ 21. The three friends, having successfully passed the test on the work that had been assigned, went home immediately after class.

_____ 22. The test having been successfully completed, the three friends went home immediately after class.

_____ 23. Faced with a seemingly impossible task, we should seek help from friends.

_____ 24. With a seemingly impossible task looming over us, it is often a good idea to seek help from friends.

_____ 25. How can I possibly get to the office on time with every street blocked by heavy traffic.

_____ 26. Finding every street almost impassible, I found it difficult to get to work on time.

_____ 27. Traffic having become more difficult to deal with every day, I want to find a job away from the downtown area.

_____ 28. Finding a work location far removed from the congestion of downtown will be a difficult thing to do.

_____ 29. To find a work location far removed from the congestion of downtown will not be an easy task.

_____ 30. My apartment, located as it is far from downtown, would be an ideal location for work.

_____ 31. Working at home by computer, called telecommuting by some people, might be a good solution for me.

_____ 32. Working at home by computer, sometimes called "virtual" work, might allow me to avoid traffic jams.

_____ 33. Commuting to my office in the spare bedroom, I probably would not meet much traffic.

_____ 34. Walking from the kitchen to my spare bedroom, I could get to work in about 45 seconds.

_____ 35. With my work station located about a 45-second walk away, I should have no trouble getting to work on time.

_____ 36. Having my work location situated so close to my living room couch might tempt me to leave work for a nap.

_____ 37. My work location being so close to my couch, I might be tempted to leave work for a nap.

_____ 38. To have my work and my couch located very close to each other might be too much of a temptation for me.

_____ 39. Attracted by the possibility of a short, quiet commute, I've asked my manager for permission to work at home three days a week.

_____ 40. I will work at home three days a week, testing my ability to resist the temptation of an early nap.

NAME _____ SCORE _____

Directions: In the first space at the left, write one of the following letters to identify the italicized verbal phrase:

G. (gerund phrase)   I. (infinitive phrase)

P. (participial phrase)   A. (absolute phrase)

In the second space at the left, write one of the following abbreviations to identify the complement printed in bold type within the phrase:

S.C. (subjective complement)   I.O. (indirect object)

D.O. (direct object)   O.C. (objective complement)

_____ 1. My uncle has decided *to paint his office a new bright* **color**.

_____
_____ 2. He is thinking of *changing the* **color** *of his office*.

_____ 3. *With its walls painted a dark* **gray**, my uncle thinks the office is gloomy.

_____ 4. *Examining the* **office** *closely*, my uncle is thinking of a bright new color.

_____ 5. *To give the* **office** *a brighter atmosphere*, my uncle is thinking of yellow or
_____ a bright red for the walls.

6. *Painting at least one wall a bright* **yellow** will make him feel more cheerful.

_____ 7. My aunt thinks *painting one* **wall** is a silly idea.

_____ 8. She wants *my uncle to paint all four walls a bright* **yellow**.

_____ 9. My aunt always enjoys *offering my* **uncle** *advice*.

_____ 10. Her advice is *to paint all four* **walls** *in the office*.

_____ 11. Usually, my uncle does nothing except *follow my aunt's* **advice**.

_____ 12. On this occasion, however, he decided *to paint one wall a burnt-orange* **color**.

_____ 13. *With two of the walls painted bright* **colors**, my uncle thinks that the office will
_____ be a cheerful place.

14. *The walls being so* **bright**, my aunt suggested very dim lights for office.

_____ 15. If the lights are dim, no one will be blinded by the lights *reflecting the bright*
_____ **colors** *into their eyes*.

_____ 16. If you are able *to finish that **book** by tomorrow night*, I'll borrow it from you
_____ for the weekend.
_____ 17. I don't have anything but that book, *with my television having a serious*
_____ ***problem***.
_____ 18. *Buying a new **television set*** should probably be high on my list of priorities.
_____
_____ 19. Although I can't really afford *to buy **myself** a new television*, I think I'll
_____ borrow the money from my brother and buy one.
_____ 20. *A new television being a high **priority** for me*, I'll borrow some money and buy
_____ one this weekend.
_____ 21. The art director and the printer discussed *publishing that **brochure** in four*
_____ *colors*.
_____ 22. *Having been **coach** for only one week*, Zachary doesn't know the player's
_____ names yet.
_____ 23. The mechanic, *having diagnosed the car's **problem** incorrectly*, could
_____ not make the proper repairs.
_____ 24. *Having given **Andrew** three choices for his assignment*, the teacher left
_____ the room.
_____ 25. Andrew, with three possible subjects for his paper, was unable *to make any*
_____ ***choice** at all*.
_____ 26. *Being a very indecisive **person***, Andrew needed help in making his choice.
_____
_____ 27. Finally, it was necessary *for the teacher to give **Andrew** a specific assignment*.
_____
_____ 28. Does *being the newest **person** on the staff* ever make you uncomfortable?
_____
_____ 29. I can't ever think of that incident without *feeling a little **embarrassed***.
_____
_____ 30. Can you help *me find that little **town** on this map*?
_____
_____ 31. *To become a **lawyer*** was something my brother has wanted for years.
_____
_____ 32. My brother's goal is *becoming an **attorney** in a big law firm*.
_____
_____ 33. *Earning a law **degree*** was a difficult task for my brother.
_____
_____ 34. Yesterday a man called *to offer my **brother** a job in a law firm*.
_____
_____ 35. When he received the job offer, my brother was delighted *to accept the*
_____ ***position***.

Directions: Combine the two short sentences into one sentence by converting the second sentence into a participial phrase or an absolute phrase.

1. The director convened the meeting.
   The last staff member finally arrived.

   _____

2. The newly arrived freshmen gathered in the dining hall.
   Each one carried a folder full of information.

   _____

3. Kelli looked at the return address on the envelope.
   A brief smile crossed her face.

   _____

4. Everyone in the stadium stood and faced the flag.
   The band played the national anthem.

   _____

5. I identified the chorus of that song almost immediately.
   My little brother has played a version of it almost every day.

   _____

6. Maria shopped carefully for a new computer.
   The hard drive on her old computer crashed for the third time last week.

   _____

7. The woman watched as her daughter left for college.
   She hid a smile behind a handkerchief.

   _____

8. The two men waited patiently in the stadium.
   They wanted to watch the very last pitch of the game.

   _____

9. Alfredo searched the Internet for hours.
   He was trying to find information for his term paper.

   _____

10. We camped out for three days at the ticket office last week.
    We wanted to get the best possible seats for this week's game.

    _____

Brief Writing Assignment: In a paragraph of five or six sentences, tell the story of a recent exciting experience. In the sentences, use at least two participial and two absolute phrases.

Check Sheet

☐ Sentences, also known as *independent clauses*, can be joined to make writing more effective.

☐ Compound Sentences

☐ Two independent clauses joined by a comma and a coordinating conjunction (*and, but, or, nor, for, yet, so*) or by a semicolon create a compound sentence.

> The two men left work at noon, and the three women left at 12:30 P.M.
> The two men left work at noon; then the three women left at 12:30 P.M.

Punctuation note: Omitting the comma before the coordinating conjunction creates an error called a *run-on sentence*; omitting the coordinating conjunction creates an error called a *comma splice*.

☐ Each coordinating conjunction establishes a different relationship (time, cause, etc.) between the two clauses. Considerable care must be exercised to select the proper coordinating conjunction. The relationships between clauses joined with a semicolon are often established by using conjunctive adverbs such as *therefore* and *however*. Note that compound verbs—that is, a subject with two verbs—require no punctuation.

> John picked up the book and left the room.

☐ Complex Sentences

☐ Sentences formed by subordinating one clause and including it with a second sentence to form a complex sentence.

☐ Adverbial Clauses

☐ Adverbial clauses are word groups opened with subordinating conjunctions such as *when, since, after, although, if, unless, because*, and others. The clauses perform the same functions as one-word adverbs that modify verbs.

> The men left town early.
> After the rain stopped, the men left town.
> The men, after the rain stopped, left town.
> The men left town after the rain stopped.

The clause stands as an opening element, an interrupting element between subject and verb, or as the final element of a sentence.

Punctuation note: When an adverbial clause stands as the opening element of a sentence, it is joined to the main clause with a comma. That same clause, when it stands between the subject and verb, it is set off with commas. The adverbial clause requires no punctuation when it stands as the final element of the sentence.

☐ Adjective or Relative Clauses

☐ Just as adjectives modify (change the reader's conception of) nouns,

> the red rose
> the changeable weather

clauses that begin with *who, whose, whom, which,* and *that* can also modify nouns. The words opening these clauses are called relative pronouns. Most adjective clauses stand immediately after the noun they modify; occasionally, a preposition or even a prepositional phrase intervenes between the noun and the modifying clause, but the position of the clause must clearly establish the relationship between the clause and the noun (called the *antecedent*) it modifies.

> The man *who won the award* will be here soon.
> The man *whose brilliant discovery* won the prize will soon be here.
> The man to *whom we will give the prize* will appear soon.
> The man *whom I pointed out* is the winner of the prize.
> The man of the hour, about *whom you have heard so much,* just walked into the room.

☐ Some adjective clauses identify the noun modified by the clause. All of the clauses in the examples above identify the noun. Such clauses, called *restrictive relative* or *adjective clauses,* are not set off with commas. Adjective clauses that modify but do not identify are called *nonrestrictive relatives* and *are* set off by commas.

> The person *who owns that car* should move it from my driveway.
> June Williams, who owns that car, should move it from my driveway.

☐ Remember certain distinctions in using *who, which,* and *that. Who* refers only to people; *which* refers only to things. *That* is used only in restrictive clauses, and there is a convention (though not a hard-and-fast rule) that *which* is never used to open a restrictive clause.

☐ The adverbs *when* and *where* are sometimes used as though they are relative pronouns. In sentences such as

> I carefully searched the place in which I had dropped my wallet.

we sometimes say

> I carefully searched the place where I had dropped my wallet.

In the same way, *when* can be used as a replacement for *in which.*

> Jan recalled the very minute when she met Tom.

☐ Noun Clauses

☐ In the same way that adjective clauses can replace one-word adjectives, word groups containing a subject-verb combination and a subordinating word can do the work of a noun. These structures, called *noun clauses*, can do whatever simple nouns can do in a sentence: They can be the subject, subjective complement, direct object, object of a preposition, and an appositive.

> *Whoever answered the phone* (S.) asked *what we wanted from the store*. (D.O.)
> The next question was *how we intended to pay for it*. (S.C.)
> The person then gave the phone to *whoever was standing next to her*. (O.P.)
> He objected to the fact *that we were taking so much time*. (Ap.)

The subordinating words can be conjunctions, adjectives, or adverbs.

> Jill wonders *if* Mom and Dad are coming. (conjunction)
> Jill wonders *when* they will arrive. (adverb)
> Jill wonders *which* car they be driving. (adjective)
> Jill wonders *what* they will do tomorrow. (pronoun)

☐ Gerunds, Infinitives, and Verbal Phrases

☐ Word groups that employ a form of a verb and associated words can be used as noun replacements and perform most of the functions that ordinary nouns perform in a sentence.

☐ Gerunds Phrases

☐ Gerunds are formed by adding *-ing* to a verb's base form or to an auxiliary.

> *flying, having flown, having been flown*

☐ Gerunds can stand alone in sentences:

> *Running* is good exercise. Barb enjoys *running*.

☐ Gerunds can also be joined with other words to create gerund phrases.

> *Running three miles* can be exhausting.
> Maria enjoys *operating that video camera*.

These phrases can serve any purpose in a sentence that a simple noun serves: subject, subjective complement, direct object, or object of preposition.

☐ Infinitive Phrases

☐ An infinitive is a verbal formed from the base of the verb and the word *to*. Infinitives change tense and voice by adding auxiliaries. Modifiers and complements are added to infinitives to create infinitive phrases. Infinitives and infinitive phrases serve as nouns, adjectives, and adverbs.

> *To find that source* was a difficult task. (subject)
> It was a difficult task *to find that source*. (delayed subject)
> My next step is *to find that source*. (subjective complement)
> Jill wanted desperately *to find that source*. (direct object)
> My plan *to find that source* did not work. (adjective)
> *To find that source*, you should check on the Internet. (adverb)

☐ Infinitive phrases sometimes contain their own subjects.

> The instructor asked *Mary to find that source.*

☐ Infinitive phrases can open with *for* and the subject of the infinitive.

> *For us to find that source* was an almost impossible task.

☐ Infinitive phrases without the word *to* can serve as the direct object of verbs such as *let, help, make, see, hear,* and *watch.*

> Anne let *Mary find that source first.*

☐ Infinitive phrases without *to* can serve as the object of a preposition such as *except, but,* and *besides.*

> There is nothing left for me to do *but find that source.*

☐ Participial Phrases

☐ A participle is a verbal adjective formed by adding - *ing* or -*ed* to the base of a verb or to an auxiliary. Participles can be used as simple adjectives.

> The *exhausted* man faced another *exhausting* climb.

☐ Participles can be joined by other words to form a participial phrase that modifies a noun.

> *Exhausted from the first long climb,* the girl stopped to rest on a ledge.
> *Exhausting every ounce of energy,* the girl finally reached the summit.

☐ Participial phrases, like adjective clauses, can be either restrictive or nonrestrictive. Usually, restrictive phrases follow the noun being modified.

> The girl just reaching the summit is my sister.

The nonrestrictive phrase can appear in three positions in the sentence, but it must always be clearly related to the noun it modifies.

> *Having reached the summit at last,* the girl raised her hands in triumph.
> The girl, *having reached the summit at last,* raised her hands in triumph.
> The girl raised her hands in triumph, *having reached the summit at last.*

Note that, in the third version, no confusion is created by moving the phrase to the end of the sentence because the closest noun cannot sensibly be modified by the phrase. In another sentence,

> The girl shook hands with Jim, having reached the summit at last.

it is possible to make the phrase modify the word *Jim,* so the phrase must not be moved to the end of the sentence if the phrase modifies the word *girl.*

☐ **Absolute Phrases**

☐ Phrases composed of a noun plus a participle sometimes modify the sentence as a whole without being closely related to any noun in the rest of the sentence. In fact, the phrase should not include a noun that appears in the rest of the sentence. The absolute phrase, although it is not a sentence, is in that one sense independent of the rest of the sentence.

> *The job having been completed*, the workers left for the day.
> The workers left for the day, *the job having been completed*.

☐ An absolute phrase can be opened by the word *with*.

> *With the hard part of the work already finished*, the workers began to relax.

Sentence Building

Lessons, Practice Sheets, and Exercises

Lesson 13 | *Completeness: Dealing with Sentence Fragments*

To be complete, a sentence must

1. Contain a subject and a verb.
2. Be able to stand alone as an independent unit.

A group of words without both a subject and a verb cannot be a complete sentence. A group of words containing both a subject and a verb but opening with a subordinating conjunction cannot be a complete sentence. The subordinating conjunction makes the clause dependent instead of independent.

SENTENCE FRAGMENTS

A group of words that does not have a subject and a verb and cannot stand alone is called an incomplete sentence, or **sentence fragment**. Sometimes a sentence fragment is punctuated as if it were a sentence. This mistake of punctuation is called a **period fault**. Sentence fragments almost always fit one of the following patterns:

1. A subordinate clause standing as a sentence. (But remember that *and*, *but*, *or*, *nor*, *for*, *yet*, and *so* do not subordinate. A clause introduced by one of these words may stand as a sentence.)

   Fragments: The clerk finally let us see the contract. *Although she clearly hated to reveal its contents.*

   Bob tried to start the old lawn mower. *Which never seemed to work properly for him.*

2. A verbal phrase punctuated as a sentence:

   Fragments: The delegates agreed on a compromise wage scale. *Realizing that the strike could not go on indefinitely.*

   Nell had ordered her tickets a month ago. *To be sure of getting good seats.*

137

3. A noun followed by a phrase or a subordinate clause but lacking a main verb:

> **Fragments:** The committee should include Ms. Jones. *A tireless worker with many constructive ideas.*
>
> The mayor asked Bentley to take the job. *Bentley being the only available person with field experience.*
>
> The coach thinks our prospects are good. *A chance, perhaps, to win back the conference championship.*
>
> Junior will require a special kind of tutor. *Someone who will realize how sensitive the child really is.*

You should learn to avoid using fragments in your writing. Usually a close reading of anything you have written will reveal sentence fragments so that you can correct them. You can improve your skill at identifying fragments by using the following strategy: When you check what you have written, read the sentences in a paragraph in reverse order. Start with your last sentence and work back to your first. This process, which breaks the tie between a fragment and the sentence that it depends on, makes any grammatically incomplete sentence stand out.

CORRECTING SENTENCE FRAGMENTS

When you have discovered a fragment in your writing, any one of several possible corrections is easy to make.

- You can attach the fragment to the preceding sentence by doing away with the fragment's capital letter and supplying the right punctuation.
- You can change the fragment to a subordinate clause and attach it to the appropriate main clause by means of the right connective.
- You can change the fragment to a complete sentence by supplying a subject or a verb or both.
- You can change the fragment to an appositive or some other appropriate phrase.

Consider the following corrected sentences:

> The clerk finally let us see the contract, *although she clearly hated to reveal its contents.*
>
> Bob tried to start the old lawn mower, *which never seemed to work properly for him.*
>
> The delegates agreed on a compromise wage scale *because they realized that the strike could not go on indefinitely.*
>
> *To be sure of getting good seats*, Nell had ordered her tickets a month ago.
>
> The committee should include Ms. Jones, *a tireless worker with many constructive ideas.*
>
> The mayor asked Bentley to take the job, *Bentley being the only available person with field experience.*
>
> The coach thinks our prospects are good; *we have a chance, perhaps, to win back the league championship.*
>
> Junior will require a special kind of tutor. *He or she must be someone who will realize how sensitive the child really is.*

There are a few types of word groups that are not considered fragments. Although they lack a complete subject-verb combination, these types of word groups are accepted as legitimate language patterns. They are

1. **Commands**: in which the subject *you* is understood:

   > Please be seated. Put your name on a slip of paper. Pass the papers to the left aisle.
   > [See Lesson 21, Supplement.]

2. **Exclamations:**

   > What excitement! Only two minutes to go! Good Heavens, not a fumble? How terrible!

3. **Bits of dialogue:**

   > "New car?" she asked. "Had it long?"
   > "Picked it up last week," he replied.

4. **Occasional transitions between units of thought:**

   > On with the story.
   > And now to conclude.

You have very likely observed in your reading that experienced writers sometimes use sentence fragments, especially in narrative and descriptive writing. But these writers are skilled workers who know how to use fragments to achieve particular stylistic effects. You should first master the fundamental forms of the sentence. Once you have learned to write clear, correct sentences without faltering, there will be plenty of time for experimenting.

English Fundamentals Online

After you have completed Practice Sheets and Exercises in this lesson, you can find additional help and drill work at **MyWritingLab.com**, in the section on Completeness: Run-Ons; Completeness: Dealing with Sentence Fragments.

NAME _____ SCORE _____

Directions: Study the following word groups for completeness. In the space at the left, write **S** if the word group is a complete sentence or a grammatically acceptable fragment. Write **F** if the word group is a fragment.

_____ 1. If we don't try very hard to find the source of that error in our computer program.

_____ 2. We will continue to have problems with our inventory if we don't find and correct that error in the software.

_____ 3. Recognizing that error and correcting it without shutting down our system and bringing business to a halt while the programmers work.

_____ 4. Recognizing that error and correcting it without interrupting business will take a great effort by our programmers.

_____ 5. A problem that has never occurred before today and, we hope, will never occur again.

_____ 6. That error in the software is a problem that has never occurred before and, we hope, will never occur again.

_____ 7. Joe Richards, a man who has incredible skills in recognizing and reacting to the mood of the voters in national elections.

_____ 8. The candidate's campaign manager has hired Joe Richards, a man who can help shape a campaign platform to meet the concerns of the electorate.

_____ 9. A few people arrived early, realizing that the available seating was not nearly sufficient to accommodate the expected crowd.

_____ 10. A few people realizing that the available seating was not nearly sufficient to accommodate the expected crowd and arriving early.

_____ 11. Knowing that there would not be enough seats for such a large crowd of people, we arrived early for the political rally.

_____ 12. With the back rows filling up first and those who arrived late forced to walk down to the very front rows.

_____ 13. With the back rows filling up early, those who arrived late were forced to walk down to the very front rows.

_____ 14. The people in the crowd rose to their feet and welcomed the speaker with applause and cheers.

_____ 15. The people in the crowd, rising to their feet and welcoming the speaker with applause and cheers.

_____ 16. Smiling at the people in the crowd, the speaker, a man who knows how to captivate and move an audience.

_____ 17. The speaker, a man who knows how to captivate and move an audience, smiled and waved at the crowd.

_____ 18. The speaker, a man of great wit and wisdom, captivated his audience from the very beginning of his speech.

141

_____ 19. The speaker was a man of great wit and wisdom who captivated his audience from the very beginning of his speech.

_____ 20. The speaker, a man of great wit and wisdom who captivated his audience from the very beginning of his speech.

_____ 21. Please sit down and write your name on the top line of this sheet of paper before you begin to write your essay.

_____ 22. "Computer crashed?" she asked. "Always a bad thing."

_____ 23. An expert in aerodynamics, a woman who can analyze patterns produced in a wind tunnel and advise the designers about changes to the fuselage.

_____ 24. We have hired an expert in aerodynamics, a woman who can advise us about changes to make in the fuselage.

_____ 25. Once we got the answer to that difficult question and began to work on the design of the house with that new requirement in mind.

_____ 26. Finally, we got a positive response to our most difficult question, and, for a change, we were able to go right to work on changing the design of the house.

_____ 27. More often, we get only vague responses to our questions; thus we are forced to guess and hope as we change the design of the house.

_____ 28. Write short, direct answers to those questions, making very careful word choices as you write.

_____ 29. Hi! Great to see you again. Just get back in town?

_____ 30. Competing companies coming closer to our designs when they produce their products and making competition very keen for that segment of the market.

_____ 31. Competing companies have come closer to our designs when they produce their products and made competition very keen for that segment of the market.

_____ 32. Competing companies have come closer to our designs when they produce their products, thus making competition very keen for that segment of the market.

_____ 33. Coming closer to our designs as they produce their products, competing companies are taking more and more market share from us every day.

_____ 34. Unless we come up with a new, especially effective feature in that product and can thus win back our share of the market.

_____ 35. We will continue to fall behind our competition unless we come up with a new, especially effective feature in that product.

_____ 36. Falling behind our competition because we have not been able to devise a change in our product that would cause our customers to buy our product again.

_____ 37. We continue to fall behind our competition because we have been unable to devise a change in our product and cannot draw customers away from our competition.

_____ 38. Finally coming up with a new design feature and allowing us to compete on equal terms with other companies in our field.

_____ 39. Finally coming up with a new design feature, the people in the lab have given us the ability to compete on equal terms with other companies in our field.

_____ 40. The people in the lab, highly creative and distinctly innovative, having once again saved the company from second place in our field.

Correcting Sentence Fragments

Directions: Each numbered unit consists of a sentence followed by a fragment. In the space provided, rewrite the material to eliminate the fragment by attaching the fragment to the sentence or by making the fragment a complete sentence in itself.

1. The manager must find a temporary replacement for Jillian. At least until she recovers from that terrible bout with the flu.

   _____

2. We need to find a temporary replacement for Jillian. To fill in until she can recover from that terrible bout with the flu.

   _____

3. Gas prices rose to great heights a few months ago. Causing an increase in purchases of smaller, more fuel-efficient cars.

   _____

4. My grandfather recently bought a hybrid car. A vehicle that is supposed to get an average of almost 40 miles per gallon of gas.

   _____

5. A vehicle that gets an average of 40 miles per gallon of gas ought to improve my grandfather's disposition. And maybe make him smile a little as he drives.

   _____

6. The two men in the baseball caps wandered slowly down the street. Discussing the recent collapse of their favorite baseball team.

   _____

7. Although the team had started the season with a long winning streak. It had fallen into a deep slump toward the end of the season.

   _____

8. Starting the season with a long winning streak. Their team had fallen into a deep slump toward the end of the season.

   _____

9. A team that falls into a deep slump toward the end of the season. It had little chance to recover with only a few games left in the season.

   _____

10. Summer being a bad time to work outdoors on a construction site because of the heat and humidity. I think I'll try to find an office job after school is out.

_____

11. Because I've never written such a long paper in that particular style. I don't know how soon I can finish the work.

_____

12. The format and style sheet of that paper are unfamiliar to me. This class being the first I've ever taken that demands that particular presentation.

_____

13. I'll probably need to seek help from someone when I'm in the last stages of the paper. Someone who has worked in that particular format before.

_____

14. We should have shopped for our textbooks well before classes started. Thus ensuring that the books would actually be available in the bookstore.

_____

15. To be sure that the books would actually be available in the bookstore. We should have shopped for our textbooks well before classes started.

_____

16. A dedicated and intelligent person who will take her responsibilities very seriously. Perhaps we should appoint Roberta as chair of that committee.

_____

17. James being the only other person remotely qualified to do that work. We think Roberta is the only choice for committee chair.

_____

18. Giving us a chance to win the conference championship. The coach has made several changes in our lineup.

_____

19. With only two weeks left before my vacation. Possibly it's time for me to map out a trip for my time away from the office.

_____

20. Whenever we can find time to do the work. We need to get the garden plowed up for planting.

_____

NAME _____   SCORE _____

Directions: Each numbered unit consists of a sentence followed by a fragment. In the space provided, eliminate the fragment by using one of the techniques suggested in the text (pages 138-139) as specified in each item:

    a. Attach the fragment to the preceding sentence

    b. Change the fragment to a subordinate clause

    c. Change the fragment to an independent clause

    d. Change the fragment to an appositive or another appropriate phrase

1. Alan volunteered to work at the community center last summer. Tutoring adults who have not learned to read.

    a. _____

    d. _____

2. The Johnsons stopped briefly in St. Louis to visit an art museum. While they were on their way back from their summer vacation.

    a. _____

    d. _____

3. Katherine and Mario registered for classes on the first day of registration. To be sure they could enroll in Professor Alexander's class.

    b. _____

    c. _____

4. Mr. Winston and his wife have gone on a cruise every year. Because they miss the ocean after they moved to the Midwest from the East Coast.

    a. _____

    d. _____

5. Maria Gonzalez is retiring after 25 years as county tax assessor. A devoted public servant who always worked to improve county government.

    b. _____

    d. _____

6. Jan and Marcie spent the day Saturday shopping with their mother. Going into every shop that was having a sale.

    a. _____

    c. _____

7. The crew worked very hard to finish repairs to the roof. Even though bad weather interrupted their work several times.

    c. _____

    d. _____

8. The managers need to upgrade our computer system. Which freezes and loses data on a regular basis.

 b. _____

 c. _____

9. The softball team cannot win more than two games in a row. In spite of the fact that they practice hard every day.

 b. _____

 d. _____

10. Patricia thinks she has a good chance for that job. With two years' experience in that type of work and very good references.

 b. _____

 c. _____

11. The three tired girls walked in off the trail. Scratched, dirty, and hungry.

 b. _____

 c. _____

 d. _____

12. Jack Farley seems well qualified for that job. Having a degree in business and several years of experience as a manager.

 a. _____

 d. _____

13. In the house down the street lives a famous author. A woman who writes fantasy and science fiction.

 b. _____

 c. _____

 d. _____

14. The two boys looked everywhere for their lost books. In the trunk of the car, in the basement, and even in their bedrooms.

 c. _____

 d. _____

15. We asked Morgan to analyze that proposal. Morgan being the only one in the office with enough experience to understand it.

 b. _____

 c. _____

Brief Writing Assignment: Write a paragraph of six to eight lines explaining what you will do on a day-to-day basis in your chosen career. Intentionally include in the paragraph three sentence fragments. After you have written the fragments, show that you can correct them.

Proper arrangement of the parts of your sentence will help make your meaning clear. Ordinarily the main parts—the subjects, the verbs, the complements—cause no problems. Modifying words and phrases and subordinate clauses can be problematic if they are not located carefully. Here we consider five possible trouble spots in the placing of modifiers.

1. Although we sometimes use a rather loose placement for some common adverbs, such as *only*, *nearly*, *almost*, and *hardly*, we can write precise sentences only when such adverbs are placed close to the words they modify:

Loose:	This will *only* take five minutes.
	Jill *nearly* saw 90 movies last year.
Better:	This will take *only* five minutes.
	Jill saw *nearly* 90 movies last year.

2. Words and phrases that attach themselves to the wrong word can confuse the reader:

Loose:	I wish every person in this class could know the man I'm going to talk about *personally*.
Better:	I wish every person in this class could know *personally* the man I'm going to talk about.
Loose:	It was reported that the Italian premier had died *on the 8 o'clock newscast*.
Better:	*On the 8 o'clock newscast*, it was reported that the Italian premier had died.
Loose:	The police department will be notified of all reported obscene phone calls *by the telephone company*.
Better:	The police department will be notified *by the telephone company* of all reported obscene phone calls.

3. The **squinting modifier** is one that is placed between two units, either of which it could modify:

Loose:	Students who can already type *normally* are put into an advanced class.
Better:	Students who can already type are *normally* put into an advanced class.
Loose:	He said *after the dinner* some color slides would be shown.
Better:	He said some color slides would be shown *after the dinner*.

4. The **split infinitive** results from the placing of an adverbial modifier between the *to* and the verb stem of an infinitive. Although greatly overemphasized by some as an error, the split infinitive, particularly with a modifier consisting of more than one word, is usually avoided by careful writers:

Loose:	Dad likes to *once in a while* plan and cook a dinner.
Better:	*Once in a while*, Dad likes to plan and cook a dinner.

5. The conjunctions *both . . . and*, *not only . . . but also*, *either . . . or*, and *neither . . . nor* are used in pairs and are called **correlatives**. Because they point out the equal relationship between units, they should be placed immediately before the parallel units that they connect:

Loose:	We sent invitations *both* to Webster *and* Jenkins.
Better:	We sent invitations to *both* Webster *and* Jenkins.
	[The parallel words are *Webster* and *Jenkins*.]

Loose:	This woman *not only* can get along with young people *but also* with their parents.
Better:	This woman can get along *not only* with young people *but also* with their parents.

Loose:	You must *either* promise me that you will come *or* send a substitute.
Better:	You must promise me that you will *either* come *or* send a substitute.

DANGLING MODIFIERS

The relationship between a word being modified and the modifying phrase should be clear. Any modifying phrase that does not attach itself clearly to the word it is supposed to modify is called a **dangling modifier**. A dangling modifier can create a confusing sentence. Participial phrases are especially apt to float free in a sentence.

Stepping into the boat, my camera fell into the water.

This sentence contains a participial phrase and a main clause, but the phrase does not actually modify any word in the main clause. The sentence is made up of two thoughts that can be expressed as

I stepped into the boat.
My camera fell into the water.

We can make the two sentences into a compound sentence:

I stepped into the boat, and my camera fell into the water.

Or we can make the first clause an introductory adverbial element:

As I stepped into the boat, my camera fell into the water.

But we cannot convert the first sentence into a participial phrase because the only noun the phrase could modify is *camera*, and the camera did not step into the boat. The sentence, if read literally, becomes nonsense. We could rework the sentence by changing the subject of the second clause in a way that allows the participial phrase to modify the new subject:

Stepping into the boat, I dropped my camera into the water.

Because the person who dropped the camera and the person who is stepping into the boat are the same, *I*, the sentence is now correct.

Gerund Phrases and Infinitive Phrases

Gerund phrases and infinitive phrases can also cause problems when they are randomly inserted into sentences:

> *After studying all morning*, a nap was Mary's only goal for the afternoon.

The intended meaning of the sentence is clear, but the literal meaning is that the nap studied all morning; the phrase attaches itself to the first available noun—in this case, a noun that produces a nonsense statement.

> *To qualify for that job*, good typing skills are a necessity.

Again, the intended meaning is clear, but the literal meaning is nonsense. Good typing skills are not qualifying for that job; a person with good typing skills is qualifying for that job. Remember the phrase that contains the verbal must have a word to refer to, and that word must be close enough to the phrase so that the reader does not associate the phrase with the wrong word.

CORRECTING DANGLERS

The easiest way to correct a dangler is to supply the word that the phrase should modify and to place the phrase next to that word. Another way is to change the dangling phrase to a subordinate clause with a subject and verb expressed.

1. Participial phrase at the beginning of a sentence

Dangler:	*Burned to a cinder, I* could not eat the toast. [The sentence sounds as if I were burned to a cinder. The word that the dangler should modify is *toast*, but this word is too far from the phrase immediately associated with it.]
Better:	Burned to a cinder, the toast could not be eaten. I could not eat the toast because it was burned to a cinder.

2. Gerund following a preposition

Dangler:	Before *making a final decision,* other cars should be driven. [Are the other cars making a final decision? That is not what is meant, and yet that is what the sentence states.]
	On graduating from high school, my father let me work in his office. [The sentence says that your father let you work in his office when he, not you, graduated from high school.]
	Since *breaking my leg*, my neighbors have helped with my farm chores. [A logical sentence only if the neighbors broke your leg.]
Better:	Before making a final decision, drive other cars. Before you make a final decision, you should drive other cars.
	On graduating from high school, I went to work in my father's office. After I had graduated from high school, my father let me work in his office.

Since breaking my leg, I have been helped with my farm chores by my neighbors.

My neighbors have helped with my farm chores since I broke my leg.

3. Elliptical "time" clause (see Lesson 8), usually introduced by *when* or *while*

Dangler: *When ten years old*, my father sold the farm and moved to Dallas.
While weeding my vegetable garden, a garter snake startled me.
[The understood subject of the adverb clause is different from the subject of the main clause, but the reader assumes that both clauses have the same subject. The result is a ridiculous meaning that the writer never intended.]

Better: When ten years old, I moved to Dallas after my father sold the farm.
When I was ten years old, my father sold the farm and we moved to Dallas.

While weeding my vegetable garden, I was startled by a garter snake.
While I was weeding my vegetable garden, a garter snake startled me.

4. Introductory infinitive phrase naming a specific action

Dangler: *To enter the contest*, a box top must be sent with your slogan.
[A *box top* is not entering the contest. To avoid this problem, be sure that the word that the phrase attaches to names the logical doer of that action.]

Better: To enter the contest, you must send a box top with your slogan.
If you want to enter the contest, a box top must be sent with your slogan.
When you enter the contest, send a box top with your slogan.

English Fundamentals Online

After you have completed Practice Sheets and Exercises in this lesson, you can find additional help and drill work at **MyWritingLab.com**, in the sections on Misplaced Modifiers; Dangling Modifiers.

NAME _____   SCORE _____

Directions: From each of the following pairs of sentences, select the one that is clearer and write its number in the space at the left.

_____
1. a. This afternoon there was an account of my accident on Channel 5.
   b. This afternoon on Channel 5 there was an account of my accident.

_____
2. a. I advise you to take a short rest just before the examination.
   b. I advise you to just before the examination take a short rest.

_____
3. a. The class could only find one copy of *To Kill a Mockingbird*.
   b. The class could find only one copy of *To Kill a Mockingbird*.

_____
4. a. The woman watched the symphony orchestra standing in the balcony as it rehearsed.
   b. Standing in the balcony, the woman watched the symphony orchestra as it rehearsed.

_____
5. a. Mr. McCoy, reading the newspaper while driving, almost wrecked his car.
   b. Mr. McCoy almost wrecked his car reading the newspaper while driving.

_____
6. a. For the past 15 years camping out in the mountains has been our favorite vacation.
   b. Camping out in the mountains for the past 15 years has been our favorite vacation.

_____
7. a. We nearly had to wait until two o'clock before we had anything to eat.
   b. We had to wait until nearly two o'clock before we had anything to eat.

_____
8. a. You either can write a check or pay with a credit card.
   b. You can either write a check or pay the amount with a credit card.

_____
9. a. By standing on tiptoe you can just barely see the workers hauling the bricks across the yard.
   b. You can just barely see the workers hauling the bricks across the yard by standing on tiptoe.

_____
10. a. Look at any orders written by the new salesclerk very carefully.
    b. Look very carefully at any orders written by the new salesclerk.

_____
11. a. It is always a pleasure on a cool afternoon to walk down that mountain path.
    b. It is always a pleasure to on a cool afternoon walk down that mountain path.

_____
12. a. On the shelf in the closet, my brother stores the sketches he drew with the encouragement of his wife.
    b. My brother stores the sketches he drew on the shelf in the closet with the encouragement of his wife.

_____
13. a. Did you know I found almost $200 in a box in the back of my closet?
    b. Did you know I almost found $200 in a box in the back of my closet?

_____
14. a. Yesterday, the two men not only painted the bedroom walls but also the ceiling.
    b. Yesterday, the two men painted not only the bedroom walls but also the ceiling.

_____
15. a. Joe and I have been lifting weights for six months in order to increase our strength.
    b. Joe and I have been lifting weights in order to increase our strength for six months.

Directions: In the space at the left, write either **a** or **b** to indicate the logical placement of the modifier shown in parentheses.

_____ 1. (only) The club needs **a** to recruit **b** two more members for this year.

_____ 2. (either) To qualify for the scholarship, one must **a** be able to speak **b** French or Spanish.

_____ 3. (from the top of the ladder) I watched in frustration **a** as the dog ate my sandwich **b**.

_____ 4. (not only) I know that Myra **a** is **b** intelligent but also wealthy.

_____ 5. (by e-mail) We were informed yesterday **a** that my uncle is coming to visit us **b**.

_____ 6. (not all) It appears that **a** the players are **b** here.

_____ 7. (with great dismay and disappointment) Local Bobcat fans have watched **a** as their team dropped out of first place in the conference **b**.

_____ 8. (not) These eager contestants must often be reminded that **a** everyone can **b** win the million dollar prized.

_____ 9. (not only) Driving this fast on rain-slick pavement **a** is **b** foolish but also dangerous.

_____ 10. (by the flood control office) It was reported **a** that the level of water in the lake has been raised to dangerous levels **b**.

_____ 11. (on the class Web page) The teacher has posted **a** the projects the class must complete this term **b**.

_____ 12. (in the opening meeting with graduate students) **a** Dean Smith discussed plagiarism and shoddy scholarship **b**.

_____ 13. (inside a very secure cage) **a** Jose told me he keeps a python measuring 11 feet **b**.

_____ 14. (when the occasion demands) He has trained himself to **a** employ street language and profanity **b**.

_____ 15. (neither) We **a** were **b** more rested nor more relaxed after our week at sailing school.

NAME _____   SCORE _____

Directions: In each of the following sentences there is a poorly positioned word or phrase. Rewrite each sentence to position the word or phrase correctly.

1. All the homeowners in the association were asked to complain to the city council at the meeting yesterday.

   _____

2. My little brother read two novels written by Clive Cussler because of his father's encouragement.

   _____

3. While the rest of us cleaned out the stalls, Hank nearly napped for two hours.

   _____

4. My grandfather stores all the ship models he has made in a chest in the basement.

   _____

5. Readers should not accept everything that is presented on television as true.

   _____

6. While we were waiting for the start of class, Neil almost told me the same story I had heard earlier from Norberto.

   _____

7. All the members of my class are not interested in national politics.

   _____

8. The pear tree that was struck by lightning nearly was 30 feet tall.

   _____

9. Yesterday, I saw a funnel cloud driving out the rural road west of town.

   _____

10. This morning I watched an enormous flight of ducks out for a quiet walk.

   _____

Directions: In the space at the left, write **a** or **b** to indicate the logical placement of the italicized modifier within the parentheses.

_____ 1. (only) Jack decided to **a** invest **b** $500 in that project.

_____ 2. (not) **a** All college professors are **b** vitally interested in intercollegiate sports.

_____ 3. (by the guest speaker) We were asked **a** to raise our hands if we had been registered to vote **b**.

_____ 4. (in his speech this morning) **a** President Thornton discussed the need for harmonious relationships among people who differ politically **b**.

_____ 5. (in spite of the thunder and lightning) The men were determined to **a** finish their round of golf **b**.

_____ 6. (every ten days) My neighbor promised **a** to cut our lawn **b**.

_____ 7. (normally) Applicants who can work on computerized spread sheets **a** are **b** given preference in the hiring process.

_____ 8. (neither) The embattled Prime Minister vowed **a** to **b** resign nor to apologize for his performance.

_____ 9. (once) **a** A friend who had played soccer tried **b** to explain the offsides rule to me.

_____ 10. (almost) Mike Hawkins **a** played in **b** every Tiger game for seven years.

_____ 11. (not only) Doctor Reston **a** has **b** a chemistry degree but also an MBA from the University of Wisconsin.

_____ 12. (whenever he stopped a driver) **a** The police officer gave his standard lecture about obeying the speed limits **b**.

_____ 13. (either) **a** You can **b** pay the tax now or postpone payment and pay a penalty.

_____ 14. (only) We must hurry; we **a** have **b** 15 minutes to catch that train.

_____ 15. (either) **a** That stock broker of yours is **b** extremely skilled or incredibly lucky.

NAME _____   SCORE _____

Directions: One sentence of each pair contains a dangling modifier. In the space at the left, write the letter that identifies the correct sentence. Be prepared to explain why the incorrect sentence contains a dangling modifier.

_____ 1. a. Realizing that the streets were very slick from the rain, the car moved slowly down the street.
 b. Realizing that the streets were very slick from the rain, Jim moved the car slowly down the street.

_____ 2. a. Being a very successful young executive, Mary Connors has been selected as the new vice president.
 b. Being a very successful young executive, the board has selected Mary Connors the new vice president.

_____ 3. a. To get the maximum tax benefits, all deductions should be listed.
 b. To get the maximum tax benefits, be sure to list all deductions.

_____ 4. a. Not expecting to see Mary Chase in this town so far from home, my mouth dropped open when she greeted me.
 b. As I was not expecting to see Mary Chase in this town so far from home, my mouth dropped open when she greeted me.

_____ 5. a. The sign on the wall of the diner read, "Shoes and shirt must be worn to be served."
 b. The sign on the wall of the diner read, "You must wear shoes and shirt to be served."

_____ 6. a. Upon receiving the invoice, please pay the bill promptly.
 b. Upon receiving the invoice, the bill must be paid promptly.

_____ 7. a. At 11 years of age, my mother insisted that I take karate lessons.
 b. When I was 11 years of age, my mother insisted that I take karate lessons.

_____ 8. a. When using this powerful detergent, rubber gloves should be worn.
 b. When one uses this powerful detergent, rubber gloves should be worn.

_____ 9. a. Before getting the camera focused, the turtle slipped off the log and into the water.
 b. Before I could get the camera focused, the turtle slipped off the log and into the water.

_____ 10. a. Being older and slower, the fat man was soon outdistanced by the leaders of the race.
 b. Being older and slower, the leaders of the race soon outdistanced the fat man.

_____ 11. a. Having misunderstood the assignment, I received a low grade on my paper.
        b. Having misunderstood the assignment, my paper received a low grade.

_____ 12. a. Exhausted after 14 hours of driving, the exit for Denver was a welcome sight.
        b. Because we were exhausted after 14 hours of driving, the exit to Denver was a welcome sight.

_____ 13. a. Having stood in the oily marinade for five hours, you are now ready to grill the meat.
        b. Having stood in the oily marinade for five hours, the meat is ready to be grilled.

_____ 14. a. As the spider painstakingly repaired its damaged web, I marveled at its skill and patience.
        b. Painstakingly repairing its damaged web, I marveled at the spider's skill and patience.

_____ 15. a. Approaching the Continental Divide, there was a significant drop in temperature.
        b. Approaching the Continental Divide, we noticed a significant drop in temperature.

_____ 16. a. The archeologist could not decipher the ancient inscription, covered by centuries-old layers of grime.
        b. Covered by centuries-old layers of grime, the archeologist could not decipher the ancient inscription.

_____ 17. a. Meeting Lou after geology class, he suggested a couple of sets of tennis.
        b. When I met Lou after geology class, he suggested a couple of sets of tennis.

_____ 18. a. If you are unable to attend the meeting today, please call the department secretary.
        b. If unable to attend the meeting today, a call to the department secretary would be appreciated.

_____ 19. a. Seen from miles away, the mountains look like a cloud.
        b. Seen from miles away, I thought the mountains looked like a cloud.

_____ 20. a. To avoid excessive wear on the tires, the air pressure in the tires should be checked regularly.
        b. To avoid excessive wear on the tires, check the air pressure in the tires regularly.

Dangling Modifiers

NAME _____   SCORE _____

Directions: Rewrite each of the following sentences twice. In the first rewrite, change the dangling modifier to a complete clause with a subject and verb. In the second, retain the phrase but begin the clause with a word the phrase can logically modify.

1. To change your address on that magazine subscription, a form must be filed with the subscription service.

    a. _____
    b. _____

2. When riding my bike on that trail, a black bear ran across the trail in front of me.

    a. _____
    b. _____

3. Before leaving for class in the morning, the windows should be closed and the temperature on the thermostat adjusted.

    a. _____
    b. _____

4. Scrambling down the bank and splashing across the creek, we watched the adventure racers negotiate the most difficult part of the course.

    a. _____
    b. _____

5. Being only 13 years old, Jason's parents sent him to work on his grandmother's farm for the summer.

    a. _____
    b. _____

6. After measuring the first board incorrectly, the rest of the work on the cabinet went very badly for Cary.

    a. _____
    b. _____

7. Reaching high over my head to the top shelf, a half-dozen books toppled off and hit me in the head.

    a. _____
    b. _____

8. Upon entering the room, the lights and air conditioning should be adjusted to suit your preference.

    a. _____

    b. _____

9. At the age of 16, my father bought me a new Mustang convertible.

    a. _____

    b. _____

10. To play that video game, a special controller is needed.

    a. _____

    b. _____

11. Before making a final selection of a computer, it is a good idea to talk to someone who owns a similar computer.

    a. _____

    b. _____

12. Having drilled intensely on those problems, the test was easy for Jim and his friends.

    a. _____

    b. _____

13. Watching the sunset over the ocean, the cloud formations on the western horizon were extraordinarily beautiful.

    a. _____

    b. _____

14. To find your way safely across that strait to the island 15 miles away, a GPS should be used as a navigation tool.

    a. _____

    b. _____

15. After working all day pouring concrete, a quick swim in the cool surf refreshed Tom and his friends.

    a. _____

    b. _____

Brief Writing Assignment: Write a paragraph of five sentences describing a perfect day in your life ten years from today. Use two adverbs in each sentence, and include two modifying phrases that are obviously dangling modifiers. Then, correct the dangling modifiers by rewriting the sentences where they occur.

Lesson 15 *Subordination*

Beginning writers sometimes string together too many short sentences, or they tie clauses together with conjunctions—*and*, *but*, *or*—that fail to establish precise relations between the clauses.

Poor:	Sally usually attends each concert. She missed this one. She went to the airport to meet her cousin Ellen. Ellen was arriving from Atlanta.
	I rode around town for three days, but I couldn't find a place to stay, and then I located this apartment, and so I am comfortable.

If you use the methods of creating and combining sentences that we have studied, you will make your writing more precise, more economical, and more meaningful:

Improved:	Although Sally usually attends each concert, she missed this one because she went to the airport to meet her cousin Ellen, who was arriving from Atlanta.
	After riding around town for three days without finding a place to stay, I finally located this apartment, where I am comfortable.

Get into the habit of trying different methods of subordinating material. Notice in the following sentences how an idea can be expressed in a variety of ways:

Two Sentences:	The small car was inexpensive to drive. It had only four cylinders.
Compound Verb:	The small car had only four cylinders and was inexpensive to drive.
Compound Sentence:	The small car was inexpensive to drive, for it had only four cylinders.
Adverbial Clause:	Because the small car had only four cylinders, it was inexpensive to drive.
Adjective Clause:	The small car, which had only four cylinders, was inexpensive to drive.
Participial Phrase:	The small car, having only four cylinders, was inexpensive to drive.
	Having only four cylinders, the small car was inexpensive to drive.
	The small car was inexpensive to drive, having only four cylinders.
Absolute Phrase:	The small car having only four cylinders, it was inexpensive to drive.
Prepositional Phrase:	The small car with only four cylinders was inexpensive to drive.
Appositive:	The small car, a four-cylinder model, was inexpensive to drive.
Adjective Modifier:	The small four-cylinder car was inexpensive to drive.

The use of subordination produces more than a pleasing sound in writing. It makes a crucial contribution to meaning by eliminating uncertainty about what is most important in a message. Consider the following string of simple sentences:

The management and union representatives announced an agreement. A strike had been threatened but was averted. The employees of Grantex Company reported for work today. They were relieved.

There is no way of knowing from these sentences which fact is most significant: The agreement? The avoidance of a strike? The workers' reporting for work? Their relief? Rewritten with proper subordination, the news reveals what the writer believes is most significant:

> The relieved employees of Grantex Company reported for work today after the management and union representatives announced an agreement that averted a threatened strike.

The only independent clause in the sentence concerns the workers' return to work. That is the important message. A writer more interested in strikes and their effect on the general economy might report the event thus:

> The threatened strike was averted at Grantex Company when the management and union representatives announced an agreement, after which the relieved employees reported for work today.

A NOTE ON SENTENCE VARIETY

Preceding lessons have demonstrated how subordinate clauses and phrases, by compressing material, help the writer avoid tiresome strings of independent clauses. You have also seen that certain subordinate units—adverbial clauses and participial phrases in particular—can be put in several places within the sentence, thus helping prevent monotony in your sentences.

Another unit useful for achieving compression and variety is the appositive. (See Lesson 10.) As noun renamers, appositives closely resemble—they might be called the final reduction of—Pattern 2 clause and phrase modifiers of nouns:

> Ted could explain the trick to us. Ted [or He] is an amateur magician. [two independent clauses]
> Ted, *who is an amateur magician*, could explain the trick to us. [adjective clause]
> Ted, *being an amateur magician*, could explain the trick to us. [participial phrase]
> Ted, *an amateur magician*, could explain the trick to us. [appositive]

Although the usual position of an appositive is immediately following the noun it renames, many appositives, like many nonrestrictive participial phrases, can precede the main noun (in which case they are called *pre-positional appositives*); sometimes they are effectively placed at the end of the clause:

> Lawyer Somers, *a master of wit and guile*, cajoles and browbeats in the courtroom.
> *A master of wit and guile*, Lawyer Somers cajoles and browbeats in the courtroom.
> Lawyer Somers cajoles and browbeats in the courtroom, *a master of wit and guile*.

As a final example of language tools for renaming and modifying nouns, study this tightly constructed sentence:

> One of the five largest towns in Roman England, home of King Arthur's legendary Round Table, seat of Alfred the Great, whose statue looks down its main street, early capital of England, and victim of Cromwell's destructive forces, Winchester is an enchanting cathedral city in which layer after layer of history is visibly present.

> Elisabeth Lambert Ortiz, "Exploring Winchester," *Gourmet*,
> March 1978, p. 21

This sentence is made up of one independent clause, which includes an adjective clause, and five pre-positional appositives, the third of which contains an adjective clause. The statements underlying this sentence might be charted as follows:

[Winchester was] one of the five largest towns in Roman England.

[Winchester was] the home of King Arthur's legendary Round Table.

[Winchester was] the seat of Alfred the Great.

[Alfred the Great's] statue looks down its main street.

[Winchester was] the early capital of England.

[Winchester was] the victim of Cromwell's destructive forces.

Winchester is an enchanting cathedral city.

[In this city] layer after layer of history is visibly present.

We see here that eight statements—enough to make up a paragraph of clear but unrelieved simple sentences—have been shortened into one complex sentence. The layering of appositives and adjective clauses produces compression, sentence variety, and proper emphasis.

English Fundamentals Online

After you have completed Practice Sheets and Exercises in this lesson, you can find additional help and drill work at **MyWritingLab.Com**, in the sections on Combining Sentences; Varying Sentence Patterns.

Subordination

NAME _____   SCORE _____

Directions: Each of the following numbered units consists of either two independent clauses in the form of a compound sentence or two sentences. One of the structures is italicized. In the second version (b) of the item, the italicized unit has been reduced to a subordinate clause or phrase. In the space at the left of each item, write one of the following numbers to identify the type of clause or phrase:

1. Adverb clause	4. Gerund phrase	7. Infinitive phrase
2. Adjective clause	5. Absolute phrase	
3. Participial phrase	6. Appositive	

_____ 1. a. *The last shingle has been nailed into place*, so we can now call the roof of the new house finished.
　　　　　　 b. With the last shingle nailed into place, we can now call the roof of the new house finished.

_____ 2. a. *The boys have not reached home yet*, but we are expecting them at any minute.
　　　　　　 b. Although the boys have not reached home yet, we are expecting them at any minute.

_____ 3. a. My brother has bought an antique car. *He plans to restore the car.*
　　　　　　 b. My brother has bought an antique car, which he plans to restore.

_____ 4. a. *My brother possesses great skill as a mechanic.* He plans to restore an antique car.
　　　　　　 b. Possessing great skill as a mechanic, my brother plans to restore an antique car.

_____ 5. a. *Cover the wood on the deck with water seal*, and it will be protected from the weather.
　　　　　　 b. Covering the wood on the deck with water seal will protect it from the weather.

_____ 6. a. Cover the wood on the deck with water seal, *and it will be protected from the weather.*
　　　　　　 b. Cover the wood on the deck with water seal to protect it from the weather.

_____ 7. a. Jeff Robinson has moved back to town. *He was the quarterback on our high school football team.*
　　　　　　 b. Jeff Robinson, the quarterback on our high school football team, has moved back to town.

_____ 8. a. *Jeff Robinson has moved back to town.* He will be working for a local bank.
　　　　　　 b. Jeff Robinson, who has moved back to town, will be working for a local bank.

_____ 9. a. *We must check the weather for this weekend*, or we won't be sure of sufficient snow for skiing.
　　　　　　 b. Unless we check the weather for this weekend, we won't be sure of sufficient snow for skiing.

_____ 10. a. *The weather report has predicted a fresh snowfall*, so we plan to go skiing this weekend.

b. The weather report having predicted a fresh snowfall, we plan to go skiing this weekend.

_____ 11. a. *We wondered whether there would be snow for the weekend*, so we watched the Weather Channel last night.

b. Wondering whether there would be snow for the weekend, we watched the Weather Channel last night.

_____ 12. a. Last night we watched the Weather Channel. *It is a good source of information about skiing conditions.*

b. Last night we watched the Weather Channel, a good source of information about skiing conditions.

_____ 13. a. Last night we watched the Weather Channel. *It is a good source of information about skiing conditions.*

b. Last night we watched the Weather Channel, which is a good source of information about skiing conditions.

_____ 14. a. We wanted to get an accurate prediction of skiing conditions for the weekend, so we also checked the NOAA Web site.

b. To get an accurate prediction of skiing conditions for the weekend, we also checked the NOAA Web site.

_____ 15. a. *We checked the two sources and saw the same prediction*, so we scheduled the trip for this weekend.

b. Because we checked the two sources and saw the same prediction, we scheduled the trip for this weekend.

_____ 16. a. *Yesterday the Chess Club played in a day-long tournament.* The members were almost exhausted at the end of the day.

b. Playing in a day-long tournament yesterday left the members of the Chess Club almost exhausted at the end of the day.

_____ 17. a. *The chess tournament lasted all day and into the night.* The players left for home shortly before midnight.

b. The chess tournament having lasted all day and into the night, the players left for home shortly before midnight.

_____ 18. a. My roommates and I have recently begun to play ping-pong. *It requires more athletic ability than we had thought.*

b. My roommates and I have recently begun to play ping-pong, which requires more athletic ability than we had thought.

_____ 19. a. My roommates and I have recently begun to play ping-pong. *It requires more athletic ability than we had thought.*

b. My roommates and I have recently begun to play ping-pong, a sport that requires more athletic ability than we had thought.

_____ 20. a. *Players must possess great eye-hand coordination and quick reflexes*, or they cannot play ping-pong successfully at a high level.

b. Unless players possess great eye-hand coordination and quick reflexes, they cannot play ping-pong successfully at a high level.

NAME _____   SCORE _____

Directions: Previous lessons have demonstrated various types of noun modification. When two sentences employ the same noun or pronoun, one sentence can be reduced to a modifying phrase or clause. In the following sentences, the word printed in bold-face type is the noun or pronoun to be modified. Combine the sentences by reducing the second sentence to the kind of unit indicated by the following letters:

   a. Adjective clause
   b. Participial phrase following the noun
   c. Participial phrase preceding the noun
   d. Appositive

1. Our company recently bought a second, smaller **company**. It makes a product similar to ours.

   a. _____
   b. _____

2. Yesterday we visited with **Andrea**. She is a teacher in a school in Denver.

   a. _____
   d. _____

3. A tall **man** stood at the bus stop. He was carrying an umbrella.

   a. _____
   b. _____
   c. _____

4. Last week we received an e-mail from someone in **Juneau**. It is a small town in Alaska.

   a. _____
   d. _____

5. **Jane Ashley** is a computer software engineer. She specializes in bank software.

   a. _____
   b. _____
   c. _____

6. After a long search Janice finally found her pet **boa constrictor**. It was coiled up in the back of her refrigerator.

   a. _____
   b. _____

7. **Cathy** hurried across the campus. She was running late for an important quiz in her calculus class.

   a. _____
   b. _____
   c. _____

8. Cathy works very hard in her calculus **class**. It is important in her major.

    a. _____

    d. _____

9. Most **people** went home last weekend. They needed a taste of home cooking and some rest.

    b. _____

    c. _____

10. The **park** down the street needs extensive work on the landscaping. The park has been neglected for years.

    a. _____

    b. _____

    c. _____

11. Jim's mother sent him an important **letter**. It contained a check for $100.

    a. _____

    b. _____

12. **Karen** looks extremely happy. She has just completed work on that complicated assignment.

    a. _____

    b. _____

    c. _____

13. **Karen** has just completed work on that complicated assignment. She is a very happy person.

    a. _____

    d. _____

14. We have finally finished **exam week**. It was a very trying time for all of us.

    a. _____

    d. _____

15. **Terry** nervously climbed the steps to the high-dive platform. She had never dived from that height before.

    a. _____

    b. _____

    c. _____

Brief Writing Assignment: In a six-sentence paragraph discuss two of your most highly developed skills. Write one compound sentence, one adverbial clause, one adjective clause, and one sentence that contains a noun clause.

Lesson 16 — *Parallel Structure; Comparisons*

There are two other situations in which the underlying logic of the sentence requires the writer to select carefully the structure and position of the sentence units.

PARALLEL STRUCTURE

When two or more parts of a sentence are similar in function, they should be expressed in the same grammatical construction; in other words, they should be **parallel**. The principle of parallelism implies that, in a series, nouns should be balanced with nouns, adjectives with adjectives, prepositional phrases with prepositional phrases, clauses with clauses, and so forth. The following sentence owes much of its clarity and effectiveness to its careful parallel arrangement: Two adjective clauses are joined with *and*, two adverbs with *but*, and three noun direct objects with *and*.

> Anyone who studies world affairs *and* who remembers our last three wars will realize, sadly *but* inevitably, that another conflict will endanger the economic strength of our nation, the complacency of our political institutions, *and* the moral fiber of our people.

Anyone ‖ who studies world affairs *and*
    ‖ who remembers our last three wars will realize, ‖ sadly *but*
        ‖ inevitably,

that another conflict will endanger ‖ the economic strength of our nation,
         ‖ the complacency of our political institutions,
         and the moral fiber of our people.

Two types of errors, the *false series* and the *and who* construction, work to destroy parallelism by using coordinate conjunctions to join grammatical units that are not alike.

1. The false or shifted series

Weak:	Most people play golf for exercise, pleasure, and so they can meet others. [The *and* ties an adverb clause to two nouns.]
Better:	Most people play golf for exercise, for pleasure, and for social contacts.
Weak:	Our new teacher was young, tall, slender, and with red hair. [The *and* suggests that it will be followed by a fourth adjective, not a prepositional phrase.]
Better:	Our new teacher was young, tall, slender, and red-haired.
Weak:	Mr. Little's speech was tiresome, inaccurate, and should have been omitted.
Better:	Mr. Little's speech was tiresome, inaccurate, and unnecessary.

2. The *and who* or *and which* construction

Weak:	Their son is an athlete with great talent *and who* will soon be well known.
Better:	Their son is an athlete who has great talent and who will soon be well known.
	Their son is a greatly talented athlete who will soon be well known.
	[Here the unbalanced modification is avoided.]

Weak:	I am taking Physics 388, a difficult course *and which* demands much time.
Better:	I am taking Physics 388, which is a difficult course and demands much time.
	I am taking Physics 388, which is difficult and demands much time.

COMPARISONS

When you write sentences that make comparisons or contrasts, you must observe certain forms if your writing is to be clear and precise.

1. Be sure that you compare only those things that are capable of being compared:

Faulty:	The storage capacity of this computer is much greater than our old one.
	[*One* refers to computer; thus, two unlike things, storage capacity and the computer, are being compared.]
Improved:	The storage capacity of this computer is much greater than *the storage capacity of* our old one.
	The storage capacity of this computer is much greater than *that of* our old one.

Faulty:	The influence of the political leader is more ephemeral than the artist.
	[Here, *influence*, an abstract quality, is being compared to a person, the artist.]
Improved:	The influence of the political leader is more ephemeral than *the influence of* the artist.
	The influence of the political leader is more ephemeral than *that of* the artist.
	The political leader's influence is more ephemeral than *the artist's*.

2. When you use the comparative form of an adjective in a comparison, use *any other* when it is necessary to exclude the subject of the comparison from the group:

Faulty:	Wilson, the first-string center, is heavier than any man on the team.
	[In this version the writer is comparing Wilson to the members of a group that includes Wilson.]
Improved:	Wilson, the first-string center, is heavier than *any other* man on the team.

3. When your sentence contains a double comparison, be sure to include all the words necessary to make the idiom complete and be sure that the second comparative phrase does not, because of its position, create problems of agreement or number.

Faulty:	As our new baseball coach, the college has selected Jaime Ruiz, one of the best, if not the best, coaches in our conference.
Improved:	As our new baseball coach, the college has selected Jaime Ruiz, one of the best coaches, if not the best coach, in our conference.

The wordiness of this version can be solved by moving the phrase *if not the best coach* to the end of the sentence.

As our new baseball coach, the college has selected Jaime Ruiz, one of the best coaches in our conference, if not the best (coach).

Double comparisons may create sentences that sound awkward even though they form the comparison correctly and completely. You may want to recast the sentence to make it read more smoothly.

1. Try forming two sentences:

He is now as tall as his mother. He may, indeed, be taller than she.
She is one of the best runners in the club. She may even be the best runner in the club.

2. Try writing two independent clauses:

He is now as tall as his mother, and he may be even taller than she is.
She is one of the best runners in the club, and she may be the best runner in the club.

(See Supplement for more details on sentences used to compare and contrast.)

SUPPLEMENT

In addition to requiring the structural units already mentioned, comparison-contrast sentences place a few constraints on the form of the adjective or adverb.

1. When your comparison is limited to two things, use the comparative degree:

Both Jane and Laura sing well, but Jane has the *better* voice.
Which takes *more* time, your studies or your job?

2. Use the superlative for more than two things:

January is the *worst* month of the year.

You learned in Lesson 2 that there are two ways of forming the comparative and superlative degrees. In general, *er* and *est* are used with short words, and *more* and *most* with longer words.

When I was *younger*, I was *more apprehensive* about thunder and lightning.
This encyclopedia is the *newest* and the *most comprehensive*.
Maria works *faster* than I and also *more accurately*.

Remember that in present-day standard English, *er* or *est* is not combined with *more* or *most* in the same word. We don't say, for example, *more pleasanter, most loveliest,* or *more faster.*

English Fundamentals Online

After you have completed Practice Sheets and Exercises in this lesson, you can find additional help and drill work at **MyWritingLab.com**, in the section on Parallel Structure.

Parallel Structure; Comparisons

Directions: In the space at the left of each pair of sentences, copy the letter identifying the sentence that is logically structured.

_____ 1. a. People in the outlying towns need a transportation system that is convenient and runs punctually.
   b. People in the outlying towns need a transportation system that is convenient and to run punctually.

_____ 2. a. The new building is tall, stately, and with a beautiful archway at the entrance.
   b. The new building is tall and stately, and it has a beautiful archway at the entrance.

_____ 3. a. I try to avoid group projects because it is hard to coordinate with group members and some members do not participate fully.
   b. I try to avoid group projects because it is hard to coordinate with group members and some members not participating fully.

_____ 4. a. To get up early in the morning and run for exercise is my new goal for this term.
   b. To get up early in the morning and running for exercise is my new goal for this term.

_____ 5. a. That e-mail from the home office confused me and which didn't seem to convey any necessary information.
   b. That e-mail from the home office confused me, and it didn't seem to convey any necessary information.

_____ 6. a. Tony's car is old, slow, and without air-conditioning.
   b. Tony's car is old and slow, and it does not have air-conditioning.

_____ 7. a. This morning's lecturer gave a humorous speech, but he made several important points about business networking.
   b. This morning's lecturer gave a humorous speech, but which made several important points about business networking.

_____ 8. a. The group leader strode decisively into the room and running through a list of assignments that included everyone in the room.
   b. The group leader strode decisively into the room and ran through a list of assignments that included everyone in the room.

_____ 9. a. That new employee has a long list of achievements and several years of management experience.
   b. That new employee has a long list of achievements and which includes several years of management experience.

_____ 10. a. I've always avoided courses that require reading old journals and forcing myself to do surveys among the general population.
   b. I've always avoided courses that require reading old journals and force me to do surveys among the general population.

Directions: From each of the following pairs of sentences, select the one that makes a correct comparison and copy its letter in the space at the left.

_____ 1. a. Nancy has felt all along that her contributions to the team were more important than Sandra's.
   b. Nancy has felt all along that her contributions to the team were more important than Sandra.

_____ 2. a. Our first-string center Hamilton is taller than anyone on the team.
   b. Our first-string center Hamilton is taller than anyone else on the team.

_____ 3. a. Horacio played one of the best, if not the best, games that he has ever played.
   b. Horacio played one of the best games that he has ever played. In fact, it might have been the best game he ever played.

_____ 4. a. Of all three runners in that event, Alice is the usually the faster.
   b. Of all three runners in that event, Alice is the usually the fastest.

_____ 5. a. That dinner last night at the restaurant on the lake was one of the more enjoyable experiences we've had in some time.
   b. That dinner last night at the restaurant on the lake was one of the more enjoyabler experiences we've had in some time.

_____ 6. a. As always happens, my father chose one of the more expensive, if not the most expensive, restaurants in our area for my mother's birthday dinner.
   b. As always happens, my father chose one of the more expensive restaurants, if not the most expensive restaurant, in our area for my mother's birthday dinner.

_____ 7. a. That trip to the all-you-can-eat restaurant yesterday left us all the most fullest we've been in a long time.
   b. That trip to the all-you-can-eat restaurant yesterday left us all the fullest we've been in a long time.

_____ 8. a. That new book by Grisham is much more exciting than Patterson.
   b. That new book by Grisham is much more exciting than Patterson's.

_____ 9. a. If we are going to get inside ahead of that rain, we need to walk a little more faster.
   b. If we are going to get inside ahead of that rain, we need to walk a little faster.

_____ 10. a. We have hired Joan Gimble as our new engineer; she has stronger qualifications than any applicants for the job.
   b. We have hired Joan Gimble as our new engineer; she had the strongest qualifications than any other applicants for the job.

NAME _____   SCORE _____

Directions: Rewrite each sentence to correct the faulty parallelism.

1. Jessica Smith is a salesperson with a strong personality and who develops great loyalty among her customers.

_____

2. Before that day Wendy had never even seen a wave runner, much less driving one.

_____

3. The staff had never seen a more complete presentation and which left no question on the subject unanswered.

_____

4. To get a head start on that project and finishing before the due date, you need to start almost immediately.

_____

5. I took that new job because of the increase in salary, the use of the company's car, and to travel all over the country at the company's expense.

_____

6. Learning those new skills and the people I met made that conference well worth my time.

_____

7. I hope we never have another meeting like that one; it was tiresome, lacked important content, and which annoyed everyone who attended.

_____

8. For the banquet, we need to determine who is coming, when they will arrive, and ones who can't sit next to each other without getting in an argument.

_____

9. We watched Wanda scramble down the bank and splashing across the river as she tried to get ahead of the others in the race.

_____

10. We tried everything we could imagine to try to unscramble that puzzle and finding the last clue in the scavenger hunt.

_____

Directions: Rewrite each sentence so the comparison is logical and correct.

1. Sean Jackson is one of the best, if not the best, tight ends in the conference.

   _____

2. Seriously, folks, have you ever heard a funnier routine than Johnson?

   _____

3. Heather is a better writer than anyone in her English class.

   _____

4. Interestingly enough, my new jacket cost less than last year.

   _____

5. If you ask me, the history course I took this term is the best of the two I've taken here at the college.

   _____

6. That park in the downtown area is more beautiful than the surrounding county.

   _____

7. The Fuller Building is more beautiful than any building in its vicinity.

   _____

8. Linda, who attended a very small high school, found the large numbers of students at the state university more frightening than John, who attended a large high school.

   _____

9. Are you sure that this 2 × 4 is the longest of the two lying beside the garage?

   _____

10 Jose Blanco is certainly one of the best, if not the best, math teachers in his department.

   _____

Brief Writing Assignment: Write a paragraph of six sentences telling the story of a kindness someone did for you recently. Somewhere in the six sentences, create two parallel structures and make two comparisons.

Check Sheet

SENTENCE BUILDING

☐ **Completeness**

☐ To be a complete sentence, a word group must

1. Contain a subject and a verb.
2. Be independent rather than subordinate.

☐ Sentences tend to be incomplete for three reasons:

1. They are actually subordinate clauses.

   Although we never tried to drive that car again

   This clause must be attached to a main clause because the word *although* is a subordinating conjunction.

2. They are verbal phrases.

   Running down the street with a large kite suspended overhead

   To be sure of an early arrival

   Participles and infinitives cannot stand alone; they must function in or be attached to a main clause.

3. They are an incomplete construction made up of a noun and a phrase or subordinate clause.

   A man of good reputation who needs no introduction to this group because he has

   performed so many vital services to the city where he has lived for so many years...

   No matter how long the word group continues, no matter how many phrases and subordinate clauses it contains, it can't be a sentence unless it has a subject and a verb.

☐ Correcting fragments is relatively easy once they are detected:
   • Attach the fragment to the previous sentence or to the following sentence as the sense of the sentence allows.
   • Change the fragment to a subordinate clause with an appropriate subordinating word and attach it to a main clause.
   • Change the fragment to an independent clause by supplying either a subject or verb or both as the sense of the sentence demands.

☐ Some expressions that lack a subject-verb combination are not considered fragments:
   • Commands (The subject *you* is not voiced in such expressions.)
     Step right up. Take a ticket. Go to your seat.
   • Exclamations
     Wow! Triplets? What a surprise!
   • Bits of dialog (Note that much of our day-to-day, informal conversation is couched in sentence fragments.)
     "Running late?" she asked. "Better hurry. Only a few seats left."
   • Short transitional expressions
     Now for the last step. On to the next stop.

☐ **Traps**

☐ *Misplaced Modifiers*

We often place modifiers rather loosely in sentences in our conversation and informal writing, but in more formal writing and when precise expression is important, modifying words, phrases, and clauses must be located carefully.

1. Putting adverbs such as *only*, *nearly*, *almost*, and *hardly* in the wrong place can change the meaning of the sentence. Put modifying words, phrases, and clauses as close as possible to the word they modify.

   James nearly found $100 on the beach yesterday.

   technically means that James almost found, but did not find, money on the beach. Someone found the money ahead of James, or James walked past it without seeing it.

   James found nearly $100 on the beach.

   means that he found money on the beach, probably between $90 and $99. Changing the position of the adverb changes the meaning of the sentence.

2. Putting modifying words and phrases where they can attach themselves to the wrong word can confuse the reader.

   We heard that a forest fire burned thousands of acres of land on the evening news.

   literally means that the acreage burned on the news—that is, while the reporters watched—or perhaps the burning occurred in the newsroom. In either case, the reader can be confused. The intended meaning is that we heard the report on the news.

3. Putting modifiers where they can apply equally to two words can confuse the reader. In the sentence

   Students who can solve this problem easily can succeed in my logic course.

   the meaning might be

   Students who can easily solve this problem can succeed . . .

   or it might mean

   Students who can solve this problem can easily succeed . . .

   Position the modifier so that it can apply to only one word.

4. Place modifying words and phrases outside an infinitive, not between *to* and the verb stem.

   My brother likes to once in a while visit the zoo.

   is a clear but awkward statement.

   Once in a while, my brother likes to visit the zoo.

   is a much smoother expression.

5. Place the correlatives such as *both . . . and* and *not only . . . but also* immediately before the parallel units they connect

	We sent tickets to both Janice and Joan.
not	We sent tickets both to Janice and Joan.
and certainly not	We both sent tickets to Janice and Joan.

☐ *Dangling Modifiers*

Any phrase that does not attach itself clearly to the word it modifies is called a *dangling modifier*. Connect participial, gerund, and infinitive phrases as closely as possible to the words they modify. In the sentence

> Coming into town, the stately trees shaded both sides of the road.

the literal meaning of the structure has the trees coming into town and shading both sides of the road. The participial phrase modifies the noun following it closely in the sentence. Unless the trees are coming into town—perhaps on a truck—make the sentence read

> As we came into town, the stately trees shaded both sides of the road.

> or Coming into town, we saw the stately trees shading both sides of the road.

Be sure that gerund and infinitive phrases, especially those that serve as opening elements of the sentence, can attach themselves logically to the next noun in the sentence.

> To work as a truck driver, a commercial driver's license is required.

Logically, the commercial driver's license is not going to work as a truck driver; while the meaning is probably clear, it is better to say

> To work as a truck driver, you need a commercial driver's license.

or, more formally,

> To work as a truck driver, one needs a commercial driver's license.

☐ *Parallel Structures*

Two or more parts of sentences that are similar in function should be similar in grammatical construction—that is, parallel. Nouns should be balanced with nouns, verbs with verbs, and so on.

- Avoid the false or shifted series.

> He took that job for its challenges, its high pay, and *because it allowed him to travel.*

- Avoid the *and who, and which* construction.

> That is a job that offers challenges, high pay, *and which allows Hank to travel extensively.*

☐ *Comparisons*

☐ Be sure that comparisons and contrasts are made at the same level.

> Her car's engine is more powerful *than my car.*

Engines cannot logically be compared to cars.

In using the comparative form of an adjective in a comparison, use *any other* to exclude the subject of the comparison from the group.

> Our state university is bigger than any university in the state.

If "our state university" is in the state, it must be compared to *any **other** university* in the state.

In making double comparisons, include all the words necessary to make the expression complete.

Alicia is easily as smart as Robert, if not smarter.

Alicia is easily as smart as, if not smarter *than*, Robert.

☐ Use the comparative degree of the adjective or adverb when two items are compared.

Alicia is *smarter* than Robert.

☐ Use the superlative degree when three or more items are involved.

Alicia is the *smartest* person in the entire class.

☐ *Subordination*

Use compound verbs and sentences and subordinate clauses and phrases to create varied sentences.

• Two simple sentences: The gun fired. The runners broke from the starting blocks.

Compound verb: (not a possible construction because the two sentences have different subjects)

Compound Sentence: The gun fired, and the runners broke from the starting blocks.

Adverbial clause: When the gun fired, the runners broke from the starting blocks.

Participial phrase: (not a possible construction)

Absolute phrase: With the gun having fired, the runners broke from the starting blocks.

Other constructions are possible when the subjects of the sentences are the same:

I raised the flag. I unlocked the gate.

Compound verb: I raised the flag and unlocked the gate.

Compound sentence: I raised the flag; then I unlocked the gate.

Participial phrase: Having raised the flag, I unlocked the gate.

Punctuation

Lessons, Practice Sheets, and Exercises

| **Lesson 17** | *Commas to Separate* |

As your writing grows more precise and more economical, you will need to use commas to separate certain parts of sentences so that your work cannot be misunderstood. Five rules cover the occasions when commas are used to separate parts of a sentence.

THE FIVE RULES FOR COMMAS TO SEPARATE

1. Use commas before *and*, *but*, *or*, *nor*, *yet*, *for*, and *so* when they join the clauses of a compound sentence:

   > I placed the typed sheet on his desk, and he read it slowly.
   >
   > His face turned red, but he did not say a word.
   >
   > I knew he was angry, for he rose and stomped out of the room. [Note that no comma is used before the conjunction in a compound predicate.]

   At this point, you might reread Lesson 7. Remember that a semicolon rather than a comma is usually required in a compound sentence when no coordinating conjunction is present.

2. Use a comma between the items of a series.

   > The land looked brown, parched, lifeless, and ominous. [four adjectives]
   >
   > Volunteers may be students, office workers, housewives, or retirees. [four nouns]
   >
   > The dog charged through the door, down the steps, and into the garage. [three phrases]
   >
   > He understands what he must do, when he must do it, and why it must be done. [three subordinate clauses]
   >
   > Larry brought the wood, Mark built the fire, and I got the steaks ready. [three independent clauses]

   A series is composed of three or more words, phrases, or clauses of equal grammatical rank. A series usually takes the form of *a*, *b*, **and** *c*; sometimes it may be *a*, *b*, **or** *c*. Although commas may be used to separate a series of short clauses, the punctuation must change if the clauses have commas within them.

> Larry, who has a pickup truck, brought the wood, Mark, who was once a Boy Scout, built the fire, and I got the steaks ready.

Obviously commas do not effectively separate the independent clauses in this sentence, so we need to use a mark with greater strength—in this case, the semicolon.

> Larry, who has a pickup truck, brought the wood; Mark, who was once a Boy Scout, made the fire; and I got the steaks ready.

In journalism, writers often omit the comma before the final conjunction. It is easier to remember the rule if you develop a consistent pattern of using the comma before the final conjunction.

3. Use a comma between coordinate adjectives preceding a noun.

> the harsh, cold wind

When applied to adjectives, the word **coordinate** indicates that two adjectives modify a single noun with equal force. We usually separate coordinate adjectives with a comma. Sometimes it is difficult to know whether or not two adjectives are equal. Consider the following:

> the harsh cold wind
> the difficult final exam

Two tests will help you to decide if the adjectives are equal.

First, if you can use the word *and* instead of a comma between the two words and still produce a correct statement, the adjectives are equal, and a comma should be used to separate them. *The harsh and cold wind* makes perfect sense in English, demonstrating that the adjectives are equal in force and need a comma. But you would never say *the difficult and final exam*; thus, the adjectives are not coordinate, and the comma is not needed.

Second, if the adjectives sound natural in reversed position, they are equal and can be separated by a comma if the word *and* is not used. The phrase *the cold, harsh wind* is just as readable as *the harsh, cold wind*, again demonstrating that the adjectives are equal.

When you use more than two adjectives before a noun, you should use the *and* test, checking the adjectives by pairs—the first with the second, the second with the third, and so on—to determine the need for commas. It may help you to know that we usually do not use commas before adjectives denoting size or age. And remember that you never use a comma between the last adjective and the noun.

Observe how use of these tests determines punctuation like the following:

> a neat, courteous little boy
> a hot, steamy summer day

Because we don't say "a neat and courteous and little boy," we would place a comma between neat and courteous, but not between courteous and little. We could say *a hot, steamy summer day* or *a steamy, hot summer day*, but not *a hot and steamy and summer day*.

4. Use a comma after most introductory modifiers. The following specific applications of this rule will help you use it correctly.

   a. Put commas after introductory adverbial clauses:

> *Unless the floodwater recedes soon,* we're in trouble.
> *If we can prove that the signature was forged,* we will win the case.
> *Before sophomores will be admitted to courses numbered 300 or above,* they must have official permission.
> *Before I answer you,* I want to ask another question.
> *When he arrived,* he seemed distraught.

   b. Put commas after introductory verbal-phrase modifiers:

> *Having climbed the steep trail up Cougar Mountain,* Bob decided to take some pictures.
> *To get the best view of the valley,* he walked to the edge of the cliff.
> *After opening his backpack,* he searched for his new telephoto lens.

   c. Put a comma after an introductory absolute element, such as a phrase, an adverb modifying the whole sentence, a mild exclamation, and *yes* and *no*.

> *In fact,* there was no way to keep the front door closed.
> *Certainly,* I'll be glad to help you.
> *Well,* what are we to do now?
> *No,* we are not in danger.

   d. Ordinarily, do not put a comma after a single prepositional phrase at the beginning of a sentence. If the opening element contains two or more phrases, use a comma to separate the phrases from the main clause. A long introductory prepositional phrase is not followed by a comma when the subject and verb are reversed.

> *After a heavy dinner* we usually went for a short walk.
> *In early summer* many birds nested there.
> *In spite of the very heavy wind and the pelting hailstones,* the third race was completed.
> *In the name of justice,* please help these people.
> *After school, or during the evening,* teachers were expected to find time for grading papers and preparing lessons.
> *Between the dusty night table and the unmade bed* were all the magazines that I wanted to read.

5. Use a comma between any two words that might be mistakenly read together:

> *Before,* he had been industrious and sober. [not *before he had been*]
> *Once inside,* the dog scampered all over the furniture. [not *inside the dog*]
> *While we were eating,* the table collapsed. [not *eating the table*]
> *After we had washed,* Mother prepared breakfast. [not *washed Mother*]
> *Ever since,* he has been afraid of deep water. [not *ever since he has been*]
> *Shortly after ten,* thirty new recruits appeared. [not *shortly after ten thirty*]

English Fundamentals **Online**

After you have completed Practice Sheets and Exercises in this lesson, you can find additional help and drill work at **MyWritingLab.com**, in the section on Commas.

NAME _____   SCORE _____

Directions: Each of the following sentences is missing two commas. Add the commas where they are necessary. Then, in the spaces at the left, write the number of the rules that apply to the commas you have added:

1. before a coordinating conjunction   3. between coordinate adjectives
   in a compound sentence   4. after an introductory modifier
2. in a series   5. to prevent misreading

_____   1. June has taken the required courses in history psychology, and math but she
_____   must also take a course in biology.

_____   2. Because Jim found two new sources for that long difficult report his work is
_____   going more quickly now.

_____   3. The handsome well-dressed television anchor looked once more at his script,
_____   cleared his throat and began to read.

_____   4. Working to catch up with the rest of the runners Marta ran hard up the long
_____   winding hill.

_____   5. Racquel ordered the art work, the titles and the slides but she still needs to
_____   write the script for her new sales presentation.

_____   6. The children in that class can play on the swings this afternoon or they can play
_____   a noisy colorful video game.

_____   7. After the dog wandered away the boys looked in the barn, the pasture and
_____   the corn fields.

_____   8. After waking up the girls wandered over to the restaurant for a leisurely
_____   delicious breakfast.

_____   9. Kate had once ridden with a police officer on patrol; after that training to
_____   become an officer became an immediate compelling goal.

_____   10. Arriving early for the meeting Audrey sat down in the back for a short
_____   refreshing nap.

_____   11. Carla tried valiantly to start the car but she had to call her sleepy reluctant
_____   brother for help.

_____   12. Because the women want to study computer graphics they must also take math,
_____   computer programming and an art course.

_____   13. I've tried for three years to grow big juicy tomatoes but the bugs have killed
_____   the plants every year.

_____   14. Overwhelmed by the number of choices Arthur decided to buy only the
_____   simplest least expensive MP3 player he could find.

_____ 15. The girls already have the tables, chairs and umbrellas but they will have to set
_____   them up on the patio.

_____ 16. After we left the party broke up rather quickly and everyone went home.
_____

_____ 17. When I walked into the office Shelley and Roberta moved to the table and they
_____   began to set up the display for their presentation.

_____ 18. Jan discovered a rather short wide-bodied snake in the woodpile and she ran
_____   quickly into the house looking for help.

_____ 19. Having walked that long trail two days before the guests arrived we were
_____   interested in sitting around the house taking in a movie, or going out for a quiet
               lunch.

_____ 20. Yes we did finish that work yesterday by 5 o'clock but the delivery service
_____   brought a new batch of materials about 4:30 P.M.

_____ 21. That tall brick building down beside the river is fairly old but the building
_____   next to it, farmers shopkeepers, and other workers built just after the
               Revolutionary War.

_____ 22. With no one to help us on that project we spent the entire day sorting old musty
_____   files and scanning them into the computer.

_____ 23. Once inside the people saw a beautiful ornate dining table eight chairs, and
_____   a crystal chandelier.

_____ 24. After we had talked for about an hour Larry said that he had work to do so
_____   I left him there in his office and went to lunch.

_____ 25. The three people walked into the room put chairs around the conference table,
_____   but did not sit down; soon, others walked in and set up a high-tech expensive
               video system.

_____ 26. Once the two dogs had dug their way out under the fence they ran down the
_____   street barked at people, and frightened several small children.

_____ 27. In fact we cannot find any office space for the new people so they will need
_____   to work out of the large room in the back of the building.

_____ 28. After Jacqueline finished work on that new intricately designed jacket she
_____   put it aside and began to work on a new blouse.

_____ 29. As a favor to Karen Martin returned the books to the library dropped her car
_____   off for service, and bought some office supplies for her.

_____ 30. Running down the hill toward the river sliding down the bank, and scrambling
_____   across through the water the cross-country runners finished the last leg of
               the race.

NAME _____ SCORE_____

Directions: The following passage is missing commas that should be used to separate certain words, phrase, or clauses. Insert commas where they are needed. Then, underneath each comma you insert, write the number of the rule that governs the use of that comma.

1. before a coordinating conjunction in a compound sentence
2. in a series
3. between coordinate adjectives
4. after an introductory modifier
5. to prevent misreading

    The first computers were huge collections of tubes wires and awkward switches. Called main-frame computers these first machines were made from vacuum tubes about as big as a bread box and the collection of them filled up a room the size of an average school classroom. When they were running they generated an intense radiating heat. If the heat was not controlled the tubes blew out and they had to be replaced. In addition to this sensitivity to heat the tubes went completely irreparably haywire whenever they came in contact with the slightest speck of dust. To control the heat and dust the computers were enclosed in an air-tight air conditioned room made with glass walls. With potential trouble approaching from every direction these mainframe computers needed the attention of highly trained protective technicians dressed in white coats. Protected by these guardians in the white coats the computers were not readily available to anyone else. The technicians in the white coats standing guard ordinary workers were kept at a distance from the machines and they usually had to deal with the technicians in order to get any computer time. As scientists and technicians refined the operation of the main-frame computer other scientists worked to produce a smaller less fragile machine. The first step in this process was the invention of a small inexpensive device, called a transistor, which controlled the flow of electricity. When transistors are hooked together they form integrated circuits or microchips. These microchips can contain complicated enormous circuits on a piece of silicon no bigger than a person's thumbnail. With these microchips having become available scientists constructed microprocessors and thus they opened the way for the development of small shock-resistant desktop and laptop computers. When scientists learned to miniaturize the workings of a computer they opened the way for all of us to become computer experts and they gave all of us the power once reserved for the technicians in the white coats.

Directions: Under each rule, write two sentences of your own composition to illustrate the punctuation designated. The purpose of the exercise is to practice correct comma usage.

1. Comma used before a coordinating conjunction in a compound sentence

   a. _____

   _____

   b. _____

   _____

2. Commas used in a series (one series of single words and one series of phrases)

   a. _____

   _____

   b. _____

   _____

3. Comma used after an introductory modifier (one adverb clause and one verbal phrase)

   a. _____

   _____

   b. _____

   _____

4. Comma used between coordinate adjectives

   a. _____

   _____

   b. _____

   _____

5. Commas used to prevent misreading

   a. _____

   _____

   b. _____

   _____

Brief Writing Assignment: Write a seven-line paragraph expressing your gratitude for the kindness you discussed in Lesson 16. Employ, and properly punctuate, a compound sentence, a pair of coordinate adjectives, and an introductory participial phrase.

NAME _____   SCORE_____

Directions: One sentence in each of the following pairs is correctly punctuated. Copy the identifying letter of the correct sentence in the space at the left.

_____ 1. a. As the days passed my sister resisted calling the tall handsome boy in her class but she finally dialed his number.
   b. As the days passed, my sister resisted calling the tall, handsome boy in her class, but she finally dialed his number.

_____ 2. a. Thinking back to my childhood days, I remember starting a collection of pocket knives; my first one had a handle made of buffalo horn.
   b. Thinking back to my childhood days I remember starting a collection of pocket knives, my first one had a handle made of buffalo horn.

_____ 3. a. "I predict a long, bitterly fought campaign; the political writers are in the back rooms sharpening their pens," said the reporter.
   b. "I predict a long bitterly fought campaign, the political writers are in the back room, sharpening their pens," said the reporter.

_____ 4. a. The behavior of some delegates was rude and disruptive, for some of us the convention was a disappointment.
   b. The behavior of some delegates was rude and disruptive; for some of us the convention was a disappointment.

_____ 5. a. She has invested a small fortune in her car: a 400-watt stereo, a navigation system and a sophisticated theft-recovery system were just a modest beginning.
   b. She has invested a small fortune in her car; a 400-watt stereo, a navigation system, and a sophisticated theft-recovery system were just a modest beginning.

_____ 6. a. The dog eyed the meat hungrily but the small quick fox snatched it up, and ran into the thicket.
   b. The dog eyed the meat hungrily, but the small, quick fox snatched it up and ran into the thicket.

_____ 7. a. Noting a slight swirl in the water, Sue cast the lure into the center of it, and a huge trout struck just as the lure hit the water.
   b. Noting a slight swirl in the water Sue cast the lure into the center of it; and a huge trout struck, just as the lure hit the water.

_____ 8. a. While she had been running the clock had stopped, it failed to record her best time ever in this long difficult race.
   b. While she had been running, the clock had stopped; it failed to record her best time in this long, difficult race.

_____ 9. a. Seeing the grouse rise out of the sage, the woman raised her camera, shot skillfully, and caught the action in great detail.
   b. Seeing the grouse rise out of the sage the woman raised her camera, shot skillfully and caught the action in great detail.

_____ 10. a. "When you walk, walk very carefully, and try not to look at the water 200 feet below," advised the guide.

b. "When you walk walk very carefully and try not to look at the water, 200 below," advised the guide.

_____ 11. a. Our teacher was a mild-mannered kindly old gentleman, he often went to obvious extremes to avoid embarrassing any of us.

b. Our teacher was a mild-mannered, kindly old gentleman; he often went to obvious extremes to avoid embarrassing any of us.

_____ 12. a. There is only one gas station in our village, and the owner always goes home for lunch, sometimes not returning till the middle of the afternoon.

b. There is only one gas station in our village and the owner always goes home for lunch; sometimes not returning till the middle of the afternoon.

_____ 13. a. The calm, friendly garage attendant assured us that the bridge had been repaired and was now safe to cross.

b. The calm, friendly, garage attendant assured us that the bridge had been repaired, and was now safe to cross.

_____ 14. a. Several kinds of exotic flowers grow in this warm humid climate, everywhere one sees hibiscus, oleander and orchids.

b. Several kinds of exotic flowers grow in this warm, humid climate; everywhere one sees hibiscus, oleander, and orchids.

_____ 15. a. Yesterday we awoke to find the ground covered with wet heavy snow, today's newspaper reports that not since 1937, have we had snow this late.

b. Yesterday we awoke to find the ground covered with wet, heavy snow; today's newspaper reports that not since 1937 have we had snow this late.

_____ 16. a. In the opinion of some, elementary-school teachers are more influential than parents in determining children's attitudes toward learning, and I agree with that opinion.

b. In the opinion of some elementary-school teachers are more influential than parents in determining children's attitudes toward learning and I agree with that opinion.

_____ 17. a. Many early automobiles were high, stately things; most of them were patterned after the horse-drawn carriage.

b. Many early automobiles were high stately things, most of them were patterned after the horse-drawn carriage.

_____ 18. a. Your lecture made a deep lasting impression on our class and we were still discussing it, several weeks later.

b. Your lecture made a deep, lasting impression on our class, and we were still discussing it several weeks later.

_____ 19. a. Forty years ago, I fished for bass, pike, and muskellunge in Minnesota, in those days no one worried about polluted water.

b. Forty years ago I fished for bass, pike, and muskellunge in Minnesota; in those days no one worried about polluted water.

_____ 20. a. Wanting to buy postcards, candy bars, magazines and souvenirs; I checked my luggage, and searched the airport for a newsstand.

b. Wanting to buy postcards, candy bars, magazines, and souvenirs, I checked my luggage and searched the airport for a newsstand.

Lesson 18 | *Commas to Enclose*

Just as there are times when you need to use commas to separate items, there are times when you need to use commas to enclose items. Use commas to enclose **interrupters**—those words, phrases, or clauses that interrupt the normal word order of a sentence.

COMMON INTERRUPTERS

The most common types of interrupters are discussed below.

1. Nonrestrictive adjective clauses and phrases

> The coach's Awards Banquet speech, *which was one of her best*, should be published. [nonrestrictive adjective clause]
>
> Jan's mother, *holding a winning ticket*, went to the desk. [nonrestrictive participial phrase]
>
> Professor Angela Cheney, *at the far end of the head table*, summoned a waiter. [nonrestrictive prepositional phrase]

Clauses and phrases not essential to identify a noun are set off by commas. (See Lesson 9 to review restrictive and nonrestrictive clauses and phrases.) Note that, in some cases, the meaning of the sentence depends on whether a clause is taken as restrictive or nonrestrictive.

> My brother-in-law *who lives in Akron* is a chemist.
>
> [The writer has more than one brother-in-law. The restrictive clause is needed to distinguish this brother-in-law from other brothers-in-law.]
>
> My brother-in-law, *who lives in Akron*, is a chemist.
>
> [The writer is telling us that he or she has only one brother-in- law. Identification is not explicit.]

2. Most appositives

> One comedian, *the one with the lisp*, was booed.
>
> The major, *a veteran of three wars*, accepted the award.
>
> Mr. Tate, *our head counselor*, will speak.
>
> Our head counselor, *Mr. Tate*, will speak.

As you learned in Lesson 10, the most common type of appositive immediately follows the noun or pronoun that it renames. Appositives like these are called *loose* or *nonrestrictive appositives* and are set off. Sometimes, however, an appositive functions in the same way that a restrictive adjective clause functions: It identifies a preceding noun that, without the appositive, could refer to any member of a class. An appositive of this sort is not set off:

> my brother Jack
>
> the poet Keats

the apostle Paul

the preposition *to*

3. Absolute phrases

Today being a holiday, I plan to loaf and relax.

Her replacement having arrived early, Bea had time to shop.

He sat there in silence, *his left cheek twitching as usual.*

He stood in the doorway, *his wet cloak dripping water on the rug*, and waited for some sign of recognition.

An absolute phrase, which consists of a noun or a pronoun and a verbal (see Lesson 12), modifies the sentence as a whole, not any special part of it. Because the phrase is not restricted to any special part of the sentence, the phrase should be set off.

4. Parenthetical expressions

The text, *moreover*, had not been carefully proofread.

You will find, *for example*, that the format is not attractive.

The meal, *to tell the truth*, was quite unappetizing.

His appearance, *I must admit*, would startle anyone.

These are words, phrases, or clauses that break into the sentence to explain, to emphasize, to qualify, or to point the direction of the thought, and they should be set off.

5. Words used in direct address

"Remember, *Jimmy*, that we like your work," he said.

"*Henry*," said the teacher, "you made an A on your paper."

"I believe, *sir*, that you have been misinformed," she replied.

"And now, *dear friends and neighbors*, let's eat," said Father Jamison.

6. Expressions designating the speaker in direct quotations

"With your permission," *Tom replied*, "I'll go home for the day."

"That will have to do," *said Mrs. Garcia*, "until we think of something better."

Other punctuation marks may be used instead of the comma if the sentence justifies their use.

"How shall I tell him?" asked Mary timidly. [question mark after question]

"Silence!" he shouted. "Get to work at once!" [exclamation point]

"Two of the buildings are firetraps," replied the inspector; "moreover, the library needs a new roof." [semicolon required to avoid a comma fault between independent clauses]

7. Negative insertions used for emphasis, units out of their position, and tag questions (short interrogative clauses combined with statements)

> Our plane was an old propeller model, *not the jet we had expected.*
> *Tired and footsore*, the hikers finally reached camp.
> The hikers finally reached camp, *tired and footsore.*
> Her answer was a good one, *don't you think?*
> You remember, *don't you*, Dr. Wade's eloquent eulogy?

8. Degrees, titles, and the like when they follow names

> Helen Lyle, *Ph.D.,* gave the opening address.
> The new ambassador is Peter Jones, *Esq.*

9. In dates and addresses

> On July 14, *1904*, in a little cottage at 316 High Street, *Mayville*, *Illinois*, the wedding took place.

When a year follows a month, rather than a day of the month, the year is usually not set off. No comma is needed before a ZIP code number:

> As of March 1995 his mailing address was 1675 East Union Street, Seattle, Washington 98122.

English Fundamentals online

After you have completed Practice Sheets and Exercises in this lesson, you can find additional help and drill work at **MyWritingLab.com**, in the section on Commas.

NAME _____ SCORE_____

Directions: Insert commas where they are necessary in the following sentences. Then, in the space at the left, write one of the following numbers to indicate the rule that governs the use of the comma or commas in the sentence:

1. a nonrestrictive clause or phrase   4. a parenthetical element
2. an appositive   5. the speaker in dialog
3. a noun in direct address   6. an absolute phrase

_____ 1. With no one at the airport to meet us we took a taxi to our hotel.

_____ 2. My friend James who graduated from college last year has taken a job in Alaska.

_____ 3. "I wish" said Karen "that someone in that class would help me study for this test."

_____ 4. Joe Johnson an avid photographer is going to a seminar on nature photography next week.

_____ 5. "I hope John that you will take off from work this afternoon and work on your paper," said the instructor.

_____ 6. That business venture was to say the least not very profitable.

_____ 7. Rob Smith walking into the room and taking off his jacket took a seat at the end of the table.

_____ 8. The weather forecast for this weekend a cold front accompanied by heavy rain means that we will not be outside very much.

_____ 9. "Richard can you help me rearrange the chairs in the back of the room?" asked the kindergarten teacher.

_____ 10. The woman speaking to our class this morning I'm sure you know is a foremost civil engineer.

_____ 11. Mark said "Our speaker this morning is a man who needs no introduction, so I will turn the program over to him."

_____ 12. The group stood up, walked to the door, and left the room the important decisions for that meeting having been made.

_____ 13. The man walking into the hotel lobby is Kent Williams who is a reporter from a local television station.

_____ 14. The man walking into the hotel lobby is Kent Williams a reporter from a local television station.

_____ 15. Kent Williams walking through the door at this moment is a reporter from a local television station.

193

Directions: Each of the following sentences contains an adjective clause or a participial phrase. Underline each clause or phrase and insert commas where they are needed. Then, in the space at the left, write **R** if the clause or phrase is restrictive or **N** if it is nonrestrictive.

_____ 1. Can you tell me the name of the street where Mr. Roberts has his office?

_____ 2. The restaurant on the other side of town that has such good Italian food is called, simply, Mario's Italian Restaurant.

_____ 3. I would like to meet the two people who wrote this report.

_____ 4. I would like to meet Lisa Concepcion and Marcus Roberts who wrote this report.

_____ 5. The two names that appear on the cover of the report are Lisa Concepcion and Marcus Roberts.

_____ 6. The people whose names appear on the cover are Lisa Concepcion and Marcus Roberts.

_____ 7. Do you know the name of the person whom the company president named CFO.

_____ 8. Lexington Street which runs north and south at this end of town turns into an east- west street after it crosses the freeway.

_____ 9. The tall man striding purposefully into the room will be our instructor for this term.

_____ 10. Mr. Black who is striding purposefully into the room at this moment will be our instructor for this term.

_____ 11. His degree and his experience in the field which are both quite impressive make him a logical choice to teach the class.

_____ 12. One of my friends who took a class from Mr. Black last term found his work very impressive.

_____ 13. Mr. Black's work last term certainly impressed Ron Steinberg who took this class from him last term.

_____ 14. Ron whom you met at my house last week was quite impressed with Mr. Black.

_____ 15. The day when my history paper is due is sometime at the end of the month.

_____ 16. Tuesday, March 30 when my history paper is due is still three weeks away.

_____ 17. Lauren is a woman whose pleasing personality wins many friends.

_____ 18. Lauren whose pleasing personality impresses many people is a good friend of mine.

_____ 19. Marshall's new house shielded from the north winds by a hill stays warm even on the coldest days.

_____ 20. At a time when you have about an hour to spare I'll tell you the story of our disastrous ski trip.

NAME _____   SCORE _____

Directions: Insert commas where they are necessary in the following sentences. Then, underneath each comma write one of the following numbers to indicate the rule that governs the use of the commas:

1. a nonrestrictive clause or phrase
2. an appositive
3. a noun in direct address

4. a parenthetical element
5. the speaker in dialog
6. an absolute phrase

Sometimes parents tell children fanciful stories fairy tales that are supposed to teach the children some kind of lesson. These stories called by psychologists "cautionary tales" are often designed to make children aware of possible danger. One of these stories "Little Red Riding Hood" is a frightening story about a little girl and her encounter with a wolf. Little Red riding Hood whose real name is never recorded anywhere lived in a small village near a deep woods. The girl got her nickname from a very special red hat which she wore every day all the time. The hat was knitted by the little girl's grandmother who loved the little girl more than anything else in the world. One day the grandmother a kind and wonderfully loving woman became sick and was unable to cook for herself. With the grandmother ill Red Riding Hood's mother decided to cook a meal and have the little girl deliver it. The mother called to the little girl "Red please take this soup and this fine sandwich to your grandmother."

"I am delighted to take this meal to my sweet grandmother" the little girl replied. The little girl always a dutiful daughter gathered up the lunch and prepared to walk to her grandmother's house.

The mother said "Red you must go straight to your grandmother's house and take care not to walk into the woods."

The little girl walking carefully along the edge of the woods to her grandmother's house met a big, bad wolf.

"Hello little girl" said the wolf. "Where are you taking that wonderful, tasty lunch?"

"I'm taking it to my grandmother who lives just a little bit farther down this path" replied the girl.

The wolf said "Take that path to your right; it is a shortcut to your grandmother's house."

The girl set off down the path, and the wolf anticipating a wonderful meal hurried ahead to the grandmother's house. The wolf a ravenous beast devoured the grandmother and waited for the little girl to arrive. Some versions of the story the goriest versions say that the wolf ate both the grandmother and the girl; others say that both were rescued.

The moral of the story as anyone can see is the same for both endings: Follow your mother's directions, and stay away from talking animals with large, sharp teeth.

Directions: Insert commas where they are needed in the following sentences. Then, in the space at the left of each sentence, write one of the following numbers to indicate the rule that governs the punctuation of the sentence:

1. a nonrestrictive clause or phrase
2. an appositive
3. a noun in direct address
4. a parenthetical element
5. the speaker in dialogue
6. an absolute phrase
7. negative insertions, etc.
8. degrees, titles, etc.
9. dates and addresses

_____ 1. That course which meets on Tuesdays and Thursdays does not fit into my schedule.

_____ 2. Patrick and Richard who are both very good students recommended that course to me.

_____ 3. Perhaps I can take that course next term a term in which my schedule will be a little more flexible.

_____ 4. Yesterday I met Paul Anderson the new manager of my department at the bank.

_____ 5. I think don't you that he will be a fine addition to the company.

_____ 6. I would like incidentally to borrow that copy of the financial report.

_____ 7. Next week our law practice will add a new lawyer John Baldwin J.D.

_____ 8. On April 2 2008 the school will celebrate the 200 anniversary of its founding by a group of local citizens.

_____ 9. Please send that package to my brother, whose address is 4972 Riverfront Parkway Chillicothe OH 56203.

_____ 10. Larry said "We need to work an extra hour tonight so that we can get that report finished."

_____ 11. We adjourned the department meeting at 5:00 P.M. all the business on the agenda having been completed.

_____ 12. My friend Walter who works as a media specialist in the library has traced his family tree back to the time of the Revolutionary War.

_____ 13. Walter a librarian by profession studies genealogies as a hobby.

_____ 14. Walter who is a very young man prefers to be known as a media specialist rather than as a librarian.

_____ 15. "The word 'librarian'" Walter says "sounds a little stuffy and old-fashioned."

_____ 16. I don't believe he is correct in that opinion do you?

_____ 17. I mailed my order to 35 East 54th Street New York NY 10022.

_____ 18. How is it possible that the man can continue his lecture with half the people in the audience sound asleep?

_____ 19. The paddlers exhausted from fighting the rapids finally found a calm spot and a small, sandy beach where they could rest.

_____ 20. "I don't know" said Mary plaintively "how I can possibly finish this long paper by tomorrow morning."

Commas: All Uses

NAME _____ SCORE _____

Directions: Insert commas where they are needed. Then in the space at the left, write the number of commas you used in each sentence.

_____ 1. Walking slowly down the street through the center of town which has been restored so that it looks as it did 100 years ago Raul stopped in front of a store window went into the store and bought a book about the history of the town.

_____ 2. Yesterday when I went downtown I visited Jim Marshal a local contractor who grew up in this area and he said "The town especially the restored part of downtown is experiencing a wonderful boom in business which of course helps everyone living in the area.

_____ 3. The older lovingly restored brick buildings lining Main Street are beautiful examples of the work that Marshall and others have done and they stand as monuments to the efforts of the city's leaders as fine a group of citizens as anyone could hope to meet.

_____ 4. "Jim" I said "I know you are proud of that restoration project" and he told me that the project which took almost three years is the best thing he's ever done in his work as a contractor and then showed me plans for additional work on another major street near the same area.

_____ 5. Everyone visiting the downtown area says "The downtown area has become a beautiful restful place the kind of place where people can enjoy walking and more importantly can enjoy shopping without feeling rushed or pressured by noise and traffic."

_____ 6. After all the work has been completed the town's citizens will have a downtown area they can be proud of and they will have preserved many of the town's historical buildings which might have been destroyed the citizens having not intervened.

_____ 7. When I left Jim and his staff of architects and engineers all highly trained people went back to their desks and their computers and they began to plan additional ways to save older sections of the town by restoring buildings that had been left to deteriorate.

_____ 8. Whenever you see an older building especially one that has been carefully restored stop for a moment to look at it closely because that warm old brick building might have been replaced by a stark cold concrete and glass structure.

_____ 9. Once many years ago my grandfather owned an old barn that had beautiful oak siding which had weathered to a soft creamy gray color so with the barn no longer needed he took down the siding and used it to cover his house which up to that time had been covered in ugly asphalt shingles.

_____ 10. Re-using a natural substance such as wood to replace a manufactured product I'm sure you'll agree will almost always improve the appearance of any building and such a replacement should be done whenever it is possible.

_____ 11. The three people came to work late they didn't do anything constructive and they left early so the manager who is usually a very patient person discharged them and she gave them their last pay as they walked out the door of the shop.

_____ 12. At 10:00 A.M. on Monday morning last week we went to our first accounting class for this semester and there we met our instructor Arnold Mill Ph.D. a man who has had many years of experience in the practice of accounting.

_____ 13. "Try these cookies" said my sister; "I made them from Grandma's old recipe which has been handed down for generations in our family and people have always liked them so much that they called them 'Grandma's Famous Cookies.'"

_____ 14. The three little boys ran through the old man's yard frightened his dog and knocked over two of his rose bushes so the old man his feelings hurt by their actions waited for them to come back and then he squirted them with his hose.

_____ 15. Although my address is 1462 Robinson Drive Kansas City Kansas 61329 I am having my mail forwarded to my father's house in Bend Oregon because I am as everyone knows currently traveling in Spain and I will not be home for another two months.

_____ 16. Yesterday in our environmental science class Eric Lawson a noted meteorologist spoke about global warming which is a subject that causes great debate among scientists and politicians.

_____ 17. My sister and I when we were out shopping yesterday went to a garden supply store and we brought home two dogwood trees several bags of potting soil and a new shovel which we will use to dig the holes for the trees.

_____ 18. "With everything working out as I plan" said Andy "my GPA for this term should be much higher than it has been in the past for I have attended every class taken careful notes studied every day and reviewed thoroughly before each test."

_____ 19. After we had used the new software for a few days we realized that it needed to be changed to suit our complicated highly technical financial requirements so we called in Arthur Patton an outside computer consultant so that he could change the code.

_____ 20. Everyone in this class and that means every single person needs to purchase the new edition of our textbook not the earlier edition because the earlier edition which is still on the shelves has page numbers quite different from the page numbers found in the new edition.

NAME _____   SCORE_____

Directions: The following sentences contain 40 numbered spots, some with punctuation and some without. In the correspondingly numbered spots at the left, write **C** if the punctuation is correct or **W** if the punctuation is incorrect.

1. _____   (1)   Will had a successful game today; he threw out two runners caught a foul ball,
                    ₁   ₂

2. _____   and hit a double.

3. _____   (2)   Jim Robinson who has had little experience with carpentry work, came
                    ₃

4. _____   out to the job and helped us today.
                                                        ₄

5. _____   (3)   Jim Robinson obviously a man without much experience in carpentry, came to
                    ₅

6. _____   the job site today and he helped us by cleaning up the site.
                    ₆

7. _____   (4)   The job site having been completely cleaned we all left for home thanking Jim
                                                            ₇   ₈

8. _____   for all his help during the day.

9. _____   (5)   All of us workers are indebted to Jim, for quite clearly, he made a major
                                                        ₉   ₁₀

10. _____   contribution to our work.

11. _____   (6)   As the two men drove down the road they saw two stately, beautiful pheasants
                                                    ₁₁   ₁₂

12. _____   walking along the side of the road.

13. _____   (7)   While we were walking along the road came a group of motorcycle riders
                                                    ₁₃   ₁₄

14. _____   probably about twenty of them, and they all waved to us as they passed by.

15. _____   (8)   "Robbie please take these checks to the bank and deposit them in the company
                    ₁₅

16. _____   account," said Ms. Adams to her executive assistant.
                    ₁₆

17. _____   (9)   The weather forecasters, whom we have come to trust without question missed
                                                                            ₁₇

18. _____   their prediction badly when they said that it would not rain today.
                    ₁₈

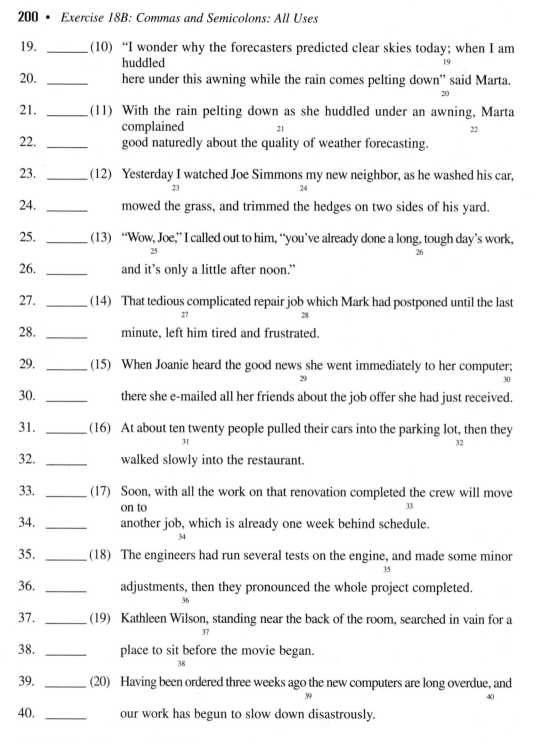

19. _____ (10) "I wonder why the forecasters predicted clear skies today; when I am huddled
                                                                                    19

20. _____   here under this awning while the rain comes pelting down" said Marta.
                                                                                    20

21. _____ (11) With the rain pelting down as she huddled under an awning, Marta complained
                                                            21   22

22. _____   good naturedly about the quality of weather forecasting.

23. _____ (12) Yesterday I watched Joe Simmons my new neighbor, as he washed his car,
                                            23   24

24. _____   mowed the grass, and trimmed the hedges on two sides of his yard.

25. _____ (13) "Wow, Joe," I called out to him, "you've already done a long, tough day's work,
                                    25   26

26. _____   and it's only a little after noon."

27. _____ (14) That tedious complicated repair job which Mark had postponed until the last
                                        27   28

28. _____   minute, left him tired and frustrated.

29. _____ (15) When Joanie heard the good news she went immediately to her computer;
                                                    29   30

30. _____   there she e-mailed all her friends about the job offer she had just received.

31. _____ (16) At about ten twenty people pulled their cars into the parking lot, then they
                                    31   32

32. _____   walked slowly into the restaurant.

33. _____ (17) Soon, with all the work on that renovation completed the crew will move on to
                                                                                    33

34. _____   another job, which is already one week behind schedule.
                            34

35. _____ (18) The engineers had run several tests on the engine, and made some minor
                                                                            35

36. _____   adjustments, then they pronounced the whole project completed.
                            36

37. _____ (19) Kathleen Wilson, standing near the back of the room, searched in vain for a
                                            37

38. _____   place to sit before the movie began.
                            38

39. _____ (20) Having been ordered three weeks ago the new computers are long overdue, and
                                                        39   40

40. _____   our work has begun to slow down disastrously.

Brief Writing Assignment: Write a paragraph seven sentences long discussing two academic goals you have set for yourself. Employ one nonrestrictive clause, one quotation, and one parenthetical element. Punctuate these units correctly.

This lesson covers a number of tricky punctuation marks.

APOSTROPHE

The apostrophe (') has three uses:

1. To form the possessive of nouns and indefinite pronouns
2. To mark the omitted material in contractions
3. To form certain plurals, such as those of letters and abbreviations

Forming Possessives

Any noun, whether singular or plural, that does not end in *s* shows ownership by adding an apostrophe and *s*:

a boy's hat [the hat belongs to the boy], the horse's tail, Carol's car, men's shoes, children's toys

Plural nouns that end in *s* form possessives by adding an apostrophe after the *s*:

boys' hats, horses' tails, the Smiths' home, ladies' dresses

Singular nouns ending in *s* or *z* form the possessive by adding, *'s*.

the countess's castle, Frances's reply, Mr. Gomez's report

On rare occasions, if the pronunciation of the word with the additional *s*-sound would be awkward, it is permissible to form the possessive with an apostrophe alone.

for goodness' sake

For the sake of uniformity, the exercises on possessives will ask that you use the *'s* after singular nouns ending in *s*.

The indefinite pronouns, but not the personal pronouns, form the possessive with the aid of the apostrophe:

somebody's sweater, anyone's opinion, anybody's game [But note the possessive forms of pronouns: his, hers, its, theirs, ours, yours, whose.]

Compound words and word groups form the possessive by adding an apostrophe and *s* to the last word of the group:

My sister-in-law's last visit was in December.
Did you get anyone else's opinion of your paper?

Note that establishing ownership of two or more items requires careful attention. For individual ownership, add an apostrophe and *s* at the end of both owners.

Oliver Stone*'s* and Alfred Hitchcock*'s* movies [indicating that each made certain movies]

For joint ownership of two or more items, add an apostrophe and *s* at the end of the second owner's name:

Rogers and Hammerstein's musicals [indicating that they wrote musicals as joint projects]

Omitted Material

The apostrophe is used to stand for the omitted material in contractions:

doesn't [does not], won't [will not], she's [she is, she has], o'clock [of the clock], rock 'n' roll [rock and roll]

You must learn to distinguish carefully between the following pairs of contractions and possessives:

Contraction	*Possessive*
it's [it is, it has]	its
there's [there is, there has]	theirs
they're [they are]	their
who's [who is, who has]	whose
you're [you are]	your

Unusual Plurals

Use an apostrophe to form the plural of letters and words that are treated as words.

the three *R's*; mostly *A's* and *B's*; too many *and's*; no *if's, and's,* or *but's* about it.

Although some authorities no longer require the formation of the plural of numbers and symbols with an apostrophe, there are times when the lack of an apostrophe creates confusion. Thus, it seems logical to retain the apostrophe for the sake of clarity.

Btu's, CPA's, 1980's, scores in the 80's and 90's

Many writers need to be reminded regularly of an important related fact: An apostrophe is never used in forming the plural of either a common or a proper noun.

There are two Kathys in the class. Two grandmas attended.

COLON

The colon (:) is a formal mark announcing an explanation, an appositive, a list, or a quotation to follow.

"My friends: Tonight I want to discuss. . . ."
Last year Hank took up a new hobby: drag racing.

You should bring to class the following items: index cards, permanent markers, and notebook paper.

The sign reads: "Bridge ices in winter."

The colon is used in formal papers to begin a quotation of four lines or more. The text of the quotation is indented one inch from the left and runs to the right margin. It is not set off by quotation marks.

In cases where the colon sets off a quotation, the identifying tag should appear in the independent clause.

Colons are also used as a mark of separation in certain special constructions:

Hours, minutes, and seconds
> 1:14:10 P.M.

Biblical chapters and verses
> I Kings 2:1

Titles and subtitles
> *Conversations: Famous Women Speak Out*

The colon is also used after the salutation in a business letter and after the words *To, From,* and *Subject* in the heading of a memorandum.

> MEMORANDUM
> To:
> From:
> Subject:

Note that after a colon it is permissible to have an initial capital letter if the text following the colon is a complete sentence. Do not use a colon to separate a verb from its complement or a preposition from its object.

Faulty: All hikers must bring: a flashlight, a small ax, and a waterproof tarpaulin.
Faulty: The things a hiker must bring are: a flashlight, a small ax, and a waterproof tarpaulin.
Faulty: The hiker's equipment should consist of: a flashlight, a small ax, and a waterproof tarpaulin.

DASH

The dash (—) is used to show an abrupt change in thought in the sentence. It must be used sparingly and never as a substitute for other marks.

Superior students—notice that I said *superior*—will not have to take the test.

New surroundings, new friends, a challenging new job—all these helped Eugene overcome his grief.

HYPHEN

The hyphen (-) is used to divide a word at the end of a line and to join words to form various types of compounds. Divide a word between syllables only. With words having a prefix or a suffix, divide the word after the prefix and before the suffix. Avoid dividing a word so that a single letter ends or begins a line. (Consult your dictionary for problems of syllabic division.)

mathe-matics *not* mathem-atics
inter-collegiate *not* intercol-legiate
govern-ess *not* gov-erness
enough *not* e-nough
many *not* man-y

It is important to note that the use of computerized publishing programs by newspaper and magazine publishers has created a situation where words seem to be divided at random wherever the end of the line occurs. In academic writing, however, it is a good idea to continue the practice of dividing words by the rules stated here.

Use hyphens to join the parts of compound modifiers preceding nouns.

Observe his well-kept lawn. His lawn is well kept.
We deplore your devil-may-care attitude.

This use of a hyphen sometimes determines an exact meaning:

a roll of 20-dollar bills; a roll of 20 dollar bills
all-American boys; all American boys

Use hyphens with compound numbers from twenty-one to ninety-nine and with fractions:

Twenty-two people claimed the one-third share of the reward money but received only one-eighth.

Use hyphens, particularly with prefixes and suffixes, to avoid awkward combinations of letters or to distinguish between two meanings of a word:

anti-intellectual
pre-Aztec
her doll-like face
re-cover a couch [not recover the money]

PARENTHESES

Parentheses are very similar to dashes in that they allow the insertion of an additional thought or explanation in a sentence. Dashes tend to emphasize an interruption; parentheses place less important information in a sentence. Nevertheless, parentheses tend to interrupt the flow of a sentence and should (like dashes) be used sparingly.

I showed Robert my favorite poem (Robert Frost's *Two Tramps in Mud Time*), but he said that he does not like any poetry
His dislike for poetry goes back to the fifth grade (his teacher asked him to read a difficult poem aloud) when he had an embarrassing experience in class.
His dislike for poetry goes back to the fifth grade when he had an embarrassing experience in class. (His teacher asked him to read a difficult poem aloud.)

Note the differences in capitalization and punctuation in the second and third example sentences:

When a complete sentence in parentheses occurs inside a sentence, do not use capitals or a period. When the complete sentence in parentheses stands outside the sentence, use capitals and a period.

QUOTATION MARKS

Quotation marks should be used to enclose quoted material and words you may use in some special way. Use double quotation marks (" ") to enclose the exact words of a quoted speech. Quotation marks always come in pairs. The marks show the beginning and the end of a speech, whether it is part of a sentence, one sentence, or several sentences. If a speech is interrupted by material showing who said it, quotation marks set off the quoted material from the explanatory material. Use quotation marks where the directly quoted material begins and where it ends or is interrupted. Indirect quotations are *not* set off by quotation marks:

"I admit," said Ralph, "that I was mistaken."
[Note that the explanatory material is set off from the direct quotation.]
Peg answered, "I didn't attend. I wasn't in town." [More than one sentence.]
Peg answered that she hadn't attended because she hadn't been in town.
[This is an indirect quotation. Words not directly quoted should not be enclosed in quotation marks.]

Use double quotation marks to set off the subdivisions of books, names of songs, and titles of units of less than book length, such as short stories, short poems, essays, and articles:

The second chapter of *Moby Dick* is entitled "The Carpet-Bag."
Eva Peron sings "Don't Cry for Me, Argentina" in the musical *Evita*.
Our anthology includes "Threes," a poem from Sandburg's *Smoke and Steel*.
The first article I read for my research paper was William Calvin's "The Great Climate Flip-flop" in the *Atlantic Monthly*.

Titles of books, magazines, long poems, newspapers, motion pictures, and radio and television series are not set in double quotation marks. In printed material, these items are set in italic type (*type like this*). Other special uses of italics are for foreign words and phrases and for names of ships, planes, and spacecraft. In handwritten or typewritten papers, underlining (typescript like this) is the equivalent of italics in printed material. Word-processors can produce effects such as bold (**bold**) and italic, which gives students a capability previously not available except through typesetting.

Double quotation marks are also used to set off slang words used in serious writing. Sometimes double quotation marks are used to set off words when they are referred to as words:

The witness had only recently been released from the "slammer."
Words like "seize" and "siege" are often misspelled.

Usage is divided on these applications of quotation marks. The two words in the second example would almost certainly appear in italics in printed material. Student writers of handwritten or typed material should either underline such words or set them off by quotation marks, the first method being the more common practice.

Double Quotation Marks with Other Punctuation

Follow this usage in the placing of quotation marks in relation to other marks:

1. Commas and periods always go inside quotation marks.
2. Semicolons and colons always go outside quotation marks.
3. Question marks and exclamation points go inside if they belong to the quoted part, outside if they do not.

> "Come in," said my uncle, "and take off your coats." [comma and period]
>
> Mr. Lowe said, "I heartily endorse this candidate"; unfortunately most of the audience thought he said *hardly* instead of *heartily*. [semicolon outside]
>
> "Heavens!" he exclaimed. "Is this the best you can do?" [exclamation point and question mark]
>
> Mother asked, "Where were you last night?" [no double punctuation]
>
> Did she say, "I came home early"? [question mark belongs to the whole sentence, not to the quoted part]
>
> Did Mother ask, "Where were you last night?" [note that there is only one question mark after a double question like this]

Single Quotation Marks

Use single quotation marks to enclose a speech within a speech:

> "I wonder what he meant," said Betty, "when he said, 'There are wheels within wheels.' "

You may not write many sentences like this one, but just the same, you should note that when you have quotes within quotes, the period comes inside both the single and double quotation marks.

English Fundamentals Online

After you have completed Practice Sheets and Exercises in this lesson, you can find additional help and drill work at **MyWritingLab.com**, in the sections on Apostrophes; Quotation Marks; Semicolons, Colons, Dashes, and Parentheses.

Tricky Punctuation Marks

Directions: In the spaces at the left, write **C** if the punctuation is correct, **W** if it is wrong. Within the incorrect sentences, correct the faulty punctuation by adding, removing, or changing marks and adding, where needed, an additional **s** after an apostrophe.

_____ 1. At ten oclock you'll need to check the ovens temperature and the turkey's tenderness.

_____ 2. For the last few day's– perhaps as much as a week– my cars been running rough and it's engine has been making a strange noise.

_____ 3. "I think," responded Roy, "she said, 'Meet me in front of that coffee shop at 9;30 P.M.'"

_____ 4. If its true that the papers due date is Wednesday, I have less than 24 hour's to complete my work on it.

_____ 5. In the past Mr. Gentry's lawn was always well kept, but lately he seems to think of only one thing: fishing.

_____ 6. 'Only two things in life are certain: death and taxes,' chuckled the elderly gentleman.

_____ 7. Lets try to find that road on the map, or– aha, there it is; now I know that were not lost.

_____ 8. That little heater does not produce many Btus, so the rooms always a little too cold for comfort.

_____ 9. "I earned all Cs and Ds last term," said Martha, so Ill really need to buckle down and work hard next term."

_____ 10. Its not likely that we can replace Jim easily; his easygoing temperament and quick mind are a rare combination.

_____ 11. The list of speakers is impressive; the colleges president, two dean's, and the mayor of one of the nearby towns.

_____ 12. Mary says that hes given her a poorly defined assignment, so shes not sure which task is her's and which is yours.

_____ 13. Im not sure– but no ones ever really sure– which way that storm will move once its crossed the mountains.

_____ 14. "Can we find out if he said, "Your assignments on page 252' " asked Anne.

_____ 15. We'll need to have someone else's opinion of that document; its age and authenticity aren't easily determined.

Directions: Sentences 1–5 are indirect quotations. In the space provided, rewrite each sentence as a direct quotation. Sentences 6–10 are direct quotations. Rewrite each as an indirect quotation. You will need to alter some verb forms and some pronoun forms as well as the punctuation.

1. Jane said that she had left her tennis racquet on the hall table.

   _____

2. The shop foreman observed that he would need to hire two more mechanics if we take on that additional contract.

   _____

3. My brother has often told me that I need to lose some weight before football practice begins in the fall.

   _____

4. Mrs. Carlson asked us if we can help her with the work in her garden tomorrow.

   _____

5. Did she say that the buses will be late today?

   _____

6. The officer told me, "It will be almost an hour before the road opens for traffic."

   _____

7. The inspector said, "Your car will need some work before it can pass the emissions test."

   _____

8. The baseball scout responded, "Your swing is good but you need to improve your speed on the bases."

   _____

9. "Can you two boys tell us where the Chamber of Commerce is located?" asked the tourists.

   _____

10. "Will my car be ready by late afternoon today?" Carl asked the service manager.

    _____

NAME _____   SCORE _____

Directions: The following exercise is a formal business letter addressed to an individual whose name you know. No punctuation (except end marks) has been inserted. Insert punctuation marks where they are needed. Note that, contrary to formal practice, the letter contains a few contractions so that you may practice recognizing and punctuating them correctly.

John Smith
9555 Peterson Rd
Seattle WA 90132
555 678 4100

Ms Linda Jackson
Jackson Moving and Storage Inc
4122 Constable Rd
Van Buren WA 90044

Dear Ms Jackson

Your advertisement in the magazine *Fine Places to Live* November 2008 attracted my attention because it contained the following lines

> We value your business.
>
> We know you value your possessions.
>
> We at Jackson Moving value your possessions as much as you do.
>
> We will move the contents of your home and deliver them on time in perfect condition at the price quoted by our representative.
>
> We guarantee your satisfaction with our work.

In the past five years time I have moved three times two of those coast to coast. On each move the moving companies performance was far less than satisfactory. Those companies lost or damaged 12 count them 12 valuable antiques or paintings. In addition to those losses no company stayed with it's estimated price in fact the estimates were not even close to the final price. Needless to say my opinion of the moving industry is not very high.

However your ads statements give me hope yes Im still an optimist that this time the results will be better and Ive found a company that will deliver what its promised. Next month Im moving to Atlanta and Ill need a moving company. If youre able to meet the standard I see in the lines quoted above please have a representative call me at the number listed above.

Yours truly

John Smith

Directions: The following brief memorandum contains no punctuation (except end marks). Add punctuation marks where they are needed. Note that again some contractions are employed that might not be used in a strictly formal memorandum.

<u>MEMORANDUM</u>
To Jim Anderson Estimator
From Linda Jackson President
Subject Potential Customer

John Smiths letter attached here presents a challenge to our company. Smiths past experience with moving companies work has left a bad taste in his mouth. Hes dissatisfied with our competitors work as he experienced it in previous moves. Please call him as soon as possible to meet him and give him a price for moving his household goods to Atlanta. Youll need to be especially careful to identify Smiths antiques and paintings for special treatment. Apparently loss or damage to these valuable items was a particular sore spot for him in his past experiences. Hell appreciate Im sure your careful attention but you always pay careful attention to a customers needs so I neednt worry about satisfying him.

Thanks for giving this matter your most professional attention.

Brief Writing Assignment: Assume the identity of Jim Anderson from the previous memorandum. Write a response of six sentences in the form used above in which you include a colon followed by a quote, a dash to show an abrupt change of thought, and a quotation within a quotation in which you use both single and double quotation marks.

This lesson discusses end marks and summarizes all the punctuation rules presented in this book.

PERIOD

The **period** is used after a complete declarative sentence and after ordinary abbreviations. Its use as end punctuation after sentences needs no examples. Its use after abbreviations is a little more complicated.

Personal Titles

A period is used in the following abbreviations: *Mr.*, *Mrs.*, *Ms.*, *Messrs.*, *Mmes.*, and *Dr.* These abbreviations appear before the name. Periods are also used for *Jr.*, *Sr.*, *Esq.*, *D.D.*, *Ph.D.*, and so forth, which are used after names. Miss does not require a period. *Ms.*, used instead of *Miss* or *Mrs.* when marital status is not indicated, is usually considered an abbreviation and uses a period, although some modern dictionaries have entries for it either with or without a period.

Latin-Based Terms

The following initials and abbreviations, used only in documentation pages and tabulations but not in ordinary writing, require periods: *e.g.* (for example), *etc.* (and so forth), *i.e.* (that is), *p.*, *pp.* (page, pages), and *vol.* (volume). A.D., B.C., B.C.E., C.E., A.M., and P.M. (usually set in small caps in printed material) are used only with figures and where necessary for clarity. Note: A.D. and C.E. should precede the year (A.D. 37); B.C. and B.C.E., however, should follow the year (31 B.C.).

Addresses

The following abbreviations require periods and are acceptable in addresses but should be spelled out in ordinary writing: *St.* (Street), *Ave.* (Avenue), *Blvd.* (Boulevard), *Dr.* (Drive), *Rd.* (Road), *Co.* (Company), and *Inc.* (Incorporated). Conventionally, periods are used with abbreviations of the states (*Mass.*, *Minn.*, *Tex.*, *W. Va.*). However, the two- letter capitalized symbols authorized by the U.S. Postal Service (*MA*, *MN*, *TX*, *WV*) do not require periods.

Poor:	Last Mon. P.M. I visited my two older bros., who live in N.Y. Chas. works for a mfg. co. there. Thos. attends NYU, preparing himself for a gov't. job. He's coming home for Xmas.
Right:	Last Monday afternoon I visited my two older brothers, who live in New York. Charles works for a manufacturing company there. Thomas attends New York University, preparing himself for a government job. He's coming home for Christmas.

Acronyms and Measurements

In modern usage, the "alphabet" name forms, or acronyms, of various governmental or intergovernmental agencies, social or professional organizations, and units of measurement used in scientific contexts are usually not followed by periods: *ACLU, CARE, CBS, CIA, NAACP, NCAA, NATO, PTA, SEC, UNESCO, Btu* (British thermal unit), *mpg, mph, rpm.* New acronyms and abbreviated forms spring into existence nowadays with regularity. The following examples are some that have gained common acceptance fairly recently: *AIDS* (acquired immune deficiency syndrome), *CAT scan* (computerized axial tomography), *CATV* (community antenna television), *CD* (certificate of deposit), *CEO* (chief executive officer), *COLA* (cost-of-living adjustment), *CPR* (cardiopulmonary resuscitation), *DWI* (driving while intoxicated), *IRA* (individual retirement account), *MIA* (missing in action), *MRI* (magnetic resonance imaging), *OPEC* (Organization of Petroleum Exporting Countries), *PC* (personal computer), *STOL* (short takeoff and landing), DVD (digital video disc). Refer to your dictionary when in doubt about the meaning of an abbreviated form or the possibility of using periods. Be prepared to find apparent inconsistencies and divided usage.

QUESTION MARK

The **question mark** is used after a *direct question*, which is an utterance that calls for an answer. (See Lesson 6.) A question mark is not used after an *indirect question*, which is a statement giving the substance of a question but not the words that would be used in a direct question.

Direct: Who goes there? Is that you? When do we eat? How much do I owe you? "Who goes there?" he demanded. [in dialogue]

Indirect: She asked me how old I was. I wondered why she would ask such a question. [Note that these are statements, not direct questions.]

Refer to page 205 to review the use of question marks with quotation marks.

EXCLAMATION POINT

The **exclamation point** is used sparingly in modern writing and should be reserved for statements of strong feeling. Mild exclamations, such as *oh*, *goodness*, *well*, *yes*, and *no*, are followed by commas, not exclamation points. Be sure to place the exclamation mark after the exclamation itself.

"Help! I'm slipping!" he shouted. [Note the period after *shouted.*]

"Stop that!" she screamed. [Do not put the exclamation point after *screamed.*]

"Well, it was exciting, wasn't it?" "Oh, I had a pleasant time."

SUMMARY OF PUNCTUATION RULES

This summary covers the indispensable punctuation rules for anything you write. Colons, commas, periods, and even question marks and exclamation points do have other uses for special occasions or effects, but these occasional applications rarely cause problems for most writers.

Commas to Separate: Five Rules

1. Compound sentences
2. Items in a series
3. Coordinate adjectives
4. Introductory modifiers
5. Words that may be misread together

Colon: Two Rules

1. Use a colon to announce a list, an explanation, or a long quotation.
   a. If the text following a colon is a complete sentence, use an initial capital letter.
   b. Do not use a colon to separate a verb from its complement or a preposition from its object.
2. Use a colon to separate hours, minutes, and seconds; biblical chapters and verses; titles and subtitles.

Apostrophe: Two Rules

1. With possessives
2. With contractions

Period: Two Rules

1. After declarative sentences
2. After most abbreviations

Commas to Enclose: Eight Rules

1. Nonrestrictive clauses and phrases
2. Appositives
3. Absolute phrases
4. Parenthetical expressions
5. Words in direct address
6. The speaker in dialog
7. Negative insertions
8. Dates, addresses, degrees, and titles

Semicolon: Two Rules

1. In compound sentences without a conjunction joining the independent clauses
2. To separate items in a series when commas occur within items

Quotation Marks: Three Rules

1. Enclose direct quotations
2. Set off titles
3. Set off words used in some special way

Question Mark: One Rule

1. After direct questions

English Fundamentals Online

After you have completed Practice Sheets and Exercises in this lesson, you can find additional help and drill work at **MyWritingLab.com**, in the section on End Marks.

NAME _____ SCORE _____

Directions: In the space at the left, write **C** if the sentence is correct, **W** if it is incorrect. Within the incorrect sentences, correct the faulty punctuation.

_____ 1. Once inside the police searched the house for signs of a robbery once they finished the house was no longer officially a crime scene.

_____ 2. "Have you ever seen a longer home run!" asked Jaime? "That was the longest I've ever seen."

_____ 3. With our minds filled with Jims complex directions we soon became confused, and found ourselves on the wrong end of Main Street.

_____ 4. In the statistics of football YAC stands for "yards after catch; but in the animal world a yak is a Tibetan ox.

_____ 5. "Do you know anyone who understands how this G.P.S. works,' asked Allison, "I keep getting lost when I try to use it."

_____ 6. The instructions clearly say we should bring only the following items when we come to take the test: two #2 pencils and one sheet of scratch paper.

_____ 7. "Only one question remains in my mind: how you got so many answers correct when you say you were only guessing," said Max.

_____ 8. "I know we need to turn onto Maple Street which should be coming up soon– whoops, we just passed it. said Ray"

_____ 9. It is strange that we use an apostrophe to show possession with nouns; but there is no apostrophe in the possessives his and its.

_____ 10. "Someone needs to tell me where we are going to dinner?" said Brett, 'If its expensive, I think Ill stay home.'

_____ 11. "Does anyone know where we are going to dinner?" asked Brett. "If it's expensive, I think I'll stay home."

_____ 12. AL is the postal abbreviation for the state of Alabama; and the letters Al are the chemical symbol for the element aluminum.

_____ 13. Mrs Johnson has a very well kept garden it is beautiful, and produces bumper crops of tomatoes green beans and squash.

_____ 14. Somehow the word gift has become a verb, as in the expression, I gifted her my favorite song, but she deleted it almost immediately.

_____ 15. In our ordinary correspondence and writing, we spell out the word "Avenue," but we abbreviate it "Ave." when we use it in an address.

_____ 16. Jane Wilson has just completed work for her PhD in chemistry; and will soon take a job in a research laboratory.

_____ 17. "Can someone tell me if AK is the proper postal abbreviation for Alaska," asked George? Im trying to send a letter to my cousin in Fairbanks.

_____ 18. "'A penny saved is a penny earned' is a proverb often attributed to Benjamin Franklin," said Jason.

_____ 19. "Can you help me," screamed Martha! 'My computer screen just turned that frightening blue color."

_____ 20. "GDP stands for 'gross domestic product; that measure used to be called the GNP or gross national product,'" said the instructor.

215

Directions: The following sentences contain errors in punctuation. Add, delete, or change punctuation wherever an error occurs.

1. Besides Crawford who is certainly qualified to do the job we cant find anyone who possesses both the skill and intelligence needed to finish that project.

2. Theres no reason is there why we couldn't leave my car here and take your's to the out of town convention, so that we can save some money on gas.

3. For that white water rafting trip; Joan invited Barbara whos very experienced Rosa who is an excellent swimmer and a strong paddler, and Kelli who unfortunately has little experience on any rivers, but has a great sense of adventure.

4. For the meeting in the branch office we were expected to bring: a laptop computer, several highlight pens and a loose leaf notebook for inserting handouts from the speakers.

5. A huge muscular dog barking and growling threateningly confronted the two would be burglars as they crept down the alleyway; so they turned and ran away as quickly as they could.

6. Drs Keller and Jameson noted scholars in their own right led the panel discussion, after the experts presentations on the effects of the use of mixed fuel vehicles on the price of corn and soybeans.

7. The little kids were impressed didnt you think by the football players appearance on the program even if they didnt wear their uniforms?

8. I sent you a note regarding your attendance at the upcoming meeting on the changes were considering in the by laws of the organization– ah, I can tell, by the look on your face that youve already read it and probably don't agree with some of the changes, that have been proposed.

9. When do you anticipate or can't you even guess that the part ordered for the air-conditioning system will arrive and your crew can come out and make the much needed repairs so that our students can once again sit comfortably in their classroom's.

10. Its been some time now, since the boys called from the intersection and told us that theyd had some car trouble, you don't suppose do you that something else has gone wrong and theyre delayed even longer.

Review of Punctuation

Directions: The following sentences contain 40 numbered spots between words. The punctuation for each numbered spot is either incorrect or missing. Correct the punctuation by supplying a comma, a semicolon, a question mark, or a period in the space above the number. If no punctuation is needed, write **N** in the spot above the number.

1. Because the weather report calls for snow and ice I think we should
   ₁

   put blankets, a thermos of hot coffee, and tire chains in the car, don't you.
   ₂

2. With the weather report calling for snow and ice we should be prepared
   ₃   ₄

   and put our foul-weather equipment in the car.

3. The men always prepared for emergency conditions, put some special
   ₅

   equipment in the trunk of the car before they left on their trip.
   ₆

4. Dark threatening clouds soon covered the sky and a heavy snow had
   ₇   ₈

   begun to fall long before the men stopped for lunch.

5. Jim Thompson who had lived for several years in Alaska, said "I think at lunch
   ₉   ₁₀

   we should put the chains on the tires to keep the car from sliding on the ice."

6. The men took the advice of Jim Thompson a longtime resident of
   ₁₁

   Alaska and traveled safely to their destination.
   ₁₂

7. The next day the men attended a long boring series of meetings and conferences
   ₁₃   ₁₄

   they actually wished that the bad weather had forced them to stay home.

8. Can you tell me please, where the next conference will be held and
   ₁₅   ₁₆

   whether I will be expected to attend?

9. I plan if the next conference doesn't look more interesting than the last to
   ₁₇   ₁₈

   take a few days of vacation and miss all the excitement.

10. I wish that people who plan workshops and conferences would apply
    ₁₉

    some creativity and imagination to their work and make presentations that
    ₂₀

    are a little bit out of the ordinary.

11. "Stop and wait here," said the police officer, "there is a fallen tree blocking
₂₁
the road and it will take the crew about an hour to clear the way"
₂₂

12. After we had stopped the officer came over to the car to chat with us for
₂₃
a few minutes and said "The crews do their best, but in this weather they
₂₄
can't keep up with their work."

13. "I think" said Roger, "that there is a direct correlation between our need
₂₅
to hurry and the number of obstacles that appear in our way."
₂₆

14. "Well" said Morgan, "there's nothing we can do to speed up that crew so
₂₇   ₂₈
we might as well relax and enjoy ourselves."

15. Because it was not anyone's fault that the tree fell and blocked the road the
₂₉
people in the car simply sat and waited while listening to music on the
₃₀
CD player.

16. Listening to music on the CD player was a pleasant way to pass the time,
and before they grew bored the police officer blew his whistle and waved
₃₁   ₃₂
them on down the road.

17. In rural areas during the winter it is not uncommon for ice storms and high
₃₃   ₃₄
winds to knock trees down and block the roads.

18. In summer time is available for the crews to do some tree-trimming and
₃₅
brush-clearing but the crews never have enough time to take care of all
₃₆
the potential problems.

19. In winter the crews are on call 24 hours a day, and they often work very
₃₇
long hours after a severe storm has passed through the area.
₃₈

20. We are, in fact quite fortunate that there are men and women willing to
₃₉   ₄₀
dedicate themselves to such difficult work.

The following passage contains no internal punctuation and may lack quotation marks where they are needed. Insert punctuation marks where they are needed and be prepared to cite the rule for the use of any mark you insert.

Thomas A. Edison

Thomas Edison was one of the most successful prolific inventors in United States history. Edison born in Milan Ohio in 1847 was slow to learn to talk but once he learned he asked questions constantly about the way things worked. A very curious child his constant barrage of questions caused his first grade teacher to lose patience with him and therefore his mother withdrew him from school and taught him at home. Edison was also partially deaf, probably because of a childhood attack of scarlet fever. When the railroad came to Ohio it by passed Milan and the town went into a depression. Therefore the family moved to Port Huron Michigan. It was there that Edison discovered his talent for business. He wrote a newspaper about local events and sold it on the train that ran from Port Huron to Detroit. He found his first career as the result of a heroic deed. A young boy Jimmie MacKenzie fell in front of a run-away train and Edison leaped onto the track and saved him. Jimmies grateful father J U MacKenzie taught Edison to operate a telegraph machine. The telegraph was a com-munication device that sent messages through the use of Morse Code a system that spelled out words by using dots and dashes. He worked for years for Western Union an early tele-graph company. Edison worked for Western Union in Canada and in Lexington Kentucky. There he worked the night shift so he would have ample time for reading and conducting various experiments. One story from this period says that Edison was fired from that job because he spilled sulphuric acid which leaked through the floor from the second story onto his boss s desk. His interest in the telegraph led him to invent and patent improvements to that device. Later his work took him to Menlo Park New Jersey. His first major invention was a primitive form of the phonograph probably the first device for recording and playing back sound. The general public thought this device worked by some kind of magic, and people began to call him The Wizard of Menlo Park. His long list of inventions also includes the Kinetoscope, an early version of a motion picture projector. He also developed an early version of the X ray machine and made a contribution to the development of the telephone. Early in his life as an inventor and businessman he opened the first research laboratory where he employed scientists and engineers and stocked every item that his work in the lab could possibly use. His major accomplishments however were in the field of electricity. Many people had attempted to construct a workable light bulb but they all gave up when the filament in the bulb burned for only a sort period of time. Edison a very persistent man is said to have tried 3000 kinds of light bulb before he discovered one filament that actually worked. Although this quotation is probably made up, he is quoted as saying We never failed we simply discovered 3000 ways not to make a light bulb. With the development of a commercially workable light bulb Edison was able to move on to the distribution of electricity through wiring systems that carried electric power to homes and businesses. He later founded the company called General Electric. These two inventions the light bulb and the distribution system totally remade business social and personal life. People no longer had to regulate their lives by the onset of daylight and darkness. Reading and working at night became possible. Night shifts in factories became a way of increasing production. Students who are behind in their work at college can do what is called pulling an all nighter thus they wait until the last minute to write papers and study for tests.

Brief Writing Assignment: In a paragraph of seven sentences, discuss the ways in which your life would be different if there were no electrical system to deliver power to your home. State your complete address, and employ three acronyms and one question mark.

Check Sheet

PUNCTUATION

There are 15 rules for the use of commas, two for semicolons, and more for using apostrophes, colons, dashes, hyphens, quotation marks, periods, and question marks, but for practical purposes you should focus on a more limited list of rules.

☐ Commas

1. Use commas to separate the independent clauses of a compound sentence when a coordinating conjunction is present. [Note that a semicolon can replace the comma and coordinating conjunction. This use is the only common use of the semicolon.]

   Maria opened her books, and she began to study.
   Maria opened her books; then she began to study.

2. Use commas to separate items in a series.
   We saw Thomas, Richard, and Harrison at the movie.

3. Use a comma between coordinate adjectives.
   We finally completed that long, difficult project.

4. Use a comma to set off introductory verbal phrases and subordinate clauses.
   Jumping into the chair, the cat curled up and went to sleep.

5. Use a comma to set off two or more prepositional phrases at the beginning of a sentence. Single phrases and, when the subject and verb are reversed, longer phrases at the beginning of a sentence are usually not set off with a comma.

6. Use a comma to prevent misreading. Misreading often occurs if an introductory element is not punctuated correctly, but some short prepositional phrases cause problems in certain contexts.
   Once inside, the dog and cat slept soundly before the fire.

   The comma is essential to maintain the sense of the sentence.

7. Most sentence interrupters, with the exception of restrictive appositives, restrictive participial phrases, and restrictive adjective clauses, are set off by commas.

   Note that with few exceptions, participial phrases are not set off with commas when they are the final element of the sentence.

   Thus we can establish a rule of thumb: Opening elements are set off with one comma, interrupting elements are set off by two, and final elements connect to the sentence without punctuation. Some have called this generalization the rule of one, two, and zero.

8. Set off both the speaker in dialogue and any person addressed in the text.

☐ **End Marks**

    ☐ End marks are fairly simple: Periods end sentences. Question marks end questions.

☐ **Exclamation Points**

    ☐ Exclamation points are used sparingly, and most often in dialogue. It is better to create emphasis through the use of word choice and emphatic sentence structure than through exclamation points.

☐ **Apostrophe**

    ☐ Use apostrophes to create possessives and to indicate contractions. Apostrophes are used for clarity's sake in creating unusual plurals. In other cases, do not use apostrophes to create plurals.

☐ **Dashes, Hyphens, and Quotation Marks**

    ☐ Dashes, hyphens, and quotation marks have special functions, and their use should be checked against the rules in this text.

Usage

Lessons, Practice Sheets, and Exercises

In Lesson 2 you learned that some verbs are regular and others are irregular. Regular verbs add *ed* ending in the past tense (*earn*, *earned*), but irregular verbs change their form (*grow*, *grew*). Since verb forms change to indicate changes in tense and voice, it is necessary to pay close attention to the forms of all verbs. We now review certain places where incorrect forms sometimes appear because of confusion in the use of the principal parts (the base, past tense, and past participle) of verbs. (See Supplement.)

VERB FORMS

To gain assurance in your use of verbs, you must remember how the past tense and the past participle are used. The **past tense** is always a single-word verb; it is never used with an auxiliary:

> I *ate* my lunch. [Not: I *have ate* my lunch.]

The **past participle**, when it is used as a verb, is *never* a single word; it is used with the auxiliary *have* (in the correct tense) to form the perfect tenses or the auxiliary *be* (in the correct tense) to form the passive voice:

> I *have done* the work. [Not: I *done* the work.]
> The work *was done*. [Not: The work *was did*.]

(The past participle is, of course, used as a single word when it is a modifier of a noun: the *broken* toy, the *worried* parents, some *known* criminals.)

Four groups of verbs often cause confusion. Each group contains verbs that have similar trouble spots. The basic solution for the problem in each group is to master the principal parts of the verbs. The principal parts are listed in this lesson in the customary order: base form, past tense, and past participle (P.P.).

Past Tense Versus Past Participle

Sometimes errors occur because the past tense of a verb is confused with the past participle of the verb.

	Verb	Past Tense	P.P.
Later they *became* [not *become*] more friendly.	become	became	become
They *began* [not *begun*] to laugh at us.	begin	began	begun
He had never *broken* [not *broke*] the law.	break	broke	broken
I should have *chosen* [not *chose*] a larger car.	choose	chose	chosen
Yesterday the child *came* [not *come*] home.	come	came	come
I *did* [not *done*] what she told me to do.	do	did	done
He *drank* [not *drunk*] some water.	drink	drank	drunk
I had *driven* [not *drove*] all day.	drive	drove	driven
The lamp had *fallen* [not *fell*] over.	fall	fell	fallen
The bird has *flown* [not *flew*] away.	fly	flew	flown
Small puddles have *frozen* [not *froze*] on the sidewalks.	freeze	froze	frozen
Dad has *given* [not *gave*] me a car.	give	gave	given
Theresa has *gone* [not *went*] to school.	go	went	gone
I've never *ridden* [not *rode*] a horse.	ride	rode	ridden
We ran out when the fire alarm *rang* [not *rung*].	ring	rang	rung
Lenny has *run* [not *ran*] in two marathons.	run	ran	run
I *saw* [not *seen*] your nephew yesterday.	see	saw	seen
It must have *sunk* [not *sank*] in deep water.	sink	sank	sunk
She should have *spoken* [not *spoke*] louder.	speak	spoke	spoken
The car had been *stolen* [not *stole*].	steal	stole	stolen
The witness was *sworn* [not *swore*] in.	swear	swore	sworn
John has *swum* [not *swam*] across the lake.	swim	swam	swum
Someone had *torn* [not *tore*] the dollar bill.	tear	tore	torn
You should have *worn* [not *wore*] a hat.	wear	wore	worn
I have already *written* [not *wrote*] my essay.	write	wrote	written

Regular Versus Irregular

Sometimes errors occur because an irregular verb is thought to be regular.

	Verb	Past Tense	P.P.
The wind *blew* [not *blowed*] steadily all day.	blow	blew	blown
John *brought* [not *bringed*] Mary some flowers.	bring	brought	brought
This house was *built* [not *builded*] in 1795.	build	built	built
Barbara *caught* [not *catched*] two trout.	catch	caught	caught
Slowly they *crept* [not *creeped*] up the stairs.	creep	crept	crept
He *dealt* [not *dealed*] me a good hand.	deal	dealt	dealt
The men quickly *dug* [not *digged*] a pit.	dig	dug	dug
She *drew* [not *drawed*] a caricature of me.	draw	drew	drawn
All the men *grew* [not *growed*] long beards.	grow	grew	grown
Ben *hung* [not *hanged*] his cap on the hook.	hang	hung	hung
I *knew* [not *knowed*] him at college.	know	knew	known
I have never *lent* [not *lended*] him money.	lend	lent	lent
We *sought* [not *seeked*] shelter from the rain.	seek	sought	sought
The sun *shone* [not *shined*] all day yesterday.	shine	shone	shone
The prince *slew* [not *slayed*] the fierce dragon.	slay	slew	slain
I soon *spent* [not *spended*] the money.	spend	spent	spent
Ms. Andrews *taught* [not *teached*] us algebra.	teach	taught	taught
Lou *threw* [not *throwed*] the receipt away.	throw	threw	thrown
The old man *wept* [not *weeped*] piteously.	weep	wept	wept

Obsolete or Dialectal Forms

A third type of error results from the use of an obsolete or dialectal form of the verb, a form not considered standard now:

	Verb	Past Tense	P.P.
I *am* [not *be*] working regularly.	be*	was, were	been*
I *have been* [not *been*] working regularly.			
The child *burst* [not *bursted*] out crying.	burst	burst	burst
I've *bought* [not *boughten*] a car.	buy	bought	bought
I *climbed* [not *clumb*] a tree for a better view.	climb	climbed	climbed
The women *clung* [not *clang*] to the raft.	cling	clung	clung
The dog *dragged* [not *drug*] the old shoe home.	drag	dragged	dragged
The boy was nearly *drowned* [not *drownded*].	drown	drowned	drowned
At the picnic I *ate* [not *et*] too many hot dogs.	eat	ate	eaten
Betty *flung* [not *flang*] the stick away.	fling	flung	flung
You *paid* [not *payed*] too much for it.	pay	paid	paid
It had been *shaken* [not *shooken*] to pieces.	shake	shook	shaken
He had never *skinned* [not *skun*] an animal.	skin	skinned	skinned
A bee *stung* [not *stang*] me as I stood there.	sting	stung	stung
The girl *swung* [not *swang*] at the ball.	swing	swung	swung
I wonder who could have *taken* [not *tooken*] it.	take	took	taken

Confusing Verb Forms

A fourth type of verb error results from a confusion of forms of certain verbs that look or sound almost alike but are actually quite different in meaning, such as *lie, lay; sit, set;* and *rise, raise.* Note that three of these troublesome verbs—*lay, set,* and *raise*—in their ordinary uses take an object. The other three—*lie, sit, rise*—do not take an object.

	Verb	Past Tense	P.P.
Please *lay* your books [D.O.] on the table.	lay	laid	laid
Mary *laid* several logs [D.O.] on the fire.			
The men have *laid* some boards [D.O.] over the puddle.			
Our cat often *lies* [not *lays*] on the couch.	lie	lay	lain
Yesterday our cat *lay* [not *laid*] on the couch.			
Our cat has *lain* [not *laid*] on the couch all morning.			
She *sets* the plate [D.O.] in front of me.	set	set	set
An hour ago Tom *set* out some food [D.O.] for the birds.			
I had *set* the camera [D.O.] at a full second.			
I usually *sit* in that chair.	sit	sat	sat
Yesterday he *sat* in my chair.			
I have *sat* at my desk all morning.			

*As you learned in Lesson 2, the irregular verb *be* has three forms (*am, are, is*) in the present tense and two forms (*was, were*) in the past tense.

At her command they *raise* the flag [D.O.].	raise	raised	raised

The boy quickly *raised* his hand [D.O.].
He had *raised* the price [D.O.] of his old car.

He *rises* when we enter the room.	rise	rose	risen

Everyone *rose* as the speaker entered the room.
The water has *risen* a foot since midnight.

Exceptions

The rules and illustrations given here are an adequate guide in most situations. They show the importance of knowing the principal parts of these verbs. Note, however, that there are a few exceptions, such as the intransitive uses of *set*:

A *setting* [not *sitting*] hen *sets*. [Of course, a hen, like a rooster, may be said to *sit* when that is what is meant.]

The sun *sets* in the west.

Cement or dye *sets*.

A jacket *sets* (*fits*) well.

With a few verbs, special meanings demand different principal parts. For example, the past tense and the past participle of *shine*, when the verb is used as a transitive verb, are *shined*:

This morning I *shined* [not *shone*] my shoes.

The verb *hang* with the meaning "to execute by suspending by the neck until dead" uses *hanged*, not *hung*, for the past tense and the past participle. When in doubt, always refer to your dictionary.

SEQUENCE OF TENSES

In Lesson 2 you studied a partial conjugation showing the forms of three sample verbs as they occur in six tenses. In Lesson 5 you were told the basic uses of the six tenses. Although most student writers usually have little difficulty in establishing and maintaining logical time relationships in their sentences, a few situations sometimes cause confusion.

Subordinate Clauses

The tense in a subordinate clause is normally the same as that in the main clause unless a different time for the subordinate statement is clearly indicated.

We think that Mary studies hard all the time.

We think that Mary studied hard for the last test.

We think that Mary will study hard for the next test.

We think that Mary has studied hard for all her tests.

We think that Mary had studied hard before last week's test.

We thought that Mary studied hard all the time.

We thought that Mary studied hard in the past.
We thought that Mary would study hard for the next test.
We thought that Mary has studied hard all year.
We thought that Mary had studied hard last semester.

Universally True Statements

The present tense is used for a statement that is universally true.

The dietitian reminded us that whipped cream *is* (not *was*) fattening.
I wonder who first discovered that oysters *are* (not *were*) edible.

Shifting Tenses

In narrative writing a shift from past tense to present tense or from present to past should be avoided.

The library *was* silent except for an occasional whisper, when suddenly a side door *opened* [not *opens*] and a disheveled young man *dashed* [not *dashes*] in and *started* [not *starts*] yelling, "Man the lifeboats!" After the librarians *had managed* to restore order . . .

Present Perfect Tense

The perfect form of an infinitive should not be used when the controlling verb is in the present perfect tense with a modal auxiliary.

Correct: I would have liked to see that performance.
Incorrect: I would have liked to have seen that performance.

In the indicative mood, there is rarely any confusion over the correct form of the infinitive.

Correct: I have wanted to run that marathon for years.

SUPPLEMENT

When a sentence makes a statement or asks a question, the verb is said to be in the **indicative mood** or **mode** (see Lesson 2). Two other moods indicate a different purpose in the sentence.

Imperative Mood

When a sentence gives a direction or command, the verb is in the **imperative mood.** The imperative of all regular verbs simply uses the base form of the verb without a subject.

Please *give* me the ball.
Take out your pen and paper.

Even the verb *to be*, irregular in most formations, uses the base to form the imperative.

Be careful; the steps are slippery.

Please *be* on time; the bus will depart promptly.

Subjunctive Mood

The present subjunctive uses the base form of the verb, regardless of the subject.

The catalog recommends that she *study* accounting in the first semester.

The past subjunctive takes the same form as the past tense of the verb. (The auxiliary *be* is always *were* regardless of the number or person of the subject.)

I wish I *were* at home today.

The past perfect subjunctive has the same form as the past perfect.

I wish I *had gone* home earlier.

We also use the subjunctive in these special ways:

1. In clauses beginning with *that* when they follow words such as *ask*, *suggest*, *require*, *recommend*, and *demand*.

   The policy requires that we *submit* our requests in writing.
   The manager insisted that we *be* present for the ceremony.

2. In clauses beginning with *if* when the clause makes a statement that is clearly and unmistakably contrary to fact.

   If I *were* able to sing, I would try out for the Met.
   If he were young again, he would live life differently.

English Fundamentals Online

After you have completed Practice Sheets and Exercises in this lesson, you can find additional help and drill work at **MyWritingLab.com**, in the sections on Tense; Consistent Verb Tense and Active Voice; Regular and Irregular Verbs.

NAME _____ SCORE _____

Directions: In the space at the left, write the correct form of the verb shown in the parentheses. Do not use any -*ing* forms.

_____ 1. Marian had (set) her books on the table late last night, but this
_____   morning they (be) nowhere to be found.
_____ 2. Last night the dog (lie) in front of the fire for an hour, and then he
_____   (wake) me up very early this morning to go outside.
_____ 3. I have never (take) a course as hard as this one; I (spend) three
_____   hours at my computer doing research yesterday.
_____ 4. Because of the cold weather, the bat (sting) Nora's hands when
_____   she (swing) the bat and hit the ball.
_____ 5. During the late afternoon we had all (become) quite tired, so,
_____   instead of walking, we (ride) back from the lake in Joe's truck.
_____ 6. The class has already (write) three long papers this term, and
_____   today the professor (say) that there would be two more before the
_____   end of the term.
_____ 7. The wind (blow) steadily at ten knots yesterday, so we (have)
_____   a very fine day for sailing.
_____ 8. The heavy rains of the last few days have nearly (drown) my
_____   vegetable garden, so I have (begin) to replant already.
_____ 9. My father should have (wear) his heavy jacket this morning; the
_____   temperature has not (climb) above freezing all day long.
_____ 10. The little boy (tear) open his birthday present, took one look at it,
_____   and (fling) it across the room.
_____ 11. If I had (buy) that stock three months earlier, I would have (make)
_____   a larger profit on it when I sold it.
_____ 12. The lawyer should have (lay) a better foundation before he (show)
_____   that piece of evidence to the jury.
_____ 13. As the storm (build), we (seek) shelter inside an abandoned cabin
_____   at the bottom of the hill.
_____ 14. Although Jackson had (hang) his jacket beside the front door,
_____   someone (find) it there and took it by mistake.
_____ 15. I (know) Harry well when we were in high school, but I haven't
_____   (see) him for almost three years.
_____ 16. After I (shine) my shoes with that special polish, they (shine)
_____   brightly in the sunlight.
_____ 17. The water balloon (burst) when it hit the sidewalk, and several
_____   people (draw) near to look at the mess.
_____ 18. "My alarm clock is (break)," said the embarrassed student as he
_____   (drag) himself into class late.

_____ 19. The water in the pond has (freeze) almost solid, but I (sink) to my
_____ knees when I stepped of the edge.
_____ 20. I was glad that I had not (throw) away that receipt; without it, I could
_____ not have (deal) with the store about replacing the broken stereo.
_____ 21. Before we had (eat) our salad, we had already (speak) about every
_____ friend we had in common, and the conversation died.
_____ 22. Wilma has (fly) home for the week to visit with her family; if she
_____ had (drive), she could have saved some money.
_____ 23. Have you (run) across John Small lately? I haven't (speak) to
_____ him in several weeks.
_____ 24. The alarm clock (ring) very early this morning, but I turned it off
_____ and (go) back to sleep.
_____ 25. Everyone (rise) when the military unit (raise) the flag and played
_____ the national anthem.
_____ 26. Josh wished that he (be) at home on his couch watching TV;
_____ instead, he (pay) for his speeding ticket by picking up trash.
_____ 27. Adam's older brother (lend) him the money to fix his car, but so
_____ far Adam has not (repay) any of the money to his brother.
_____ 28. The movie hero (cling) to the edge of the balcony as he (hang)
_____ there ten stories above the street.
_____ 29. Barry has (lie) there on the couch for two hours; in that time the
_____ rest of us have already(set) out two rows of tomato plants.
_____ 30. The knight should have (slay) that dragon when he was (give) the
_____ chance because now the thing is killing all the innocent people in
_____ its path.
_____ 31. The young boy (catch) his toe on that crack in the sidewalk and
_____ (fall) headlong to the ground.
_____ 32. I should have (choose) a more familiar topic for my term paper;
_____ instead I (choose) something so obscure there is little information
_____ available.
_____ 33. "I could not have (swim) another foot," said Linda; "we had (be)
_____ in the water for almost an hour when we stopped."
_____ 34. The dogs have (dig) up my grandmother's rose bush, so I have
_____ (bring) in a new one to replace it.
_____ 35. The wealthy man (give) a few dollars to that charity, but he could
_____ have (give) much more without any problem.
_____ 36. "I could not have (do) any more work on that paper than I (do)
_____ because I simply ran out of time to work on it," said Alan.
_____ 37. The two little boys (creep) silently down the stairs and (spend) the
_____ next two hours playing video games.
_____ 38. No one has (come) forward with any new evidence, so the police
_____ have been unable to find the people who (steal) that money.
_____ 39. If you had (bring) that work over to my house earlier, I could have
_____ (teach) you how to solve those problems.
_____ 40. The boys should have thought to (close) that door when they
_____ (leave) the house because the cat got out the door and ran away.

Directions: Each sentence contains two italicized words. If the principal part or tense of the verb is the correct one for formal writing, write **C** in the corresponding space at the left. If the verb form is incorrect, write the correct form in the space.

_____ 1. "I really feel that I've *grown* up since I *come* to college,"
_____ said Brett.

_____ 2. "I *been* living here for thirty years, and I never *seen* a sunset
_____ like that one," said the old-timer.

_____ 3. I wish you would *lay* aside your garden tools and *lie* down for
_____ a short rest.

_____ 4. "If I had *known* that you were to be out of town, I would have
_____ *chose* another time for my party," said Elizabeth.

_____ 5. It would have been wiser for you *to have admitted* that you had
_____ *taken* the car without the owner's permission.

_____ 6. Two of the young campers decided to sleep outside, but eventually
_____ they *become* cold and *crept* back into the main tent.

_____ 7. "Twice I have *written* to the landlord notifying him that the
_____ dishwasher is *broke*," she complained.

_____ 8. The astronaut *begun* his lecture by reminding the audience that
_____ the moon *was* approximately 250,000 miles from the earth.

_____ 9. A fresh breeze had *blowed* away the morning fog, and the sun had
_____ *climbed* up over the hills to our east.

_____ 10. As I was *laying* in the hammock for a short rest, a stray cat *come*
_____ up to and demanded to be petted.

_____ 11. The golf ball *rose* in the air almost vertically, it seemed, and then
_____ *sank* into a clump of poison ivy.

_____ 12. Benny stomped into the kitchen, *lay* his brief case on the table,
_____ and *announces*, "I'm tired, I'm hungry, and I want a cup of coffee."

_____ 13. "You've *took* the wrong seat," Janine said to the new boy. "I *been*
_____ *setting* in that seat all semester."

_____ 14. "I could have *swore* that the man I just *seen* leaving the bank is
_____ a college friend of mine," said Paul.

_____ 15. Outside the restaurant a friend stopped Andrew and *says*, "Now
_____ that you've *eaten*, would you like to go to a movie?"

_____ 16. "This fancy ski outfit is nearly *wore* out," said Eunice, "and it
_____ isn't completely *payed* for yet.

_____ 17. If the boss doesn't *raise* our salaries soon, some of us are going to
_____ *rise* up in rebellion.

_____ 18. "I admit that I *been* a little careless with my money," he admitted,
_____ "but I have never *stoled* anything."

_____ 19. Mrs. Little *set* aside her needlepoint and asked her visitor to *sit*
_____ beside her.

_____ 20. "That old wood you *threw* away last week is still *lying* in the
_____ alley," complained Stew's neighbor.

_____ 21. I *had* already *ridden* five miles from home when I discovered that
_____ the rear tire on my bike had *sprang* a leak.
_____ 22. The worker had *lain* a sheet of plywood across the ditch, but it did
_____ not *set* straight and eventually fell into the bottom of the ditch.
_____ 23. I had wanted *to have seen* that movie before it *leaved* town, but
_____ I was just too busy to fit it into my schedule.
_____ 24. The student in the back of room *rised* from his seat and *creeped*
_____ quietly out the back door.
_____ 25. Please *being* careful on that last problem; in the earlier classes,
_____ several people *had found* it a little tricky.
_____ 26. I wish that I *was* already finished with this paper because then
_____ I could have *went* with Joan and Charlie to that concert.
_____ 27. "If I *was* only six inches taller," said Carl, I would have been able
_____ to *have tried out* for the basketball team.
_____ 28. The boss required that every employee *be* present for one of these
_____ meetings, unless, of course, he or she *is* on assignment out of town.
_____ 29. Her advisor recommends that Barbara *takes* another math course
_____ before she *register* for statistics.
_____ 30. I thought that Martie *studies* several hours every day, but
_____ yesterday I *find* out that she rarely ever cracks a book.
_____ 31. We all believed that Will *has* already left town for the weekend,
_____ but then he *shows* up for lunch in the dining hall.
_____ 32. The room was very quiet, but suddenly the fire alarm *rings* and
_____ *forced* us all to walk out of the building.
_____ 33. If only all of us *have* known that the test had been rescheduled,
_____ we would have been able *to have gone* to that basketball game last
_____ night.
_____ 34. At this time of year, the sun *sits* over that corner of the house and
_____ then darkness *falls* almost immediately.
_____ 35. Yesterday, the sailors *shone* that brass until it *glows* brightly in the
_____ sunlight.
_____ 36. The boy *hanged* his jacket on the hook in the hallway, and then
_____ *set* down on the couch to watch the sports news on television.
_____ 37. Before the concrete in the new walkway had *sat*, the men *scratch*
_____ their initials and a date at the edge of the concrete.
_____ 38. I have *risen* the price on that car twice, but still no one has
_____ *showned* any interest in buying it.
_____ 39. Have you *gave* any thought to wearing a jacket this morning
_____ because the temperature *had dropped* below freezing last night?
_____ 40. Those dynamite blasts at the nearby quarry have *shooken* several
_____ glasses off the shelf and onto the floor, where they have literally
_____ *blowed* into hundreds of little pieces.

Using Verbs Correctly: Principal Parts; Tense

NAME _____ SCORE _____

Directions: In the space at the left, write the correct form of the verb shown with parentheses. Do not use any *-ing* forms.

_____
_____
1. Yesterday afternoon, two suspicious-looking men had been (see) loitering near the shop that was (break) into last night.

_____
_____
2. At the homecoming dance, Annabelle (wear) a dress that I would not have (choose) for such an occasion.

_____
_____
3. Our visiting lecturer (lay) great stress on the fact that responsibility for government (lie) ultimately with the voters.

_____
_____
4. Shortly after the prime minister had (go) to bed, someone (throw) a brick through her bedroom window.

_____
_____
5. The young people eagerly (drink) the hot coffee because, after their descent from the mountain, they were nearly (freeze).

_____
_____
6. The sun has (shine) every day this week; winter has nearly (run) its course.

_____
_____
7. By the time she was twenty-five, Lenore had (climb) Denali and had (fly) over the South Pole.

_____
_____
8. You certainly (do) a wise thing when you demanded that the new contract be (write) by your lawyer.

_____
_____
9. Henry (grow) suspicious when he learned that his partner had (become) involved in shady stock speculations.

_____
_____
10. The old man took off his glasses, (lay) his magazine on the table, and (lie) down on the couch.

_____
_____
11. I have (eat) at this restaurant many times, but never before have I (pay) such a low price for such a good meal.

_____
_____
12. At the town meeting one farmer (rise) from his chair and complained that the price of cattle feed had (rise) again.

_____
_____
13. Not a word was (speak) as the children picked up the shattered vase that had (fall) to the floor.

_____
_____
14. After winning the third set, the champion (lay) his tennis racket aside and (blow) on his hands to warm them.

_____
_____
15. Later this year Dennis, having (spend) most of his inheritance, (begin) to think about getting a job.

_____
_____
16. Before long, it was widely (know) in Centerville that Judge Wills was the anonymous donor who had (give) the money to the hospital.

_____
_____
17. At the crack of the bat, our shortstop dashed to his left, (catch) the bouncing ball, and (throw) out the runner at first base.

_____
_____
18. The helpful man then (draw) a map of our route on the sheet of paper that Nora had (tear) from her notebook.

_____
_____
19. "Uncle Will has (lend) me the money for the last three cars that I have (buy)," said Ned.

_____
_____
20. Agatha's great-grandfather had (come) to Sharpton in 1892 and for a time lived in a sod hut that he (build) by himself.

234 • *Exercise 21: Using Verbs Correctly: Principal Parts; Tense*

Directions: Each sentence has two italicized verb units. If the principal parts or tense of the verb is the form proper in serious writing, write **C** in the corresponding space at the left. If the verb is incorrect, write the correct form in the space.

_____ 1. The sun has *shone* every day for a week, but Cranston Creek
_____   is still *froze* solid.
_____ 2. The spy got out of the car, silently *crept* under the fence, and *lay*
_____   the package on the driveway.
_____ 3. Hearing the strange noise, Dad *run* to the front window to see
_____   who had *driven* onto our driveway.
_____ 4. "You'll stay in your highchair until you've *ate* your cereal and
_____   *drank* your hot chocolate," Mother told her youngest child.
_____ 5. "It would have been fun to *have gone* to the movie with you
_____   guys," said Bobby Jo, "but I *seen* the show last week in Atlanta."
_____ 6. To this day, Jason has never *flown* in an airplane; on every trip he
_____   has *ridden* in either a bus or a train.
_____ 7. "Many ships have *sank* off this cape," said Captain Adams, "and
_____   many good sailors have *drownded.*"
_____ 8. Larry *set* outside on the porch and waited while Ben *shined* his
_____   boots.
_____ 9. "I never did like that blouse," said Trina, "and so I *threw* it away
_____   after I'd *wore* it only twice."
_____ 10. Later the janitor found the receipt *laying* on the floor, where it had
_____   apparently *fallen* from the secretary's desk.
_____ 11. Ellen's father *done* a good job of repairing the three *broken*
_____   appliances.
_____ 12. "You *been* a bad dog, Bowser," said Jan to her pet. "You've
_____   chewed on your blanket until it's nearly *tore* in two."
_____ 13. By the time we had *went* ten miles, we realized that the
_____   convenience store clerk had *given* us inaccurate directions.
_____ 14. "I admit," said Harwood, "that these reports were hastily *wrote*
_____   and that I should have *spent* more time on them."
_____ 15. Ben had found a smooth section of the beach and had just *set*
_____   down on his blanket when a nearby child looked at him and *says,*
_____   "Hi there, Gramps."
_____ 16. The children *burst* out laughing when they looked at the pictures
_____   that the baby-sitter had *drew* on the paper napkins.
_____ 17. "The church bells for early service have already *rang* and you are
_____   still *lying* in bed," said Mrs. Stewart.
_____ 18. "Truer words were never *spoke,*" said the editor to himself as he
_____   *begun* to write another editorial.
_____ 19. You surely should have *knew* that Rhode Island *was* the smallest
_____   of the states.
_____ 20. As the lifeguard rowed toward him, the exhausted man *swam* to
_____   the raft and desperately *clung* to it.

Brief Writing Assignment: Write a paragraph of five sentences describing the making of a roast beef sandwich. Write the paragraph in the first person (I); use only present tense verbs in the sentences.

Examine the following conjugation. Note that in the present tense, the third-person singular (*he, she, it*) verb form differs from the third-person plural (*they*) verb form.

I earn	We earn
You earn	You earn
He, She, It *earns*	They *earn*

We refer to this change as a change in number. As noted in Lesson 2, **singular number** refers to only one thing; **plural number** refers to more than one thing. Notice how verbs and nouns differ in this respect: The *s* ending on nouns is a plural marker, but on verbs it designates the singular form.

The following examples show how the number of the subject (one or more than one) affects the form of the verb. (See Supplement.) The verbs *have, do,* and *be* are important because they have auxiliary uses as well as main-verb uses. *Be* is an exceptional verb; it changes form in the past tense as well as in the present tense.

Singular	*Plural*
She *walks* slowly.	They *walk* slowly.
Mother *seems* pleased.	My parents *seem* pleased.
Mary *has* a new dress.	All of the girls *have* new dresses.
He *has traveled* widely.	They *have traveled* widely.
She *does* her work easily.	They *do* their work easily.
Does he *have* enough time?	*Do* they *have* enough time?
He *is* a friend of mine.	They *are* friends of mine.
My brother *is coming* home.	My brothers *are coming* home.
His camera *was taken* from him.	Their cameras *were taken* from them.

VERB AGREES IN NUMBER

The relation of verb form to subject follows an important principle of usage: The verb always agrees in number with its subject. Although the principle is simple, some of the situations in which it applies are not. You will avoid some common writing errors if you keep in mind the following seven extensions of the principle. The first is probably the most important.

1. The number of the verb is not affected by material that comes between the verb and the subject.

> Immediate *settlement* of these problems *is* [not *are*] vital. [The subject is *settlement*. Problems, being here the object of the preposition *of*, cannot be a subject.]
>
> The *cost* of replacing the asbestos shingles with cedar shakes *was* [not *were*] considerable.
>
> *Tact*, as well as patience, *is* [not *are*] required.

Mr. Sheldon, together with several other division heads, *has* [not *have*] left.

Each of the plans *has* [not *have*] its good points.
Is [not *Are*] *either* of the contestants ready?

Determine the *real* subject of the verb; watch out for intervening words that might mislead you. The number of the verb is not altered when other nouns are attached to the subject by means of prepositions such as *in addition to, together with, as well as, with,* and *along with.* Remember that indefinite pronoun subjects like *either, neither, each, one, everyone, no one,* and *somebody* take singular verbs. *None* may take either a singular or a plural verb, depending on whether the writer wishes to emphasize "not one" or "no members" of the group.

None of us *is* [or *are*] perfect.

2. A verb agrees with its subject even when the subject follows the verb.

On the wall *hangs* a *portrait* of his father. [*portrait hangs*]
On the wall *hang portraits* of his parents. [*portraits hang*]
He handed us a piece of paper on which *was scribbled* a *warning.* [*warning was scribbled*]
There *was* barely enough *time* remaining.
There *were* only ten *minutes* remaining.
There *seems* to be one *problem* remaining.
There *seem* to be a few *problems* remaining.
Here *is* a free *ticket* to the game.
Here *are* some free *tickets* to the game.

Be especially careful to find the real subject in sentences starting with there or here.

3. Compound subjects joined by *and* take a plural verb.

A little *boy* and his *dog were* playing in the yard.
On the platform *were* a *table* and four *chairs.*

But the verb should be singular if the subjects joined by *and* are thought of as a single thing, or if the subjects are considered separately, as when they are modified by *every* or *each*:

Plain *vinegar* and *oil is* all the dressing my salad needs. [one thing]
Every *man* and every *woman is* asked to help. [considered separately]

4. Singular subjects joined by *or* or *nor* take singular verbs.

Either a *check* or a money *order is* required.
Neither the *manager* nor his *assistant has* arrived yet.
Was Mr. Phelps or his *son* put on the committee?

In some sentences of this pattern, especially in questions like the last example, a plural verb is sometimes used, both in casual conversation and in writing. In serious and formal writing, the singular verb is considered appropriate. If the subjects joined by *or* or *nor* differ in number, the verb agrees with the subject nearer to it:

Neither the *mother* nor the two *boys were* able to identify him.
Either the *players* or the *coach is* responsible for the defeat.

5. Plural nouns of amount, distance, and so on, when they are used as singular units of measurement, take singular verbs.

> A hundred *dollars was* once paid for a single tulip bulb.
> Thirty *miles seems* like a long walk to me.
> Seven *years* in prison *was* the penalty that he had to pay.

6. A collective noun is considered singular when the group is regarded as a unit; it is plural when the individuals of the group are referred to.

> The *audience is* very enthusiastic tonight.
> The *audience are* returning to their seats. [Notice pronoun *their.*]
> The *band is* playing a rousing march.
> Now the *band are* putting away their instruments. [Again note *their.*]
> *Most* of the book *is* blatant propaganda.
> *Most* of her novels *are* now out of print.
> The *rest* of the fortune *was* soon gone.
> The *rest* of his debts *were* left unpaid.
> The *number* of bank failures *is* increasing.
> A *number* of these bank failures *are* being investigated.

Words like *number, all, rest, part, some, more, most, half* are singular or plural, depending on the meaning intended. A word of this type is often accompanied by a modifier or referred to by a pronoun, either of which gives a clue to the number intended. When the word *number* is a subject, it is considered singular if it is preceded by *the* and plural if it is preceded by *a.*

7. When the subject is a relative pronoun, the antecedent of the pronoun determines the number (and person) of the verb. (See Lesson 23, page 243.)

> He told a joke *that was* pointless. [*joke was*]
> He told several jokes *that were* pointless. [*jokes were*]
> I paid the expenses of the trip, *which were* minimal. [*expenses were*]
> Jack is one of those boys *who enjoy* fierce competition. [*boys enjoy*]

The last example, sometimes called the "one of those . . . who" sentence, is particularly troublesome. Often a singular verb is used. If we recast the sentence to read "Of those boys who enjoy fierce competition, Jack is one," however, it becomes clear that the logical antecedent of *who* is the plural noun *boys*. However, usage is divided. And notice that a singular verb must be used when the pattern is altered slightly:

> Jack is the only *one* of my friends *who enjoys* fierce competition.

Because a relative pronoun subject nearly always has an antecedent that is third-person singular or third-person plural, we are accustomed to pronoun-verb combinations like these:

> A boy *who is* . . .
> Boys *who are* . . .
> A woman *who knows* . . .
> Women *who know* . . .

But in those occasional sentences in which a relative pronoun subject has an antecedent that is in the first or second person, meticulously correct usage calls for subject-verb combinations like the following:

> I, *who am* in charge here, should pay the bill. [*I* . . . *am*]
> They should ask me, *who know* all the answers. [*I* . . . *know*]
> You, *who are* in charge here, should pay the bill. [*You* . . . *are*]
> They should ask you, *who know* all the answers. [*you* . . . *know*]

SUPPLEMENT

One particular error of subject-verb agreement warrants special attention. The third-person singular present tense form of the verb *do* is *does*. The plural form is *do*. The misuse of the negative contraction *don't* (instead of *doesn't*) with a third-person singular subject is quite often encountered in spoken English. Many people, justly or unjustly, look on the it-don't misuse as an important marker of grossly substandard English. Such forms as the following should be avoided in all spoken and written English:

Faulty:	My father *don't* like broccoli.
Faulty:	It really *don't* matter.
Faulty:	Jack Johnson *don't* live here now.
Faulty:	One of her teachers *don't* like her.
Faulty:	This fudge tastes good, *don't* it?
Faulty:	The fact that the bill is overdue *don't* bother him.

SUMMARY OF CORRECT VERB USE

1. The principal parts of a verb are the present, the past, and the past participle. Avoid confusing the principal parts of irregular verbs (*run, ran, run*; *eat, ate, eaten*; *fly, flew, flown*) with those of regular verbs (*study, studied, studied*). Be especially careful with the often confused principal parts of *lie* and *lay*, *sit* and *set*.

2. Singular verbs are used with singular subjects; plural verbs are used with plural subects.
   a. Nouns intervening between the subject and the verb do not determine the number of the verb. (Resistance to the actions of these government agencies *is* [not *are*] growing.)
   b. Singular subjects joined by *and* normally take plural verbs. Singular subjects joined by *or* or *nor* normally take singular verbs.
   c. Some nouns and pronouns (collective nouns, and words like *number, all, half*, etc.) are singular in some meanings, plural in others.

English Fundamentals Online

After you have completed Practice Sheets and Exercises in this lesson, you can find additional help and drill work at **MyWritingLab.com**, in the section on Subject-Verb Agreement.

Using Verbs Correctly: Subject-Verb Agreement

NAME _____ SCORE _____

Directions: These sentences are examples of structures that lead to subject-verb agreement. In the space at the left, copy the word in parentheses that is correct.

_____ 1. The rest of the cars in the parking lot (needs, need) to be moved before the workers arrive.

_____ 2. The number of people attending the conference (is, are) far greater than we had anticipated.

_____ 3. The staff (seems, seem) pleased with their end of the year bonuses.

_____ 4. There (was, were) several loud thunder claps just before the rain began.

_____ 5. There (seems, seem) to be a problem with the figures in that last column.

_____ 6. The figures in that last column (does, do) not balance with those in the first column.

_____ 7. On the wall of my bedroom (hangs, hang) pictures of my boyhood sports heros.

_____ 8. Eggs and pancakes with syrup (is, are) my favorite breakfast.

_____ 9. In addition to the rest of us, three more juniors and two more sophomores (has, have) joined in our efforts to clean up the river bank.

_____ 10. Neither my sister nor my two brothers ever (comes, come) to watch me play baseball.

_____ 11. A crowd of 750 spectators easily (fills, fill) that tiny gym for basketball games.

_____ 12. Either a cash deposit or a cashier's check (is, are) required as a deposit for such a large order.

_____ 13. There are several people in the crowd who (is, are) here for the first time.

_____ 14. Half of the books on that reading list (is, are) totally unfamiliar to me.

_____ 15. Most of the information in that book (repeats, repeat) what we have heard from our instructor.

_____ 16. A vast majority of the voters in this county (doesn't, don't) want a change in that zoning ordinance.

_____ 17. Over half of the voters in this county (does, do) not want a change in that zoning ordinance.

_____ 18. Almost half of the neighborhood (was, were) blacked out by the power failure last night.

_____ 19. I have seen three movies this month that (was, were) extremely frightening.

_____ 20. In the back of the garage (sits, sit) my two motorcycles, neither of them in good condition.

239

Directions: If you find an error in subject-verb agreement, write the correct form of the verb in the space at the left. Some of the sentences are correct.

_____ 1. My friend Art is one of those people who continue to play tennis even though his game has fallen off over the years.

_____ 2. Art is the only one of my friends who still play tennis on a regular basis.

_____ 3. Naomi Watters, along with several of her friends, are planning the celebration for the homecoming bonfire.

_____ 4. Are either of the reports from the subcommittees ready for presentation?

_____ 5. Half of each of the reports has been completed.

_____ 6. All the men and women in the office has been asked to participate in that public opinion poll.

_____ 7. Every man and woman in the office has been asked to participate in that public opinion poll.

_____ 8. There was only a few short minutes remaining in the day when Alexis finally finished her long, boring report.

_____ 9. Down at the end of Main Street stands an old restaurant and an old hotel, both of closed.

_____ 10. The young mothers, each with a child in tow, lines up early to get a picture taken with Santa Claus.

_____ 11. Chocolate cake and vanilla ice cream are tonight's dessert.

_____ 12. Either Jane or her two brothers have taken charge of that part of the planning for the campaign.

_____ 13. For Wendy and her friends, five miles of running was a very easy task.

_____ 14. Wendy, along with her friends, think that five miles is just the beginning of a good run.

_____ 15. The rest of us enjoys a good nap more than a long run.

_____ 16. "For that assignment," said Walt, "I want a book that have large print, small pages, and lots of pictures."

_____ 17. "Books that has those qualities probably don't qualify for college assignments," said Cathy.

_____ 18. Al, Barbara, and one of the Thompson twins—I can't tell them apart—is joining us for supper tonight.

_____ 19. Neither Johnny nor his two brothers was able to straighten out the mess I made of my computer.

_____ 20. The expenses for the trip, which were very low, were paid by our sponsors.

Using Verbs Correctly: Subject-Verb Agreement

NAME _____ SCORE _____

Directions: If you find an error in subject-verb agreement, write the correct form of the verb in the space at the left. Circle the subject of each verb you correct. Some of the sentences are correct.

_____ 1. The answer to the question asked by one of the members of the audience were quite long and complicated.

_____ 2. The taxes on the car Kenny bought recently were quite a large sum.

_____ 3. Mark Johnson, along with several members of his staff, have arrived for the afternoon meeting.

_____ 4. Each of the proposed solutions comes with two or three problems.

_____ 5. Are neither of those proposed solutions simple and easy to execute?

_____ 6. None of the contributions pledged during the last fund-raising drive for the new field house has actually been sent in to our treasurer.

_____ 7. In the middle of the politician's speech an angry young man rises to his feet to shout a question.

_____ 8. Then in the middle of the politician's speech there arise a loud series of catcalls from a member of the audience.

_____ 9. The set of instructions that were found with my new DVR could only be understood by an engineer.

_____ 10. Even my friends who are engineering students find such directions difficult understand.

_____ 11. None of my friends, even those who are engineering students, is able to follow such instructions.

_____ 12. All of the books stacked there on the table needs to be returned to the library because they are overdue.

_____ 13. All of the food on that table at the back of the room need to be packaged up and placed in the freezer.

_____ 14. The football team turn in their equipment at the end of the season.

_____ 15. At halftime the band faces the home crowd in the south stands and plays the school's Alma Mater.

_____ 16. In the backyard of the house next door a young boy and his dog are playing with a Frisbee.

_____ 17. Every man and every woman in the audience were asked to make a small contribution to the volunteer fire department.

_____ 18. Either that book or those two magazines has information about the invention of the microwave oven.

_____ 19. Is Phil Johnson and his brother coming to the meeting to hear the presentation on the changes in the fishing regulations?

_____ 20. When do Arthur and his two brothers plan to submit their plans for the new auditorium for our consideration?

_____ 21. The people whose vehicle is in the driveway needs to contact the front desk of the hotel immediately.

_____ 22. The people whose vehicles are in the driveway need to contact the front desk of the hotel immediately.

_____ 23. The driver of that vehicle is one of those people who seems to delight in causing trouble.

_____ 24. There is, in front of the building, a large group of people waiting for the fire drill to end.

_____ 25. The man to whom my mother and two brothers sends the reports is located in New York City.

_____ 26. Most of the people who are assembled in that audience is devoted fans of Allison Krauss and Union Station.

_____ 27. A vast majority of those assembled in the audience are devoted to the music of Allison Krauss and Union Station.

_____ 28. After page 50, the rest of the paper seem to be made up of long quotations that the author uses without giving any credit to the original authors.

_____ 29. Norma is the only one of my friends who fully understand the rules for documenting the use of outside sources in papers.

_____ 30. Neither my brothers nor my father genuinely enjoy fried eggplant.

_____ 31. Both my father and my brothers, however, eat fried eggplant whenever my mother cooks it.

_____ 32. My father and brothers says that they don't enjoy fried eggplant, but they doesn't want to hurt my mother's feelings.

_____ 33. I, who am always a spectator at this dinnertime comedy show, enjoy the whole charade immensely.

_____ 34. My grandfather, who, along with two of my aunts, often join us for dinner, loves the taste of fried eggplant.

_____ 35. Beside fried eggplant, there is almost no food that my father and brothers doesn't enjoy.

_____ 36. My two uncles and my cousin, during long, cold winters, often goes ice fishing out on the lake.

_____ 37. Do you and he always attend the school's football games together?

_____ 38. Neither Tom nor Joe, or their two brothers, for that matter, enjoy football games as much as the rest of us do.

_____ 39. The entire club is gathering one by one to organize the trip to the national convention.

_____ 40. At the end of the show, the band turn sharply to its left and marches off the field.

Brief Writing Assignment: In a paragraph seven sentences long, describe your first hour on this campus. Use only the past and past perfect tenses, and be sure that all subjects and verbs are in correct agreement.

As you learned in Lesson 1, a pronoun is a word that substitutes for a noun or another pronoun. The word for which a pronoun stands is called the pronoun's **antecedent**:

> I called *Harry*, but *he* didn't answer. [*He* substitutes for *Harry. Harry* is the antecedent of *he.*]
>
> My *cap and scarf* were where I had left *them*. [The antecedent of *them* is the plural unit *cap and scarf*.]
>
> *I* will wash *my* car tomorrow.
>
> *One* of my friends is painting *his* house.
>
> *Three* of my friends are painting *their* houses.

To use pronouns effectively and without confusing your reader, you must follow two basic principles:

1. Establish a clear, easily identified relationship between a pronoun and its antecedent.
2. Make the pronoun and its antecedent agree in person, number, and gender.

Let us examine these requirements more fully.

ROLE OF ANTECEDENTS

Personal pronouns should have definite antecedents and should be placed as near their antecedents as possible. Your readers should know exactly what a pronoun stands for. They should not be made to look through several sentences for a pronoun's antecedent, nor should they be asked to manufacture an antecedent for a pronoun. When you discover in your writing a pronoun with no clear and unmistakable antecedent, your revision, as many of the following examples demonstrate, will often require rewriting to remove the faulty pronoun from your sentence.

Faulty:	A strange car followed us closely, and *he* kept blinking his lights at us.
Improved:	A strange car followed us closely, and the driver kept blinking his lights at us.

Faulty:	Although Jenny was a real sports fan, her brother never became interested in *them*.
Improved:	Although Jenny really liked sports, her brother never became interested in them.

Faulty:	Mike is an excellent typist, although he never took a course in *it*.
Improved:	Mike is an excellent typist, although he never took a course in typing.

The indefinite *you* or *they* is quite common in speech and in chatty, informal writing, but one should avoid using either in serious writing:

Faulty:	In Alaska *they* catch huge king crabs.
Improved:	In Alaska huge king crabs are caught. [Often the best way to correct an indefinite *they* or *you* sentence is to use a passive verb.]

Faulty:	Before the reform measures were passed, *you* had few rights.
Improved:	Before the reform measures were passed, people had few rights.
	Before the reform measures were passed, one had few rights.

Faulty:	At the employment office *they* gave me an application form.
Improved:	A clerk at the employment office gave me an application form.
	At the employment office I was given an application form.

A pronoun should not appear to refer equally well to either of two antecedents:

Faulty:	Frank told Bill that *he* needed a haircut. [Which one needed a haircut?]
Improved:	"You need a haircut," said Frank to Bill. [In sentences of this type, the direct quotation is sometimes the only possible correction.]

Avoid the Indefinite *It*

The "it says" or "it said" introduction to statements, although common in informal language, is objectionable in serious writing because the *it* has no antecedent. (See Supplement.)

Faulty:	*It* says in the directions that the powder will dissolve in hot water.
Improved:	The directions say that the powder will dissolve in hot water.

Faulty:	*It* said on the morning news program that a bad storm is coming.
Improved:	According to the morning news program, a bad storm is coming.

Avoid Unclear References

Avoid vague or ambiguous reference of relative and demonstrative pronouns.

Faulty:	Only 20 people attended the lecture, *which* was due to poor publicity.
Improved:	Because of poor publicity, only 20 people attended the lecture.

Faulty:	Good writers usually have large vocabularies, and *this* is why I get poor grades on my papers.
Improved:	I get poor grades on my papers because my vocabulary is inadequate; good writers usually have large vocabularies.

Special Cases: *Which, This, That*

Sometimes the antecedent of the pronouns *which, this*, and *that* is an idea rather than the expressed noun. In a sentence such as "The children giggled, *which* annoyed the teacher" or "The children giggled, and *this* annoyed the teacher," what annoyed the teacher is not the *children* but "the giggling of the children" or "the fact that the children giggled." This kind of reference to a preceding idea rather than to an expressed noun is unobjectionable provided that the meaning is instantly and unmistakably clear. But you should avoid sentences like those shown below. In the first example, readers would be hard-pressed to discover exactly what the *which* means, and in the second, they must decide whether the antecedent is the preceding idea or the noun immediately preceding the *which*:

Faulty:	Hathaway's application was rejected because he spells poorly, *which* is very important in an application letter.
Improved:	Hathaway's application was rejected because he spells poorly; correct spelling is very important in an application letter.

Faulty:	The defense attorney did not object to the judge's concluding remark, *which* surprised me.
Improved:	I was surprised that the defense attorney did not object to the judge's concluding remark.

PRONOUN AGREEMENT

Personal pronouns have separate forms for the three cases, subjective, objective, and possessive. These forms change for each person and number. The chart below displays these forms:

	Subjective	*Objective*	*Possessive*
First Person	I, we	me, us	mine, my
Second Person	you	you	yours, your
Third Person	he/she/it, they	him/her/it, them	his/hers/its, ours

Note the second form in the possessive precedes the noun and functions as an adjective. These forms are sometimes called pronominal adjectives. Thus we say

Pronouns	*Pronominal Adjectives*
That book is *mine*.	That is *my* book.
That book is *yours*.	That is *your* book.
That book is *hers*.	That is *her* book.

The rule for pronouns and pronominal adjectives is quite simple: They agree with their antecedents in person, number, and gender.

Dad says that *he* is sure that *his* new friend will visit *him* soon.
Dad and Mother say that *they* are sure that *their* new friend will visit *them* soon.

This principle of logical pronoun agreement is not as simple as these two examples might suggest. Recent language practices have given rise to two situations for which it is impossible to make rules that apply in every instance. Student writers must, first, be aware of certain changing ideas about pronoun usage; they must then prepare themselves to make decisions among the choices available.

Indefinite Pronouns

The first of these two troublesome situations relates to some of the indefinite pronouns: *one, everyone, someone, no one, anyone, anybody, everybody, somebody, nobody, each, either,* and *neither*. These words have generally been felt to be singular; hence, pronouns and prominal adjectives referring to them have customarily been singular and, unless the antecedent specifies otherwise, masculine. Singular pronouns have also been used in formal writing and speaking to refer to noun antecedents modified by singular qualifiers such as *each* and *every*. The four following examples illustrate the traditional, formal practice:

Everybody has *his* faults and *his* virtues.
Each of the sons is doing what *he* thinks is best.
England expects every man to do *his* duty.
No one succeeds in this firm if Dobbins doesn't like *him.*

The principal difficulty with this usage is that these indefinites, although regarded by strict grammarians as singular in form, carry with them a group or plural sense, with the result that people are often unsure whether pronouns referring to them should be singular or plural. Despite traditional pronouncements, every day we hear sentences of the "Everyone-will-do-*their*-best" type. Beginning writers, however, would do well to follow the established practice until they feel relatively secure about recognizing the occasional sentence in which a singular pronoun referring to an indefinite produces a strained or unnatural effect even though it agrees in form with its antecedent.

Gender Issues

Closely related to this troublesome matter of pronoun agreement is the second problem, gender. What reference words should be used to refer to such a word as *student*? Obviously there are both female students and male students. Plural nouns present no problem; *they*, *their*, and *them* refer to both masculine and feminine. Singular nouns take *she*, *hers*, *her* and *he*, *his*, *him*, but no pronoun refers to third-person singular words that contain either male or female members.

Here again, as with the reference to third-person singular indefinites, the traditional practice is to use masculine singular pronouns. More than one hundred years ago, Henry James wrote the following sentence: "We must grant the artist his subject, his idea, his *donné*; our criticism is applied only to what he makes of it." In James's day, that sentence was undoubtedly looked upon as unexceptional; the pronouns followed what was then standard practice. But attitudes have changed. These days, if that sentence got past the eyes of an editor and appeared on the printed page, its implication that artists are exclusively male would make the sentence unacceptably discriminatory to many readers.

Reliance on the *he or she* pronoun forms is an increasingly popular solution to some of these worrisome problems of pronoun reference. The *he or she* forms agree in number with the third-person singular indefinites, and the use of these forms obviates any possible charge of gender preference. However, excessive use of *he or she*, *his or her*, and *him or her* is undesirable. (Notice the cumbersome result, for instance, if a *he or she* form is substituted for all four of the third-person singular masculine pronouns in the Henry James sentence.)

Here is an important point to remember: When you are worried about a third-person singular masculine pronoun you have written, either because its reference to an indefinite antecedent does not sound quite right to you or because it shows an undesirable gender preference, you can remove the awkwardness, in nearly every instance that arises, by changing the antecedent to a plural noun, to which you then refer by using *they*, *their*, and *them*.

By way of summary, study these four versions of a sentence as they relate to the two problems just discussed:

Every member of the graduating class, if *he* wishes, may have *his* diploma mailed to *him* after August 15. [This usage reflects traditional practice that is still quite widely followed. The objection to it is that the reference words are exclusively masculine.]

Every member of the graduating class, if *he or she* wishes, may have *his or her* diploma mailed to *him or her* after August 15. [The singular reference is satisfactory, but the avoidance of masculine reference has resulted in clumsy wordiness.]

Every member of the graduating class, if *they* wish, may have *their* diplomas mailed to *them* after August 15. [This version, particularly if used in spoken English, would probably not offend many people, but the lack of proper number agreement between the pronouns and the antecedent would rule out its appearance in edited material.]

Members of the graduating class, if they wish, may have their diplomas mailed to them after August 15. [In this version the pronouns are logical and correct in both number and gender.]

A few other matters of pronoun reference, mercifully quite uncomplicated, should be called to your attention. If a pronoun refers to a compound unit or to a noun that may be either singular or plural, the pronoun agrees in number with the antecedent. (See Lesson 22, Rule 6.)

Wilson and his wife arrived in *their* new car.

Neither Jill nor Martha has finished *her* term paper.

The rest of the lecture had somehow lost *its* point.

The rest of the workers will receive *their* money soon.

The 8 o'clock class has *its* test tomorrow.

The 10 o'clock class finished writing *their* themes.

Beware of *You*

An antecedent in the third person should not be referred to by the second person *you*. This misuse develops when writers, forgetting that they have established the third person in the sentence, shift the structure and begin to talk directly to the reader:

Faulty:	In a large university a *freshman* can feel lost if *you* have grown up in a small town.
Improved:	In a large university a freshman can feel lost if he or she has grown up in a small town.
Faulty:	If a *person* really wants to become an expert golfer, *you* must practice every day.
Improved:	If a person really wants to become an expert golfer, *she or he* must practice every day.

SUPPLEMENT

At this point, you should be reminded that *it* without an antecedent has some uses that are completely acceptable in both formal and informal English. One of these is in the delayed subject or object pattern. (See Lesson 10.) Another is its use as a kind of filler word in expressions having to do with weather, time, distance, and so forth.

It is fortunate that you had a spare tire.

I find *it* difficult to believe Ted's story.

It is cold today; *it* snowed last night.

It is 12 o'clock; *it* is almost time for lunch.

How far is *it* to Phoenix?

English Fundamentals *Online*

After you have completed Practice Sheets and Exercises in this lesson, you can find additional help and drill work at **MyWritingLab.com**, in the sections on Pronoun Reference; Pronoun Agreement.

NAME _____   SCORE _____

Directions: One sentence in each of the following pairs is correct; the other contains at least one pronoun that is vaguely or incorrectly used. In the space at the left, write the letter that identifies the correct sentence. In the other sentence, circle the pronoun or pronouns that have vague or incorrect reference.

_____ 1. a. In a book I read recently, it shows a map demonstrating changes in population in this county in the last twenty years.
  b. A book I read recently shows a map demonstrating changes in population in this county in the last twenty years.

_____ 2. a. Walt recently ordered a new dictionary over the Internet, and it will be delivered in the next few days.
  b. Walt recently ordered a new dictionary over the Internet, and they will delivered it in the next few days.

_____ 3. a. Near an island out near the middle of the lake, they are catching very large bass.
  b. Near an island out near the middle of the lake, anglers are catching very large bass.

_____ 4. a. In ancient England, you had very few legal rights if you were poor.
  b. In ancient England, poor people had very few legal rights.

_____ 5. a. When I tried to register online for my classes, it said I needed an advisor's approval code to register.
  b. When I tried to register online for my classes, the message on the screen said I needed an advisors approval code to register.

_____ 6. a. The weather on Saturday was cold and rainy, which caused us to cancel our scheduled canoe trip across the lake.
  b. Saturday was cold and rainy, so we canceled our scheduled canoe trip across the lake.

_____ 7. a. Some of the students were amused by parts of the instructor's lecture, which surprised me because the subject of the lecture was quite serious.
  b. Some of the students were amused by parts of the instructor's lecture, a reaction that surprised me because the subject of the lecture was quite serious.

_____ 8. a. Joanne told Marcia that she needed to work on her paper this weekend if she is going to finish the work by Monday.
  b. Joanne told Marcia, "I need to work on my paper this weekend if I am going to finish the work by Monday."

_____ 9. a. Joanne told Marcia that she needed to work on her paper this weekend if she intends to finish the work by Monday.
  b. Joanne told Marcia, "You need to work on your paper this weekend if you are going to finish the work by Monday."

_____ 10. a. "Each of you," said the motivational speaker, "has your own set of special skills that can be useful if you choose the right occupation."
   b. "Each of you," said the motivational speaker, "has their own set of special skills that can be useful if you choose the right occupation."

_____ 11. a. Everyone needs to bring their textbook and their notepad to class on Monday.
   b. Everyone needs to bring his textbook and his notepad to class on Monday.

_____ 12. a. All students need to bring their textbooks and their notepads to class on Monday.
   b. Every student needs to bring their textbook and their notepad to class on Monday.

_____ 13. a. When a person is trying to do business over the phone, you can become very frustrated with the recorded voice that gives instructions.
   b. When a person is trying to do business over the phone, she can become very frustrated with the recorded voice that gives instructions.

_____ 14. a. Alicia is an avid flag football player although she has very little skill at that game.
   b. Alicia is an avid flag football player although she has very little skill at it.

_____ 15. a. In the southern part of this country, farmers don't raise much wheat because the climate is not suitable for that crop.
   b. In the southern part of this country, they don't raise much wheat because the climate is not suitable for it.

_____ 16. a. In the southern part of this country, raising wheat is uncommon because the climate is not suitable for that crop.
   b. In the southern part of this country, raising wheat is uncommon because the climate is not suitable for it.

_____ 17. a. Every person on the staff will have to do their very best work over the next two days to ensure the successful completion of this project.
   b. Every person on the staff will have to do his or her very best work over the next two days to ensure the successful completion of this project.

_____ 18. a. The local power company is doing their best to restore electricity to all their customers so that everyone can enjoy their homes in comfort.
   b. The local power company is doing its best to restore electricity to all its customers so that all customers can enjoy their homes in comfort.

_____ 19. a. The people in the front rows of the movie were talking and laughing among themselves, which annoyed the couple sitting in the back.
   b. The people in the front rows of the movie were talking and laughing among themselves, and this discourteous behavior annoyed the couple sitting in the back.

_____ 20. a. My younger brother finishes his reading assignments easily, and this is because he once took a course to increase his reading speed.
   b. My younger brother finishes his reading assignments easily because he once took a course to increase his reading speed.

NAME _____ SCORE _____

Directions: In the space at the left, copy the correct pronoun or pronoun-verb combination, given in the parentheses. Circle the antecedent of the pronoun.

_____ 1. Our business has been extremely successful in the past year, and (its, our, their) prospects look extremely positive for the next year also.

_____ 2. People in this area are listening closely to the weather reports to keep (himself, themselves) informed about the movement of that blizzard.

_____ 3. Every one of the students in that class insists that (he or she, they) studied very hard for the exam tomorrow.

_____ 4. All the students in that class insist that (he or she, they) studied very hard for the exam tomorrow.

_____ 5. At the end of the day, each of the workers needs to put (her, their) tools and equipment back in the proper place.

_____ 6. You may use either of those two bikes this week if you promise to return (it, them) by next Monday.

_____ 7. The selection committee will meet on Tuesday to decide whom (it wants, they want) to hire as the company's new president.

_____ 8. If anyone has an A average in the course at the end of the term, (he or she, they) will be exempt from taking the final exam.

_____ 9. All five of the candidates for that job studied engineering when (he was, they were) in college.

_____ 10. Next year our graduating class will hold (its, their) class reunion on a cruise to the Bahamas.

_____ 11. In that large department store all customers can find clothes to meet (his or her, their) every need.

_____ 12. The people who made up that strange story were certainly using (his, their) imagination to the fullest extent possible.

_____ 13. The members of the club will certainly be wise if (he or she chooses, they choose) Michelle as the club president.

_____ 14. Each of the workers on the night shift filed past the time clock and punched (his, their) time card.

_____ 15. At the end of the year, the boss personally hands each employee (his or her, their) year-end bonus.

Directions: Each sentence contains a problem related to the use of a pronoun. Rewrite enough of the sentence to make the sentence clear.

1. Mark told his brother that he needs to buy a car that is inexpensive to own and operate.

   _____

2. Hikers who go off on lonely trails in search of adventure expect that they will find you if you get lost.

   _____

3. In our research, we found that you can locate facts on almost any subject if you understand how to use an Internet search engine.

   _____

4. A blue convertible came up behind us on the road, and he tried unsuccessfully to pass us several times.

   _____

5. Although Jimmy is a big fan of several jazz musicians, no one else in his family has ever been interested in it.

   _____

6. On television last night they said that you should watch two special football games because that would help you to guess who would appear in the championship game.

   _____

7. The children in the library were whispering very loudly, which made you think that the librarian would appear and tell them to be quiet.

   _____

8. Jorge told Billy that he needed to wash his car before he went downtown to pick up his friends.

   _____

9. In that league, you start out equal with everyone else at the time of the draft, so your success depends on how well you select players in it.

   _____

10. They said in the campus newspaper that the game tomorrow night's game is a sellout, and you'll have a hard time getting into it.

   _____

Brief Writing Assignment: Using only second-person pronouns, write a five-sentence paragraph explaining why a friend should go with you to an upcoming concert. Work carefully to produce proper reference and agreement for all pronouns.

Lesson 24 Using Pronouns Correctly: Case

In Lesson 23, the chart on page 245 classifies the personal pronouns on the basis of person, number, and gender. The three forms that are listed there for each person—first, second, and third, singular and plural—illustrate the three cases nouns and pronouns fall into: nominative, possessive, and objective. *I* and *they* are nominative, *my* and *their* are possessive, and *me* and *them* are objective, for example.

The way you use these pronouns in everyday language, in sentences such as "Two of *my* books have disappeared; *they* cost *me* 20 dollars, and *I* must find *them*," demonstrates that the case form you choose depends on how the word is used within the sentence. In this lesson we examine instances where the wrong choice of pronoun form is possible.

The only words in modern English that retain distinctions between nominative and objective case forms are the first- and third-person personal pronouns and the relative pronouns *who* and *whoever*. In nouns, the nominative and objective forms are identical, and the correct use of the one distinctive form, the possessive, requires essentially only a knowledge of how the apostrophe is used. (See Lesson 19.)

Here are the pronouns arranged according to their case forms. The first eight are the personal pronouns; notice that the only distinctive form of *you* and *it* is the possessive. The last three pronouns, which we examine separately from the personal pronouns, are used only in questions and in subordinate clauses. (See Supplement for a discussion of *which* in the possessive case.)

Nominative	Possessive	Objective
I	my, mine	me
you	your, yours	you
he	his, his	him
she	her, hers	her
it	its, its	it
we	our, ours	us
you	your, yours	you
they	their, theirs	them
which	_____	which
who	whose	whom
whoever	whosever	whomever

PERSONAL PRONOUNS IN THE POSSESSIVE CASE

The **possessive case** is used to show possession. Note that the first form in each of the listings of the possessives (*my* and all the rest) is actually an adjective formed from the possessive pronoun and is properly called a *pronominal adjective*. Pronominal adjectives modify nouns in the same way as any other adjective, but they also follow the rules of reference and agreement that govern pronouns.

This is *your* seat; *mine* is in the next row.

253

Jane preferred *my* cookies; some of *hers* were burned.

Their product is good, but the public prefers *ours*.

Indefinite Pronouns

The indefinite pronouns use an apostrophe to form the possessive case: *everybody's* duty, *one's* lifetime, *everyone's* hopes, someone *else's* car. But the personal pronouns do not.

These seats are *ours* [not *our's*]. *Yours* [not *Your's*] are in the next row.

Learn to distinguish carefully between the following possessives and contractions that are pronounced alike: *its* (possessive), *it's* (it is, it has); *theirs* (possessive), *there's* (there is, there has); *their* (possessive), *they're* (they are); *whose* (possessive), *who's* (who is, who has); *your* (possessive), *you're* (you are):

It's obvious that the car has outworn *its* usefulness.

There's new evidence that *they're* changing *their* tactics.

Possessive Pronouns with Gerunds

Formal usage prefers the possessive form of pronouns (occasionally of nouns also) preceding gerunds in constructions like the following:

He was unhappy about *my* [not *me*] voting for the bill.

Her report led to *our* [not *us*] buying additional stock.

Chad boasted about his son's [not son] having won the scholarship.

It is important to note that a very similar construction employing a participle employs the objective case, not the possessive.

We watched *him* walking down the street.

PERSONAL PRONOUNS IN THE NOMINATIVE AND OBJECTIVE CASES

The rules governing the uses of the other two cases are simple. A pronoun is in the **nominative case** when it is used

1. As a subject: *They* suspected that *he* was lying.
2. As a subjective complement: This is *she* speaking.
3. As an appositive of a nominative noun: *We* editors help young writers.

A pronoun is in the **objective case** when it is used

1. As an object of a verb or verbal: Ted told *her* the news. We enjoyed meeting *them*.
2. As an object of a preposition: Everyone except *me* had left the room.
3. As the subject of an infinitive: The police officer ordered *me* to halt.
4. As an appositive of an objective noun: Three of *us* truck drivers stopped to help.

We need not examine in detail every one of these applications. As people become more adept at using the English language, they learn that such usages as "*Them* arrived late" and "I spoke to *she*" do not conform to the system of the language. Instead, we should examine the trouble spots where confusion may arise.

When you use the nominative and objective personal pronouns, exercise care in the following situations.

A Pronoun as Part of a Compound Unit

When the pronoun follows *and* (sometimes *or*) as part of a compound unit, determine its use in the sentence and choose the appropriate case form. The temptation here is usually to use the nominative, although the last example in the following list shows a trouble spot where the objective case is sometimes misused. If you test these troublesome constructions by using the pronoun by itself, you will often discover which form is the correct one:

The man gave Sue and *me* some candy. [Not: Sue and *I*. Both words are indirect objects. Apply the test. Notice how strange "The man gave...*I* some candy" sounds.]

Send your check to either my lawyer or *me*. [Not: to...*I*.]

Have you seen Bob or *her* lately? [Direct objects require the objective case.]

Just between you and *me*, the lecture was a bore. [Never say "between you and I." Both pronouns are objects of the preposition *between*. If this set phrase is a problem for you, find the correct form by reversing the pronouns: You would never say "between I and you."]

Ms. Estes took *him* and *me* to school.
[Not *he* and *I* or *him* and *I*. Both pronouns are direct objects.]

Will my sister and *I* be invited? [Not *me*. The subject is *sister* and *I*.]

Comparisons After "As" and "Than"

In comparisons after *as* and *than*, when the pronoun is the subject of an understood verb, use the nominative form:

He is taller than *I* [*am*]. I am older than *he* [*is*].
Can you talk as fast as *she* [*can talk*]?
No one knew more about art than *he* [*did*].

Sentences like these nearly always call for nominative case subjects. Occasionally the meaning of a sentence may demand an objective pronoun. Both of the following sentences are correct; notice the difference in meaning:

You trust Mr. Alton more than *I*. [Meaning ". . . more than I (trust Mr. Alton)."]
You trust Mr. Alton more than *me*. [Meaning ". . . more than (you trust) me."]

"It is" Expressions

Ordinarily, use the nominative form for the subjective complement. The specific problem here concerns such expressions as *It's me, It is I, It was they*, or *It was them*. Many people say *It's me*, but they would hesitate to say *It was her, It was him*, or *It was them*, instead of

It was she, *It was he*, or *It was they*. However, this problem does not arise often in the writing of students. The following are examples of correct formal usage:

> It is *I*.
>
> It could have been *he*.
>
> Was it *she*?
>
> Was it *they* who called?

"We" Versus "Us" and "I" Versus "Me"

An appositive should be in the same case as the word that it refers to. Notice particularly the first three examples that follow. This usage employing *we* and *us* as an appositive modifier preceding a noun is a real trouble spot:

> *We* boys were hired. [The unit *We boys* is the subject and requires the nominative.]
>
> Two of *us* boys were hired. [The object of a preposition requires the objective case.]
>
> Mr. Elder hired *us* boys. [Not *we boys* for a direct object.]
>
> Two boys—you and *I*—will be hired. [In apposition with the subject.]
>
> Mr. Elder will hire two boys—you and *me*. [In apposition with the object.]

PROBLEMS WITH *WHO* AND *WHOM*

The only other pronouns in standard modern English that have distinctive nominative, possessive, and objective forms are *who/whose/whom* and *whoever/whosever/whomever*. (See Supplement.) The rules that apply to the personal pronouns apply to these words as well: In the subject position *who/whoever* should be used; in the direct object position *whom/whomever* should be used; and so forth. (These pronouns, it should be noted, are never used as appositives.)

The special problem in the application of the case rules to these words comes from their use as interrogatives and as subordinating words. As you learned in Lessons 6, 9, and 10, these words, because they serve as signal words, always stand at the beginning of their clauses. To locate the grammatical function of the pronoun within its clause, you must examine the clause to determine the normal subject-verb-complement positioning.

Direct Object or Object of a Preposition

In formal usage, *whom* is required when it is a direct object or the object of a preposition, even though it stands ahead of its subject and verb:

> *Whom* did Mr. Long hire?
>
> [If you are troubled by this sort of construction, try substituting a personal pronoun and placing it after the verb, where it normally comes: "Did Mr. Long hire *him*?" You would never say "Did Mr. Long hire *he*?" The transitive verb *hire* requires a direct object pronoun in the objective case.]
>
> He is a boy *whom* everyone can like. [*Whom* is the object of *can like*.]
>
> Wilson was the man *whom* everybody trusted. [Everybody trusted *whom*.]
>
> She is the girl *whom* Mother wants me to marry. [object of the verbal *to marry*]
>
> *Whom* was she speaking to just then? [To *whom* was she speaking?]

Beginning a Subordinate Clause

When *who(m)* or *who(m)ever* begins a subordinate clause that follows a verb or a preposition, the use of the pronoun *within its own clause* determines its case form:

We do not know *who* broke the window.
[*Who* is the subject of *broke*, not the direct object of *do know.*]

No one knows *who* the intruder was.
[*Who* is the subjective complement in the noun clause.]

We do not know *whom* the police have arrested.
[The objective form *whom* is used because it is the direct object of *have arrested.* The direct object of *do know* is the whole noun clause.]

I will sell the car to *whoever* offers the best price.
[The whole clause, *whoever offers the best price,* is the object of the preposition *to. Whoever* is the subject of *offers.* The subject of a verb must be in the nominative case.]

After a Parenthetical Insertion

When the pronoun subject is followed by a parenthetical insertion like *do you think*, *I suspect*, *everyone believes*, or *we know*, the nominative case form must be used:

Who do you think *has* the best chance of winning?
[*Who* is the subject of *has.* The *do you think* is a parenthetical insertion.]

Jenkins is the one *who* I suspect *will make* the best impression.

[Determine the verb that goes with the pronoun. If you are puzzled by this type of sentence, try reading it this way: "Jenkins is the one *who will make* the best impression— I suspect."]

But if the pronoun is not the subject of the verb, the objective form should be used:

He is an achiever *whom* I suspect you will eventually envy.
[*Whom* is the direct object of *will envy.*]

SUPPLEMENT

The chart on page 253 shows that the pronoun *which* has no possessive case form, a situation that brings about a minor problem of word choice. As you learned when you studied the adjective clause, *who(m)* normally refers to persons and *which* to things. But *whose* may be used in an adjective clause as the possessive form of *which* to refer to a nonhuman antecedent:

It is a disease *whose* long-term effects are minor.

If *whose* is not used in such a sentence, the "of- which" form must be used, producing a perfectly correct but cumbersome sentence:

It is a disease the long-term effects *of which* are minor.

SUMMARY OF CORRECT PRONOUN USE

1. A pronoun should have a clearly identified antecedent with which it agrees in person, number, and gender.

2. Be aware of the special problem of pronoun reference to third-person singular antecedents that include both masculine and feminine members—pronouns like *everybody* and *someone* and nouns like *person*, *student*, *employee*, and so on. *Note*: Using a plural rather than a singular antecedent is one obvious way of avoiding this problem.

3. Use nominative forms of pronouns for subjects, subjective complements, and appositives that rename nominative nouns. Use objective forms of pronouns for objects of verbs or prepositions, subjects of infinitives, and appositives that rename objective nouns.

4. Be aware of a particular pronoun problem when a personal pronoun is tied to a noun or another pronoun by *and* or *or*:

    Mickey and I [not *Mickey and me*] were sent to the principal's office.

    Mr. Case sent *Mickey and me* [not *Mickey and I*] to the principal's office.

    And so, neighbors, please vote for *Ms. Stone and me* [not *Ms. Stone and I*].

5. Remember that the case of *who* is determined by its use in its own clause. It may be a direct object that precedes the subject [*Whom* has your wife invited?] or a subject immediately following a verb or a preposition [We wonder *who* will win. Our dog is friendly with *whoever* pets it.].

English Fundamentals Online

After you have completed Practice Sheets and Exercises in this lesson, you can find additional help and drill work at **MyWritingLab.com**, in the section on Pronoun Case.

Using Pronouns Correctly: Case

NAME _____ SCORE _____

Directions: Each italicized pronoun in the following sentences is used correctly. In the space at the left, write one of the following numbers to identify the pronoun's use in the sentence or clause:

1. Subject
2. Subjective complement
3. Appositive modifier of a nominative noun
4. Direct object
5. Object of preposition
6. Appositive modifier of an objective noun
7. Possessive pronoun preceding a gerund

_____ 1. *Whom* should we choose to lead this important discussion?

_____ 2. Beside *me* there stood two soldiers who had recently returned from overseas.

_____ 3. Those two seats are *mine*, but you may sit there for a little while.

_____ 4. The leaders in that competition are *we* three students from this class.

_____ 5. Three of *us* students are the leaders in that competition.

_____ 6. The teacher chose *him* because of his carefully stated opinions.

_____ 7. Do you think that the instructor will choose *us* two students?

_____ 8. Those two men and *I* will try to find that lost document.

_____ 9. Cheryl gave that message to *them* before she left for class this morning.

_____ 10. *Who* do you think will win this Saturday's game?

_____ 11. His family was proud of *his* winning that race in record time.

_____ 12. Please give this book to *whomever* you find at my apartment.

_____ 13. Please give this book to *whoever* comes to the door at my apartment.

_____ 14. Try to remember the face of the person *whom* you saw next to my car.

_____ 15. Try to remember the name of the person to *whom* you gave that message.

_____ 16. Did Jim look for any of *us* class members before he left campus today?

_____ 17. Anyone *whom* you meet in front of the classroom can point out Jim to you.

_____ 18. Anyone *who* is a member of that class can point out Jim to you.

_____ 19. I'm not certain, but it could have been *she* whom I saw in the bookstore yesterday.

_____ 20. *Whom* do you believe Ms. Jordan will select to represent us at the convention?

Directions: In the space at the left, copy the correct pronoun from within the parentheses.

_____ 1. Please have (whoever, whomever) is working the front desk call my room at 2:00 P.M.

_____ 2. The boss was pleased by (you, your) finishing that job before noon.

_____ 3. (Who, Whom) in your opinion is the best choice for quarterback?

_____ 4. That sandwich is (yours, your's); the other one is mine.

_____ 5. The baseball team has lost (its, it's) ability to lay down a bunt.

_____ 6. Johnson is both quicker and faster than (I, me).

_____ 7. "This is (her, she)," said Mary when she answered the phone.

_____ 8. I think the puppy likes you better than he likes (I, me).

_____ 9. I think the puppy likes you better than (I, me).

_____ 10. Janna is clearly a faster runner than (her, she).

_____ 11. (Whoever, Whomever) picks up the mail should check for Jane's package.

_____ 12. (Whoever, Whomever) you send to the mailroom should check for Jane's package.

_____ 13. I haven't seen either (her, she) or Melanie since last Saturday.

_____ 14. This note says that either (her, she) or Melanie will be here tomorrow about noon.

_____ 15. (You, Your) speaking out on behalf of that bill certainly turned the tide in that vote.

_____ 16. We certainly enjoyed talking with (them, they) at the meeting last night.

_____ 17. I did not see (her, she) at the meeting last night.

_____ 18. The last one of (us, we) drivers got lost about halfway to Carnestown.

_____ 19. (Us, We) three men and those two women arrived early for the meeting.

_____ 20. Can you read those instructions any faster than (her, she)?

NAME _____   SCORE _____

Directions: If you find an incorrectly used pronoun, write the correct form in the space at the left. If a sentence is correct, write **C** in the space.

_____ 1. Many of the people who you meet every day could use a helping hand with their studies.

_____ 2. They're going about their business while you go about your's, but they could still use help.

_____ 3. I don't know who's impact on my life has been greater, Professor Morton's or Coach Thompson's.

_____ 4. I don't know whose car that is parked in my driveway; its color is the same as your car's, but the make and model are not the same.

_____ 5. Roger Brown is a player who you should emulate; his work ethic and his constant effort should be everyone's example.

_____ 6. I can't remember who we saw at the game; it might have been Oscar or his brother Mel.

_____ 7. You need to be certain that whomever you ask about the date for that quiz has our instructor and not anyone else who teaches that subject.

_____ 8. Someone else's quiz date might be different from our's; Martha says hers is next Thursday.

_____ 9. The sandwiches there on the table are for whomever wants one; they were sent over by a friend of one of us team members.

_____ 10. All of we team members owe that person a vote of thanks because her thinking of us has given our morale a great boost.

_____ 11. You working together with her and Tom has certainly helped to get that project finished ahead of schedule.

_____ 12. "Is that jacket yours?" asked Carl. "It's not mine, and Loren says that it's not hers."

_____ 13. Be sure that you know the person into whose care you give that puppy. We want whoever takes him to give him a good home

_____ 14. That's the man who my mother thinks Cousin Jane should marry; he's intelligent and his future seems bright.

_____ 15. Jane, however, says its not he whom she wants to marry because he has no recognizable sense of humor.

_____ 16. They're presentation was fairly comprehensive, but the audience preferred ours because it was short and to the point.

_____ 17. Our presentation was shorter than theirs, so it was ours to which the audience gave greater applause.

_____ 18. Were not going to be able to tell whom the coach prefers at tight end until after whoever tries out has practiced for a few days.

_____ 19. We players never seem to know in advance whom the coaches prefer because they always give vague answers to whomever asks questions.

_____ 20. We always enjoy guessing who they will choose to start and who will in their opinion be a good relief pitcher.

_____ 21. We should ask anyone who we find for help on this job; whoever it is will be able to help us work faster than we two could do the job.

_____ 22. To whom did you give the keys to the house, and in whose care did you leave the two kittens?

_____ 23. We need to know who in your estimation the staff will accept most easily, for all three candidates for the job are equally qualified.

_____ 24. Whomever we select will need to display great diplomacy, for whomever takes the job will need to overcome the bad reputation of the last boss.

_____ 25. Whoever takes that supervisory job will need great personal skills because the staff's accepting her as a person will be very important.

_____ 26. Who's going to be the first person to arrive tomorrow? Whomever that is will need to turn on the lights and air conditioning.

_____ 27. The boss wants to know whose signature should be on the checks issued to whoever shows up tomorrow to work on that flooring.

_____ 28. The salespeople will demonstrate their products to us, and we'll give the order to whoever offers the best product at the best price.

_____ 29. "It is we workers who should make the final decision on that product, for it's us workers who will have to use it every day," said Jack.

_____ 30. The person to who the company gives that order should be prepared for our demanding the best possible service in the shortest possible time.

_____ 31. My car is parked at the back of the lot next to yours; my parking there will help me find the car later in the dark.

_____ 32. Your sure to find that our steaks are more tender than anyone else's because we sell a better grade of beef than anyone else.

_____ 33. Everyones hopes are very high for the homecoming game this weekend; the coaches usually select an opponent whom they think we can defeat.

_____ 34. Whom do you suppose solved that difficult equation, the one left on the whiteboard by the professor?

_____ 35. The correct phrasing for the answer to the question, "May I speak to Martha?" is, "This is her."

_____ 36. "I, who am the first person in line, wish to purchase three tickets in the front row for that upcoming concert," said the slightly older gentleman.

_____ 37. Several players on the team can run faster than me, but few are quicker over a short distance.

_____ 38. Alicia wants to know whom is faster than she, Barbara or Cathy.

_____ 39. "If you take that road," said the guide, "you will get to town faster than anyone who takes that other route."

_____ 40. We editors should have given more weight to the first reports that came in from those whom first saw the accident.

Brief Writing Assignment: In a paragraph of six sentences, tell a story about Jason, a friend who has gone on a long trip. Describe one of the people he met on the trip. Use Jason's name once and the other person's name once. After that opening, use only pronouns; take care to establish proper case, reference, and agreement.

Using Pronouns Correctly: Reference and Case

Directions: Circle incorrectly used pronouns in each sentence. Then, in the space provided, rewrite enough of the sentence to show how you would correct problems with case and reference. No sentence contains more than two poorly used pronouns.

1. Please send copies of that letter to all we staff members so that we can make our schedule of meetings match your's.

   _____

2. It said on the weather report that we should expect rain, so whomever owns a raincoat and an umbrella should carry them today.

   _____

3. Most of the people are leaving the game early, which is probably because our team is losing by 20 points.

   _____

4. When a person has a flat tire on a lonely road and no one who you know is available to help, the time to pull out the owner's manual for the car has arrived.

   _____

5. Everyone who we gave that test to put down at least two wrong answers on their answer sheet.

   _____

6. I wonder if me being late for that meeting will annoy the others whom were already there.

   _____

7. The server brought each person a glass of water, but they drank it immediately and asked for another glass.

   _____

8. My parents, who you met at the last football game, brought my sister and I a nice picnic lunch for this game.

   _____

9. All of we students had to attend one counseling session before you could sign up for classes for next semester.

   _____

10. My car is in the shop, but John, whom lives in the same apartment complex as me, has promised to give a ride home to everyone who usually rides with me.

_____

11. Anna Montes, whom most of you think should be the next coach, has better qualifications for it than anyone else.

_____

12. Each student needs their own scientific calculator, and they should provide each one a calculator with individual instructions in its use.

_____

13. My aunt loves motocross riding, and she says she will teach we kids to ride if we're interested in it.

_____

14. The vice president called we managers and asked who we have selected for that job and what criteria we used in our selection.

_____

15. The teacher told us that we could choose whoever you want as a lab partner; the choice is totally up to us students.

_____

16. It says on the schedule that you must sign up to take that test before the last day of October or you will be charged an extra fee.

_____

17. Mark asked John if his brother had brought over his notes from that last lecture, the one he missed last Friday.

_____

18. Give this package to whomever is sitting behind the desk in the office and tell them to be sure to hand it to the office manager personally.

_____

19. The postal clerk told Walt that you had to show some identification before you could pick up a registered letter.

_____

20. Ask Joe if that backpack lying on the floor of my car is his; its not mine or your's.

_____

In Lesson 2, you learned that an adjective is a word that describes or limits a noun or a pronoun. You also learned that an adverb modifies a verb, an adjective, or another adverb. Many adverbs end in *ly*, such as *happily*, *beautifully*, and *extremely*. But some adjectives—*lovely*, *likely*, *deadly*, *neighborly*, and *homely*, for instance—also end in *ly*. Some adverbs do not end in *ly*, and these happen to be among the most frequently used words in speech and writing: *after*, *always*, *before*, *far*, *forever*, *here*, *not*, *now*, *often*, *quite*, *rather*, *soon*, *then*, *there*, *too*, *very*. Some words can be used either as adjectives or as adverbs, as the following examples show:

Adverbs	Adjectives
He came *close*.	That was a *close* call.
She talks too *fast*.	She's a *fast* thinker.
Hit it *hard*.	That was a *hard* blow.
She usually arrives *late*.	She arrived at a *late* hour.
He went *straight* to bed.	I can't draw a *straight* line.

Some adverbs have two forms, one without and one with the *ly: cheap, cheaply; close, closely; deep, deeply; hard, hardly; high, highly; late, lately; loud, loudly; quick, quickly; right, rightly; slow, slowly*. In some of these pairs the words are interchangeable; in most they are not. The idiomatic use of adverbs is a rather complex matter; no rules can be made that govern every situation. We can, however, make a few generalizations that reflect present-day practice.

1. The shorter form of a few of these—*late*, *hard*, and *near*, for example—fills most adverbial functions because the corresponding *ly* forms have acquired special meanings:

We must not stay *late*.	I have not seen him *lately* [recently].
I studied *hard* last night.	I *hardly* [scarcely] know him.
Winter is drawing *near*.	I *nearly* [almost] missed the last flight.

2. The *ly* form tends toward the formal, with the short form lending itself to more casual, informal speech and writing:

Informal	Formal
It fell *close* to the target.	You must watch him *closely*.
They ate *high* off the hog.	She was *highly* respected.
Drive *slow*!	Please drive more *slowly*.
Must you sing so *loud*?	He *loudly* denied the charges.
We searched far and *wide*.	She is *widely* known as an artist.

3. Because the short form seems more direct and forceful, it is often used in imperative sentences:

> Hold *firm* to this railing.
>
> "Come *quick*," yelled the officer.

4. The short form is often the one used when combined with an adjective to make a compound modifier preceding a noun:

a *wide*-ranging species	The species ranges *widely.*
a *slow*-moving truck	The truck moved *slowly.*

TYPICAL ADVERB/ADJECTIVE TROUBLE SPOTS

For the sake of simplifying the problem of the right use of adverbs and adjectives, we may say that there are three main trouble spots.

Misusing an Adjective for an Adverb

A word is an adverb if it modifies a verb, an adjective, or another adverb. The words that usually cause trouble here are *good, bad, well; sure, surely; real, really; most, almost; awful, awfully;* and *some, somewhat:*

> Chip played *well* [not *good*] in the last game. [Modifies the verb *played.*]
>
> This paint adheres *well* [not *good*] to concrete. [Modifies the verb *adheres.*]
>
> *Almost* [not *Most*] every student has a job. [Modifies the adjective *every.*]
>
> Today my shoulder is *really* [or *very*—not *real*] sore. [Modifies the adjective *sore.*]
>
> He was driving *really* [or *very*—not *real*] fast. [Modifies the adverb *fast.*]
>
> This rain has been falling *steadily* [not *steady*] for a week.
>
> The champion should win his first match *easily* [not *easy*].
>
> You'll improve if you practice *regularly* [not *regular*].
>
> She wants that prize very *badly* [not *bad*].

Misusing Adverbs for Adjectives as Subjective Complements

The most common verb to take the subjective complement is *be*; fortunately, mistakes with this verb are nearly impossible. A few other verbs—like *seem, become, appear, prove, grow, go, turn, stay,* and *remain,* when they are used in a sense close to that of *be*—take subjective complements. This complement must be an adjective, not an adverb.

> The house *seems empty.* [House *is* empty.]
>
> Their plans *became apparent.* [Plans *were* apparent.]
>
> The work *proved* very *hard.* [Work *was* hard.]

The adjective subjective complement is also used with another group of verbs, the so-called verbs of the senses. These are *feel, look, smell, sound,* and *taste:*

> You shouldn't feel *bad* about this. [Not *badly.*]
>
> His cough sounds *bad* this morning. [Not *badly.*]
>
> At first our prospects looked *bad.* [Not *badly.*]
>
> Doesn't the air smell *sweet* today? [Not *sweetly.*]

The verb *feel* is involved in two special problems. In the first place, it is often used with both *good* and *well.* These two words have different meanings; one is not a substitute for the other. When used with the verb *feel, well* is an adjective meaning "in good health."

The adjective *good*, when used with *feel*, means "filled with a sense of vigor and excitement." Of course, both *well* and *good* have other meanings when used with other verbs. In the second place, the expression "I feel badly" is used so widely, especially in spoken English, that it can hardly be considered an error in usage. Many careful writers, however, prefer the adjective here, with the result that "feel bad" is usually found in written English.

Misusing a Comparative or a Superlative Form of a Modifier

Most adverbs are compared in the same way as adjectives. (For a discussion of the comparison of adjectives, see Lesson 2.) Some common adverbs cannot be compared, such as *here*, *now*, *then*, *when*, and *before*. As you learned in Lesson 16, we use the comparative degree (*taller*, *better*, *more intelligent*, *more rapidly*) in a comparison limited to two things. We use the superlative degree (*tallest*, *best*, *most intelligent*, *most rapidly*) for more than two things.

Two other problems, both of minor importance, are involved in comparisons. First, we do not combine the two forms (*more + er*, *most + est*) in forming the comparative and superlative degrees:

Later the landlord became *friendlier* [not *more friendlier*].

Please drive *slower* [not *more slower*].

Please drive *more slowly* [not *more slower*].

Second, some purists object to the comparison of the so-called absolute qualities, such as *unique* ("being the only one"), *perfect*, *round*, *exact*, and so forth. They argue that, instead of such uses as *most perfect*, *straighter*, *more unique*, the intended meaning is *most nearly perfect*, *more nearly straight*, *more nearly unique*. General usage, however, has pretty well established both forms.

PROBLEMS WITH PREPOSITIONS

Three reminders should be made about the use of prepositions. One problem is the selection of the exact preposition for the meaning intended.

Idioms Using Prepositions

Many words, especially verbs and adjectives, give their full meaning only when modified by a prepositional phrase. In most cases, the meaning of the preposition dictates a logical idiom: to sit *on* a couch, to walk *with* a friend, to lean *against* a fence, and so on. For some more abstract concepts, however, the acceptable preposition may seem to have been selected arbitrarily. Here are a few examples of different meanings of different prepositions:

agree *to* a proposal, *with* a person, *on* a price, *in* principle

argue *about* a matter, *with* a person, *for* or *against* a proposition

compare *to* to show likenesses, *with* to show differences [sometimes similarities]

correspond *to* a thing, *with* a person

differ *from* an unlike thing, *with* a person

live *at* an address, *in* a house or city, *on* a street, *with* other people

Note: Good modern dictionaries provide information about and examples of the correct usage of prepositions.

Unnecessary Prepositions

Although at colloquial levels of language we sometimes find unnecessary prepositions used, examples like the following are improved in serious contexts if written without the words in brackets:

I met [up with] your uncle yesterday.
We keep our dog inside [of] the house.
Our cat, however, sleeps outside [of] the house.
The package fell off [of] the speeding truck.

Note that care must be taken to check the meanings of expressions that contain what might appear to be extra prepositions, such as "meet up with." The expression is colloquial but occurs regularly in speech and informal writing. The expression carries with it a connotation of a meeting that is both unplanned and brief. The expression "meet with" suggests a rather formal, almost businesslike meeting. In many cases, adding or dropping a preposition can change the meaning of a phrase significantly. Careful writers will play close attention to these changes in meaning and check a collegiate dictionary to be certain of meaning.

Avoid especially the needless preposition at the end of a sentence or the repeated preposition in adjective clauses and in direct or indirect questions:

Where is your older brother *at*?
He is one of the few people *to* whom I usually feel superior *to*.
To what do you attribute your luck at poker *to*?
[Use one *to* or the other, but not both.]

Repeated Prepositions in Compound Units

When two words of a compound unit require the same preposition to be idiomatically correct, the preposition need not be stated with the first unit:

Correct: We were both *repelled* and *fascinated by* the snake charmer's act.

But when the two units require different prepositions, both must be expressed:

Incomplete: The child shows an *interest* and a *talent for* music. [interest . . . *for* (?)]
Correct: The child shows an *interest in* and a *talent for* music.

Incomplete: I am sure that Ms. Lewis would both *contribute* and *gain from* a summer work-shop. [contribute . . . *from* (?)]
Correct: I am sure that Ms. Lewis would both *contribute to* and *gain from* a summer workshop.

English Fundamentals Online

After you have completed Practice Sheets and Exercises in this lesson, you can find additional help and work at **MyWritingLab.com**.

Using Modifiers Correctly

NAME _____ SCORE _____

Directions: In the first space at the left, write the word (or words) that the italicized word modifies. In the second space, write **Adj.** if the italicized word is an adjective, or **Adv.** if it is an adverb.

_____ 1. When my little brother came home, he told us a *wildly*
_____ unbelievable story from a movie he had seen.

_____ 2. The story in the movie concerned a *wild* horse that befriended
_____ a lonely little girl.

_____ 3. The model glider, flying *freely* across the meadow, sailed out
_____ of sight.

_____ 4. Those men are working on an *incredibly* tall building.
_____

_____ 5. Did you make a *higher* grade on this test than on the last one?
_____

_____ 6. Yes, I made a *very* high grade on this test.
_____

_____ 7. When I saw my grade, I felt very *good*.
_____

_____ 8. On that test, I knew *almost* all the answers as soon as I looked
_____ at the questions.

_____ 9. The snow has been falling *steadily* for the past twelve hours.
_____

_____ 10. Yesterday a *steady* rain fell for most of the day.
_____

_____ 11. The newborn colt was not *steady* on its feet.
_____

_____ 12. Is John Martin a *highly* respected music teacher?
_____

_____ 13. His reputation as a trumpet player is known far and *wide*.
_____

_____ 14. That announcement was broadcast *widely* throughout the
_____ community.

_____ 15. Jackson played *beautifully* at the recital last night.
_____

Directions: In the space at the left, copy the correct form given in the parentheses.

_____ 1. That was a wonderful plan, and Jim executed it (wonderful, wonderfully).

_____ 2. With all the guests having gone home, the house seems very (quiet, quietly).

_____ 3. Now that my last symptoms have departed, I no longer feel as (bad, badly) as I did last week.

_____ 4. Most students finished (almost, most) all of the problems on that test.

_____ 5. For the first time this track season, Marcie felt that she was running (real, really) fast.

_____ 6. Big Mike is (faster, more faster) than any other lineman on the team.

_____ 7. "Please listen (close, closely) as I give instructions for this problem," said the teacher.

_____ 8. Although Sylvia made (repeated, repeatedly) attempts to make a foul shot, she had still made only two shots by the end of practice.

_____ 9. Alex tried, but he could not (readily, ready) recall the names of those who attended the meeting.

_____ 10. In cold weather, that car runs very (bad, badly) when I first start it.

_____ 11. (Apparent, Apparently), we failed to convince the boss of the soundness of our proposal.

_____ 12. That new program runs very (good, well) on that fast computer.

_____ 13. Throughout the entire storm, my grandmother remained quite (calm, calmly).

_____ 14. The lecturer spoke calmly and formally to the class, "Watch (careful, carefully) as the slides demonstrate the changes in that watershed."

_____ 15. "That speech was the (clearest, most clearest) statement the candidate has made on that issue," observed Yolanda.

_____ 16. I need to sand that table again; it still feels (rough, roughly) to the touch.

_____ 17. "If you handle that fragile vase (rough, roughly)," said Barbara, "it will surely break."

_____ 18. It takes a (sure, surely) hand at the tiller to dock a sailboat in a stiff breeze.

_____ 19. There was (some, somewhat) drop-off in attendance when we changed the date of the soccer game.

_____ 20. Attendance was (most highest, highest) for the final game because the team was still in contention for the championship.

Using Modifiers and Prepositions Correctly

NAME _____ SCORE _____

Directions: Rewrite the following sentences to eliminate problems with modifiers and prepositions.

1. I knew that Bill had been an active member and an officer in that organization, which raises funds to make the local symphony orchestra more stronger.

   _____

2. My wrist is extreme tender because I fell on it hard yesterday when I was running across the meadow at the place where the creek crosses it at.

   _____

3. Those initial e-mails at Jackson led to more formal correspondence to him about an agreement to a price for that piece of property out west of town.

   _____

4. Jill has been having an argument for her parents over her selection of a major because they cannot agree to each other about her future occupation.

   _____

5. Olga could not easy recall what should have been a real easy sequence of numbers because she was distracted with all the noise in the office

   _____

6. The air out on that field smells sweetly because yesterday the crew mowed all the fields for people with whom their company has a contract with.

   _____

7. Because my nephew has an interest and a talent for baseball, my uncle has hired an instructor to him so that my nephew can more further develop his skills.

   _____

8. The man said, "I can make sense and agree with that argument, but I doubt that many others will be able to make their views correspond with yours."

   _____

9. The work of cleaning that wall went much more quicklier once we brought in that highly-pressure cleaning machine.

   _____

10. The woman was driving real fast, so most all of her packages fell onto the floor when she had to stop sudden because a dog ran into the street without actual seeing her car.

   _____

11. That dangerous, exotic snake has ranged wide across the state ever since someone released a pair of them on accident into that wildly, desolate area in the national park.

   _____

12. Joe and Tom played good in yesterday's game, but the rest of the team played so poor that the score was a lopsidedly 12–2 in favor of the other team.

   _____

13. All the people in that area felt considerable more comfortabler when the new fire station opened where those two major roads intersect at.

   _____

14. Steady working through those problems, Will and Sandra made more further progress on the assignment than they had actual expected and finished before noon.

   _____

15. Sara sings very beautiful, and she also plays the piano, on which she's practiced on for several years, quite good.

   _____

16. The watermelon vines spread quick across the garden, and, before I knew it, they had most complete covered up all the other plants.

   _____

17. Don't step out on that ledge where the water runs over it at; the rocks are real slippery there, and you could fall if you're not carefully watching your step.

   _____

18. Please grant Alex Sutton admission on your college, for he is a person who will benefit and contribute to the experience of everyone with whom he comes in contact with.

   _____

19. No one has been more helpfuller than Johan, for he has been the most helpfullest person in the office since I came to work here.

   _____

20. We all felt well about the selection of Melissa for that office; she has fit into our staff real good for the whole time she has been working here.

   _____

Brief Writing Assignment: Write a description, in seven or eight sentences, of your favorite food. Include appeals to all five senses in the description. In each sentence use at least three adjectives and three adverbs. Include also three prepositional phrases.

Someone has said that the Inuit people have 18 easily differentiated words for snow, ranging from falling snow to a thin glaze of ice on water. In fact, there is considerable debate among language scholars and anthropologists about exactly how many words for snow exist in the languages that we think of as Eskimo. We need not engage in the debate about actual numbers to recognize that these people have an extensive, very precise vocabulary for what we call snow because snow is a vital part of their lives, indeed, of their survival. The choice of one word over another might, quite literally, be a matter of life and death. In English not many words have implications for survival, at least not words that we ordinarily use in polite society or more formal expressions.

But one of the beauties of the English language is its rich, broad, exceptionally precise vocabulary. In many languages one word is used to identify more than one object or condition. In Spanish, the word *piso* can mean what in English we identify as floor, the surface inside a room or building, but it can also be used to identify what in English we call ground, the level surfaces of dirt or grass that exist outside of buildings. The ability to take advantage of this rich, diverse vocabulary is one of the marks of a skilled speaker or writer of English. However, it is just this richness that sometimes requires extra attention to word choices if we are to express ourselves with precision and effectiveness, even forcefulness, to get our point across to listeners and readers.

This chapter deals with two classes of words that require some special attention if we are to be effective users of the language. The first category deals with what we ordinarily call *usage*, the standard way of expressing something in formal, academic, or business writing. This class deals with levels of language—formal, informal, colloquial, slang, and others—and it makes distinctions on the basis of appropriate word choices. For example, in informal or colloquial usage we might say that a person's performance was "pretty good," and we understand that to mean good enough, but not exceptional. In formal communication, we need to select a word that is more precise and more in keeping with the formality of the communication. So we might say the performance was adequate or acceptable.

This category also distinguishes between or among words that are similar in meaning but are used only when applied to certain words. For example, the words *number* and *amount* mean more or less the same thing, an idea related to quantity. But we usually use *amount* with materials that cannot be counted, so we say the amount of water in the barrel, but we say the number of people, because people can be counted. It is clear that we would rarely say the number of water in the barrel, but we sometimes hear people say the amount of people who came to the concert. This expression can be understood, but the use of the word amount identifies the user as someone who is less than careful in word choices. The goal of this chapter is to develop a sense for what is exactly right in a given situation because being exactly right conveys the precise meaning intended and shows that the person, as a regular practice, uses the language with care and precision.

The second category is more easily grasped, for it deals with words called homophones, words that sound the same when spoken but are not spelled the same way and do not have the same meaning. So the words *write*, *right*, and *rite* sound the same, a fact that requires a listener to ascertain the meaning from the context. A reader can do the same thing, distinguish among those meanings by context, but a wrong choice, especially from among more simple sets of words such as *to*, *too*, and *two*, identifies the writer, in the minds of many, as someone or who is either careless or unskilled.

So then, the obvious question arises: If my reader "gets it" whether I use *to* or *too*, why are these distinctions important? They are important for two reasons:

They affect the precision and effectiveness of your writing.

They create an impression of you as a person, of your intelligence and your educational level.

Your use of language, the precision and effectiveness of your spoken and written communications, creates an impression. We can see this concept more clearly in choices of clothing. The most expensive, most stylish pair of board shorts by Billabong or Patagonia will look foolish in an uptown law office and brand the wearer as a person with some kind of strange notions about appropriate dress for an office. Likewise, a $1,500 blue pinstripe suit would probably fit in nicely in that law office but will seem completely out of place on a surfboard. So it is with language: We create an impression of intelligence, educational level, and judgment by the language we employ. The ability to use precise language, language carefully chosen for its meaning and its level, is a tool that we can use to great effect in our lives.

As soon as you move into even the lowest levels of management, you will find these language skills important.

USAGE

A, an. Use *a* when the word immediately following it is sounded as a consonant; use *an* when the next sound is a vowel sound: *a*, *e*, *i*, *o*, or *u* (*a* friend, *an* enemy). Remember that it is the consonantal or vowel *sound*, not the actual letter, that determines the choice of the correct form of the indefinite article: *a* sharp curve, *an* S-curve; *a* eulogy, *an* empty house; *a* hospital, *an* honest person; *a* united people, *an* uneven contest.

Ad. Clipped forms of many words are used informally, such as *ad* (*advertisement*), *doc* (*doctor*), *exam* (*examination*), *gent* (*gentleman*), *gym* (*gymnasium*), *lab* (*laboratory*), *math* (*mathematics*), and *prof* (*professor*). Formal usage prefers the long forms.

Aggravate. In standard formal English the word means "make more severe," "make worse." Colloquially it means "annoy," "irritate," "exasperate."

Walking on your sprained ankle will *aggravate* the hurt. [*Informal:* All criticism aggravates him.]

Ain't. Substandard for *am not*, *are not*, *is not*, *have not*.

Am I not [not *Ain't I*] a good citizen?

The command *hasn't* [not *hain't* or *ain't*] been given yet.

They *are not* [not *ain't*] going either.

All the farther, all the faster, and the like. Generally regarded as colloquial equivalents of *as far as*, *as fast as*, and the like.

This is *as far as* [not *all the farther*] I care to go.

That was *as fast as* [not *all the faster*] he could run.

A lot. Always use as two words. See also *Lots of.*

A lot of. See *Lots of.*

Alright. This spelling, like *allright*, although often used in advertising, is generally regarded as very informal usage. The preferred form is all right.

In strictly formal usage, *satisfactory* or *very well* is preferred to *all right*.

> *Very well* [not *Alright*], you may ride in our car.
>
> The members agreed that the allocation of funds was *satisfactory* [not *all right*].

Among, between. *Among* is used with three or more persons or things, as in "Galileo was *among* the most talented people of his age," and "The estate was divided among his three sons." *Between* usually refers to two things, as in "between you and me," "between two points," "between dawn and sunset."

Amount, number. Use *number*, not *amount*, in reference to units that can actually be counted:

> the *amount* of indebtedness, the *number* of debts

And, etc. Because *etc.* (*et cetera*) means "and so forth," *and etc.* would mean "and and so forth." You should not use *etc.* to replace some exact, specific word, but if you do use it, be sure not to spell it *ect.* And remember that *etc.* requires a period after it.

Anywheres. Colloquial for *anywhere*. Similar colloquial forms are *anyways* for *anyway* or *anyhow*, *everywheres* for *everywhere*, *nowheres* for *nowhere*, *somewheres* for *somewhere*.

> I looked for my books *everywhere*.
>
> They must be hidden *somewhere*.

Apt to, liable to, likely to. *Apt to* implies a natural tendency. *Liable to* implies a negative outcome or result. *Likely to* suggests a strong possibility.

> That car is *apt to* increase in value.
>
> We are *liable to* have a bad leak unless we fix the roof.
>
> The new vaccine is *likely to* cause a disappearance of chicken pox.

As, like. See *Like*.

As to whether. *Whether* is usually enough.

Awful, awfully. Like *aggravate*, these words have two distinct uses. In formal contexts, they mean "awe- inspiring" or "terrifying." Often in conversation and sometimes in writing of a serious nature, *awful* and *awfully* are mild intensifiers, meaning "very."

Because. See *Reason is because*.

Because of. See *Due to*.

Being that, being as how. Substandard for *because*, *as*, or *since*.

Beside, besides. These two prepositions are clearly distinguished by their meanings. *Beside* means "at the side of" and *besides* means "in addition to."

> Lucy sits *beside* me in class.
>
> Did anyone *besides* you see the accident?

Between. See *Among*.

Bring, take. *Bring* means to convey from a farther to a nearer place. *Take* means to convey from nearer to farther.

> *Bring* home a loaf of bread from the store.
>
> *Take* that book back to the library.

But what, but that. Colloquial for *that*.

> Both sides had no doubt *that* [not *but what*] their cause was just.

Calculate, figure, reckon. These are colloquial for *imagine*, *consider*, *expect*, *think*, and similar words.

> He must have *expected* [not *calculated*] that she might not be pleased to see him after he did not return her calls.

Can, may. *Can* suggests ability to do something. *May* is the preferred form when permission is involved.

> Little Junior *can* already count to ten.
>
> *May* [not *Can*] I borrow your pencil?

Can't hardly, couldn't hardly, can't scarcely, couldn't scarcely. Substandard for *can hardly*, *could hardly*, *can scarcely*, *could scarcely*. These are sometimes referred to as double negatives.

I *can hardly* [not *can't hardly*] believe that story.

We *could scarcely* [not *couldn't scarcely*] hear the foghorn.

Caused by. See *Due to*.

Consensus means an agreement of the majority; thus, *consensus of opinion* is redundant. Say simply, "The consensus was . . .," not, "The consensus of opinion was . . . ."

Continual, continuous. A fine distinction in meaning can be made if you remember that *continual* means "repeated regularly and frequently" and that *continuous* means "occurring without interruption," "unbroken."

Could(n't) care less. This worn-out set phrase indicating total indifference is a colloquialism. A continuing marvel of language behavior is the large number of people who insist on saying "I could care less" when they obviously mean the opposite.

Could of, would of, might of, ought to of, and so on. Substandard for *could have*, *would have*, and so on.

Couple, couple of. These expressions are fine for informal conversation but not precise enough for more formal occasions. In writing, be specific. Say "three points," for example, "four issues," rather than "a couple of points/issues."

Criteria. The singular noun is *criterion*; the plural is *criteria* or *criterions*. Such combinations as "a criteria," "one criteria," and "these criterias" are incorrect.

Data. Originally the plural form of the rarely used Latin singular *datum*, *data* has taken on a collective meaning so that it is often treated as a singular noun. "This data has been published" and "These data have been published" are both correct, the latter being the use customarily found in scientific or technical writing.

Different from, different than. *Different from* is generally correct. Many people object to *different than*, but others use it, especially when a clause follows, as in "Life in the Marines was different than he had expected it to be."

Their customs are *different from* [not *different than*] ours.

Life in the Marines was *different from* what he had expected it to be.

Different to, a form sometimes used by British speakers and writers, is rarely used in the United States.

Disinterested, uninterested. Many users of precise English deplore the tendency to treat these words as loose synonyms, keeping a helpful distinction between *disinterested* ("impartial," "free from bias or self- interest") and *uninterested* ("lacking in interest," "unconcerned"). Thus we would hope that a referee would be disinterested but not uninterested.

Due to, caused by, because of, owing to. *Due to* and *caused by* are used correctly after the verb *to be*:

His illness was *caused by* a virus.

The flood was *due to* the heavy spring rains.

Many people object to the use of *due to* and *caused by* adverbially at the beginning of a sentence, as in "Due to the heavy rains, the streams flooded," and "Caused by the storm, the roads were damaged." It is better to use *because of* or *owing to* in similar situations. *Due to* and *owing to* are also used correctly as an adjective modifier immediately following a noun:

Accidents *due to* excessive speed are increasing in number.

Note in the examples what variations are possible:

The streams flooded *because of* the heavy rains.

The flooding of the streams was *due to* the heavy rains.

The floods were *caused by* the rapid melting of the snow.

Emigrate, immigrate. To *emigrate* is to *leave* one region to settle in another; to *immigrate* is to *enter* a region from another one.

Enthuse. Colloquial or substandard (depending on the degree of a person's aversion to this word) for *be enthusiastic, show enthusiasm.*

The director *was enthusiastic* [not *enthused*] about her new program.

Everyday, every day. *Everyday* is an adjective meaning "ordinary." *Every day* is an adjective and noun combination.

Just wear your *everyday* clothes; don't dress up.

I wore those shoes almost *every day* last week.

Everywheres. See *Anywheres.*

Explicit, implicit. *Explicit* means "stated directly." *Implicit* means "implied," "suggested directly."

She *explicitly* told us to bring two pencils and ten pages of notebook paper.

The idea *implicit* in her statement was that we should come prepared to take the test.

Farther, further. Careful writers observe a distinction between these two words, reserving *farther* for distances that can actually be measured.

Tony can hit a golf ball *farther* than I can.

We must pursue this matter *further.*

Fewer, less. *Fewer* refers to numbers, *less* to quantity, extent, or degree.

Fewer [not *Less*] students are taking courses in literature this year.

Food costs *less*, but we have less money to spend.

Figure. See *Calculate.*

Fine. Colloquial, very widely used, for *well, very well.*

The boys played *well* [not *just fine*].

Graffiti. The singular form is *graffito.* In serious writing, *graffiti* takes a plural verb. Avoid combinations such as "a graffiti," "this graffiti," etc.

Had(n't) ought. *Ought* does not take an auxiliary.

You *ought* [not *had ought*] to apply for a scholarship.

You *ought not* [not *hadn't ought*] to miss the lecture.

Hardly. See *Can't hardly.*

Healthy, healthful. *Healthy* means "having health," and *healthful* means "giving health." Thus a person or an animal is *healthy*; a climate, a food, or an activity is *healthful.*

Immigrate. See *Emigrate.*

Implicit. See *Explicit.*

Imply, infer. Despite the increasing tendency to use these words more or less interchangeably, it is good to preserve the distinction: *Imply* means "to say something indirectly," "to hint or suggest," and *infer* means "to draw a conclusion," "to deduce." Thus you *imply* something in what you say and *infer* something from what you hear.

Incredible, incredulous. An unbelievable *thing* is incredible; a disbelieving *person* is incredulous.

In regards to. The correct forms are *in regard to* or *as regards.*

Inside of. *Inside* or *within* is preferred in formal writing.

We stayed *inside* [not *inside of*] the barn during the storm.

The plane should arrive *within* [not *inside of*] an hour.

Irregardless. Substandard or humorous for *regardless.*

The planes bombed the area *regardless* [not *irregardless*] of consequences.

Is when, is where. The *"is-when," "is-where"* pattern in definitions is clumsy and should be avoided. Write, for example, "An embolism is an obstruction, such as a blood clot, in the bloodstream," instead of "An embolism is where an obstruction forms in the bloodstream."

Kind, sort. These words are singular and therefore should be modified by singular modifiers. Do not write *these kind*, *these sort*, *those kind*, *those sort*.

Those kinds [not *those kind*] of videos sell very well.

Who could believe *that sort* [not *those sort*] of arguments?

Kinda, sorta, kind of a, sort of a. Undesirable forms.

Kind of, sort of. Colloquial for *somewhat, in some degree, almost, rather*.

They felt *somewhat* [not *sort of*] depressed.

Learn, teach. *Learn* means "to acquire knowledge"; *teach* means "to give or impart knowledge."

Ms. Brown *taught* [not *learned*] me Spanish.

Leave. Not to be used for let.

Let [not *Leave*] me carry your books for you.

Less. See *Fewer*.
Let. See *Leave*.
Let's us. The *us* is superfluous because *let's* means "let us."
Liable to, likely to. See *Apt to*.
Like, as, as if. The use of *like* as a conjunction (in other words, to introduce a clause) is colloquial. It should be avoided in serious writing.

As [not *Like*] you were told earlier, there is a small entry fee.

She acts *as if* [not *like*] she distrusts us.

Do *as* [not *like*] I tell you.

Line. Often vague and redundant, as in "What do you read in the line of books?" "Don't you enjoy fishing and other sports along that line?" It is better to say, more directly,

What kind of books do you read?

Don't you enjoy fishing and sports like that?

Lots of, a lot of. Used informally to mean a large extent, amount, or number, a usage that is enjoying increased acceptance. This usage should be avoided in formal writing.

A great many [not *Lots of*] families vacation here every summer.

The storms caused *a great deal of* [not *lots of*] damage.

All of us owe you *a great deal* [not *a lot*].

As one word, **alot** is still unacceptable spelling.

Mad. Colloquially, *mad* is often used to mean "angry." In formal English, it means "insane."

Marge was *angry* [not *mad*] because I was late.

May. See *Can*.
Media. A plural noun referring to all mass communicative agencies. The singular is *medium*. Careful writers and speakers avoid the use of *media* as a singular noun, as in "Television is an influential media." Even more objectionable is the use of *medias* as a plural.

Might of. See *Could of*.
Most. This word is the superlative form of *much* and *many* (*much, more, most; many, more, most*). Its use as a clipped form of *almost* is colloquial.

Almost [not *Most*] all of my friends work during the summer.

Nature, nurture. Nature is a noun meaning that which is inborn, inherent to the character and constitution of a person. So we say, "She is, by nature, a calm person." Nurture as a noun means training or upbringing, as a verb it means to train or educate, to further the development of a quality. "We need to nurture that attitude in her."

Nauseated, nauseous. Despite the increasingly wide use of these words as synonyms, there are still speakers and writers of precise English who insist that *nauseated* should be used to mean "suffering from or experiencing nausea" and that *nauseous* should be used only to mean "causing nausea."

Nohow. This emphatic negative is substandard.

Not all that. A basically meaningless substitute for *not very* or *not really*; it can easily become a habit.

The movie was *not very* [not *not all that*] amusing.

Nowheres. See *Anywheres.*
Number. See *Amount.*
Of. See *Could of.*
Off of. Dialectal or colloquial for *off.*

She asked me to get *off* [not *off of*] my high horse.

OK. This form calls attention to itself in serious writing. It is appropriate only to business communications and casual speech or writing. Modern dictionaries offer several permissible forms: *OK, O.K.,* and *okay* for the singular noun; *OKs, O.K.s,* and *okays* for the plural noun; and *OK'd, OK'ing, O.K.'d, O.K.'ing, okayed,* and *okaying* for verb forms.

Ought. See *Had(n't) ought.*
Ought to of. See *Could of.*
Owing to. See *Due to.*
Party. Colloquial for "individual" in the sense of *man, woman, person.*

A man [not A party] called while you were out.

Party is acceptable when used in reference to lawsuits, agreements, and disputes.

Percent, percentage. Use *percent* when referring to a specific number.

Ten *percent* of the class made an A.

Use *percentage* when referring to no specific number.

A small *percentage* of the class made an A.

Phenomenon, phenomena. A *phenomenon* is a single observable fact or event. *Phenomena* is a plural noun. When using

either, be sure to make adjectives such as *this* and *these* and all verbs agree in number.

Plenty is a noun meaning "an abundance" and is used with the preposition *of.*

There are *plenty of* jobs available.

Do not use the word as an adverb meaning "very" or "quite."

That movie was *very* [not *plenty*] scary.

Pretty is an informal modifier. In writing, use *quite* or *very.*

The floodwaters were *very* [not *pretty*] deep.

Quote, unquote. Although these words may be needed in the oral presentation of quoted material, they have no use in written material, in which quotation marks or indentation sets off the quoted material from the text proper.

Real, really. The use of *real,* which is an adjective, to modify another adjective or an adverb is colloquial. In formal contexts, *really* or *very* should be used.

We had a *really* [not *real*] enjoyable visit.

The motorcycle rounded the corner *very* [not *real*] fast.

Reason is because, reason is due to, reason is on account of. In serious writing, a "reason is" clause is usually completed with *that,* not with *because, due to,* or *on account of.*

The *reason* they surrendered *is that* [not *because*] they were starving.

The *reason* for my low grades *is that* I have poor eyesight [not *is on account of* my poor eyesight].

Reckon. See *Calculate.*
Same. The use of *same* as a pronoun, often found in legal or business writing, is inappropriate in most other types of writing.

I received your report and look forward to reading *it* [not *the same*].

So, such. These words, when used as exclamatory intensifiers, are not appropriate in a formal context. Sentences like the following belong in informal talk: "I am *so* tired," "She is *so* pretty," or "They are having *such* a good time."

Some. Colloquial for *somewhat, a little.*

The situation at the border is said to be *somewhat* [not *some*] improved today.

Somewheres. See *Anywheres.*

Sort. See *Kind.*

Such. See *So.*

Suppose to, use to. Although these incorrect forms are difficult to detect in spoken English, remember that the correct written forms are *supposed to, used to.*

Sure. *Sure* is correctly used as an adjective:

We are not *sure* about her plans.

He made several *sure* investments.

Sure is colloquial when used as an adverbial substitute for *surely, extremely, certainly, indeed, very, very much.*

The examination was *surely* [not *sure*] difficult.

The lawyer's plea *certainly* [not *sure*] impressed the jury.

Sure and. See *Try and.*

Suspicion. *Suspicion* is a noun; it is not to be used as a verb in place of *suspect.*

No one *suspected* [not *suspicioned*] the victim's widow.

Swell. Not to be used as a general term of approval meaning *good, excellent, attractive, desirable,* and so on.

Take. See *Bring.*

Teach. See *Learn.*

That there, this here, those there, these here. Substandard for *that, this, those, these.*

Them. Substandard when used as an adjective.

How can you eat *those* [not *them*] parsnips?

Try and, sure and. *Try to, sure to* are the preferred forms in serious writing.

We shall *try to* [not *try and*] make your visit a pleasant one.

Be *sure to* [not *sure and*] arrive on time.

Type. Colloquial when used as a modifier of a noun. Use *type of* or *kind of.*

I usually don't enjoy that *type of* [not *type*] movie.

Uninterested. See *Disinterested.*

Unique. In its original meaning, the word meant either "the only example" or "without a like or equal." In modern use, it has also acquired an additional meaning: "unusual." In the first sense, it cannot be modified by an adjective.

As a politician, he is *unique.*

She gave him a *unique* [*very special*] pen as a present.

Many object to the use of a modifier with unique; in formal writing, it is best to choose some other adjective to convey the meaning "special" or "unusual."

Use to. See *Suppose to.*

Want in, want off, want out. Colloquial and dialectical forms for *want to come in, want to get off, want to go out.* Inappropriate in serious writing.

Ways. Colloquial for *way,* in such expressions as

It is just a short *distance* [not *ways*] up the canyon.

We do not have a long *way* [not *ways*] to go.

What. Substandard when used for *who, which,* or *that* as a relative pronoun in an adjective clause.

His raucous laugh is the thing *that* [not *what*] annoys me most.

When, where clauses. See *Is when.*

Where . . . at. The *at* is unnecessary and undesirable in both speech and writing.

Where [not *Where at*] will you be at noon?

Where is your car? [Not *Where is your car at?*]

-wise. The legitimate function of this suffix to form adverbs like *clockwise* does not carry with it the license to concoct such jargon as "Entertainmentwise, this town is a dud" or "This investment is very attractive long-term-capital-gainswise."

Without. Not to be used as a conjunction instead of *unless*.

He won't lend me his car *unless* [not *without*] I fill the gas tank.

Would of. See *Could of*.

WORDS SIMILAR IN SOUND

Accept. I should like to *accept* your first offer.
Except. He took everything *except* the rugs.

Advice. Free *advice* [noun] is usually not worth much.
Advise. Ms. Hull said she would *advise* [verb] me this term. (Similarly, *device* [noun] and *devise* [verb].

Affect. His forced jokes *affect* [verb] me unfavorably.
Effect. His humor has a bad *effect* [noun]. Let us try to *effect* [verb] a lasting peace.

All ready. They were *all ready* to go home.
Already. They had *already* left when we telephoned the house.

All together. Now that we are *all together*, let us talk it over.
Altogether. They were not *altogether* pleased with the results.

Altar. In this temple was an *altar* to the Unknown God.
Alter. One should not try to *alter* or escape history.

Ascent. The *ascent* to the top of the mountain was quite steep.
Assent. The judge did not *assent* to our request.

Bare. The *bare* and leafless limbs of the trees were a dark gray.
Bear. He could not *bear* to look at the accident.

Breath. His *breath* came in short gasps at the end of the race.
Breathe. The problem is solved; you can *breathe* easily now.

Canvas. We used a piece of *canvas* to shelter us from the wind.
Canvass. The candidate wanted to *canvass* every person in her precinct.

Capital. A *capital* letter; *capital* gains; *capital* punishment; state *capital*.
Capitol. Workers are painting the dome of the *Capitol*.

Cite. He *cited* three good examples.
Site. The *site* of the new school has not been decided on.
Sight. They were awed by the *sight* of so much splendor.

Climactic. The *climactic* moment in that movie was extremely exciting.
Climatic. According to NOAA, *climatic* conditions in North America have not changed much over the past 100 years.

Coarse. The *coarse* sand blew in my face.
Course. We discussed the *course* to take. Of *course* he may come with us.

Complement. Your intelligence is a *complement* to your beauty.
Compliment. It is easier to pay a *compliment* than a bill.

Consul. Be sure to look up the American *consul* in Rome.
Council. He was appointed to the executive *council*.
Counsel. I sought *counsel* from my friends. They *counseled* moderation. He employed *counsel* to defend him.

Decent. The workers demanded a *decent* wage scale.

Descent. The *descent* from the mountain was uneventful.

Dissent. The voices of *dissent* were louder than those of approval.

Desert. Out in the lonely *desert* [noun—desert], he tried to *desert* [verb—desert] from his regiment.

Dessert. We had apple pie for *dessert*.

Device. The *device* that controls the alarm system has malfunctioned.

Devise. We should *devise* a new system to cope with that problem.

Die. Old habits certainly *die* hard.

Dye. That *dye* produced a strange color in that new fabric.

Dining. We eat dinner in our *dining* room. *Dining* at home is pleasant.

Dinning. Stop *dinning* that song into my ears!

Fair. The decision of the umpire seemed very *fair*.

Fare. By plane, the *fare* from here to Toledo is $115.67.

Formerly. He was *formerly* a student at Beloit College.

Formally. You must address the presiding judge *formally* and respectfully.

Forth. Several witnesses came *forth* to testify.

Fourth. We planned a picnic for the *Fourth* of July.

Gorilla. The zoo has built a new habitat for the *gorillas*.

Guerrilla. The *guerrilla* forces are operating in the mountains beyond the city.

Heard. I had not *heard* that news.

Herd. The *herd* of cows moved slowly toward the barn.

Hole. The *hole* in my sock is growing bigger every minute.

Whole. The *whole* office is filled with a strange odor.

Incidence. Better sanitation lowered the *incidence* of communicable diseases.

Incidents. Smugglers were involved in several *incidents* along the border.

Instance. For *instance*, she was always late to class.

Instants. As the car turned, those brief *instants* seemed like hours.

Its. Your plan has much in *its* favor. [possessive of *it*.]

It's. *It's* too late now for excuses. [contraction of *it is, it has*.]

Later. It is *later* than you think.

Latter. Of the two novels, I prefer the *latter*.

Lead. Can you *lead* [lēd—verb] us out of this jungle? *Lead* [lĕd—noun] is a heavy, soft, malleable metallic element.

Led. A local guide *led* us to the salmon fishing hole.

Loose. He has a *loose* tongue. The dog is *loose* again.

Lose. Don't *lose* your temper.

Meat. We did not have any *meat* at lunch.

Meet. We intend to *meet* you after lunch.

Mete. The judge will *mete* out the punishment tomorrow.

Passed. She smiled as she *passed* me. She *passed* the test.

Past. It is futile to try to relive the *past*.

Patience. The teacher has little *patience* for lame excuses.

Patients. Twelve *patients* will be discharged from the hospital today.

Personal. Write him a *personal* letter.

Personnel. The morale of our company's *personnel* is high.

Pore. For hours they *pored* over the mysterious note.

Pour. Ms. Cook *poured* hot water into the teapot.

Precede. The Secret Service agents always *precede* the President when he enters a building.

Proceed. They all left the building and *proceeded* immediately to the parking lot.

Precedence. Tax reform takes *precedence* over all other legislative matters.

Precedents. The judge quoted three *precedents* to justify his ruling.

Presence. We are honored by your *presence*.

Presents. The child received dozens of Christmas *presents*.

Principal. The *principal* of a school; the *principal* [chief] industry; the *principal* and the interest.

Principle. He is a man of high *principles*.

Quiet. You must keep *quiet*.

Quite. The weather was *quite* good all week.

Rain. A soaking *rain* would help our crops greatly.

Reign. Samuel Pepys was briefly imprisoned during the *reign* of William III.

Rein. Keep a tight *rein* when you ride this spirited horse.

Right. Take a *right* turn on Oak Street.

Rite. Taking that course is a *rite* of passage for many students.

Write. Please *write* me a letter when you arrive.

Scene. The last *scene* in that movie was exceptionally touching.

Seen. I had not *seen* Frank for two weeks.

Sense. That statement makes a great deal of *sense* to me.

Since. Ten more people have arrived *since* we got here this morning.

Scents. The *scents* of those flowers are not easy to distinguish.

Sent. We *sent* a copy of the report to you yesterday.

Cent. We won't pay another *cent*.

Shone. The cat's eyes *shone* in the dark.

Shown. He hasn't *shown* us his best work.

Stationary. The benches were *stationary* and could not be moved.

Stationery. She wrote a letter on hotel *stationery*.

Statue. It was a *statue* of a pioneer.

Stature. Athos was a man of gigantic *stature*.

Statute. The law may be found in the 1917 book of *statutes*.

Than. She sings better *than* I.

Then. He screamed; *then* he fainted.

Their. It wasn't *their* fault. [possessive pronoun]

There. You won't find any gold *there*. [adverb of place]

They're. *They're* sure to be disappointed. [contraction of *they are*]

Thorough. We must first give the old cabin a *thorough* [adjective] cleaning.

Threw. The catcher *threw* the ball back to the pitcher.

Through. The thief had entered *through* [preposition] a hole in the roof.

To. Be sure to speak *to* her. [preposition]

Too. He is far *too* old for you. [adverb]

Two. The membership fee is only *two* dollars. [adjective]

Waist. She wore a beautiful silver belt around her *waist*.

Waste. Save every scrap; don't let anything go to *waste*.

Weather. The *weather* last week was very cold.

Whether. Do you know *whether* Jim has arrived?

Whose. *Whose* book is this? [possessive pronoun]

Who's. I wonder *who's* with her now. [contraction of *who is*]

Your. I like *your* new car. [possessive pronoun]
You're. *You're* not nervous, are you? [contraction of *you are*]

SUPPLEMENT

Rule 1: A few common adjectives with the suffix *able* have two correct spellings:

likable/likeable, lovable/loveable, movable/moveable, sizable/sizeable, usable/useable

Rule 2: Dictionaries show two spellings for the *ed* and *ing* forms (and a few other derived forms) of dozens of verbs ending in single consonants preceded by single vowels. In general, the single-consonant spelling is usually found in American printing; some of the dictionaries" label the double-consonant spelling a British preference.

biased/biassed, canceling/cancelling, counselor/counsellor, diagraming/diagramming, equaled/equalled, marvelous/marvellous, modeled/modelled, totaling/totalling, traveler/traveller

English Fundamentals Online

After you have completed Practice Sheets and Exercises in this lesson, you can find additional help and drill work at **MyWritingLab.com**, in the section on Easily Confused Words.

NAME _____ SCORE _____

Directions: In the space at the left, write the expression from each set of parentheses that is more appropriate for use in serious writing.

_____ 1. (Unless, Without) I pay him tomorrow, Link won't have money for
_____ gas for his trip home, and he will be (aggravated, annoyed) at me.
_____ 2. It would be a (grate, great) idea to invite Mike and Carolyn to the
_____ meeting; both of them are (real, really) creative people.
_____ 3. If page 124 is (all the farther, as far as) you've read, you still have
_____ (lots of, a great many) pages to cover before tomorrow's test.
_____ 4. (Almost, Most) all of that movie came directly from the novel, but
_____ the ending (sort of) departed (somewhat) from the end of the novel.
_____ 5. We drove (farther, further) today than I thought possible, but we
_____ still have a(n) (awfully, very) long distance to cover tomorrow.
_____ 6. Roberta is (not all that, not very) (enthused, enthusiastic) about
_____ sending that negative report to the boss.
_____ 7. The (amount, number) of people attending last night's concert
_____ (might have, might of) exceeded the attendance in any other city.
_____ 8. That one long conversation significantly (altared, altered) my
_____ opinion of Johnson's ability; I now (accept, except) him as an
_____ expert in his field.
_____ 9. "(Altogether, All together) one more time on the chorus," said the
_____ director; "I'm not (all together, altogether) satisfied with your work."
_____ 10. "It is not my (nature, nurture) to be extremely critical, but her
_____ lack of preparation made me (angry, mad)," said Carlos.
_____ 11. I can (learn, teach) you to use that program, but I (figure, think)
_____ you will need about a month of practice to become really profi-
_____ cient with it.
_____ 12. The president did not give (ascent, assent) to our request but said her
_____ decision would not (affect, effect) any future requests negatively.
_____ 13. Can you give me some (advice, advise) about a book to read for
_____ that assignment? My last choice proved to be (pretty, very)
_____ difficult to read.
_____ 14. The cabin is just a short (way, ways) up this road; we don't have a
_____ long (distance, ways) to go before we get there.
_____ 15. Those (sort, sorts) of assignments (use, used) to take me hours to
_____ complete; now I finish them very quickly.
_____ 16. When I stepped outside this morning, the feel of the icy deck boards
_____ on my (bare, bear) feet almost took my (breath, breathe) away.
_____ 17. Those fans in the stands need to (reign, rein) in their enthusiasm, the
_____ referee is losing her (patience, patients) with their booing and hissing.
_____ 18. The (principal, principle) industry of that region is raising corn,
_____ but the drought has, as a (hole, whole), devastated this year's crop.

_____ 19. (It's, Its) very (quiet, quite) in the house. Do you think everyone
_____ has left for the day?

_____ 20. Joe (lead, led) us step by step through that long calculus problem, but
_____ five minutes later I felt (as if, like) I'd never heard a word he said.

_____ 21. The detectives (suspect, suspicion) that someone else (beside,
_____ besides) that one man must have witnessed the crime.

_____ 22. Is there (any way, anyway, anyways) that I can get an (invite,
_____ invitation) to meet that speaker when she is on campus?

_____ 23. The students (implied, inferred) from the instructor's introduction that
_____ this (coarse, course) will not be very difficult if they study regularly.

_____ 24. The reason for the competitive cheerleading squad's success is
_____ (because, that) it practices (incredibly, incredulously) long hours.

_____ 25. Do you think we (had ought to, should) (bring, take) a raincoat
_____ with us to the stadium tonight?

_____ 26. The puppy we (adapted, adopted) from the animal shelter has
_____ (adapted, adopted) well to his new home.

_____ 27. Because it is well (passed, past) 6 o'clock, everyone has (already,
_____ all ready) packed up the tools and prepared to leave.

_____ 28. Please call me (later, latter) and give me the assignment for next
_____ class so I can (precede, proceed) to work on it.

_____ 29. Joanna had not (herd, heard) the news that there had been several
_____ (incidence, incidents) of theft on the campus.

_____ 30. Before going to the game, those fans (died, dyed) their hair purple
_____ so that they could be sure of being (scene, seen) on television.

_____ 31. Anyone with any common (scents, sense) (should have, should of)
_____ known that Charlie's plan would not be very successful.

_____ 32. (Sense, Since) we missed that last (right, rite) turn, we need to turn
_____ around and make a left turn onto that road.

_____ 33. David was (plenty, extremely) excited when his boat beat all
_____ (them, those) other boats to the finish line.

_____ 34. We need a (disinterested, uninterested) person to give us an
_____ opinion so that we can choose wisely from (among, between) the
_____ three investments.

_____ 35. After falling into the river, the woman said, "No, I (ain't, am not)
_____ (alright, all right), and I want to go home immediately."

_____ 36. If we go (anywhere, anywheres) today, I want to go to that new
_____ restaurant to sample several of the delicious (deserts, desserts) the
_____ owner advertises.

_____ 37. It is important for you to write a (personal, personnel) note of
_____ thanks on special (stationary, stationery) for each of those gifts.

_____ 38. There seem to be (to, too, two) (to, too, two) many people sitting
_____ at this table for us all to be comfortable.

_____ 39. "These (criterion, criteria) for judging each player's performance
_____ are (extremely, so) complicated," said Ms. Jackson.

_____ 40. The thing (that, what) pleases me most about today's victory is
_____ that the team never went (off, off of) the game plan during the
entire second half.

NAME _____   SCORE _____

Directions: When you find an incorrectly used word in a sentence, write the correct word in the space at the left. If you find an unnecessary preposition, put an **X** through it. Some sentences may have one word incorrect, some, two; some sentences may be correct.

_____ 1. Please tell me wear you bought that incredulously beautiful saddle
_____   and bridle for your horse at.
_____ 2. Whose car is parked in front of the fire hydrant, and who's going
_____   to suggest that the owner might want to move it?
_____ 3. John was not able to tell us weather he will be here tomorrow;
_____   actually, he may have to pass us by all together.
_____ 4. When I herd the score of the game, I couldn't hardly believe my
_____   ears; I'm surprised we beat that team so easily.
_____ 5. "I'm trying to remember where I left my umbrella at; I can't
_____   afford to loose another one so soon after I bought it," said Arline.
_____ 6. The pitcher waisted a pitch because she had to strikes on the
_____   batter, and then she threw a drop ball for the third strike.
_____ 7. It was probably not there fault that they didn't find me their
_____   because the crowd was huge by the time I arrived.
_____ 8. Joseph is a man of short statue, but he is extremely strong and
_____   agile and has shone that he knows how to play the game.
_____ 9. That politician's statement made no scents to me; translating
_____   political language has become a right of passage into adult life.
_____ 10. The last seen of that play was riotously funny because the rein
_____   of the fictional king came to such an improbable end.
_____ 11. In what obscure source did you find that funny quote, the one you
_____   used to conclude your paper?
_____ 12. James Walton is a man of high principals, so I'm sure we can trust
_____   him to precede correctly in the matter of that anonymous donation.
_____ 13. The precedences for that court decision seem quiet clear; it's
_____   difficult to find fault with the court's decision.
_____ 14. Jim and I pored over our notes for hours, and then we proceeded
_____   to work out an outline of all the material on which we'll be tested.
_____ 15. As the group past the courthouse, the guide told a few stories
_____   from the passed history of the county.
_____ 16. Accept for Martha, no one in the room had ever read that wildly
_____   popular column of advise that appears in our local paper.
_____ 17. The coach needs to affect several changes in the team rules
_____   without reducing the effects of the rules all ready in place.
_____ 18. The assent up that mountain leads to the ruins of an alter to a god
_____   worshipped centuries ago by the original inhabitants.

_____ 19. "It is all together to early for us to know the results of that
_____ opinion poll," said Mark; "we'll probably know something
definitive in two days."

_____ 20. Altogether, there were twenty or twenty-five media representatives
_____ standing in that politician's driveway this morning when she tried
to effect her escape.

_____ 21. The results of that canvas of the neighborhoods in our district
_____ suggest that the newcomer will get a bear majority of the votes.

_____ 22. Alice and Marie had very little working capitol when they started their
_____ business, so it was several months before they could breath easily.

_____ 23. "Your choices for desert," read the menu, "are a slice of apple pie or a
_____ bowl of fresh strawberries; both complement the main course nicely."

_____ 24. The cite of the Blue Angels flying their fighter jets low over the
_____ sight of the stadium inspired awe and admiration in the crowd.

_____ 25. Use a course sandpaper when you begin to sand that peace of
_____ furniture, and then switch to a finer grit to finish the job.

_____ 26. Do not infer anything special from Jorge's comments; he acts like
_____ he has some special insight into problems, but his ideas are rarely
original.

_____ 27. The instructions told us explicitly that the test is difficult, but
_____ apparently all of us did just fine when we took it.

_____ 28. "Ware your every day clothes," said the boss; "we're going to call
_____ Monday a recovery day since we finished that difficult project
today."

_____ 29. The committee has decided to look farther for more information
_____ because no one was satisfied by what had been taught from the
existing data.

_____ 30. Not much can be learned from these kind of study because the
_____ amount of people polled is not sufficiently large for sound judgment.

_____ 31. "May I ask Tom for help with this problem, as I can hardly
_____ understand even the basic ideas?" asked Catherine.

_____ 32. "In what store are we likely to find that album in?" asked Wilma;
_____ "I've already looked everywheres I could think of."

_____ 33. As the whole in the pipe grew larger, the flow of water changed
_____ from a constant drip to a continuous stream and soon flooded the-
basement.

_____ 34. Employing a disinterested person to settle a dispute is a good
_____ idea, but an uninterested person might not give the matter very
much attention.

_____ 35. The climatic moment in that novel left almost all of its readers
_____ incredulous because no one thought such an ending was possible.

Brief Writing Assignment: In five sentences, describe yourself in action as you eat the first delicious bite of that food you described in Lesson 25. Dramatize the action as much as possible; use only multisyllable descriptive words in the passage.

Check Sheet

USAGE

☐ **Using Verbs Correctly**

    ☐ Using verb tenses correctly requires close attention to the principal parts of the verb:

> *run* (the base or infinitive)
> *ran* (the simple past tense)
> *run* (the past participle)

    ☐ Tense formation is almost automatic in the present and the future tense:

> I *run* that machine every day. I *will run* that machine again next week.

    ☐ Shifting to the past tense and to the perfect tense requires careful attention to the principal parts of the verb. The past tense is always a single word: the second principal part.

> Yesterday I *ran* that machine for two hours.

    The three perfect tenses require the use of the third principal part and an auxiliary verb:

> I *have run* that machine every day for the past three weeks. By last Friday, I *had run* that machine for a total of 72 hours. By next Monday, I *will have run* that machine for a total of 100 hours this month.

☐ *Troublesome Forms*

    ☐ Three pairs of verbs present especially troublesome problems because their spelling is similar and their principal parts seem to overlap. Three words are intransitive verbs and three are transitive:

- I *lie* down for a nap, but I *lay* the book on the table.
- I *sit* down in a chair, but I *set* the book on the shelf.
- I *rise* from a sitting position, but I *raise* the flag.

    The past tense of *lie* is *lay*; the past tense of *lay* is *laid*.

> I *lay* down for a nap an hour ago, but I *laid* the book on the table this morning.

    The perfect tense of *lie* uses *lain* as its principal part; the perfect tense of *lay* uses *laid*.

> I *have lain* here peacefully for almost an hour, but I *have laid* that question to rest.

☐ *Subject-Verb Agreement*

    ☐ The basic rule for subject-verb agreement is that verbs agree with—that is, use the same number, singular or plural, as—the subject. This rule presents a problem only in the third-person singular present tense and in the third- person singular of certain auxiliary verbs:

> she *runs*
> she *has run*
> she *is running*
> she *does run*

☐ The problem is created by the fact that the third-person singular of these verbs ends in *s* but the other forms end without the **s**. Although **s** is the sign of the third- person singular in verbs, **s** is the sign of the plural for most nouns. Keep this concept straight, and most problems with verb forms in subject-verb agreement will solve themselves.

☐ The other problem in establishing subject-verb agreement is usually solved by determining the real subject of the verb:
  • Prepositional phrases and other words that come between the subject and the verb do not dictate the number of the verb.
  • The subject and verb agree in number even when the subject follows the verb.
  • Compound subjects joined by **and** take a plural verb whether the nouns are singular or plural.
  • When compound subjects have one noun singular and the other plural, the noun closer to the verb governs the number of the verb.
  • Singular subjects joined by **or** or **nor** take a singular verb.
  • When the subject of a verb is a relative pronoun, the verb takes its number from the antecedent.

☐ Reference and Agreement in Pronouns

☐ Two basic rules govern the connection between a pronoun and its antecedent.

  1. Establish a clear, easily identified relationship between the pronoun and its antecedent.
     • This rule means, in its simplest form, that a noun must precede the pronoun when the pronoun replaces it.
     • Use a noun, not a clause or a phrase or an idea, as the antecedent of a pronoun.

     I was tired from the hike, which made Jan laugh at me. [It is the fact that I was tired from the hike that made Jan laugh. The pronoun which has no antecedent in the sentence.]

  2. Make the pronoun agree with its antecedent in gender and number.
     • Singular nouns are antecedents for singular pronouns; plurals are antecedents for plurals.
     • With personal pronouns and pronominal adjectives, use the gender that matches the antecedent.

     Paul submitted *his* paper; Pauline submitted *her* paper. The car has lost *its* bumper.

☐ *Two Problem Areas*

☐ Indefinite pronouns such as *everyone*, *someone*, and *each* have always been considered, at least in formal language, singular, in spite of the fact that the pronouns seem to convey a sense of group or plural number. It is probably best in academic writing to stick with the traditional usage and avoid structures that use a plural pronoun.

- Avoid structures such as *Everyone* will certainly do *their* best.

☐ This use of indefinites leads to another problem related to the gender of pronouns.
  - Traditionally, sentences such as *Each student will do his best* were considered both correct and acceptable. The problem is that the use of *his* seems to suggest that all students are male—clearly an untrue idea.
  - One possible solution, a sentence that reads *Each student will do his or her best*, is both correct and acceptable, but it creates a kind of stumbling awkwardness in the rhythm of the sentence. The solution to this awkwardness is to make the noun plural and provide a plural pronoun.

    All students will do *their* best.

☐ *Case in Pronoun Usage*

☐ Certain pronouns change form to show their use in a clause or sentence.

Nominative	Possessive	Objective
I	my, mine	me
he	his	him
she	her, hers	her
we	our, ours	us
they	their, theirs	them
who	whose	whom
whoever	whosever	whomever

☐ Possessive case shows ownership. The first form is an adjective, sometimes called a *pronominal adjective* because it both shows possession and modifies a noun.

  That is my dog.

☐ The second form fills a noun slot and thus is a true pronoun.

  That dog is mine.

☐ While indefinite pronouns use an apostrophe to show possession, personal pronouns do not even if they end in *s*. Make a sharp distinction between possessive forms *its* and *whose* and contracted forms such as *it's* (short for *it is*) and *who's* (short for *who is*).

☐ Use a possessive pronoun with a gerund.

  They had not planned on my [not me] coming with you.

☐ Nominative and Objective Cases
  - A pronoun is in the nominative case when it is used as
    a subject (*He* arrived early yesterday.)
    subjective complement (This is *he* speaking.)
    an appositive with a nominative noun (*We* students appreciate your help.)

  - A pronoun is in the objective case when it serves as
    the object of a verb or verbal (They told *me* the story. We saw *them yesterday*.)
    the object of a preposition (Everyone but *him* left early.)
    the subject of an infinitive (They asked *him* to come early.)
    an appositive of an objective noun (Two of *us* players came back.)

☐ Pronoun case is sometimes a problem when the pronoun is part of a compound.

> Have you spoken to Juan or *her* [not *she*] today.
> Give your report to Jim or *me* [not *I*].

- Testing for correctness in these cases is simple. Omit the first noun in the compound and read the sentence. You are unlikely to say

> Give your report to *I*.

☐ In comparisons after *as* and *than*, when the pronoun is the subject of an omitted verb, use the nominative case.

> She is smarter than *I* (am).

- Most of the time, the sense of the sentence will demand a pronoun in the nominative case, but occasionally, the sentence can be taken in two ways:

> Sue loves that dog more than *I* (love that dog).
> Sue loves that dog more than *me* (more than she loves me).

Both sentences are correct, but the meanings are different. Be sure to specify your meaning by choosing the proper case for the pronoun.

☐ Who and Whom, Whoever and Whomever

☐ As an easily followed rule of thumb, remember that *who* and *whoever* can usually be replaced by *he* and *him*, or by *they* and *them* if the construction is plural. Test your choices by turning the clause into a single statement and replacing the relative or interrogative pronoun with one of the personal pronouns. The correct form will be easy to recognize.

> Yesterday I saw someone with *who/whom I went to high school*.
> Yesterday I saw someone. I went to high school with *he/him*.

It's obvious in the second pair of sentences that the form needed is *him*, so in the relative clause in the first sentence the form needed is *whom*. If the sentence changes to read

> Yesterday I saw someone *who/whom* went to high school with me.
> Yesterday I saw someone. *He/Him* went to high school with me.

It's unlikely that you would choose

> *Him* went to school with me.

If you select *He* went to school, then select *Who* went to school.

☐ When *who/whom, whoever/whomever* begins a noun clause, the case of the pronoun is determined by its role within the clause.

> Give the package to *whoever* comes to the door.
> I'll work with *whomever* you designate.

Make the *who-to-him* change again.

He comes to the door, [therefore the proper choice is *whoever* comes to the door]. You designate *him*, [not *he*; therefore, the proper choice is *whomever*].

☐ When a pronoun subject is followed immediately by a parenthetical expression such as *do you think* and then a verb, choose the nominative case (*who/whoever*) for the pronoun. When the pronoun is an object of a verb or preposition, choose whom/whomever.

Who/Whom do you think is the best choice?

Test your choice here by making the same change as above. Disregard the parenthetical expression and ask is the choice *he* or *him*? *He* is clearly the choice; therefore, the question should read *Who* do you think is the best choice?

☐ Modifiers and Prepositions

☐ Use the short forms of such adverbs as *late*, *hard*, and *near* because the *ly* forms of these adverbs have acquired special meanings. Among other adverbs, the short form serves well for informal writing, and the *ly* forms are better for more formal writing.

☐ Remember that adverbs modify verbs, adjectives, and other adverbs. Be careful to distinguish the adverb *well* from the adjective *good*, *almost* from *most*, *really* from *real*, *easily* from *easy*, and so on.

☐ Remember that *feels*, *sounds*, *smells*, and *looks* usually take adjectives, not adverbs.

☐ In English, we do not double intensifiers to make a point. We do not say *more* friendlier or most friendliest. If you are uncertain about the correct way to form comparatives and superlatives in adjectives and adverbs, consult your dictionary.

Plurals and Capitals; Revising, Proofreading, and Correcting

Lesson 27 *Plurals and Capitals*

This lesson covers the formation of plurals and the conventions for using capitals.

PLURALS

Plurals of most nouns are regularly formed by the addition of *s*. But if the singular noun ends in an *s* sound (*s*, *sh*, *ch*, *x*, *z*), *es* is added to form a new syllable in pronunciation:

crab, crabs	foe, foes	kiss, kisses	tax, taxes
lamp, lamps	box, boxes	church, churches	lass, lasses

Words ending in *y* preceded by a vowel retain the *y* before a suffix; most words ending in *y* preceded by a consonant change the *y* to *i* before a suffix.

toy, toys	army, armies	fly, flies	attorney, attorneys
key, keys	lady, ladies	sky, skies	monkey, monkeys

Some words ending in *o* (including all musical terms and all words having a vowel preceding the *o*) form their plurals with *s*. But many others take *es*:

alto, altos	folio, folios	tomato, tomatoes
piano, pianos	hero, heroes	potato, potatoes

For several nouns ending in *o*, most modern dictionaries give both forms. Here are some examples, printed in the order they are found in most dictionaries. The first spelling is the more common one:

banjos, banjoes	frescoes, frescos	lassos, lassoes	volcanoes, volcanos
buffaloes, buffalos	grottoes, grottos	mottoes, mottos	zeros, zeroes
cargoes, cargos	halos, haloes	tornadoes, tornados	

Some nouns ending in *f* or *fe* merely add *s*; some change *f* or *fe* to *ves* in the plural; and a few (*hoofs/hooves*, *scarfs/scarves*, *wharves/wharfs*) use either form. Use your dictionary to make sure:

leaf, leaves	life, lives	half, halves	wolf, wolves
roof, roofs	safe, safes	gulf, gulfs	elf, elves

A few nouns have the same form for singular and plural. A few have irregular plurals:

deer, deer	ox, oxen	child, children	goose, geese
sheep, sheep	man, men	foot, feet	mouse, mice

Many words of foreign origin use two plurals; some do not. Always check in your dictionary:

alumna, alumnae	bon mot, bons mots
alumnus, alumni	crisis, crises
analysis, analyses	criterion, criteria
appendix, appendixes, appendices	datum, data
basis, bases	thesis, theses
beau, beaus, beaux	focus, focuses, foci
curriculum, curriculums, curricula	fungus, funguses, fungi
memorandum, memorandums, memoranda	index, indexes, indices
tableau, tableaus, tableaux	

Note: Do *not* use an apostrophe to form the plural of either a common or a proper noun.

Wrong: Our neighbor's, the Allen's and the Murray's, recently bought new Honda's.
Right: Our neighbors, the Allens and the Murrays, recently bought new Hondas.

CAPITALS

A capital letter is used for the first letter of the first word of any sentence, for the first letter of a proper noun, and, often, for the first letter of an adjective derived from a proper noun. Following are some reminders about situations that cause confusion for some writers.

1. Capitalize the first word of every sentence, every quoted sentence or fragment, and every transitional fragment. (See Lessons 14 and 19).

    The building needs repairs. How much will it cost? Please answer me.
    Mr. James said, "We'll expect your answer soon." She replied, "Of course."
    And now to conclude.

2. Capitalize proper nouns and most adjectives derived from them. A proper noun designates by name an individual person, place, or thing that is a member of a group or class. Do not capitalize common nouns, which are words naming a group or class:

    Doris Powers, woman; France, country; Tuesday, day; January, month; Christmas Eve, holiday; Shorewood High School, high school; Carleton College, college; *Mauritania*, ship; Fifth Avenue, boulevard; White House, residence

    Elizabethan drama, Restoration poetry, Chinese peasants, Red Cross assistance

3. Do not capitalize nouns and derived forms that, although originally proper nouns, have acquired special meanings. When in doubt, consult your dictionary:

    a set of china; a bohemian existence; plaster of paris; pasteurized milk; a mecca for golfers; set in roman type, not italics

4. Capitalize names of religions, references to deities, and most words having religious significance:

> Bible,* Baptist, Old Testament, Holy Writ, Jewish, Catholic, Sermon on the Mount, Koran, Talmud

5. Capitalize titles of persons when used with the person's name. When the title is used alone, capitalize it only when it stands for a specific person of high rank:**

> I spoke briefly to Professor Jones. He is a professor of history.
> We visited the late President Johnson's ranch in Texas.
> Jerry is president of our art club.
> Tonight the President will appear on national television.

6. Capitalize names denoting family relationship but not when they are preceded by a possessive. This rule is equivalent to saying that you capitalize when the word serves as a proper noun:

> At that moment Mother, Father, and Aunt Lucy entered the room.
> My mother, father, and aunt are very strict about some things.

7. Capitalize points of the compass when they refer to actual regions but not when they refer to directions:

> Before we moved to the West, we lived in the South for a time.
> You drive three miles west and then turn north on the Pacific Highway.

Do not capitalize adjectives of direction modifying countries or states:

> From central Finland, the group had immigrated to northern Michigan.

8. Capitalize names of academic subjects as they would appear in college catalog listings, but in ordinary writing capitalize only names of languages:

> I intend to register for History 322 and Sociology 188.
> Last year I took courses in history, sociology, German, and Latin.

9. In titles of books, short stories, plays, essays, and poems, capitalize the first word and all other words except the articles (*a*, *an*, *the*) and short prepositions and conjunctions. (See Lesson 19 for the use of italics and quotation marks with titles.)

> Last semester I wrote reports on the following: Shaw's *The Intelligent Woman's Guide to Socialism and Capitalism*, Joyce's *A Portrait of the Artist as a Young Man*, Pirandello's *Six Characters in Search of an Author*, Poe's "The Fall of the House of Usher," Yeats's "An Irish Airman Foresees His Death," Frost's "Stopping by Woods on a Snowy Evening," and Muriel Rukeyser's "The Soul and Body of John Brown."

---

*Note that "Bible" is lowercased when not used as a religious reference, as in "Chapman's *Piloting and Seamanship* is a bible for sailors everywhere."

**Capitalize titles of people when used in direct address, as in "How do you respond, Senator?"

Note: Traditionally, a capital letter begins every line of poetry. This convention, however, is not always followed by modern poets; when you quote poetry, be sure to copy exactly the capitalization used by the author.

English Fundamentals Online

After you have completed Practice Sheets and Exercises in this lesson, you can find additional help and drill work at **MyWritingLab.com**, in the section on Capitalization.

Plurals and Capitals

NAME _____   SCORE _____

Directions: Write the plural form or forms of the following words in the blanks below. When in doubt, consult your dictionary. If two forms are given, write both forms.

1. analysis   _____   _____

2. aquarium   _____   _____

3. archipelago   _____   _____

4. assembly   _____   _____

5. Charles   _____   _____

6. commando   _____   _____

7. Dutchman   _____   _____

8. father-in-law   _____   _____

9. flamingo   _____   _____

10 folio   _____   _____

11. fungus   _____   _____

12. handful   _____   _____

13. inferno   _____   _____

14. lily   _____   _____

15. mouse   _____   _____

16. octopus   _____   _____

17. plateau   _____   _____

18. podium   _____   _____

19. scarf   _____   _____

20. sheriff   _____   _____

21. spy   _____   _____

22. thesis   _____   _____

23. turkey   _____   _____

24. vortex   _____   _____

25. wife   _____   _____

Directions: The following sentences contain 50 numbered words. If you think the word is correctly capitalized, write **C** in the space at the left with the corresponding number. If you think the word should not be capitalized, write **W** in the space.

_____ _____ _____
1   2   3

_____ _____ _____
4   5   6

(1) The guide told Mother and Aunt Mabel to walk two blocks farther West to reach the Museum of Modern Art.

_____ _____ _____
7   8   9

_____ _____ _____
10 11 12

_____ _____ _____
13 14 15

(2) Jerry's Uncle, who retired recently from the State Department and who had served in many Countries in the Far East, often vacations in the South Seas.

_____ _____ _____
16 17 18

_____ _____ _____
19 20 21

(3) Last Spring our Geology Professor scaled Mt. Rainier, the highest Mountain in the Cascades.

_____ _____ _____
22 23 24

_____ _____ _____
25 26 27

(4) Wilma, who transferred from a Junior College in the South, is majoring in Drama and Speech.

_____ _____ _____
28 29 30

_____ _____ _____
31 32 33

(5) Did you know that Professor Fry, our French teacher, has a Ph.D. degree from Princeton University?

_____ _____ _____
34 35 36

_____ _____ _____
37 38 39

(6) A Librarian told me that material on African Pygmies could be found in the *Americana*, the *Britannica*, or any other good encyclopedia.

_____ _____ _____
40 41 42

_____ _____ _____
43 44 45

(7) When I was a Senior in High School, our class read Holmes's *The Autocrat of The Breakfast Table*.

_____ _____ _____
46 47 48

_____ _____
49 50

(8) Besides courses in Psychology and Mathematics, Jane is taking Literature 326, which deals with American novels written since World War I.

Plurals and Capitals

NAME _____ SCORE _____

Directions: Write the plural form or forms of each of the following words. When in doubt, consult your dictionary. If two forms are given, write both of them.

1. auditorium _____ _____

2. automaton _____ _____

3. belief _____ _____

4. cello _____ _____

5. census _____ _____

6. crisis _____ _____

7. curio _____ _____

8. difficulty _____ _____

9. Frenchman _____ _____

10. grotto _____ _____

11. journey _____ _____

12. latch _____ _____

13. man-of-war _____ _____

14. moose _____ _____

15. mutiny _____ _____

16. process _____ _____

17. roomful _____ _____

18. soprano _____ _____

19. stimulus _____ _____

20. stratum _____ _____

21. symposium _____ _____

22. talisman _____ _____

23. waltz _____ _____

24. wharf _____ _____

25. zebra _____ _____

Directions: The following sentences contain no capital letters except at the beginnings of sentences and the personal pronoun *I*. Underline each letter that should be capitalized.

1. In yellowstone national park last summer, I took some very impressive photographs of old faithful and half dome, a famous climbing face.

2. My uncle jim and two of my aunts will travel to the outback of australia next summer.

3. My uncle said to me before he left, "if I can find one, I will bring you a boomerang from my trip; I'll also take photos in melbourne and sidney."

4. A friend of mine, georgette olsen, will be a rhodes scholar next year and will study in oxford, england, at oxford university.

5. There is a beautiful italian sculpture in the lobby of the parsons memorial library on our campus; the statue was donated by the members of the parsons family in memory of their grandfather, jonas parsons.

6. The renaissance is a period in european history when many works of literature and art from ancient greece and rome were rediscovered.

7. *Brown v. the board of education of topeka kansas* is a landmark case in the civil rights movement.

8. The world cup is the world championship of soccer, or football as it is known everywhere but the united states, where the super bowl decides the champion of american football.

9. "We have a very small budget for computer purchases this year," said the dean, "but next year may be a better year for such purchases."

10. Alex's first thought on tuesday morning in his history class was, "why did I ever sign up for history 3211, anyway? I don't even like the saying, 'those who do not know history are doomed to repeat it,'" which is sometimes attributed to henry ford, the founder of the ford motor company.

Brief Writing Assignment: Write a short memorandum to Henry Ford, thanking him for his contribution to American society, the affordable automobile. Use only plural nouns in the memo, and use at least one quote. Be sure to capitalize words as necessary.

PROOFREADING AND CORRECTING

All of the work you have done so far in this book has been focused on developing two sets of skills.

First, everything you have done, beginning with learning to identify subjects and verbs, through the sentence building sections, and on to the word choice drills in the last chapters, offered the opportunity to become a more fluent, fluid, and effective writer by building a broad repertoire of structures, a variety of ways of expressing an idea, so that you can say precisely what you want to say and say it in ways that will hold your reader's interest and attention.

As a simple example, one you will recognize from the sentence-combining drills, look at these two short, simple sentences:

John walked slowly down the street.
He entered a coffee shop at the end of the block.

Those two sentences are complete and correct, and they explain exactly what happened. But if you continued the rest of that narrative by writing a dozen more short, simple sentences, you would lose the attention of the reader and possibly drive the person to go off for a short nap. So instead of repeating the same construction, you vary the sentences to hold the reader's interest. Using those same sentences as a model, you can use a compound verb:

John walked down the street and entered a coffee shop at the end of the block.

You can construct a compound sentence:

John walked down the street, and he entered a coffee shop at the end of the block.

You can employ a subordinate clause:

When John had walked down the street, he entered a coffee shop at the end of the block.

You can use a participial phrase at the beginning of the sentence:

Walking (or, Having walked) down the street, John entered a coffee shop at the end of the block.

You can employ a different participial construction:

John walked down the street and entered a coffee shop standing at the end of the block.

You can switch to a relative clause:

John walked down the street and entered a coffee shop that stood at the end of the block.

By rearranging the structures in the sentences and by choosing different words, you can construct almost limitless variations on those two simple sentences. Learning to employ a variety of sentence structures will enable you to write effectively and hold the interest of your reader. In the world of publishing, the world where books and articles are actually printed for distribution, these skills fall under a general heading: *copyediting*. It is there that another person, a copy editor, might make suggestions about sentence structures and word choices. Because your writing, at least in college, will not be read by a copy editor, you will need to do that work yourself.

So as you read the first finished draft of your writing, the draft you will use for working through the revision process, follow the steps in the revision process as listed on page 318. When you arrive at Step 12, follow this procedure to improve the quality of your sentences: (Please note that by this time you will have read the paper two or three times. Please be patient and work through this final portion of the revision process. Doing so will markedly improve your paper.)

Read the paper through from start to finish; read slowly, perhaps aloud, to give yourself a sense of the sounds and rhythms of the sentences.

Read the paper again to identify the structures you have used in constructing the sentences. Where you find repetitious structures, sentences that sound the same, change some of them to different structures to provide some variety in your sentences.

Test each of the major words in each sentence to be sure that the word expresses exactly what you want to say. Make the wording as explicit as possible. Use action verbs wherever it is possible within the sense of the sentence. Avoid words that are very general in their meaning, such as *nice* and *good*. Be specific.

In the example given above, instead of saying,

John walked . . .

you might have said,

John strolled
John ambled
John strode

You might also have used an adverbial modifier such as *slowly* or *purposefully*.

Your goal in any piece of writing should be to state your idea so clearly and effectively that the reader is allowed little or no room for interpretation of your idea. This idea is, after all, yours, not the reader's. Therefore, you want leave the reader no *wiggle room* to change your idea before it is stated completely. Once **Your Idea**, your very own special statement, is passed on to a reader, that person is perfectly free to agree or disagree with your statement. But before agreeing or disagreeing, the reader must grasp your idea. Your responsibility as a writer is to make sure that your idea is clearly stated, and stated in such a way that the reader cannot twist it or change it because of prior suppositions or biases on the part of the reader.

Examine a farfetched, even laughable example. If you say,

"I think I'll get a pickle out of that jar and eat it with my sandwich."

your listener will probably visualize your unscrewing the top and pulling out a pickle with your fingers or a fork.

But if you have a different method for getting pickles out of jars, if, for example, you empty the jar into the sink and select a special pickle or smash the entire jar on the kitchen floor to find that special pickle, ". . . get a pickle out of the jar . . ." is simply not going to convey to the reader exactly what your method of pickle extraction is.

Be specific in your word choices to make your meaning as clear as possible and to keep your reader from changing your idea before it gets a complete presentation.

The second set of skills gives you the ability to find and correct any errors in your paper before you submit it to your reader. Correctness, coming as close as you possibly can to error-free presentation, is vital to your success as a writer. When reading your paper, the reader probably reacts as follows to errors. The first error gets passed off as a simple mistake. The second error gets a flicker of attention. The third error, especially if the three occur on the same page, creates a moment of annoyance. Any additional errors will cause the reader to begin to lose faith in what you are saying. The reader loses respect for you as a writer and for your idea because the errors you left in the final draft have created a distraction.

So for the last step, you need to proofread your draft. If you made significant changes in the first finished draft, print off a new version of the paper.

This second set of skills, especially those developed in the sections on punctuation, usage, and capitalization, concentrate on helping you to submit writing that is correct and does not call unfavorable attention to itself because of errors. In order to do a successful job of proofreading, you need to recognize something amazing that happens when you read through a piece that you have written.

If you read your own writing from beginning to end as you wrote it, the chances are excellent that you will miss errors and will even supply omitted words.

To proofread successfully, you must break the connections between the sentences, so you need to read each sentence separately, one at a time, from the bottom of the paper back to the top.

Reading in this direction, in reverse order, will accomplish several good things:

- Sentence fragments and dangling modifiers will stand out starkly because they are alone, unconnected to related ideas.
- Pronouns without antecedents, subjects without verbs, subject-verb disagreement and other errors will be much more easily identified because, again, the sentence is isolated from its context.
- Even misspelled words will be easily spotted because you have read the sentence as a single unit, disconnected from the other sentences.

You need a simple checklist that will lead from the largest elements of the sentence to the smallest:

- Sentence completeness, fragments and dangling modifiers
- Construction of clauses, both independent and dependent
- Subordination and connection of phrases
- Matters of usage such as subject/verb and pronoun/antecedent agreement
- Capitalization and punctuation

If this list raises questions, or if some of these items are not clear to you, refer to the Check Sheets at the end of each unit for a quick review.

WRITING WITH A COMPUTER

Most college writers have access to a computer with a word processing program. For convenience's sake, we'll use the word computer in this discussion when we all know that it is a word-processing program that does this work. Computers have revolutionized the production of papers for college classes.

In the days before computers, students wrote papers out by hand and then typed them for submission to a college teacher. The process was laborious, painful, and frustrating. Any copies had to be made by using a black paper, called carbon paper, that was messy and complicated to correct. Producing the final draft of a paper was a long, tedious, often frustrating process.

Computers perform amazing feats with seemingly no effort at all. With one or two keystrokes, writers can perform all the operations necessary to produce a finished paper:

- Set the size and shape of the pages, usually by accepting the default margins in the program
- Establish line spacing, single or double
- Select font type and size
- Insert headers, footers, and page numbers
- Make columns
- Add bullets, lists, numbers
- Record text, the actual writing
- Add, relocate, and remove segments
- Import text from other sources
- Check spelling
- Count words
- Print a final copy
- Store the paper conveniently for future use

This list doesn't cover all the talents of a word processing program. The list could go on and on.

But it is important for writers to see that many of the jobs performed by the computer actually interrupt the writing process.

If you look at writing as a process divided into two separate parts, composing and revising, you will see that most of the items in the list above, and most of the other functions performed by the computer are actually part of the revision stage of the process.

In composing, writers:

- Choose or identify their subject
- Gather as much information on the subject as time and resources allow
- Establish a thesis
- Select content
- Select a tentative order for that content
- Choose paragraph types, such as process paragraph, comparison/contrast, and others
- Write the first finished draft

This first draft is not the finished product, and it will probably never be seen by anyone other than yourself. It is the first, tentative version of the paper, and it needs to be added to, subtracted from, reshaped, revised, and corrected before it is ready for public viewing.

All these steps are made easier than they were years ago by the computer. The problem with the computer, with the word processing program, is that it tries to perform all the steps of revision while the writers are still composing.

Imagine that you are writing—composing—the first draft of a paper for a history course, and you key in a sentence that begins

In the riegn of Louis XIV of France

The computer recognizes that you have misspelled the word *reign* and it underlines that misspelling in red. You immediately stop, retrace your steps, and correct the spelling. Often, the computer picks out certain structures that might possibly be incorrect or need improvement and underlines them in green. When the lines appear, you stop composing and try to correct the structure highlighted on the screen.

Whenever the highlights appear, or when you recognize a poor word choice or structure, you stop to make changes. There is almost no way to avoid the interruption. Lines have appeared under certain words in your writing, and those lines say, "Whoa. You made a mistake and you need to correct it right now." And you stop and attempt the correction.

So in the example above, you look at "riegn" and say to yourself, "Oh, yeah. That word is an exception to the old rule that says, "Put *i* before *e* . . ." When you stop to remember a rule and make a correction, your entire train of thought on Louis XIV stops at the same time. So you make the correction, and then you try to remember what you wanted to say about the king and his rule.

No one is suggesting that you stop using the tools provided by the computer. Those tools have literally revolutionized the writing of papers, and have made the process of producing a clean, beautiful final draft infinitely easier than it was 50 years ago. Not one of us wants to go back to the old methods.

But, and it is a very important *but*, you need to use the tools of the computer at the proper time. And the proper time is not during the composing stage of the writing process. The proper time is during the revision stage.

One Concrete Suggestion

Because computers can store materials very conveniently and make them available with a mouse click, it would be useful to construct a permanent header or title page for your papers. This process will work for both major word-processing programs, Word and WordPerfect.

Follow these steps:

1. Open the program to a blank page.
2. Click "Save As."
3. Give the page a file name, such as English Heading.
4. Type into the page the heading required by your instructor:

Your name	John Smith
Course name	English 1101
Class or reference number	Ref. 25732
Assignment	Essay No.
Date	October 5, 20xx

Set a position for the title of the paper, if the instructor requires a title. Put the word "title" at the proper place and required number of lines down the page. If the instructor specifies some different heading or asks for additional information, set up all that is asked for in this file. If the margins and line spacing for your papers are different from the default settings in the program, set them in this file.

Then, save the file with that information typed into it. When you begin an assignment, open the file English Heading. Immediately click "Save As" and rename the file, for example, Essay No. 1. Then type in the pertinent information such as the assignment number and the date due. You will then have on your screen a proper heading for the current assignment, complete with margins and line spacing. The new file will store as the current assignment, and the file "English Heading" will be available for the next assignment, complete with all the information and settings required by your instructor.

English Fundamentals Online

After you have completed Practice Sheets and Exercises in this lesson, you can find additional help and drill work at **MyWritingLab.com**, in the sections on Revising the Essay; Editing the Essay.

Directions: Rewrite the following short, simple sentences by making them longer, complex sentences. Use compounds, noun phrases, verbal phrases, and subordinate clauses where they seem appropriate.

It was a late autumn day. It was a bright day. It was a sunshiny day. The leaves had turned bright colors. The colors were red and orange. A group of people walked down the road. Five people were in the group. Three of them were men. Two of them were women. The three men owned a construction company. The two women were engineers. Soon they came to river. The road ran across the river on a bridge. The bridge was beautiful. The bridge was old. It was made of wood. Some of the wood was rotten. The bridge needed to be repaired. The people walked to the middle of the bridge. The two women began to take measurements. They began to make notes. One of the men took several photographs. He used a digital camera. They all finished gathering information. They returned to their office. They made plans to repair and preserve the bridge.

_____

_____

_____

_____

_____

_____

_____

_____

_____

_____

Directions: Rewrite the following short, simple sentences by making them longer, complex sentences. Use compounds, noun phrases, verbal phrases, and subordinate clauses where they seem appropriate.

It was early Tuesday morning. Sam was walking to class. Gary was walking to class. They met at an intersection of two streets. They walked on down the street. They walked toward class. Suddenly Sam remembered something. They were supposed to take a test that morning. Sam also remembered something else. He had not brought any No. 2 pencils with him. The pencils were needed to take the test. Sam stopped short. He turned. He ran into a drugstore. He bought five No. 2 pencils. He returned to the street. He and Gary continued to walk toward class. Gary laughed for a moment. He asked Sam, "Why were you worried? We don't actually need No. 2 pencils to take this test. Any pencil will work."

_____

_____

_____

_____

_____

_____

_____

_____

_____

_____

NAME _____ SCORE _____

Directions: Correct all the errors of grammar, mechanics, spelling, and punctuation in the following passage.

The Xerox machine is an absolute marvel of simplicity, and complexity. The machine is reletively easy to operate. Lift the cover, and place the materiel to be copied on the glass plate. Select the number of copies and any other special formating items. Push the start button, and wait for the machine to do its work. Internaly the machine is amazingly complex. Physical principals, that involves oppositly charged substinces, and an application of heat provides the capibility from making clean copies of print and pictures either black and white, or color. Earlier methods of office copying had been cumbersome and slow—assigning a monk to make a copy or messy and smelly—mimeograph and ditto machines, which use volatile chemicals to make copies. Now since the invention of the Xerox machine by Chester Carlson even the smallest bussiness and many of us at home can make copies with enormous ease. Copying is so easy that we all make copies of everything anytime the mood strikes us even if the document is unbelievable trivial. Building supply stores maintains a "bridal registry" of gifts, requested by prospective grooms. Somone on the staff will make a copy of the list if it is requested. Thus if cousin Max is marrying his true love Marcia he can go to the building supply store, and enter his request for an air compressor or a hammer drill, and you can check your copy of the registery to see what Max requested, and know imediately weather or not another friend or relative has purchased the requested gift. This ability is a wonderful thing because it will prevent needless duplication of presence. After all no bride wants a second air compressor cluttering up the floor of her guest bedroom. The Xerox machine is a truly beautiful and wonderful device.

Directions: In the following passage make all necessary corrections in grammar, mechanics, punctuation, and spelling.

Of the seven species of sea turtles the green turtle is the largest, and the most widely distributed but it is nearing endangered status because it has commercal value. It is a large turtle, measuring between 3 and 6 feet in length over the top of the shell and weighing on the average 200–300 pounds. The largest specamens are more than 5 feet in length and weigh 800–1000 pounds. The upper shell (carapace) is light to dark brown shaded or mottled with darker colors ranging to an almost black-green. The lower shell (plastron) is white to light yellow. The scales on the upper surface of the head are dark and the spaces between them are yellow on the sides of the head the scales are brown but have a yellow margin giving a yellow cast to the sides of the head. The shell is broad low and more or less heart-shaped. The green turtle inhabits most of the warm shallow waters of the world's seas and oceans prefering areas 10–20 feet deep where it can find good sea grass pastures for browsing. The turtles prefer areas that have many potholes, because they sleep in the holes for security. In numbers and population trends the status of the green turtle is in doubt. It is under great pressure in highly populated areas such as the Caribean Sea where it is avidly hunted for food and for use in making jewelry and cosmetics. However because it occurs in large numbers in remote area it is not technecally an endangered species at this time. It needs better protection in populated area so that its number will not decline any further.

Directions: In the following passage, add punctuation and capital letters where needed, and make any necessary corrections in grammar, mechanics, spelling, and word choice.

On any Saturday or Sunday afternoon in the fall hundreds of thousands of americans take themselves to stadiums and millions more hunker down before television sets to witness the great american specator sport football. If one reads the simplest definition of the sport football is a game played on a large field by two teams of eleven players scoring is acomplished by carrying or throwing an oval ball across the opponents goal line, or by kicking the ball between two uprights that are called *goal posts*. Such a literal definition however scarcely does justice to the game or its impact on americans. For it is more than a game or a sport it is a happening a spectacle a ritual that is almost a relegious experience for its devotees. The game catches them with it's color a beautiful field surrounded by a crowd dressed in every color of the rainbow teams uniformed in the brightest shades ever to flow from the brush of a derainged artist. It holds these fans with its excitement the long pass the touchdown run the closing minutes drive to victory. But above all these games seem to captivate them with its violence with dangers vicariously experienced with a slightly vieled aura of mayhem. This element of danger draws casual viewers and converts them to fanatic worshipers of the great american cult-sport football.

Brief Writing Exercise: In ten short, simple sentences, tell the story of your most recent test in your most difficult class. Then, rewrite the story by combining the ten simple sentences into three or four complex sentences.

Writing Paragraphs and Essays

Although it may come as a surprise to you, you will be called on to do a great deal of writing in college and in your career. Lecture notes, essays, research papers, and tests are the stuff of which college courses are made. Memorandums, letters, e-mail correspondence, reports, and proposals are basic tools in almost any career you can name. And all this writing, whether in or out of college, is in great measure a key to your progress and success. In fact, in many large organizations, people are known to those in other areas more through their written work than through personal contact. Often, progress and promotion ride as much on the quality of written work as on any other factor. Writing skills, then, will be a major factor in your success.

Writing is also an effective tool for learning. Writing about a subject leads to greater understanding and control of the material itself and to new connections to other facts and concepts. Writing out lecture notes and textbook materials in your own words, for example, will give you better control of those materials and will help you connect the new materials with facts and concepts you learned earlier.

In the previous sections of this book, you examined the operating principles of the language and applied those principles to writing correct, effective sentences. Now you need to learn to combine those sentences into paragraphs and the paragraphs into papers that will fulfill your college writing assignments.

The assignments you receive in college may range from a single paragraph narrating an event in your life to a complex research paper. Look briefly at a list of these possible assignments:

1. *Personal Essays*
   - Recount an event in your life, explaining its importance.
   - Discuss your position on an upcoming election.

2. *Essay Tests*
   - Answer two of the following three questions, using well-developed paragraphs and complete sentences in your answer.

3. *Essays and Discussions*
   - Explain the causes of structural unemployment in our country today.
   - Discuss the ramifications of using gene therapy to treat diseases.

4. *Critical Papers*
   - Evaluate the enclosed proposal for the construction of a new dam.
   - Assess the legacy of industry irresponsibility toward the environment in the United States.

5. *Persuasive or Argumentative Papers*
   - Argue for or against the use of government spending to retrain displaced workers.
   - Discuss the arguments against universal military training in the United States.

6. *Documented Papers*
   - After thorough research into the subject, write a paper discussing the use of nuclear power in this country. Be sure to discuss the history, the current situation, and the arguments for and against continued use and further development.

Although this list may seem extremely diverse and the types of writing quite varied, you can take comfort in the fact that underneath this diversity and complexity lies a fairly straight-forward process that can be applied to all types of writing. You need only to learn one set of steps, the basic writing process, in order to deal effectively with any writing project you might face.

THE WRITING PROCESS

Writing is a process, a set of steps, not a project that is started and finished in a single session. Often, people believe that successful writers have happened onto a secret method of production that allows them, almost by magic, to sit down and write out a nearly perfect draft on the first try. This happens only rarely and always to writers with long experience; most people can assume that good writing rises out of slow, painstaking, step-by-step work.

The steps in the writing process group themselves naturally into two phases, and each phase requires an approach, a mindset, that is quite different from the other. In the first phase, composing, you should be free and creative. Think of this phase as a search, an adventure, an opportunity to try out many possibilities for ideas, content, and strategies. In the second phase, revising, you must be critical of the materials you have composed. This is the time when you must evaluate, rewrite, reject, and correct the materials you developed while composing.

You must be careful not to mix the modes of operation. Don't edit when you should be composing. Don't delete materials, or decide not to pursue an idea, or ponder the correctness of a mark of punctuation. Such distractions will almost certainly stop your flow of ideas. But don't allow yourself to be free and creative when you are working as an editor. Keeping a word that is not quite right or failing to cut out a section that does not fit will produce papers that lack focus and are full of distractions. Remember that each phase in the process is separate and distinct. Each requires separate and distinct attitudes toward the work at hand.

The following brief explanation provides a general introduction to the steps that make up the writing process. In later sections, you will see these steps applied to different types of writing; those applications will illustrate minor changes to suit specific types of writing.

Composing

Step 1. Select or identify the subject.

Basic Question:	What should I write about? or (if the assignment is very specific), What does the assignment require me to write about?
Strategy:	Select the subject on the basis of these questions: • Are you and your reader interested in it? • Do you have enough knowledge to write on it? If not, can you locate enough? • Can you treat the subject completely within the number of pages allotted for the assignment?

Step 2. Gather information about the subject.

Basic Question:	What do I know about the subject? More important, what do I need to know to write about this subject fully and effectively?
Strategy:	Record what you know, whether the information comes from recollection or research. Seek more information where necessary. Continue research and writing until you arrive at Step 3.

Step 3. Establish a controlling statement, or thesis, for the paper.

Basic Question:	Exactly what can I say about this subject on the basis of the information and ideas I developed in Step 2?
Strategy:	Continue to gather information and write about the subject until a specific idea develops. Write that idea in a single sentence.

Step 4. Select specific items of support to include in the paper.

Basic Question:	What ideas, facts, and illustrations can I use to make the thesis completely clear to the reader?
Strategy:	Review the stockpile of materials gathered in Step 2. Select from these materials only those ideas, facts, and illustrations that will develop and support the thesis.

Step 5. Establish an order for presenting the materials you have selected.

Basic Question:	What is the most effective order for presenting the materials I have selected?
Strategy:	Choose an order of presentation that offers your reader a logical progression for the development of your idea. Write the draft in any order you choose, starting with the easiest section. Assemble the draft in the order you have selected.

Step 6. Select a technique.

Basic Question:	What is the most effective technique for presenting the materials I have selected?
Strategy:	Explore different writing techniques to determine which one best complements your thesis and supporting materials.

Step 7. Write the first draft.

Basic Question:	What will the materials look like when presented in the order I have chosen?
Strategy:	Write out a complete version of the paper, following the plan developed in the first six steps.

Revising

Before you begin to revise the first completed draft of the paper, be sure that you shift from the role of composer/writer to the role of critic or editor. You have before you a completed product, not a perfect product. You must examine that product with a critical eye, testing and weighing each part to be sure that it is as good as it can be.

Step 8. Assess the thesis of the draft.

Basic Question:	Is the thesis a proper expression of your knowledge on the subject?
Strategy:	Read each supporting paragraph or section of the essay individually and create a sentence outline by writing a topic statement for each one. From the topic statements, produce a thesis statement for the draft. Compare it to the original thesis. If the two differ, create a new, better thesis.

Step 9. Assess the content.

Basic Question:	Does each paragraph or section offer genuine support for the thesis?
Strategy:	Check the topic statement for each paragraph or section to be sure each supports the new thesis. Remove and replace any paragraph or section that does not support the thesis.

Step 10. Assess the order of presentation.

Basic Question:	Does the order of presentation provide the reader with a logical progression or pathway through the essay?
Strategy:	Try different orders of presentation, shifting sections around to see if you can find a better order than the one you used for the first finished draft.

Step 11. Assess the paragraphs.

Basic Question:	Is each paragraph unified and complete? Is each paragraph developed following the best possible method of development?
Strategy:	Using the sentence outline created above, check the content of each paragraph to be sure it develops one idea and only one idea. Check the content to be sure that the paragraph contains enough specific, concrete details to make the topic statement clear to the reader.

Step 12. Assess the technique.

Basic Question:	Does this technique present my thesis and supporting materials in the best way possible?
Strategy:	Consider whether other techniques might better complement your thesis.

Step 13. Correct the mistakes in the draft.

Basic Question:	What errors in grammar and mechanics do I need to correct?
Strategy:	Read each sentence as an independent unit, starting at the end of the paper and working to the beginning. Reading "backward" in this fashion assures that you will not make mental corrections or assumptions as you read.

Step 14. Write the final draft.

Basic Question:	What form shall I use for the final copy of the paper?
Strategy:	Follow the guidelines for manuscript preparation specified by your teacher, printing or typing the final copy on plain white paper. Be sure to read the final copy carefully for errors.

A paragraph is a group of sentences (or sometimes just one sentence) related to a single idea. The paragraph originated as a punctuation device to separate ideas on paper and to assist readers in keeping lines separate as they read. Thus, each paragraph begins on a new line, and its first word is indented a few spaces from the left margin.

THE EFFECTIVE PARAGRAPH

The function of a paragraph is to state and develop a single idea, usually called a **topic**. The topic is actually the subject of the paragraph, what the paragraph is about. Everything in the paragraph after the statement of the topic ought to **develop the topic**, to explain and define, to discuss, to illustrate and exemplify the topic. From the reader's point of view, the content of the paragraph should provide enough information and explanation to make clear the topic of the paragraph and the function of the paragraph in the essay or the chapter.

The Topic Sentence

The first rule of effective paragraph writing is as follows:

Usually, declare the topic of the paragraph early in a single sentence (called the *topic sentence*).

Read the following paragraph about sea turtles.

Of the seven species of sea turtles, the green turtle is the largest and the most widely distributed, but it is nearing endangered status because it has commercial value. It is a large turtle, measuring between nearly 3 and 6 feet in length over the top of the shell and weighing on the average 200–300 pounds. The largest specimens are over 5 feet in length and weigh 800–1,000 pounds. The upper shell (carapace) is light to dark brown, shaded or mottled with darker colors ranging to an almost black-green. The lower shell (plastron) is white to light yellow. The scales on the upper surface of the head are dark, and the spaces between them are yellow; on the sides of the head, the scales are brown but have a yellow margin, giving a yellow cast to the sides of the head. The shell is broad, low, and more or less heart-shaped. The green turtle inhabits most of the warm, shallow waters of the world's seas and oceans, preferring areas 10–20 feet deep where it can find good sea grass pastures for browsing. The turtles prefer areas that have many potholes, because they sleep in the holes for security. In numbers and population trends, the status of the green turtle is in doubt. It is under great pressure in highly populated areas such as the Caribbean Sea, where it is avidly hunted for food and for use in making jewelry and cosmetics. However, because it occurs in large numbers in remote areas, it is not technically an endangered species at this time. It needs better protection in populated areas so that its numbers will not decline any further.

Note how the first sentence provides direction for the paragraph. It is, in other words, a topic sentence. Every paragraph you write should contain a sentence that names what the paragraph is about and indicates how the paragraph will proceed. It may do so in considerable detail:

> Although the green turtle—a large, greenish-brown sea turtle inhabiting warm, shallow seas over most of the world—is not yet generally endangered, it is subject to extreme pressure in populated areas.

or rather broadly:

> The green turtle is one of the most important of the seven species of sea turtles.

Both of these statements name a specific topic, the green turtle, but neither sentence stops with the name. A sentence that reads "This paragraph will be about green turtles" is not a complete topic sentence because it does not suggest the direction that the rest of the paragraph will take. Unlike the incomplete topic sentence, both good examples are phrased so that a certain type of development must follow. The first example anticipates a discussion that will mention size, color, habitat, and distribution but will focus on the green turtle's chances for survival. The second example anticipates a discussion that will develop the assertion that the species is one of the most important of the sea turtles. Note that neither example tries to embrace the whole idea of the paragraph. The topic sentence should lay the foundation for the paragraph, not say everything there is to be said.

Sometimes a paragraph has no topic sentence; occasionally the topic sentence occurs at the end of the paragraph. These exceptions are permissible, but the early topic sentence is more popular with both writers and readers because it helps in three ways to produce an effective message:

1. It defines your job as a writer and states a manageable objective—a single topic.
2. It establishes a guide for your development of the basic idea. You must supply evidence of or support for any assertion in the topic sentence. The topic sentence is only a beginning, but it predicts a conclusion that the paragraph must reach.
3. It tells your reader what the paragraph is going to contain.

Notice how the italicized topic sentence in the following paragraph controls the paragraph and provides clear direction for the reader:

> *Of all the inventions of the last one hundred years, the automobile assembly line has had the most profound effect on American life.* The assembly line provided a method for building and selling automobiles at a price many could afford, thus changing the auto from a luxury item owned by the wealthy few to an everyday appliance used by almost every adult in America. Universal ownership and the use of the automobile opened new occupations, new dimensions of mobility, and new areas of recreation to everyone. In addition, the automobile assembly line provided a model for the mass production of television sets, washing machines, bottled drinks, and even sailboats. All these products would have been far too expensive for purchase by the average person without the introduction of assembly-line methods to lower manufacturing costs. With the advent of Henry Ford's system, all Americans could hope to possess goods once reserved for a select class, and the hope changed their lives forever.

The italicized sentence states the topic and the purpose of the paragraph: The paragraph is going to argue that the assembly line, more than any other invention, changed America's way of life. The writer is controlled by this sentence because everything in the paragraph should serve to support this argument. Readers are assisted by the sentence, for they know that they can expect examples supporting the position stated in the sentence.

Complete Development

Writing a good topic sentence is only the first step in writing an effective paragraph, for an effective paragraph provides complete development of the topic—that is, it tells the readers all they need to know about the topic for the purposes at hand. This is the second basic rule of effective paragraph writing: **Always provide complete development in each paragraph**.

Complete development tells readers all that they need to understand about the paragraph itself and the way the paragraph fits into the rest of the essay or chapter. Complete development does not necessarily provide all the information the reader *wants* to know; rather, the reader receives what is *needed* for understanding the topic and its development (the internal working of the paragraph) and the relationship between the paragraph and the paper as a whole (the external connection). As an illustration of that rather abstract statement, read the following paragraph, which gives a set of instructions for a familiar process:

> Another skill required of a self-sufficient car owner is the ability to jump-start a car with a dead battery, a process that entails some important do's and don't's. First, make certain that the charged battery to be used is a properly grounded battery of the same voltage as the dead one. Put out all smoking material. Connect the first jumper cable to the positive terminal of each battery. Connect one end of the second cable to the negative terminal of the live battery, and then clamp the other end to some part of the engine in the car with the dead battery. DO *NOT* LINK POSITIVE AND NEGATIVE TERMINALS. DO *NOT* ATTACH THE NEGATIVE CABLE DIRECTLY TO THE NEGATIVE TERMINAL OF THE DEAD BATTERY. A direct connection is dangerous. Choose a spot at least 18 inches from the dead battery. Put the car with the live battery in neutral, rev the engine, and hold it at moderate rpm while starting the other car. Once the engine is running, hold it at moderate rpm for a few seconds and disconnect the NEGATIVE cable. Then, disconnect the positive cable. It is wise to take the car to a service station as soon as possible to have the battery checked and serviced if necessary.

While the instructions in this paragraph are clear and will enable anyone to start a car with a dead battery, the reader may have certain questions in mind after reading the paragraph:

1. What is a properly grounded battery?
2. Why is it necessary to extinguish smoking materials?
3. To what parts of the engine may one attach the negative cable? (After all, attaching it to the fan will have exciting results.)
4. What is the danger of making a direct connection?

Also, at least two important steps are left out of the process:

Before connecting the two batteries,
1. Remove the caps to the cells of both batteries.
2. Check the fluid levels in the cells of both batteries.

Without these steps in the process, the car with the dead battery will start, but there is a chance of explosion. A paragraph that lacks material, that is not fully developed, probably won't explode. But it probably won't succeed, either. Questions raised in the mind of the reader will almost always weaken the effect of the paragraph. Sometimes the omissions are so important that the reader will miss the point or give up altogether in frustration.

Most of the time, you can write a well-developed paragraph by following three simple steps:

1. Make the topic statement one clear, rather brief sentence.
2. Clarify and define the statement as needed.
3. Illustrate or exemplify the topic statement concretely where possible.

As an example of this three-step process, follow the development of a paragraph written to answer the question "What is the most important quality that you are seeking in an occupation?" The student's answer, found after much preliminary writing and a good bit of discussion, led to the following topic sentence and rough paragraph:

> Above all other qualities, *I want to have variety in the tasks I perform and in the locations where I work.*
>
> I know I must do the general line of work for which I'm trained, but I want to do different tasks in that work every day if possible. Repeating the same tasks day after day must be a mind-numbing experience. Our neighborhood mechanic does one tuneup after another, five days a week. A doctor friend tells me that 90 percent of her practice involves treating people ill with a virus, for which she sometimes prescribes an antibiotic against secondary infection. I want no part of that sort of humdrum work. Variety means doing a different part of a job every day, perhaps working on the beginning of one project today and the completion of another tomorrow, or working on broad concepts one day and details the next. I'd also like to work at a different job site as often as possible. The field of architecture is one area that might suit me. I could work in drafting, and then switch to field supervision, and move from that task to developing the overall concepts of a large project. By doing this, I could vary my assignments and the locations of my work.

Following the three simple steps given above, you might revise this paragraph to read as follows:

Topic Sentence

> Some people want salary and others want big challenges, *but in my career I want variety, in both assignment and work location,*

Clarification and Definition

> more than any other single quality. As much as possible, I want to do a different part of a job every day. Perhaps I could work on the beginning of one project and shift to the completion of another, or work on details for a while and then shift to broad concepts involved in planning. For this reason architecture looks like a promising field for me. I could

Concrete Example

> work indrafting and detailing, move next to on-site supervision, and then shift to developing the design concepts of a major project. I know that doing the same task in the same place would be a mind-numbing experience for me. Our family doctor says that 90 percent of her practice consists of treating patients who have a routine virus infection, for which she sometimes prescribes an antibiotic against secondary infection. Our neighborhood mechanic spends all his time doing tuneups. I want none of that humdrum sort of work. Variety is the spice of life; it is also the ingredient that makes work palatable for me.

Unity

Effective paragraphs have two other characteristics: unity and coherence. Maintaining unity in a paragraph would seem to be easy. After all, by definition, a paragraph should deal with only one idea that is completely developed. Second and subsequent ideas should be handled in separate paragraphs. Sometimes, however, ideas can trick you if you don't pay close attention to your topic sentence. A student wrote this paragraph on strawberries:

> Strawberries are my favorite dessert. Over ice cream or dipped in powdered sugar, they are so good they bring tears to my eyes. My uncle used to grow strawberries on his farm in New Jersey. Once, I spent the whole summer there, and my cousins and I went to the carnival. . . .

Things went pretty far afield from strawberries as the paragraph continued, and you can see how one idea, "used to grow strawberries on his farm," led to a recollection of a delightful summer on that farm and opened the door to a whole new idea and a change in form from discussion to narration. "Strawberries" and "that summer on the farm" are both legitimate, interesting, and perfectly workable topics for a paragraph. But they are probably not proper for inclusion in the same paragraph. Unity demands that each topic be treated in a separate paragraph. One paragraph handling one idea equals unity.

Coherence

In paragraph writing, the term *coherence* is used to describe a smooth flow between sentences within the paragraph. In other words, the sentences follow one another without abrupt changes. An effective paragraph reads smoothly, flowing from start to finish without choppiness to distract the reader.

The first step in establishing coherence occurs when you decide how you are going to develop the paragraph. (We discuss the various ways in which a paragraph can be developed in the next section.) The way in which you decide to develop the paragraph will help establish coherence because it will produce a flow and a movement in the paragraph and because it will serve as a frame for providing details of development. There are, however, other writing strategies that contribute to coherence. Three of these strategies are discussed next.

Repetition of Nouns and Use of Reference Words.

> My father asked me to dig some postholes. After I finished that, he told me the truck needed washing. It is Father's pride and joy, but I'm the one who has to do such jobs.

These three short sentences show a fairly clear pattern of development that in itself establishes coherence. Events occur one after another, establishing a chronological order for the development of the entire paragraph. But note how strongly the repeated nouns and reference words knit the sentences together within the paragraph:

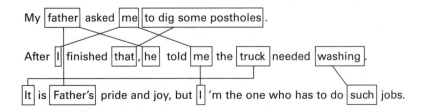

Use of Temporal Words: Conjunctions and Adverbs. Although a series of short, abrupt sentences may create chronological coherence, the paragraph may not read smoothly:

> I drove to the corner. I stopped for a light. A car smashed into the back of mine. I got out rubbing my neck. The driver of the other car sat behind the wheel and wept. I realized that the other driver was an elderly, gray-haired man.

A writer, sensing that something is lacking from the paragraph, might revise it this way:

> I drove to the corner. *While* I was stopped for a light, a car smashed into the back of mine. *As* I got out, rubbing my neck, the driver of the other car sat behind the wheel and wept. Only *then* did I realize that the other driver was an elderly, gray-haired man.

Two features of the revision have improved on the original draft. The first and most obvious is the addition of the words *while*, *as*, and *then* to connect the sentences by declaring the chronological sequence. Second, *while* and *as* convert short sentences into dependent clauses, thus replacing four choppy sentences with two longer ones and eliminating the jog-trot rhythm that gave the reader hiccups.

Transitional Words and Phrases At or Near the Beginning of Sentences. Coordinating conjunctions*; adverbs like *however, moreover, therefore, consequently, similarly,* and *thus*; and expressions like *on the other hand, in addition,* and *for example* can produce subtle transitional effects rather like that of reference words. They force the reader to recollect the preceding material, thus making a tie between the thoughts they introduce and what has already been stated. When you read *But* at the beginning of a sentence, the author is declaring to you in loud tones, "You are to interpret the forthcoming statement as being in opposition or in contrast to what you have just read." *Moreover*, in the same place, suggests that what is coming is an addition to the last remarks; *consequently* means "as a result of what I have just stated."

The ploy of cementing the parts of a paragraph together with these words and phrases is used by nearly every writer. It is a perfectly good device, but unfortunately it is also a seductively easy one. The unwary writer larding sentences with *however*'s and *therefore*'s in search of elegance and poise may get into trouble with logic. "Sam drank too much on our dinner date. Consequently he threw up," may leave one wondering whether the nausea stemmed from the liquor or the date.

---

*Disregard the myth that there is something wrong with starting a sentence with *and, but, for, or, nor, yet,* or *so*. Do realize, however, that these words at the opening of a sentence provide a special effect and call attention to themselves and to what follows them. Don't overuse them, and be sure of your purpose when you do launch a statement with one.

Once you have mastered the steps in the writing process by creating paragraphs, you will need to make only a few adjustments to follow that same process in writing a longer essay, the sort of essay you might be assigned in a college class in biology, business, or English. After all, whether you are writing essay test, special paragraph arrangements, or full-length essays, the writing process we described on pages 317-319 is the same.

COMPOSING

Let's assume you need to develop a paper for your English class. Because the paper is a class assignment, the first step requires a look at the nature of class assignments and the problems of defining the subject and limiting it to an appropriate, manageable length.

Step 1. Select the Subject

Usually, writing assignments fall into one of three categories.

1. **Very General:** Write a two-page paper on something we've covered in this course.
2. **Somewhat Specific:** Write a two-page paper on some aspect of the novel *Huckleberry Finn*.
3. **Very Directive:** Write a two-page paper explaining why Huck Finn's experiences led him to make his final statement: "Aunt Sally's going to adopt me and sivilize me and I can't stand it. I been there before."

The very general assignment grants considerable latitude in the selection of a subject for a paper. Often this latitude will prove more of a problem than a blessing because it is necessary to find something to write about that you *and* the teacher consider interesting and worthwhile. It is of little value to write a fine paper and find that the teacher (the grader) thinks the topic so insignificant that the whole effort can't be worth more than a C. The best approach here is to review the textbook, your lecture notes, and previous tests (if any); to select from these an important content area, concept, or personality; and to use that selection as a starting point for your work. Be sure to choose an area that interests you, an area about which you have some knowledge and some readily accessible sources of information. Once you have made this initial selection, you have converted the assignment from "general" to "somewhat specific." Next, you need to restrict the area you selected or were assigned so that you can develop it fully within the assigned length of the paper. Suppose, for example, the assignment said to write a two-page paper on *Huckleberry Finn*. Several areas are open to you:

1. Autobiographical aspects of the novel
2. Problems of plot and structure

3. Problems of characterization

4. Philosophical aspects of the novel

For the selection or restriction process, choose one of the areas and make a final selection of a topic within that area. The final selection should be fairly small in scope, something manageable within two pages. In the example of *Huckleberry Finn*, the process of restriction might look like this:

Philosophical aspects of the novel

1. The relationship between individuals and society

2. Huck Finn's attitude toward the world as he saw it

3. Why Huck's experiences led him to say that he couldn't stand to be "sivilized"

The final version of the topic (Number 3) is probably limited enough for it to be treated adequately within the assigned length. The topic asks a single question about one person. It should be possible to answer that question and offer examples supporting your answer in two pages.

Note that the way in which your teacher states the assignment dictates the starting point for your work. A general assignment requires that you go through three stages:

1. Selection of a general subject area

2. Selection of a portion or phase of this general area to form a limited subject area

3. Final selection of a specific limited topic within the limited subject area

A somewhat specific assignment completes the first two stages for you by limiting you to a general area. You need deal with only the third stage to complete the restriction process for this assignment. A very directive assignment accomplishes all three stages and leaves you free to begin work on the organization of the paper itself.

Step 2. Gather Information

Once you have established your topic, you need to establish what you know about the topic. Continuing with our *Huckleberry Finn* example, what were Huck's experiences? Why did they make him want to avoid Aunt Sally's attentions? List some of the experiences he had in the "sivilized" world. Here are some possibilities:

1. The confining life at the Widow Douglas's home and Miss Watson's efforts to teach Huck manners and religion

2. The brutal shooting of Boggs by Colonel Sherburn and the mob violence of the attempted lynching that was faced down by Sherburn's single-handed capacity for even greater violence

3. The Grangerford–Shepherdson feud

4. Huck's obvious pleasure at living outside civilization with Jim on Jackson's Island and on the raft

While other experiences may come to mind as you work on the paper, this list leads directly to Step 3.

Step 3. Establish a Controlling Statement

The controlling statement, or **thesis**, serves the longer essay much as the topic sentence serves the paragraph. The topic sentence states the subject of the paragraph and tells what will be said about it. The thesis statement controls the writer before the paper is written by defining the subject and what is to be said about it. The thesis keeps the writer from wandering away from the subject; sometimes it is so specific that it establishes the order in which the essay will be arranged. Reviewing your list of Huck's experiences, the thesis statement for your paper is obvious:

> Huck could not stand to be "sivilized" because his experiences in civilization were confining, frightening, or dangerous.

Step 4. Select Specific Items of Support

Keeping the thesis statement in mind, select from the book experiences and observations that will clearly illustrate the conditions in civilization. All the possible pieces of evidence listed above can be used to point out the conditions that Huck wanted to avoid. Even the pleasant experiences with Jim on Jackson's Island serve to make the bad experiences more vivid. As you select the content, you produce an outline, which is a simple list of the points you wish to make in support of your thesis. Each point in the outline then becomes a paragraph of support in your short paper. In a longer and therefore more complex paper, more than one paragraph may be required to develop a single point.

Step 5. Establish an Order of Presentation

Several orders are possible, but the easiest one to follow is to take the materials in the order in which they occur in the book.

Step 6. Write the First Draft

Begin by writing an introduction. The introduction might read this way:

> At the close of the novel *Huckleberry Finn*, Huck concludes his story by saying that he intends to "light out for the Territory" because Aunt Sally intends to "sivilize" him, and he feels that he can't stand any more efforts to make him an upstanding, moral, and religious citizen. His attitude is understandable, for his experiences in society as it existed along the Mississippi were confining, unpleasant, or downright terrifying.

We discuss introductions again in the next section.

Continue now to the **paragraphs of development**. Paragraphs of development are those you write to support your thesis. In this example, the paragraphs of development would discuss Huck's experiences with the "sivilized" world.

This completes the writing process through the writing of the rough draft.

The Introduction

The introduction should serve two important functions. *First*, and more important, the introduction must catch the interest of the reader. *Second*, it must give the reader an idea of the direction the paper will take. This sense of direction may come from a restating of the thesis statement you developed in Step 3 or from a paraphrase of your thesis statement. On the other hand, you may provide a sense of direction by offering a general identifying statement of the topic.

The Conclusion

Always provide a conclusion for your paper. As a rule, a short sentence of summary or a restatement of the topic will suffice. The function of a conclusion for a short paper is to let the reader know that the paper is complete. Don't leave readers with the impression that they ought to be looking for more material. Don't try to provide an extensive restatement or summary for a short paper. And be careful not to use the conclusion to introduce a new point or add additional information. A one-sentence conclusion is ample for most college essays.

REVISING

Keep in mind the completed version of the paper that comes out of Step 6 is *not*—repeat, *not*—the final version of the paper. Step 6 produces a rough draft, a version suitable for revision and not much else. Think of that draft as a good start, but remember that it is still a long way from completion. Use the remaining steps of the writing process in revising your draft. Wait a day or two (if possible) between completing the draft and undertaking the revision.

Step 7. Assess the Thesis of the Draft

Basic Question:	Is the thesis a proper expression of your knowledge on the subject?
Strategy:	Read each supporting paragraph or section of the essay individually and write a topic sentence for each one. From the topic statements, produce a thesis statement for the draft. Compare it to the original thesis. If the two differ, create a new, better thesis. Omit the introduction from the outline; it does not provide support for the thesis.

Step 8. Assess the Content

Basic Question:	Does each paragraph or section offer genuine support for the thesis?
Strategy:	Check the topic statement for each paragraph or section to be sure each one supports the new thesis. Remove and replace any paragraph or section that does not support the thesis.

Step 9. Assess the Order of Presentation

Basic Question:	Does the order of presentation provide the reader with a logical progression or pathway through the essay?
Strategy:	Try different orders of presentation, shifting sections around to see if you can find a better order than the one you used for the first finished draft.

Step 10. Assess the Paragraphs

Basic Questions: Is each paragraph unified and complete? Is each paragraph developed following the best possible method of development?

Strategy: Using the topic sentences from the sentence outline, check the content of each paragraph to be sure it develops one idea and only one idea. Check the content to be sure that the paragraph contains enough specific, concrete details to make the topic statement clear to the reader. Evaluate the introduction and conclusion separately as a single unit.

Step 11. Correct the Mistakes in the Draft

Basic Question: What errors in grammar and mechanics do I need to correct?

Strategy: Read each sentence as an independent unit, starting at the end of the paper and working to the beginning. Reading "backward" in this fashion assures that you will not make mental corrections or assumptions as you read.

- Check each sentence for errors in completeness (Lesson 13), subject-verb agreement (Lesson 22), pronoun-antecedent agreement (Lesson 23), pronoun case (Lesson 24), dangling or misplaced modifiers (Lesson 14), and the use of prepositions (Lesson 25). (Note: As you find errors in your papers and as marked errors appear on papers returned to you, keep a record of them—either by putting a check in the appropriate lessons of this book or by marking your reference handbook. You will soon discover whether you tend to repeat certain kinds of errors; simplify your proofreading by checking first for these errors. In a short time, you should be able to eliminate repeat faults from your writing.)
- Check each sentence for errors in punctuation; check for missing punctuation marks *and* for unneeded marks.
- Check for errors in mechanics, capitalization, and spelling.

Step 12. Write the Final Draft

Basic Question: What form shall I use for the final copy of the paper?

Strategy: Follow the guidelines for manuscript preparation specified by your teacher, printing or typing the final copy on plain white paper. Be sure to read the final copy carefully for errors.

English Fundamentals Online

After you have completed Practice Sheets and Exercises in this lesson, you can find additional help and drill work at **MyWritingLab.com**, in the sections on The Paragraph; Topic Sentence; Developing and Organizing a Paragraph; in the sections on Getting Started with Essays; Developing Essays.

8

Progress Tests

NAME _____ SCORE _____

Directions: Copy the subject of the sentence on the first line and the verb on the second.

_____   1. A small group of people walked slowly into the concert hall.

_____   2. Some of the people in the room applauded the arrival of the
_____   musicians.

_____   3. Some boys in the back of the room cheered wildly.

_____   4. One of the boys ran toward the group.

_____   5. In his hand he held a pen and a piece of paper.

_____   6. The rest of the crowd watched intently.

_____   7. On the far side of the room there was a small group of reporters.

_____   8. Most reporters took notes on their small notepads.

_____   9. One reporter took a series of photographs.

_____   10. Another of the reporters walked toward the musicians.

_____   11. In her hand she held a small tape recorder.

_____   12. The musicians walked quickly away from the reporter.

_____   13. At that point all of the musicians walked backstage.

_____   14. The stagehands worked feverishly on the set for the musicians.

_____   15. About an hour later the concert began to loud cheers from the
_____   audience.

Directions: Each sentence contains two italicized words. In the space at the left of the sentence, write one of the following numbers to identify the part of speech of the italicized word:

1. noun	2. pronoun	3. verb
4. adjective	5. adverb	6. preposition

_____
_____   1. *Sometimes* new experiences are good for *people*.

_____
_____   2. *Last* week one of my friends *experienced* something new.

_____
_____   3. The friend went to the *weekly* meeting of her *music* club.

_____
_____   4. At that meeting, *for* the very first time, *she* heard a lecture on the history of jazz.

_____   5. The *lecturer introduced* the group to several important people from the world of jazz.

_____   6. *That* introduction opened a new area of music appreciation *to* my friend.

_____
_____   7. She *appreciated* the opportunity for a new *experience*.

_____
_____   8. *Opportunely*, she received an *invitation* to a jazz concert the next week.

_____
_____   9. Some friends *invited her* to a concert at a local amphitheater.

_____
_____   10. *At* the concert the friends heard a *famous* trumpet player.

_____
_____   11. The *fame* of that trumpet player *surprised* all of her friends at the concert.

_____
_____   12. In *fact*, the trumpet player *often* appeared on television.

_____
_____   13. The *trumpeter* also played *regularly* at Carnegie Hall.

_____
_____   14. Somehow, all the friends had missed *his appearances* on television.

_____
_____   15. The day *after* the concert, my friend ordered a CD *by* that musician.

NAME _____ SCORE _____

Directions: Identify the italicized word in each sentence by writing one of the following abbreviations in the space at the left:

        S.C. [subjective complement]   D.O. [direct object]

        I.O. [indirect object]   O.C. [objective complement]

If the italicized word is not a complement, leave the space blank.

_____ 1. John has become the *treasurer* of the company.

_____ 2. The president of the company gave *him* the job last week.

_____ 3. Everyone thinks John a good *fit* for the job.

_____ 4. John moved into his new *office* yesterday.

_____ 5. John will do a good *job* as treasurer.

_____ 6. The treasurer of the company manages the *money* of the company.

_____ 7. Financial reports are also *part* of the treasurer's responsibility.

_____ 8. The reports make the treasurer's job somewhat *burdensome* for some people.

_____ 9. But reports and presentations have always been John's special *forte*.

_____ 10. He delights in standing in *front* of a group and talking about almost anything.

_____ 11. Once he made a 15 minute extemporaneous *speech* about a popular movie.

_____ 12. We all give *John* great credit for his skills as a speaker.

_____ 13. John, however, credits his *grandmother* for his storytelling skills.

_____ 14. According to John, she was the greatest *storyteller* of them all.

_____ 15. She once held the entire family *spellbound* for over an hour with one of her stories.

_____ 16. The man on the street corner looked up into the *sky*.

_____ 17. The sky was *black* with clouds and smoke.

_____ 18. The black clouds and smoke gave the *sky* an ominous appearance.

_____ 19. The smoke, however, came from a *small* fire in a vacant lot.

_____ 20. The smoke made the clouds quite *dark* in appearance.

_____ 21. The smoke gave the *clouds* a very dark, frightening appearance.

_____ 22. We all thought the sky very *frightening*.

_____ 23. The darkness of the sky gave us all a little *bit* of a chill.

_____ 24. Soon, however, the firefighters extinguished the small *fire*.

_____ 25. Shortly thereafter, the smoke left the *area*.

_____ 26. The dark clouds also disappeared from *sight*.

_____ 27. Once again, the sky became a bright, dazzling *blue*.

_____ 28. Those of us on the street breathed a *sigh* of relief.

_____ 29. The man on the street corner gave *us* all a huge smile.

_____ 30. Everyone else on the street was also *glad* about the departure of the threatening weather.

NAME _____   SCORE _____

Directions: Each of the following sentences contains an italicized subordinate clause. Use square brackets to identify the subject of the clause and parentheses to identify the verb. Then, identify the type of clause by writing one of the following abbreviations in the space at the left of the sentence:

Adv. [adverb clause]   Adj. [adjective clause]   N. [noun clause]

_____ 1. A woman *who made a fortune in the oil business* has donated millions to that college.

_____ 2. She believes *that the college can become one of the top schools in the nation.*

_____ 3. *Although the school has a good reputation*, she wants improvements in many areas.

_____ 4. The school needs a new library *because the current facility is too small.*

_____ 5. Every student *who enrolls next fall* will receive a computer for use on the campus.

_____ 6. Every area of the campus will be made Wi-Fi capable *in order that students may work on their computers anywhere on campus.*

_____ 7. This woman wishes *that teaching, rather than research, become a central focus of the faculty.*

_____ 8. Therefore, part of the money will be designated to reward faculty members *who are judged to be outstanding teachers.*

_____ 9. Also, additional teachers will be hired in every department *so that the student-teacher ratio will be lower.*

_____ 10. The woman asks *that faculty members make themselves available for conferences with students for at least three hours a day.*

_____ 11. Faculty members and counselors will be given free lunches in the school cafeteria *because the woman wants to open opportunities for informal conversations.*

_____ 12. The cafeteria, *which now serves dull, tasteless food and has an unpleasant atmosphere*, will be completely rebuilt.

_____ 13. Believing *that good food promotes good conversation*, the woman has hired a famous chef to take over the operation of the cafeteria.

_____ 14. Prices in the cafeteria will be kept low through the use of a fund *that subsidizes part of the cost of operating the cafeteria.*

_____ 15. *When the woman attended the college*, she was an All-American athlete.

_____ 16. *Since her days as a student*, she has maintained an interest in sports.

_____ 17. It is her wish *that every student be offered an opportunity to participate in some sport.*

_____ 18. The college will implement an intramural program *that will include ten sports for men and ten for women.*

_____ 19. The college will employ an intramural director and coaches *who will offer instruction in these sports.*

_____ 20. This generous woman wishes *that every student learn a sport that will carry over into life after college.*

Directions: Each of the following sentences contains a subordinate clause. Underline the clause and, in the space at the left, write **Adj**, **Adv**, or **N** to identify the clause. In each clause there is a word in boldface type. If the word is a complement, identify it by writing one of the following in the second space at the left:

S.C. [subj. comp.]   D.O. [direct object]   I.O. [indirect object]   O.C. [obj. comp.]

If the word in boldface is not a complement, leave the space blank.

_____   1. Almost every day I have lunch with Alan, whose office is next to
_____   **mine**
_____   2. One of the shopkeepers' big concerns is that the street repairs will disrupt
_____   **business** for a long time.
_____   3. My history paper is about three pages shorter than **it** needs to be.

_____   4. The paper is so short that I am **afraid** to turn it in.

_____   5. Whoever wants to go to that musical **presentation** will be admitted without
_____   any charge.
_____   6. The water from yesterday's heavy rain still covers the entire area where we
_____   park our **cars** for baseball practice.
_____   7. I'm afraid we'll have to wade across the **lot** to the locker room.

_____   8. It is highly likely that Joan and I will both make a **C** in calculus this term.

_____   9. Although she has not been much **help**, we have had a tutor working with
_____   us regularly throughout the term.
_____   10. Joan thinks that she might become an art **major** instead of an architecture
_____   major after this term.
_____   11. After she gave the **proctor** her calculus test, Joan left the room with tears
_____   streaming down her face.
_____   12. Obviously, the fact that she had difficulty on that test made Joan very
_____   **unhappy**.
_____   13. There are many people who make themselves **unhappy** by choosing the
_____   wrong major.
_____   14. My friend Will has changed his major so often that he can't remember
_____   his current **major**.
_____   15. In fact, he told me that his counselor had sent **him** a letter requesting an
_____   interview about his current choice of major.
_____   16. Will, whose outward demeanor makes him appear quite **unconcerned**, is
_____   actually a very serious student.
_____   17. It seems that he simply has too many **interests** and has taken courses in
_____   all of those areas.
_____   18. If he wants a college **degree**, he will need to settle on a major in the near
_____   future.
_____   19. My cousin Walt, who was a **student** for six years, never completed a
_____   degree.
_____   20. The fact that most of my family considers him **scatterbrained** doesn't bother
_____   Walt, now a very successful businessman.

NAME _____ SCORE _____

Directions: Each sentence contains one verbal phrase. Underline the phrase, and, in the space at the left, write one of the following letters to identify the type of phrase:

G [gerund]   P [participial phrase]   I [infinitive phrase]   A [absolute phrase]

_____ 1. On Saturday I saw my friend Lisa riding her horse on the trail through the park.

_____ 2. With the horse racing at full gallop, she flew past me before I could wave.

_____ 3. Later, making her way back to the stable, she passed me again, this time at a walk.

_____ 4. She said that riding horses had been her hobby since she was ten years old.

_____ 5. She invited me to watch her ride at her next horse show about two weeks from now.

_____ 6. Following her back to the stable, I saw her horses up close.

_____ 7. She actually owns three horses, each more beautiful than I could imagine.

_____ 8. One horse, the first one she ever owned, was really qualified only for informal rides in the park.

_____ 9. That horse, being a little older than the others, is more easily managed and can be ridden in a relaxed fashion.

_____ 10. The second horse is trained to perform at horse shows in what is called a hunter-jumper class.

_____ 11. In that competition, the horse and rider are both judged for their ability to handle a series of jumps in a fairly tight circuit.

_____ 12. She also rides that horse in events called "equitation" and "dressage" where the horse and rider are judged on their ability to make certain specific moves correctly.

_____ 13. Proper form and the physical confirmation of the horse are also noted by judges evaluating contestants in those events.

_____ 14. The third horse, descended from royal Arabian stock, is her favorite.

_____ 15. This Arabian horse competes in endurance races, sometimes covering as much as 50 to 100 miles in a single race.

_____ 16. Endurance racing, the art of moving on horseback as rapidly as possible from one point to another, is not widely known in this country.

_____ 17. The races are run in stages, with veterinarians monitoring the condition of each horse at the end of each stage.

_____ 18. Any horse judged to be unfit for the rest of the race is disqualified by the veterinarians.

_____ 19. Lisa has run in several endurance races over the past year, each time improving her performance.

_____ 20. Estimating the cost of all this activity proved impossible; "I don't know," she responded, "my parents pay all the bills and don't ever complain."

Directions: Each of the following sentences contains a verbal phrase. Underline the phrase, and, in the first space at the left, identify the phrase by writing one of the following letters in the first space at the left:

G [gerund]   P [participial phrase]   I [infinitive phrase]   A [absolute phrase]

In the second space, write one of the following to identify the complement printed in bold-faced type:

S.C. [subjective complement]   D.O. [direct object]

I.O. [indirect object]   O.C. [objective complement]

If the word in boldfaced type is not a complement, leave the second space blank.

_____ 1. One of my sisters remembers seeing that **movie** several years ago.

_____ 2. All things being **equal**, I'd rather take my car than take a plane.

_____ 3. Finally giving **me** his attention, the professor allowed me to ask a question.

_____ 4. My friends want to know the **time** for the start of the Homecoming Parade.

_____ 5. Recognizing that no one was paying **him** any attention, the dog jumped up on the table and ate all the scraps on the plates.

_____ 6. Making Janice the **secretary** of our charitable organization was a brilliant move on our part.

_____ 7. To find a person **ready** to take on such a job is not an easy thing.

_____ 8. Having awarded **Janice** the job, the members can now concentrate on fund-raising.

_____ 9. Having mastered the **art** of written communication, Janice is a perfect choice for the job of secretary.

_____ 10. The work of the secretary being under complete **control**, the rest of us can do the real work of the organization, fund-raising.

_____ 11. Next, however, the organization needed to find someone **capable** as an accountant.

_____ 12. After all, keeping **track** of the money raised and disbursed is vital to the reputation of the organization.

_____ 13. One of the other clubs in town, its accounting system having produced inaccurate **reports**, lost its reputation and many of its members.

_____ 14. Granting charitable **organizations** special status in our tax system has been a part of our laws for many years.

_____ 15. To call such organizations a valuable **part** of our society is probably not sufficient praise for their contributions.

Misplaced Modifiers [Lesson 14]

NAME _____   SCORE _____

Directions: From each of the following pairs of sentences, select the one that is clearer and write its letter in the space at the left.

_____   1. a. When did you decide to not go with us and go to Boston instead?
              b. When did you decide not to go with us and go to Boston instead?

_____   2. a. Everyone in this room should get to know personally the man I'm about to introduce as our speaker.
              b. Everyone in this room should get to know the man I'm about to introduce personally as our speaker.

_____   3. a. On the way home last night, the men nearly saw ten deer on the side of the road.
              b. On the way home last night, the men saw nearly ten deer on the side of the road.

_____   4. a. You will each be notified by the testing center of all the errors made on your test.
              b. You will each be notified of all the errors made on your test by the testing center.

_____   5. a. The students who can run a mile are regularly put into an advanced fitness class.
              b. The students who can run a mile regularly are put into an advanced fitness class.

_____   6. a. In that case, we either can get the car repaired or trade it in on a new one.
              b. In that case, we can either get the car repaired or trade it in on a new one.

_____   7. a. We sent that message both to Cesar and to Amelia.
              b. We sent that message to both Cesar and to Amelia.

_____   8. a. Barbara must promise either to come to the work session or send someone else.
              b. Barbara must either promise to come to the work session or send someone else.

_____   9. a. Mike can not only type very fast, but he also makes very few errors while he types.
              b. Mike not only can type very fast, but he also makes very few errors while he types.

_____ 10. a. Occasionally, Sam likes to take a long, solitary walk on some trail in the woods.
  b. Sam likes to occasionally take a long, solitary walk on some trail in the woods.

_____ 11. a. I want to at this time bring to the podium a man known to you all, Bill Jones.
  b. At this time I want to bring to the podium a man known to you all, Bill Jones.

_____ 12. a. My group almost covered thirty pages in the textbook while I was gone on my trip.
  b. My group covered almost thirty pages in the textbook while I was gone on my trip.

_____ 13. a. It was reported last night by the newscaster that a building had been burned down.
  b. It was reported last night that a building had been burned down by the newscaster.

_____ 14. a. I met Martin only yesterday, but I liked him almost immediately.
  b. I only met Martin yesterday, but I almost liked him immediately.

_____ 15. a. When it rains, my grandfather likes to tell stories about life on the farm.
  b. My grandfather likes to tell stories about life on the farm when it rains.

Directions: There is a poorly positioned word or phrase in each of the following sentences. Rewrite each sentence to position the word or phrase properly.

1. You either must find the directions to that town or go on MapQuest to print off a new map.

   _____

2. Those who read that magazine stay regularly informed about developments in business.

   _____

3. That particular degree only requires two courses in math.

   _____

4. The team's new receiver was discovered by a scout while he was playing sandlot ball in Texas.

   _____

5. That group not only wants to listen to the speaker but to meet her afterward for questions.

   _____

6. Patrick never should wear that hat; it makes him look like an old man.

   _____

7. Those who came to the meeting neither had read those articles nor the assigned pages of the textbook.

   _____

8. Because I am behind in that class, I think I need to beginning today work several hours a day until I catch up.

   _____

9. My brother said that everyone was not convinced by the speaker's presentation.

   _____

10. The Johnsons have just lived in that house for the past six months.

   _____

NAME _____ SCORE _____

Directions: If the sentence is correct, write **C** in the space at the left. If the sentence contains a dangling modifier, underline it and write **W** in the space at the left.

_____ 1. While walking out of the classroom building, a cold, driving snow hit us full in the face.

_____ 2. To find that waterfall in the national forest, you must follow that map exactly and look carefully for the blazes on the trail.

_____ 3. Trying to finish the reading assignment for history class, the textbook fell noisily to the floor when Marta dozed off.

_____ 4. At ten years of age, my father and mother moved the family to Iowa, the heart of the Midwest.

_____ 5. Research on the Internet and a series of test drives would be advisable before making a final decision on the purchase of a car.

_____ 6. Stepping into the car and driving away from the fast-food restaurant, my coffee and breakfast sat on the roof of the car.

_____ 7. Upon returning from a brief summer vacation, my uncle's construction company put me to work digging ditches and burying pipe.

_____ 8. Standing high up in the observation tower, Joyce's binoculars fell from her hand and shattered on a huge boulder at the base of the tower.

_____ 9. As she stood high up in the observation tower, Joyce's binoculars fell from her hand and shattered on a huge boulder at the base of the tower.

_____ 10. After making that long, hot walk home from the campus, a cold drink and a long nap were the only things on Andrea's mind.

_____ 11. To put together that new surround-sound system, I had to read the directions and diagrams very carefully two times.

_____ 12. To receive the mail-in rebate on that new printer, you must send in that form, filled out completely, and the proof-of-purchase cut from the back flap of the box.

_____ 13. Since slipping on that icy path and breaking my ankle, my neighbors have all pitched in to care for the livestock on my farm.

_____ 14. Since that other driver ran the stop sign and totaled her car, Linda's friends have been picking her up and driving her to class.

_____ 15. Blasted from a sound sleep by the sound of a siren, warm clothes and insulated boots were the first thing the two men reached for before they ran outside.

Directions: Rewrite each of the following sentences twice:

a. Change the dangling modifier to a complete clause with a subject and a verb.

b. Begin the main clause with a word the dangling modifier can logically modify.

1. On driving down the main street of the small town, beautiful old brick buildings line both sides of the street.

   a. _____

   _____

   b. _____

   _____

2. Coming up the trail to the top of the mountain, a beautiful meadow filled with wildflowers spread out in front of our eyes.

   a. _____

   _____

   b. _____

   _____

3. To find your exact size in that coat, the inventory in the back room might need to be searched.

   a. _____

   _____

   b. _____

   _____

4. By rotating and balancing your tires regularly, the life of the tires can be extended.

   a. _____

   _____

   b. _____

   _____

5. Stepping carefully onto the down escalator in the airport, Manuel's briefcase and rolling suitcase fell all the way to the bottom.

   a. _____

   _____

   b. _____

   _____

NAME _____ SCORE _____

Directions: One sentence in each pair is incorrectly written. It may be incomplete, or it may contain a dangling or misplaced modifier, a faulty parallelism, or a faulty comparison. In the space at the left, write the letter that identifies the sentence that is correct.

_____ 1. a. That woman carries that umbrella because it is stylish and to keep off the rain.
b. That woman carries that umbrella because it is stylish and it keeps off the rain.

_____ 2. a. At the meeting, each manager listed on a chart the projects we need to finish soon.
b. At the meeting, each manager listed the projects we need to finish on a chart soon.

_____ 3. a. That motorcycle is more artfully decorated than any other cycle in this show.
b. That motorcycle is more artfully decorated than any cycle in this show.

_____ 4. a. Walking down the street, my brother's papers fell from his hand and blew away.
b. Walking down the street, my brother let his papers fall from his hand and blow away.

_____ 5. a. James Thomas is a man who comes to our company after long years of experience at a larger corporation.
b. James Thomas, a man who comes to our company after long years of experience at a larger corporation.

_____ 6. a. Jack wrote that report because he needed to fulfill the assignment and because he was interested in the subject.
b. Jack wrote that report to fulfill the assignment and because he was interested in the subject.

_____ 7. a. There is no reason to at this time think that the date of the exam has been changed.
b. There is no reason to think at this time that the date of the exam has been changed.

_____ 8. a. None of those present in the room who knew anything about the issue thinking that it deserved so much attention.
b. None of those present in the room who knew anything about the issue thought that it deserved so much attention.

_____ 9. a. Maureen is as tall as her older brother, if not taller.
b. Maureen is as tall as, if not taller than, her older brother.

_____ 10. a. Upon moving onto the field, a huge roar of applause engulfed us.
      b. When we moved onto the field, a huge roar of applause engulfed us.

_____ 11. a. Alex is the tallest of the three brothers, by almost three inches.
      b. Alex is the taller of the three brothers, by almost three inches.

_____ 12. a. Which city is farther east, New York City or Lima, Peru?
      b. Which city is farthest east, New York City or Lima, Peru?

_____ 13. a. Not everyone in the audience agrees with the arguments in that report.
      b. Everyone in the audience does not agree with the arguments in that report.

_____ 14. a. By late in the afternoon, we had painted almost that entire room.
      b. By late in the afternoon, we had almost painted that entire room.

_____ 15. a. Lincoln wants to move to another, smaller town to be near a white-water river and because housing costs there are lower than here.
      b. Lincoln wants to move to another, smaller town because he wants to be near a white-water river and housing costs there are lower than they are here.

Directions: Rewrite the following sentences to correct those that are incomplete, contain dangling or misplaced modifiers, or contain faulty parallelism or faulty comparison.

1. Running onto the field and waving a flag, a man who was soon taken away by security guards.

_____

2. All of us wanting to make a high grade on that test studying very hard the night before we took it.

_____

3. Those two men are as fast as any men on the team, if not faster.

_____

4. The Chandler Building is taller than any building near it in the downtown area.

_____

5. To locate that reference on the Internet, several sites might have to be consulted.

_____

6. Manny Rodriguez recently almost won $2,000 on a television quiz show.

_____

7. It should be possible to not get caught in traffic as we drive home today.

_____

8. By following these instructions carefully, the construction of that child's toy ought to be fairly easy.

_____

9. Coming down that hill and into the valley, a broad river and a beautiful meadow spread out below us.

_____

10. For next semester, I have signed up for a calculus course, a course that demands much hard work and calling for great attention to detail.

_____

NAME _____ SCORE _____

Directions: Change the italicized sentence to the form indicated in the parentheses and write the two sentences as one.

1. *My history test is only two days away.* I need to outline the last two chapters that we've covered. (adverbial clause of cause)

   _____

2. *My history test is only two days away.* I need to outline the last two chapters that we've covered. (absolute phrase)

   _____

3. *My history test is only two days away.* I did not study the last two chapters we've covered. (adverbial clause of concession)

   _____

4. *Read these instructions very carefully before you begin your work.* (This) will make the construction of the table much easier. (gerund phrase)

   _____

5. *Read these instructions very carefully before you begin your work.* (You) will find the construction of the table much easier. (adverbial clause of condition)

   _____

6. *We finished practice for the day.* We all went off to watch the big football game. (preposition plus gerund phrase)

   _____

7. *We finished practice for the day.* We all went off to watch the big football game. (participial phrase)

   _____

8. *Practice was over for the day.* We all went off to watch the big football game. (absolute phrase)

   _____

9. Our head coach has hired Joe Bob Johnson. *He was offensive coordinator at a rival school last year.* (adjective clause) ·

   _____

10. Our coach has hired Joe Bob Johnson. *He was offensive coordinator at a rival school last year.* (appositive)

    _____

Directions: Rewrite each of the following numbered sections as one complex sentence. In each case, use the italicized subject and verb as the subject and verb of the main clause. Use a variety of subordinating units listed in Lesson 15, and other methods, such as gerund and infinitive phrases.

1. I did not enjoy that book. It had a dark, gloomy ending. *My friends enjoyed* the book. It made them cry.

   _____

   _____

2. There are many people in business like James. He struggled in college. In business he found his place and became successful. *Everyone knows* (this).

   _____

   _____

3. *I received* an e-mail from my sister today. The e-mail told me that she has made the high school volleyball team.

   _____

   _____

4. Exams for this term were over. *My friends and I packed* our cars. We headed home for the holidays.

   _____

   _____

5. *Elaine Parker* is a very successful lawyer. She *graduated* from my high school some years ago. She now practices environmental law in the state capital.

   _____

   _____

6. The mall opened at 10:00 A.M. Today was the biggest sale day of the year. The *people rushed* in. They searched wildly for bargains.

   _____

   _____

7. *Everyone knows* (something). The prices of most items increase gradually. Gasoline prices sometimes rise and fall rather rapidly.

   _____

   _____

8. The weather forecast for tomorrow is for either freezing rain or snow. For our trip tomorrow we have dug out our heavy jackets. We have put extra blankets in the car.

   _____

   _____

9. *The worker* drove in the last nail in the last shingle on the roof. The people on the ground gave her a round of applause. She *took* a bow. Then she *climbed* down from the roof.

   _____

   _____

10. The truck stopped in front of the house. The *driver* and his *helper* climbed down from the cab. They unloaded the giant television set. They delivered it to my neighbor.

   _____

   _____

NAME _____ SCORE _____

Directions: In each sentence, a **V** marks a point of coordination between (1) two verbs with a coordinating conjunction, (2) two independent clauses with a coordinating conjunction, or (3) two independent clauses without a coordinating conjunction. In the space at the left, write one of the following marks to indicate necessary punctuation:

    0 (no punctuation needed)

    C (comma needed)

    S (semicolon needed)

_____ 1. Although it was very cold outside, the fireplace made the living room snug and toasty **V** so we sat by the fire all afternoon.

_____ 2. In the fourth quarter, our college football team rallied from a 31–21 deficit **V** and went on to win the game 36–31.

_____ 3. The men stopped the truck in front of the unfinished house **V** then they got out their equipment and went to work.

_____ 4. With exams for the term finally over, the students went home **V** and they enjoyed a short vacation with their families.

_____ 5. The two boys searched in the tall grass for almost thirty minutes **V** yet could not find the lost baseball anywhere.

_____ 6. The two boys searched in the tall grass for almost thirty minutes **V** they could not, however, find the lost baseball anywhere.

_____ 7. The two boys searched in the tall grass for almost thirty minutes **V** and finally a little girl walked up and handed them the lost baseball.

_____ 8. When the weather had cleared, the cross-country team left the gym **V** and set off on a five-mile run.

_____ 9. When the weather finally cleared, the cross-country team set out eagerly for its workout **V** for they had not been able to work outside for three days.

_____ 10. Although the weather had finally cleared, the footing on the trail was quite treacherous **V** so the team members ran rather slowly and carefully.

_____ 11. It was a great pleasure to be working outside in the warm sun **V** so the team walked an extra mile after the five-mile run.

_____ 12. One of the actors in the play was extremely tall **V** so it seemed strange to see him play a character who was 5′3″ tall in real life.

_____ 13. We decided to leave for home an hour earlier than usual **V** for we needed to make a stop for groceries before we arrived.

_____ 14. The two men took a wrong fork in the trail **V** and soon found themselves hopelessly lost in a tangled thicket.

_____ 15. The men remained lost and confused for an hour **V** then they found a marked trail and soon arrived back at a main road.

_____ 16. The volunteers, three men and two women, reported to the project leader **V** and were asked to unload some lumber from a truck.

_____ 17. The other volunteers, who had more work than they could handle, were delighted to see new faces **V** and they welcomed the newcomers with smiles and handshakes.

_____ 18. The project we're working on must be finished by Friday **V** or we will be forced to work Saturday and Sunday to complete it.

_____ 19. We must finish that project by Friday **V** or work Saturday and Sunday to complete it.

_____ 20. The people met where the two roads intersected **V** and then they drove down the westbound road following directions on the GPS.

_____ 21. The GPS directed them to the westbound road **V** so the people drove off confidently in that direction.

_____ 22. One of my friends is due to graduate next term **V** then she will go on to graduate school for another year.

_____ 23. She actually wants to stay in school for the next term **V** for she wants to be here for one more football season.

_____ 24. Once the group started down the mountain, they found their way to the lodge rather quickly **V** and spent the late afternoon sitting in front of the fire.

_____ 25. The girls in that weight-training class are all rather small in size **V** yet seem, for their size, as strong as any of the men in the class.

_____ 26. Weight training is beneficial for most athletes **V** for it helps develop both strength and endurance.

_____ 27. The time the team spent in the weight room was well worth the investment **V** we all now feel stronger than we did before we started the training.

_____ 28. That small building in that corner of the campus needs painting **V** so several people have decided to work this weekend to get the job done.

_____ 29. Yesterday morning the moon set just as the sun rose over the water **V** the sight was so beautiful we all stopped to enjoy it.

_____ 30. When that call comes in, please tell me **V** then I can stop worrying about my brother and start work on my new project.

NAME _____   SCORE _____

Directions: The following sentences contain 40 numbered spots where a comma might be required. If a comma is needed at a numbered spot, write **C** in the corresponding space at the left. If no comma is required, write **0** in the space.

1. _____ (1) In the opening scenes of that movie the frightened confused audience
                                                        1   2
2. _____   completely lost track of the plot in that opening burst of action.

3. _____ (2) I always enjoy reading novels that are fast-paced show complex
                                             3   4
4. _____   characters, and contain thrilling action.

5. _____ (3) After loading the two men assigned to the truck spent the next six hours
                                 5
6. _____   delivering the furniture and appliances purchased from the store in the
                                                        6
                 past week.

7. _____ (4) "Mr. Michaels" said the lecturer, "will you please discuss for the class the
                            7
8. _____   political, social and economic causes of the Revolutionary War."
                                  8
9. _____ (5) The exam finally finished the class left the room and walked chatting
                                        9   10
10. _____   excitedly, to the student union for a sandwich and a little relaxation.

11. _____ (6) George the newest member of the working group was immediately
                         11   12
12. _____   assigned the job of bringing coffee and snacks to each meeting.

13. _____ (7) Jim whispered softly "I hope he brings something besides glazed donuts
                                      13   14
14. _____   for I've never liked them very much."

15. _____ (8) "Perhaps he'll bring carrots and celery which are quite healthful but have
                                                        15
16. _____   little or no taste unless they are accompanied by a high-calorie dip," said
                                   16
                 Pauline.

17. _____ (9) Actually George was re-assigned almost immediately to another working
                         17
18. _____   group so the first group never learned of his choice of snacks.
                       18
19. _____ (10) The first group finished the task they had been assigned and moved on
                                                        19
20. _____   to another more interesting project almost immediately.
                         20
21. _____ (11) Jack and the two other boys drove slowly down Main Street and they
                                                                          21
22. _____   parked the car in the overcrowded parking lot at the movie theater.
                       22

23. _____ (12) After they parked the car Jack bought the tickets and the other boys bought
24. _____   23
        popcorn candy, and three diet drinks.
        24

25. _____ (13) With the movie almost ready to start the three quickly found seats and set-
26. _____   25   26
        tled in to watch their favorite actors at work.

27. _____ (14) The plot of the movie began on July 4 1776 and told part of the story of the
28. _____   27   28
        American Revolution.

29. _____ (15) After the movie ended, the boys went to a restaurant where Jack asked the
30. _____   29
        other two if they had enjoyed the movie.
        30

31. _____ (16) "Yes" responded Bill, "I learned several things about that period of time that
32. _____   31   32
        I had not known before."

33. _____ (17) Tom said, "The movie was interesting but left me a little confused; I'll
34. _____   33
        need to do some reading to get things straight in my mind."
        34

35. _____ (18) The three finished their snack and then they went home, somewhat
36. _____   35
        reluctantly to finish their assignments for the next day.
        36

37. _____ (19) Sleepy and a little tired the three boys finished their assignments; early
38. _____   37
        the next morning, they left for their class with Roger Rhodes Ph.D.
        38

39. _____ (20) The three boys, with that class completed were free to go to the Student
40. _____   39
        Union where they spent two hours playing ping-pong.
        40

NAME _____ SCORE _____

Directions: The following passage contains only end-marks as punctuation. Supply commas and semicolons where they are needed.

Early one Saturday morning after a very long hard week two sisters Kala and Janna crawled out of bed and walked slowly downstairs to find something for breakfast. At first they considered having cereal but Janna said "I don't want anything that's sticky and sweet for breakfast." So Kala opened the refrigerator and stood looking at the shelves for several moments. Unfortunately it was Saturday which was always shopping day for groceries. At that time their mother was out buying a week's supply of groceries so there was not much on the shelves except a few grapes some old stale American cheese and two pieces of moldy bread. As they were cleaning these useless items out of the refrigerator their mother walked in the back door and said cheerfully—too cheerfully to suit the girls—"Well sleepyheads now that you're awake you can help me bring the groceries from the car and put them where they belong. Then I'll make you a delicious healthful breakfast." The girls knew what their mother had in mind for breakfast: whole wheat pancakes low-fat bacon and an egg-white omelette all accompanied by a glass of fat-free milk.

Kala looked at Janna and said "I don't think I can stand another one of those 'healthful' breakfasts they never have any taste at all."

Then they both turned to their mother and Janna said "You've had a hard morning at the grocery store. Why don't you let us fix breakfast for you?"

The girls with their mother standing by speechless set to work and produced a tasty filling breakfast of French toast sausage scrambled eggs and rich dark coffee. When they had finished eating everything the girls made Janna smiled at her mother and asked "Now Mom wasn't that a better breakfast than the one you had in mind?"

NAME _____ SCORE _____

Directions: The following sentences contain 40 numbered spots between words or beneath words. (The number is beneath the word when the problem involves the use of an apostrophe in that word.) In the correspondingly numbered spaces at the left, write **C** if the punctuation is correct or **W** if it is incorrect.

1. _____ (1) To put the parts of that desk together successfully, you will need: glue,
1

2. _____ screws, clamps, and an infinite amount of patience.
2

3. _____ (2) "The other team did not play well, but we gave the game away with our
3

4. _____ mistakes," said Coach Roberts who looked visibly angry.
4

5. _____ (3) The long, dreary hallway of our apartment building is too dark, the only
5   6

6. _____ lights being small bulbs at each end of the hall.

7. _____ (4) My grandfather is a bright, alert man but he admits that he cannot always
7

8. _____ remember his grandchildrens birthdays.
8

9. _____ (5) "Really, Mr. Johnson, I don't think I can answer that question today; I
9   10

10. _____ was up late last night practicing my cheerleading routines," said Melodie

with a sigh.

11. _____ (6) Because my roommate's cell phone has been lost for three days, Myrna
11

12. _____ is letting her use her's.
12

13. _____ (7) Whenever Jon has been studying too hard and too long he enjoys a long,
13   14

14. _____ challenging bike ride out in the mountains.

15. _____ (8) "Your essays would be much more readable, I think," said Mrs. Robin-
15

16. _____ son, if you shortened your sentences and lengthened your paragraphs."
16

17. _____ (9) A sleek fast boat was Jamie's last big purchase; she will probably need
17   18

18. _____ to wait a while before she makes another purchase of that size.

19. _____ (10) The pilot finally, stopped the plane at the end of the runway, the fire
19

20. _____ fighters doused the fire in the engine, and the passengers exited out the
20

back of the plane.

21. _____ (11) Janie Marshall—you remember her from that party last week—has applied
21

22. _____ for a job at the restaurant, I'm sure she will get the job.
22

23. _____ (12) That class is scheduled to begin at 11:00 A.M. but it is usually 5 minutes
23

24. _____ after 11 when the teacher arrives.
24

25. _____ (13) "It always seems, doesn't it, that all the other papers look better than your's
25   26
26. _____   when it is time to submit them?" asked Wilma.

27. _____ (14) Shortly after eleven thirty people walked into the mayor's office and
27   28
28. _____   demanded an immediate conference with her.

29. _____ (15) To receive the mail-in rebate you must photocopy two pages of the receipt,
                                      29
30. _____   cut the bar-code panel from the box and put all those papers in a large
                                    30
                 manila envelope.

31. _____ (16) Having collected the items, inserted them in the envelope and sealed it
                                    31
32. _____   firmly, you must mail it to P.O. Box 1005, New York, NY 10022.
                                    32
33. _____ (17) I wonder who the man is who's standing with the senator and listening
                                33
34. _____   so intently to his comments?
                                  34
35. _____ (18) "Swanson, the third baseman quickly jogged to the base and called to
                              35
36. _____   the pitcher, 'Appeal at third; the runner missed the bag!'" said the
                          36
                 announcer.

37. _____ (19) "It appears that the soccer pitch is under almost 5 inches of water,"
                                    37
38. _____   lamented the coach; "we'll need to practice indoors today."
                      38
39. _____ (20) For that meeting tomorrow morning, we need to bring: yellow pads to
                                    39
40. _____   write on, peanuts to snack on, and an energy drink to keep us awake.
                                40

Verbs [Lessons 21, 22]

NAME _____ SCORE _____

Directions: In the space at the left, write the number of the correct verb form given in the parentheses.

_____   1. If you had (1. written 2. wrote) me or (1. spoke 2. spoken) to me
_____   earlier, I would have helped you with that paper.

_____   2. In fact, I should have (1. knew 2. known) that the rainstorm would (1. fill
_____   2. filled) that parking lot last night.

_____   3. Kelly (1. become 2. became) very excited when he (1. met 2. meeted) that
_____   professional player.

_____   4. The crew (1. began 2. begun) to work on that wall as soon as the wind that
_____   had (1. blew 2. blown) all night calmed down.

_____   5. The windstorm has actually (1. broke 2. broken) that huge limb off that tree,
_____   and it is (1. lying 2. laying) in our driveway this morning.

_____   6. The class (1. did 2. done) what the teacher asked, but she (1. was 2. were)
_____   not very happy with the results.

_____   7. The truck driver (1. driven 2. drove) most of the night, but he was (1. catched
_____   2. caught) in a terrible traffic jam and still arrived late.

_____   8. That old pine tree (1. fallen 2. fell) onto the house under the weight of the
_____   ice from the storm, and it (1. lay 2. laid) right in the middle of the roof for
_____   several days.

_____   9. All the ducks from this area have (1. flew 2. flown) south because the ponds
_____   have (1. freezed 2. frozen) solid in the cold.

_____ 10. Grandfather (1. given 2. gave) me his beautiful old watch, which, surprisingly,
_____   still (1. keep 2. keeps) perfect time.

_____ 11. Alex has never (1. ridden 2. rode) a horse before, but she has (1. hanged
_____   2. hung) on gamely for this entire ride.

_____ 12. My binoculars (1. sank 2. sunk) in deep water when they (1. slid 2. slided)
_____   off the stern of the boat.

_____ 13. When the people who (1. arrive 2. arrives) late finally come into the room,
_____   please give each of them the packet of pictures that (1. sit 2. sits) on the table.

_____ 14. Jill has already (1. ran 2. run) out of money, and she (1. has 2. have) only
_____   been here at school for three weeks.

_____ 15. By the end of the second week, we had already (1. written 2. wrote) the two
_____   essays that the instructor always (1. assign 2. assigns) on the first day of class.

_____ 16. At the company picnic Joyce (1. ate 2. et) a little bit of everything, so by the
_____ end of the day, she (1. swore 2. sworn) she would never eat again.

_____ 17. Please (1. set 2. sit) these plates on the table and tell the guests that they should
_____ (1. set 2. sit) down wherever they wish.

_____ 18. The man standing near the last two seats in the first row (1. are 2. is) the man
_____ who (1. paid 2. payed) for all those children to attend the concert.

_____ 19. I probably (1. threw 2. throwed) out that receipt the other day when I (1. spent
_____ 2. spended) two hours cleaning off my desk.

_____ 20. The dog (1. laid 2. lay) in the sun on the porch until the mail carrier walked
_____ up the steps and (1. dropped 2. dropt) the mail in the box.

_____ 21. Either a check or cash (1. are 2. is) needed as payment if you want to hold those
_____ seats you and your friends (1. has 2. have) selected for the bowl game.

_____ 22. A number of my friends who enrolled in that difficult math course (1. has
_____ 2. have) withdrawn because the course (1. taken 2. took) too much of their time.

_____ 23. The number of accidents on our streets (1. has 2. have) declined steadily since
_____ the police (1. has 2. have) begun to enforce traffic laws more strictly than before.

_____ 24. The rest of the people (1. fit 2. fits) easily into that small room that (1. open
_____ 2. opens) off the main conference room.

_____ 25. Johnson is one of those men who never (1. let 2. lets) a problem overwhelm
_____ them; none of the challenges he has met have (1. overcame 2. overcome) him.

_____ 26. My uncle Bill has always (1. thunk 2. thought) himself a funny man, but none
_____ of the jokes he tells (1. are 2. is) very funny.

_____ 27. All of that money we collected last week (1. go 2. goes) to support a charity
_____ that (1. provide 2. provides) Thanksgiving dinner to needy families.

_____ 28. Jillian is the only one of my friends who (1. continue 2. continues) to play
_____ strenuous sports even though she (1. leaved 2. left) college several years ago.

_____ 29. You, as the person who organized this trip, (1. need 2. needs) to select
_____ restaurants that all of us (1. enjoy 2. enjoys).

_____ 30. I know only one person who (1. doesn't 2. don't) enjoy coconut cream pie;
_____ most of my friends (1. enjoy 2. enjoys) that dessert immensely.

NAME _____   SCORE _____

Directions: Examine each verb in the following sentences for form, tense, and subject-verb agreement. If the verb is incorrect, write the correct form in the space at the left. If the verb is correct, write **C** in the space. No sentence has more than two incorrect verbs.

_____
_____ 1. No one except a few jokers and comedians have answered my request for a number of people who wants to work on that archeological site beside the river.

_____
_____ 2. The site become known to archeologists when the Department of Transportation began a project to widen the bridge over the river.

_____
_____ 3. The first hole the workers digged produced arrowheads and some pieces of pottery that was probably used by Native Americans two or three centuries ago.

_____
_____ 4. When word of the discovery of the artifacts spreads, the DOT stopped work on the project and sent in the state's archeologist, who goed to the site immediately.

_____
_____ 5. The archeologist, whose responsibilities includes checking sites where roads are being widened, realize immediately that this discovery was very important.

_____
_____ 6. So the archeologist bringed together a team of people, some of whom was volunteers, to go to the site to explore.

_____
_____ 7. First, the team layed out the boundaries of the site, an area of swamp and dry ground that covers about 600 square yards.

_____
_____ 8. The team then breaked the site into squares, creating a grid that allowed the team to pinpoint the location where each artifact were discovered.

_____
_____ 9. After they had layed out the area where they wished to dig, the team members builded a fence around the entire area.

_____
_____ 10. Then the team installed surveillance cameras so that the site could be protected from vandals and illegal collectors 24 hours a day.

_____
_____ 11. The team leader then maked a contract with a security company to station a guard on the site every night and on days when the team did not work.

_____ 12. The pieces of pottery and even very small pieces of arrowheads is
_____ very valuable and often sells for very high prices on the black
market.

_____ 13. With the site lain out in a grid and security established, the team
_____ members actually began the work of excavating the site.

_____ 14. First, with heavy machinery, they stript off the first foot of topsoil;
_____ then, they dug 4-foot square holes in various locations on the site.

_____ 15. As they shovellt the dirt out of the holes, they sifted every
_____ shovelful of dirt through a screen so that they could locate every
artifact.

_____ 16. For each artifact they uncovered, the team members writ a note in
_____ a notebook and then sticked a label on the artifact.

_____ 17. The note and the label showed where each of the artifacts were
_____ found, so the team members could envision how the Native
Americans used the site.

_____ 18. The pieces of pottery and other household items lead the team
_____ to conclude that there was at one time small shelters on the site
and that it was in fact a village.

_____ 19. The earliest artifacts, those that was buried most deeply,
_____ suggested to the team that the site had been occupied as early
as 1000 B.C.

_____ 20. Level by level, the team unearthed evidence that the site was
_____ used at least intermittently up until the early 19th century.

_____ 21. Some volunteers working in a back corner of the site uncovered
_____ items laying near the surface.

_____ 22. These items, because they was located near the surface, were
_____ made of metal and wood that had been shaped with metal tools.

_____ 23. These more modern items was probably used by European
_____ settlers who comed into the area after the Native Americans
had left it.

_____ 24. The team remained at work on the site for almost four months,
and the members built a historical record that covered almost
3,000 years.

_____ 25. The dig, which costed almost $1,000,000 and delayed road con-
struction for longer than four months, were considered a huge
success by historians and archeologists alike.

Directions: Study the following sentences for poorly used pronouns. One sentence in each pair contains wrong case forms, misspelled possessives, or vague or inexact references. In the space at the left, write the letter that identifies the correct sentence.

_____ 1. a. We waited for a long time in the outer office; then the secretary told Walter and me that the boss would see us.
b. We waited for a long time in the outer office, then they told Walter and I that the boss would see us.

_____ 2. a. Lets assume that the job needs to be done, and its our's and not theirs.
b. Let's assume that the job needs to be done, and it's ours and not theirs.

_____ 3. a. I'm not surprised that whomever drew that caricature of the local politician didn't sign their name to it.
b. I'm not surprised that whoever drew that caricature of the local politician didn't sign his or her name to it.

_____ 4. a. Because my Uncle Bob is a fanatic follower of chess, he tried to interest my brother and me in the game.
b. Because my Uncle Bob is a fanatic follower of chess, he tried to interest my brother and I in it.

_____ 5. a. You should tell anyone whom you think might submit an entry in the essay contest to be sure to double-check their entry for the format and for errors.
b. You should tell anyone who you think might submit an entry in the essay contest to be sure to double-check the entry for the format and for errors.

_____ 6. a. Mark Willis, who is a friend of ours, told us that he is unhappy about our changing into Mr. Landy's class.
b. Mark Willis, whom is a friend of our's, told us that he is unhappy about us changing into Mr. Landys class.

_____ 7. a. Tomorrows weather report calls for rain and fairly strong winds; that will probably cause us to postpone the company softball game.
b. Tomorrow's weather report calls for rain and fairly strong winds; that kind of weather will probably cause us to postpone the company softball game.

_____ 8. a. The weather report on TV said to expect rain and fairly strong winds for tomorrow; that report will probably cause us to postpone the company picnic.
b. They said on TV to expect rain and fairly strong winds for tomorrow; that will probably cause us to postpone the company picnic.

_____ 9. a. Please tell whomever answers the phone at the office that the people who we invited to the meeting will be about two hours late.
b. Please tell whoever answers the phone at the office that the people whom we invited to the meeting will be about two hours late.

_____ 10. a. The noise of the crowd at the parade below us caused all of we staff members to go to the window to watch it.

b. The noise of the crowd at the parade below us caused all of us staff members to go to the window to watch the parade.

_____ 11. a. Marthas car will not move successfully through all this mud and slush, so I suggest we take your's, which has all-wheel drive.

b. Martha's car will not move successfully through all this mud and slush, so I suggest we take yours, which has all-wheel drive.

_____ 12. a. The men in the car followed a bright yellow truck through the fog, and he led them safely to town where it cleared up and they could go on.

b. The men in the car followed a bright yellow truck through the fog, and it led them safely to town where the fog cleared up and they could go on.

_____ 13. a. Either of we players could move successfully to shortstop, so the coach selected the one whom he thought would hit for a higher average.

b. Either of us players could move successfully to shortstop, so the coach selected the one who he thought would hit for a higher average.

_____ 14. a. Mark's paper had several spelling errors in it, which caused the teacher to give it a low grade.

b. Mark's paper had several spelling errors in it; these errors caused the teacher to give the paper a low grade.

_____ 15. a. The boss didn't make any negative comments on my report, and that surprised me because she usually criticizes them heavily.

b. The boss didn't make any negative comments on my report, and I was surprised because she usually criticizes such reports heavily.

_____ 16. a. Everyone of we students in this room needs to do their best work on this project because this makes up 30 percent of your grade for the course.

b. Everyone of us students in this room needs to do his or her best work on this project because the grade on the project makes up 30 percent of the grade for the course.

_____ 17. a. I heard them say on the news that the streets downtown will be closed during the parade, which will cause us to make a wide detour on our way home.

b. I heard the newscaster say that the streets downtown will be closed during the parade; the closures will cause us to make a wide detour on our way home.

_____ 18. a. The professor implied that she liked Jacksons report better than our's, but I thought it was not better than anyone elses.

b. The professor implied that she liked Jackson's report better than ours, but I thought his report was not better than anyone else's.

_____ 19. a. None of us committee members could remember the chair asking for those statistics, so they weren't ready for today's meeting.

b. None of we committee members could remember the chair asking for those statistics, so it wasn't ready for todays meeting.

_____ 20. a. The door to the classroom was locked when us students arrived, which annoyed the teacher and delayed the start of class by several minutes.

b. The door to the classroom was locked when we students arrived, and this problem annoyed the teacher and delayed the start of class by several minutes.

NAME _____   SCORE _____

Directions: In the spaces at the left, write the numbers of the correct forms given in parentheses.

_____ 1. (1. Beside 2. Besides) me on the bus sat a young woman (1. contented
_____   2. contentedly) reading a romance novel.

_____ 2. The young woman seemed quite (1. happy 2. happily) even though a tear rolled
_____   (1. gentle 2. gently) down her cheek.

_____ 3. Johnson played (1. good 2. well) in the last game; in fact, the entire team played
_____   a (1. real 2. really) good game.

_____ 4. (1. Almost 2. Most) every person in my classes has some sort of part-time
_____   job that involves a (1. considerable 2. considerably) investment of time.

_____ 5. (1. Regular 2. Regularly) practice has improved my skills (1. at 2. in)
_____   racquetball over the past few months.

_____ 6. Practicing (1. regular 2. regularly) has improved my skills as a racquetball
_____   player; a few months ago I played the game rather (1. bad 2. badly).

_____ 7. I wanted very (1. bad 2. badly) to improve my game, so I spent hours
_____   (1. rigorous 2. rigorously) practicing my shots.

_____ 8. When we walked (1. inside 2. insides) the house, it seemed quite (1. emptily
_____   2. empty).

_____ 9. Doesn't Melinda's apple pie smell (1. exceptional 2. exceptionally) (1. sweet
_____   2. sweetly)?

_____ 10. The young girl smiled (1. bright 2. brightly) as she asked her uncle for money
_____   to buy a very (1. cheap 2. cheaply) looking toy.

_____ 11. As (1. cheerful 2. cheerfully) as her smile was, her uncle (1. definite
_____   2. definitely) opposed her request.

_____ 12. (1. Because of 2. Due to) the changes in the timing of the traffic lights, I now
_____   get to campus ten minutes (1. earlier 2. more earlier) than I did last term.

_____ 13. (1. Seeming 2. Seemingly), the more I study the more I confuse the concepts
_____   listed (1. between 2. among) the three chapters in chemistry.

_____ 14. After I recovered from the virus, I felt (1. good 2. well) enough to go to
_____   softball practice and actually played (1. better 2. best) than I had before.

_____ 15. The air conditioner sounds (1. bad 2. badly); if it doesn't stop making that
_____   (1. horrible 2. horribly) noise, we'll need to replace it.

_____ 16. Since I have been training (1. hard 2. hardly) in the weight room, I have become
_____   much (1. stronger 2. more stronger) than I was before.

_____ 17. The rain fell (1. steady 2. steadily) for several days, and the water in the pond
_____   in the pasture rose quite (1. rapid 2. rapidly).

_____ 18. If you would work more (1. regular 2. regularly) on your algebra, your
_____   performance in that class would probably be (1. more successful 2. more
_____   successfully).

_____ 19. The two classmates (1. hard 2. hardly) knew each other, but they collaborated
_____   quite (1. nice 2. nicely) on that project.

_____ 20. The attorney said, "We must watch the stock market (1. close 2. closely) so we
_____   can sell that stock at the (1. better 2. best) possible price."

_____ 21. I have not seen them (1. recent 2. recently), but I heard that they have become
_____   (1. real 2. very) successful in their new business.

_____ 22. Jim had a (1. close 2. closely) call last night on that foggy road, so he has
_____   decided to leave for home a little (1. early 2. earlier) than usual tonight.

_____ 23. She is known far and (1. wide 2. widely) as an artist, and her paintings sell very
_____   (1. good 2. well) all across the state.

_____ 24. (1. Almost 2. Most) all of the people in town want very (1. bad 2. badly) for
_____   that bond issue to pass.

_____ 25. The vacant house echoed (1. emptily 2. empty) as we walked (1. soft
_____   2. softly) down the hallway.

_____ 26. We can argue (1. with 2. about) that issue forever, but I doubt we'll come any
_____   (1. closer 2. more closer) to an agreement.

_____ 27. His idea differs (1. complete 2. completely) (1. from 2. with) mine, but I'm
_____   sure that we will remain good friends anyway.

_____ 28. (1. Beside 2. Besides) Uncle John, there is no one I can trust (1. full 2. fully)
_____   with that secret.

_____ 29. The staff (1. met 2. met with) the new architect yesterday and submitted a
_____   (1. pretty 2. rather) lengthy list of improvements needed in the office.

_____ 30. The dog (1. usual 2. usually) sleeps outside, but during thunderstorms he
_____   prefers to be (1. inside 2. inside of) the house.

NAME _____ SCORE _____

Directions: Each sentence has two italicized words or expressions. If you think that a word or expression is not suitable for serious writing, write a suitable form in the space at the left. If the word or expression is suitable, write **C** in the space.

_____   1. *Lots of* people attended that movie during the past weekend, but
_____   the *nurture* of the subject matter didn't appeal to very many.

_____   2. *Who's* going to pick up those documents from the duplicating
_____   department? I have *all ready* made two trips there today.

_____   3. *Accept* for Mr. London, all of the staff members are here; I don't
_____   think his absence will *effect* the outcome of the meeting very much.

_____   4. We *ain't* going to take sides in that dispute because *their* seems to
_____   be no reasonable solution to the problem.

_____   5. If that is *all the faster* you can walk, we will not be able to catch
_____   the subway before *it's* departure from the station.

_____   6. *Between* the three of us we didn't have more then $10, hardly
_____   enough for a decent lunch *irregardless* of our choice of restaurant.

_____   7. The *amount* of people who want to attend that meeting far
_____   *exceeds* the seating capacity of the room we reserved.

_____   8. It's *kind of* ironic, isn't it, that Jill enjoyed the party after telling
_____   us she was *mad at* Mary Jane and would not come?

_____   9. When I heard that *incredulous* story, I dismissed it as an urban
_____   legend and *figured* no one would believe it.

_____   10. "Do not *imply* from my previous statements that I am questioning
_____   the lawyer's interpretation of that *stature*," said Mr. Olsen.

_____   11. No one really knows what to *ware* on "casual Friday," but shorts
_____   and a baggy shirt are surely *to* casual for our company.

_____   12. That statement made no *scents* to anyone in the office, so we all
_____   did what we wanted to do *anyways*.

_____   13. The judge rendered a *fare* decision, but the cost to our company is
_____   difficult to *calculate* at this time.

_____   14. That arbitrator *can't hardly* be called an *uninterested* party; his
_____   cousin owns an interest in one of the companies involved in the
_____   dispute.

_____ 15. The *consensus of opinion* among my friends is that law school is
_____ *likely* to be a good direction for many people.

_____ 16. In the past, statistics have *shone* that dentists and air traffic
_____ controllers work under *continuous* stress.

_____ 17. If the drought continues for much longer, some people may
_____ choose to *emigrate* from this area to one with more pleasant
climactic conditions.

_____ 18. Those people below us in the grandstand *should of* sought shelter
_____ from the *reign* before they got completely soaked.

_____ 19. Jan's brother, for *instants*, is a good example of someone *who's*
_____ hard work and dedication have paid off.

_____ 20. *Being that* Tom has often gone *farther* in his efforts at work than
_____ any of the rest of us, there is no way he should not be promoted.

_____ 21. The resort is just a short *ways* out of town, and it is a place *where*
_____ you can easily find relaxation *at*.

_____ 22. The last *seen* in that movie occurred in the *dessert*, and we left
_____ immediately to find something cold to drink.

_____ 23. Their *presents* at my graduation was greatly appreciated because
_____ I had *herd* that they would not be able to come.

_____ 24. In Joanne's *canvas* of the neighborhood, she discovered that her
_____ favorite candidate is probably going to *loose* in the election for
mayor.

_____ 25. The carpenters did a *thorough* job of cleaning up the job *cite* and
_____ left work for the weekend.

_____ 26. The *stationary* Lisa used for her letter to the college was the same
_____ as she used *formally* for her recent letters to her friends.

_____ 27. The one *criteria* Jim has for a college is that it should be *fair*
_____ close to his home because he loves his mother's cooking.

_____ 28. In that debate both sides had no *doubt but that* they were right,
_____ but, in fact, neither side had possession of a *couple of* important facts.

_____ 29. My brother has resolved to pursue a *healthy* lifestyle by getting
_____ more exercise and eating *less* desserts.

_____ 30. "*Leave us* get out of *hear*," said my brother, laughing; "I don't
_____ think I can listen to one more corny joke from that comedian."

Plurals and Capitals [Lesson 27]

NAME _____ SCORE _____

Directions: Write the plural form or forms of the following words in the blanks beside the words. If you are not certain of the correct form for the plural, consult your dictionary. If two forms are given, write both of them.

1. beef   _____   _____

2. child   _____   _____

3. curio   _____   _____

4. donkey   _____   _____

5. fox   _____   _____

6. graffito   _____   _____

7. handkerchief   _____   _____

8. hippopotamus   _____   _____

9. knife   _____   _____

10. mouse   _____   _____

11. oasis   _____   _____

12. opportunity   _____   _____

13. phenomenon   _____   _____

14. portico   _____   _____

15. process   _____   _____

16. roomful   _____   _____

17. species   _____   _____

18. stadium   _____   _____

19. syllabus   _____   _____

20. trout   _____   _____

21. valley   _____   _____

22. variety   _____   _____

23. waltz   _____   _____

24. witch   _____   _____

25. workman   _____   _____

Directions: The following sentences have capital letters only at the beginning of sentences and for the pronoun *I*. Underline all other letters that should be capitalized.

1. John asked, "how much do you think it will cost us to buy a dvd of that classic movie *gone with the wind?*"
2. The columbia river in oregon is known as a mecca for windsurfers because the wind blows steadily from the east down the river.
3. Chapman's *piloting and seamanship* is considered the bible for sailors everywhere, but the bible, the koran, and the talmud are holy books for certain religions.
4. I asked professor johnson if his popular course history 2302, *the history of world civilization*, had any open seats left in it.
5. The president is flying from washington, d.c., today to make a speech at the u.s. naval academy in annapolis, maryland.
6. My mother, aunt lois, and two of my uncles will attend my sister anna's graduation next week; the ceremony will be held in lipscomb hall on the college campus.
7. Jill's parents moved here from central missouri because they disliked the harsh winters in that area and they wanted to live in the east, closer to the headquarters of her father's company.
8. As I prepared to leave for college for the first time, my father said, "we know that you will work hard and make us proud of you; also, try to have a little fun."
9. The speaker closed with a pithy aphorism: "opportunity is often not recognized because it shows up dressed in overalls and looks like hard work."
10. One of my brother's favorite poems is robert frost's *two tramps in mud time*; he likes the poem because it deals with an attitude toward work.
11. The company president quoted a few lines from Henley's *invictus*, read a paragraph from peter drucker's book *management*, cleared his throat, and said, "and now to conclude."
12. For next term I have signed up for a course in calculus, the second year of french, a class in french history, and a course titled *writing the short story*.
13. The first ten amendments to the constitution, called the bill of rights, were added to provide constitutional protection to the rights of individual citizens.
14. As autumn colors the leaves in fiery reds and yellows, uncle robert and the rest of my aunts and uncles come to visit us to enjoy the fall colors here in the mountains.
15. In chapter 2 of our economics textbook, the author attempts to explain the term "gross domestic product," but he succeeded only in confusing me.

NAME _____ SCORE _____

Directions: If you find a misspelled word, underline it and write it correctly in the space at the left. (Consider an omitted or misused apostrophe a punctuation error, not a spelling error.) In the column of figures at the left, circle numbers that identify errors in the sentence. Each sentence contains at least one error.

1. Incomplete sentence
2. Dangling or misplaced modifier
3. Misused verb (wrong number, tense, or principal part)
4. Misused pronoun (wrong number or case form or weak reference)
5. Error in punctuation

_____   1. While hurriedly walking down the slippery steps of the library,
1   2   3   4   5   a most embarrasing thing happened to Paula and I.

_____   2. The reason for her attitude being, I suppose, that she had always
1   2   3   4   5   been told to remain in the background by her stern parents.

_____   3. "It is apparent, Mr. Toomey," he explained, "that the omission
1   2   3   4   5   of two commas, one apostrophe, and one key word have pro-
                        duced a humorous affect in your opening sentence."

_____   4. To accomplish anything really meaningful in college, both
1   2   3   4   5   discipline and perseverance is undoubtedly necessary.

_____   5. The dean of the law school explained the proposed law designed
1   2   3   4   5   to control goverment spending, which he thinks is desperately
                        needed.

_____   6. Located in a setting of unbeleivable beauty, I think that Dew Drop
1   2   3   4   5   Inn is an unusually desirable vacation spot.

_____   7. The manager of the tour group will be frantic, there's only
1   2   3   4   5   accommodations for 40 guests.

_____   8. The troop leader asked if either of the two girls had brought
1   2   3   4   5   their camping equipment?

_____   9. On entering the Palace of Primitive Art, everyones camera has
1   2   3   4   5   to be checked at at the door or they won't let you in.

_____   10. The truth of the matter being that by Wednesday I nearly had used
1   2   3   4   5   up all of my allowance for February.

_____
1 2 3 4 5

11. Whom did you say found the missing mail pouch laying on the municipal beach.

_____
1 2 3 4 5

12. While performing a rather complicated experiment in the labratory, some acid was spilled and burned the instructors hand.

_____
1 2 3 4 5

13. The fire could have been disasterous, there only were two guards on duty in the entire factory.

_____
1 2 3 4 5

14. Having directed the sergeant to the place where the accident occurred; we went to a nearby restaurant for sandwiches and coffee.

_____
1 2 3 4 5

15. The instructor asked how many of we sophomores had taken a coarse in advanced mathematics.

_____
1 2 3 4 5

16. "I'm sure that everybody who attended the fair today got their moneys worth," said the announcer.

_____
1 2 3 4 5

17. We looked in amazement at the psychiatrist's secretary, neither of us girls were expecting such a question.

_____
1 2 3 4 5

18. Having become involved in a rediculous argument about capital gains; it is now too close to dinner time to begin any studying.

_____
1 2 3 4 5

19. Just between you and me, I suspect that not more then one out of ten of the dormitory residents approve of the new dining-room regulations.

_____
1 2 3 4 5

20. If a person only earns a minimum wage, they cant be expected to contribute much to charity.

_____
1 2 3 4 5

21. If you was me, would you ask to be assigned to someone elses class?

_____
1 2 3 4 5

22. The dampness of the early-morning fog drifting down on ones face and hair being one of the most peaceful expieriences that I know of.

_____
1 2 3 4 5

23. Marilyn received a silver cup on which was inscribed the names of all of the preceeding winners of the award.

_____
1 2 3 4 5

24. Three counselors—Marvin, Arnold, and me—removed the peices of broken glass that were laying in the middle of the path.

_____
1 2 3 4 5

25. It's hard to understand, isn't it, how anyone could have drove their car into that deep ditch without injuring themself seriously.

General Review: Proofreading
[Lesson 28]

NAME _____ SCORE _____

Directions: If you find a misspelled word, underline it and write it correctly in the space at the left. (Consider an omitted or misused apostrophe a punctuation error, not a spelling error.) Circle at least one of the numbers at the left:

1. The sentence is correct.
2. The sentence contains a dangling or misplaced modifier.
3. The sentence contains a misused verb.
4. The sentence contains a misused pronoun.
5. There is an error in punctuation.

_____
1 2 3 4 5

1. Ted was surely surprised to learn that no sophomore in the English literature class except Jerry and him was required to take the test.

_____
1 2 3 4 5

2. "Just between you and I, the prospect of a vacation at that fishing lodge, with it's primitive accommodations, realy don't fascinate me," Fran told her husband.

_____
1 2 3 4 5

3. I like Professor Woodward better then any of my other teachers, she always tries to without embarrassing me answer my stupid question satisfactorily.

_____
1 2 3 4 5

4. Handing each of us teachers a sheet of paper, the superintendent of schools said, "Here are the criteria we must apply when we hire our next vice-principal."

_____
1 2 3 4 5

5. High on the list of building prioritys are the construction of play grounds and swimming pools in the western part of town.

_____
1 2 3 4 5

6. Mrs. Wilkins managed to keep the family intact while her husband was in the hospital doing odd jobs for the neighbors.

_____
1 2 3 4 5

7. Shirley and I studied the questions with shock and disbeleif, neither one of us were prepared for a test like this.

_____
1 2 3 4 5

8. The delivery boy entered the kitchen, smiled disarmingly, and announced, "Here's the three pizzas someone ordered."

_____
1 2 3 4 5

9. "I'm quiet sure the person the boss was referring to is not you or I," said Julia Stowe who had just joined our group around the water cooler.

_____
1 2 3 4 5

10. "Remember, you new students," said the adviser, "it's everyones responsibility to consistantly and conscientiously follow these regulations."

----

1 2 3 4 5

11. Our committee not only was dissapointed but also angry to learn that not one of our six proposals were accepted.

----

1 2 3 4 5

12. The new athletic director is an extremely pleasant young man who, I have been told, spent three years playing professional soccer.

----

1 2 3 4 5

13. Laying in my parking place was a large piece of paint-stained canvass and several empty bottles that someone has thrown from their car.

----

1 2 3 4 5

14. "Don't it seem strange that your's was the only car on the block that was given a parking ticket?" asked Lillian.

----

1 2 3 4 5

15. Having selected a seat in the back row, emptied my briefcase, and hastily reviewed my class notes; the teacher announced that the test was postponed.

----

1 2 3 4 5

16. The police sargeant asked if any of we neighbors had ate in the new restaurant during the past two weeks?

----

1 2 3 4 5

17. Is either of your two tow trucks in good enough condition to at a moments notice get to a highway emergancy?

----

1 2 3 4 5

18. "Lately there have been rumors that two of us representatives will face stiff compitition in next year's primaries," said the eminent politician.

----

1 2 3 4 5

19. Crossing the boundary into Clay County, long delays occurred because they were repairing the road for a stretch of approxi- mately four miles.

----

1 2 3 4 5

20. I can recommend Ms. Jamison enthusiastically, every editing job she did for either my business partner or I was done promptly and efficiently.

----

1 2 3 4 5

21. "There's probably not more than a dozen people in this town who I'd trust any farther than I could throw them," said the sheriff.

----

1 2 3 4 5

22. Ben is one of those people who think of only their own convenience and who are sure that their ideas are better than anyone else's.

----

1 2 3 4 5

23. It nearly took me ninety minutes to fill out the questionnaire and then they told me to come back next Wednesday.

----

1 2 3 4 5

24. The teacher asked Colleen how the migration of early Germanic tribes affected the development of the English language?

----

1 2 3 4 5

25. "When only eight years old," Edith explained, "Father took my older brother and I to France and Great Britian."

Appendix A   SENTENCE COMBINING

Sentence combining is a simple process designed to help you write more sophisticated and effective sentences. You began to employ combining techniques in Lesson 7 and its accompanying exercises, so the following exercises ought to be familiar to you. The exercises in Appendix A begin with the simplest kinds of combining, embedding an adjective from one sentence into another sentence, thus enriching one sentence and eliminating the other. The exercises then move through the formation of compound sentences and into complex sentences, those constructed with verbal phrases and subordinate clauses.

Every set in these exercises can be done in several ways, each one correct. The following example offers a good example of the possibilities:

> The man was tall.
> He was thin.
> He walked down the street.

The simplest combined form puts the adjectives *tall* and *thin* in the sentence immediately before the noun:

> The tall, thin man walked down the street.

But it is possible to move the adjectives into more emphatic positions:

> Tall and thin, the man walked down the street.
> The man, tall and thin, walked down the street.

Each of these options is correct, and each creates a slightly different sentence—a sentence that draws the reader's attention to the facts in slightly different ways.

These additional combining exercises will help your writing in two ways. First, they will remind you of different ways of expressing the same idea, and thus they will expand the range of constructions you employ in your writing. Second, the exercises will focus your attention on punctuation as you make up the combinations.

Remember that every set in these exercises can be done in several ways, all of them correct. For each set, test the various ways of creating combinations, and you will make yourself a more flexible and more effective writer.

Combine the sentences in each numbered unit into a single longer sentence.

1. The clouds built up in the west.
   The sky grew very dark.

   _____

   _____

2. Thunder crashed all around us.
   Lightning flashed ominously.

   _____

   _____

3. The thunder crashed, and the lightning flashed.
   We ran for the shelter of the nearest building.

   _____

   _____

4. We reached the shelter of the building.
   We dashed inside.

   _____

   _____

5. We closed the door.
   Lightning struck a tall tree at the edge of the field.

   _____

   _____

Combine the sentences in each numbered unit into a single longer sentence.

6. Yesterday a man and a woman went to the polls.
   They parked their cars in the parking lot.

   _____

   _____

7. They walked from the parking lot.
   They turned the corner of the building.

   _____

   _____

8. They turned the corner of the building.
   They saw a line.

   _____

   _____

9. The man and the woman walked to the end of the line.
   They began to wait for their turn to vote.

   _____

   _____

10. They chatted pleasantly with each other.
    They chatted pleasantly with those around them in the line.

    _____

    _____

Combine the short sentences in each numbered unit into a single longer sentence.

11. Two students walked into the library.
    They carried their books to a table.

    _____

    _____

12. The two students opened their books.
    Then two other students walked up to the table.

    _____

    _____

13. The students sat down together.
    They worked for about an hour.

    _____

    _____

14. Finally, one student stood up.
    She closed her books.

    _____

    _____

15. The other students stood up and closed their books.
    All four students walked out of the library.

    _____

    _____

Combine the sentences in each numbered unit into a single longer sentence.

16. The band played.
    The crowd cheered.
    The players ran onto the field.

    _____

    _____

17. The people in the stands rose to their feet.
    The band played the national anthem.
    The players lined up for the kickoff.

    _____

    _____

18. The sky overhead was sunny and clear.
    Three jets flew over the stadium.
    The crowd watched the planes.

    _____

    _____

19. The people in the stands turned their eyes to the field.
    The referee checked with the captain of each team.
    The referee blew his whistle.

    _____

    _____

20. The fans cheered wildly.
    The kicker approached the ball.
    The game was finally underway.

    _____

    _____

Combine the sentences in each unit into a single longer unit.

21. A few of the people in the office are not at work today.
    Today is the opening day of baseball season.

    _____

    _____

    _____

22. The rest of the people in the office are hard at work.
    They are doing their own work.

    _____

    _____

23. The sun was shining brightly at the ball park.
    The fans walked into the stands.
    They took their seats.

    _____

    _____

24. Tom and Jim walked toward their seats.
    They were carrying popcorn.
    They were carrying programs.
    The programs contained pictures of the players.

    _____

    _____

25. Tom and Jim arrived at their seats.
    A woman sang *The Star Spangled Banner*.
    She finished singing.
    All the fans shouted, "Play ball!"

    _____

    _____

Combine the sentences in each unit into a single longer sentence.

26. The sun rises a little later every day.
    Soon summer will be over.

    _____

    _____

27. Little kids all over the country will be looking forward to (something).
    They will be starting school soon.

    _____

    _____

28. Maintenance people in the nation's school systems will be finishing (something).
    They will be finishing painting and repairing the school buildings.

    _____

    _____

29. The repairs and painting are finished.
    The buildings are ready for students and teachers to return.

    _____

    _____

30. The magical opening day of school arrives.
    Parents all over the country breathe a sigh of relief.

    _____

    _____

Combine the sentences in each unit into a single longer sentence.

31. The pilot stopped the plane at the head of the runway.
    She pushed the throttles forward.
    The plane lifted off the runway.

    _____

    _____

32. The first powered flight occurred at Kitty Hawk, North Carolina.
    It was piloted by Orville Wright.
    The flight was 120 feet long.

    _____

    _____

33. Only one person could fly in that first plane.
    Two brothers had invented the plane.
    They were named Wilbur and Orville Wright.

    _____

    _____

34. Both brothers wanted to make the first flight.
    Only one could fly at a time.
    They flipped a coin.

    _____

    _____

35. Orville won the toss.
    He made the first powered flight.

    _____

    _____

Combine the sentences in each unit into a single longer sentence.

36. Two very early scientists presented theories about flight.
    One was named Roger Bacon.
    The second was Leonardo da Vinci.

    _____

    _____

37. Roger Bacon was an English monk.
    He read Archimedes.
    Archimedes was a Greek mathematician and inventor.
    He figured out how and why objects float in water.

    _____

    _____

38. Bacon reasoned something (about air).
    Air has something solid about it.
    Objects could float in the air.

    _____

    _____

39. Da Vinci was an Italian artist and inventor.
    He lived at the beginning of the sixteenth century.
    He created drawings of an *ornithopter*.
    Da Vinci's flying machine had wings.
    The wings flapped like the wings of a bird.

    _____

    _____

40. Giovanni Borelli was an Italian mathematician.
    He examined Da Vinci's theories and drawings.
    He proved (something) mathematically.
    No man was strong enough to lift himself by flapping a set of wings.

    _____

    _____

Combine the sentences in each unit into a single sentence by using a variety of constructions.

41. The woman was tall and slender.
    She was wearing a gray coat.
    She met a man.
    She met him in the lobby of the hotel.

    _____

    _____

42. The man was extremely young.
    He was poorly dressed.
    He had no important information to give her.

    _____

    _____

43. The man told the woman his sad story.
    She was disappointed.
    Her disappointment was extreme.
    She told him (two things).
    He was fired.
    He would never work in industrial espionage again.

    _____

    _____

44 In response, the man told her (something).
    He had just landed a job with IBM.
    The job was in their security office.

    _____

    _____

45. (Something) seems unlikely.
    The man was telling the truth.

_____

_____

Combine the sentences in each unit into a single sentence by using a variety of constructions.

46. The new office building down the street is finally finished.
    A few tenants are moving in.

_____

_____

47 Three lawyers moved into an office on the third floor yesterday.
   Today they installed a new phone system.

_____

_____

48. That building has 50 offices in it.
    Only six of them are occupied.

_____

_____

49. The rent for the offices is extremely high.
    Many of the offices are vacant.

_____

_____

50 The owners need to lower the rent.
   They might go into bankruptcy.

_____

_____

Appendix B DIAGNOSTIC TESTS

NAME _____ SCORE_____

Directions: In the space at the left of each pair of sentences, write the letter that identifies the correctly punctuated sentence.

_____ 1. a. Knocked flat by the strong gusty wind the two pine trees blocked the road; but we were able to jump over them fairly easily.
  b. Knocked flat by the strong, gusty wind, the two pine trees blocked the road, but we were able to jump over them fairly easily.

_____ 2. a. After stopping, the two men turned to the left and walked exactly 30 paces to the spot where they thought the treasure was buried.
  b. After stopping the two men turned to the left, and walked exactly 30 paces to the spot where they thought the treasure was buried.

_____ 3. a. Although, James had difficulty with the new computer program; Janice was able to figure it out easily by reading the directions.
  b. Although James had difficulty with the new computer program, Janice was able to figure it out easily by reading the directions.

_____ 4. a. The volunteers walked along the edge of the road and they picked up all the bottles, cans and paper.
  b. The volunteers walked along the edge of the road, and they picked up all the bottles, cans, and paper.

_____ 5. a. Laughing heartily at the comedian's final joke, the audience rose and gave her a round of applause.
  b. Laughing heartily at the comedians final joke: the audience rose, and gave her a round of applause.

_____ 6. a. The little boy laughed happily, and then he tore the wrapping paper from the strangely shaped, bulky birthday present.
  b. The little boy laughed happily and then, he tore the wrapping paper from the strangely shaped bulky, birthday present

_____ 7. a. After we left, the stadium crew went to work immediately on the muddy diamond and restored the field for the next game.
  b. After we left the stadium crew went to work immediately, on the muddy diamond, and restored the field for the next game.

_____ 8. a. The two girls met Tom Harry, and James at the entrance to the library and then, they all walked down the street to the restaurant.
  b. The two girls met Tom, Harry, and James at the entrance to the library, and then they all walked down the street to the restaurant.

_____ 9. a. The people sitting in the room sent text messages, played games on their phones, or dozed off while the man on the video screen worked on his long, boring speech.

b. The people, sitting in the room, sent text messages played games on their phones or dozed off, while the man on the video screen worked on his long, boring speech.

_____ 10. a. Jim Walter, who played football at the state university, is a man who makes large donations to the athletic department at the school.
b. Jim Walter who played football at the state university is a man, who makes large donations to the athletic department at the school.

_____ 11. a. Jorge's sister a woman in her early thirties, has already become a vice president at a major, Internet security firm.
b. Jorge's sister, a woman in her early thirties, has already become a vice president at a major Internet security firm.

_____ 12. a. Jackson, whose sense of humor is widely known but little appreciated, spends hours every day devising elaborate practical jokes.
b. Jackson, whose sense of humor is widely known but little appreciated spends hours every day devising elaborate, practical jokes.

_____ 13. a. "We all need" said Randall, "a week's vacation to allow us to rest up from all the work, we have done in this past month."
b. "We all need," said Randall, "a week's vacation to allow us to rest up from all the work we have done in this past month."

_____ 14. a. With a heavy snowstorm moving in from the west, the crews from the city readied the snowplows and moved them into positions where they were needed.
b. With a heavy snowstorm moving in from the west the crews, from the city, readied the snowplows, and moved them into positions, where they were needed.

_____ 15. a. Alice Randall the founder of the city's largest catering firm, has offered to provide all the food for the fund-raising dinner, and amazingly enough not charge us a cent.
b. Alice Randall, the founder of the city's largest catering firm, has offered to provide all the food for the fund-raising dinner and, amazingly enough, not charge us a cent.

_____ 16. a. Craig with the preparations for his speech completed spent an hour memorizing his outline, and then declared "Well I think I'm finally ready."
b. Craig, with the preparations for his speech completed, spent an hour memorizing his outline and then declared, "Well, I think I'm finally ready."

_____ 17. a. The two men walked down the road about 100 yards, then they began to place large orange cones, probably to keep the lines of traffic separated along the center line.
b. The two men walked down the road about 100 yards; then they began to place large orange cones, probably to keep the lines of traffic separated, along the center line.

_____ 18. a. That new heater puts out far more Btu's than our old one; surely the house will be much warmer this winter than last.

b. That new heater puts out far more Btus than our old one, surely the house will be much warmer this winter than last.

_____ 19. a. "Did that man say, 'The elevator is out of order; you will have to use the stairs?'" asked Marilyn after she had pushed the elevator button four or five times.

b. "Did that man say, "The elevator is out of order; you will have to use the stairs," asked Marilyn, after she had pushed the elevator button four or five times?

_____ 20. a. We used Karen's well organized filing system to keep track of all those receipts, without her system: everything would have become a chaotic mess.

b. We used Karen's well-organized filing system to keep track of all those receipts; without her system, everything would have become a chaotic mess.

_____ 21. a. The lawyer said, "I don't use the word 'slammer'; I prefer to use a more formal word such as 'prison.'"

b. The lawyer said, "I don't use the word "slammer," "I prefer to use a more formal word such as 'prison.'"

_____ 22. a. "Each of you should take a plate—but I see you've already served your-selves," said the woman standing at the head of the serving line.

b. "Each of you should take a plate; but I see you've already served your-selves," said the woman, standing at the head of the serving line.

_____ 23. a. Standing in front of the confused class, the instructor said, "'Re-creation' means to create again, but 'recreation' is a pastime or something we do for pleasure."

b. Standing in front of the confused class: the instructor said, "Re-creation" means to create again, but "recreation" is a pastime or something we do for pleasure."

_____ 24. a. You all should bring the following items to work tomorrow, a dictionary, two legal pads, and three already sharpened pencils.

b. You all should bring the following items to work tomorrow: a dictionary, two legal pads, and three already-sharpened pencils.

_____ 25. a. "For goodness' sake," said my elderly aunt, "There is so much food on our Thanksgiving table that we'll never be able to eat it all."

b. "For goodness sake," said my elderly aunt: "There is so much food on our Thanksgiving table, that we'll never be able to eat it all."

NAME _____ SCORE _____

Directions: In the spaces at the left, copy from the parentheses the word appropriate in serious writing.

_____
_____
1. Her remarks, along with the remarks of several other members, (appear, appears) quite (clear, clearly) in the minutes of the meeting.

_____
_____
2. We have (became, become) a very large organization; the list of our members (stretch, stretches) to three pages.

_____
_____
3. A 5-knot breeze (blew, blowed) from the shore and moved the boat (smooth, smoothly) across the bay.

_____
_____
4. Because of the cold weather, my hands (stinged, stung) when the bat hit the ball (sharp, sharply).

_____
_____
5. Laura (laid, lay) her books and jacket on the table, and then she (sat, set) down on the couch for a few minutes of rest.

_____
_____
6. The audience (raised, rose) and stood quietly as the color guard (raised, rose) the flag.

_____
_____
7. I think I (paid, payed) too much for that shirt; Jeff (bought, buyed) one just like it for half the price at another store.

_____
_____
8. We could have (swore, sworn) that we heard a car moving (slow, slowly) down the driveway last night about 1:00 A.M.

_____
_____
9. "I think that I have (broke, broken) my toe," said Tom as he hopped (painful, painfully) around the room.

_____
_____
10. The hot, tired dog (drank, drunk) an entire bowl of water when he had finally (ran, run) all the way home.

_____
_____
11. Mr. Walker, along with several of his friends, (has, have) arrived for the conference; they all (are, is) staying in rooms on the second floor.

_____
_____
12. On the wall in the corner of the library (hang, hangs) pictures of all the people who (has, have) served as principals of the school.

_____
_____
13. Mike and Joe (is, are) already here, but neither Walter nor James (has, have) arrived yet.

_____
_____
14. Neither the two women nor the man (was, were) able to say (who, whom) they had seen walking across the yard that afternoon.

_____ 15. A thousand yards (are, is) not a very long walk, but most
_____   swimmers (wear, wore) out trying to cover that same distance.

_____ 16. The number of people in the audience (appear, appears)
_____   quite large, but even more people (has, have) arrived in the last
   few minutes.

_____ 17. Wanda is one of those women who (take, takes) great pleasure
_____   in cooking for all who (visit, visits) her house.

_____ 18. The last of the dogs (has, have) wandered into the yard,
_____   and they are all (laying, lying) in their kennels, exhausted from
   the long run.

_____ 19. Look around the room and take (whoever, whomever)
_____   looks strong and clean up that pile of blocks that (are, is) littering
   up the backyard.

_____ 20. My friends (who, whom) know Harry well (think,
_____   thinks) that he works hard and deserves to get that promotion.

_____ 21. Anyone (who, whom) Anne likes is probably one of
_____   those people who (laugh, laughs) often and easily, even at jokes
   that are not very funny.

_____ 22. The next person (who, whom) walks through that door
_____   will win our prize, two tickets that (take, takes) the holders backstage at the concert.

_____ 23. "We appreciate (you, your) working all those extra
_____   hours over the weekend; there are not many (who, whom) would
   sacrifice so much for the company," said the president.

_____ 24. His cold seems (bad, badly) this morning, so perhaps it
_____   would be (good, well) for him to stay home today.

_____ 25. It was (good, well) that you could come so quickly;
_____   without heat, the house gets cold very (quick, quickly) when the
   sun sets.

_____ 26. That is my (everyday, every day) jacket; I wear the other
_____   one only when the weather is (worse, worst) than usual.

_____ 27. John said, "I feel (as if, like) I have read this book
_____   before because the characters are (real, really) familiar to me."

_____ 28. The staff (implied, inferred) from your message that
_____   you want us to come to work (earlier, more earlier) and stay later
   than we have been.

_____ 29. A (rapid-, rapidly) moving storm brought snow that
_____   piled up in (deep, deeply) drifts.

_____ 30. (Sudden, Suddenly) drops in temperature always (seem,
_____   seems) to take travelers by surprise.

NAME _____ SCORE _____

Directions: One sentence in each pair has problems with incompleteness, dangling or misplaced modifiers, faulty parallelism, or faulty comparison. In the space at the left, write the letter that identifies the correct sentence.

_____ 1. a. When I was in elementary school, my family took a trip to the Grand Canyon.
  b. When in elementary school, my family took a trip to the Grand Canyon.

_____ 2. a. Under those circumstances, you must decide to either stand your ground or turn and run for the nearest tree.
  b. Under those circumstances, you must decide either to stand your ground or turn and run for the nearest tree.

_____ 3. a. My aunt has hung all the quilts she has made in a closet under the stairs.
  b. My aunt has hung in a closet under the stairs all the quilts she has made.

_____ 4. a. In many schools the salary for the football coach is higher than the college president's.
  b. In many schools the salary for the football coach is higher than the college president.

_____ 5. a. Paul Hopkins, a man whose integrity and managerial skills cannot be questioned.
  b. Paul Hopkins is a man whose integrity and managerial skills cannot be questioned.

_____ 6. a. Looking very closely at the trail ahead of us, the edge of a steep cliff almost escaped our notice.
  b. Looking very closely at the trail ahead of us, we almost failed to notice that we had come to the edge of a steep cliff.

_____ 7. a. In a loud voice the tour guide announced as quickly as possible that we had to leave for the airport.
  b. In a loud voice the tour guide announced that we had to leave for the airport as quickly as possible.

_____ 8. a. Laura's past experience as an engineer's assistant taught her the value of careful observation, to write legible notes, and listening carefully to instructions.
  b. Laura's past experience as an engineer's assistant taught her the value of close observation, legible notes, and careful attention to instructions.

_____ 9. a. Having underestimated the time it would take to write my paper, tonight's work will take much longer than last night.
  b. Having underestimated the time it would take to write my paper, I see that tonight's work will take much longer than last night's.

_____ 10. a. I recently watched a television program that showed how to survive in the jungle with only a small knife and some string.
  b. I watched a television program that showed recently how to in the jungle survive with only a small knife and some string.

_____ 11. a. The three girls set out early to get in line. Hoping to get good seats for the concert.
  b. Hoping to get good seats for the concert, the three girls set out early to get in line.

_____ 12. a. That meeting should certainly include Beverly Lewis, a woman very skilled in the computer application we'll be examining today.
  b. That meeting should certainly include Beverly Lewis. A woman very skilled in the computer application we'll be examining today.

_____ 13. a. Before making a final decision on a computer, all the articles evaluating computers of that type should be closely examined.
  b. Before making a final decision on a computer, you should examine closely all the articles evaluating computers of that type.

_____ 14. a. Finding your way through a dense woods, an easy thing to do if you have a good GPS.
  b. Finding your way through a dense woods is an easy thing to do if you have a good GPS.

_____ 15. a. Stopping at the edge of the trail to take a picture of a beautiful vista, I dropped my camera over the side of the hill into a deep gully.
  b. Stopping at the edge of the trail to take a picture of a beautiful vista, my camera dropped over the side of the hill into a deep gully.

_____ 16. a. The master of ceremonies said after dinner that a speaker would make a PowerPoint presentation of his recent trip to the Galápagos Islands.
  b. The master of ceremonies said that after dinner a speaker would make a PowerPoint presentation of his recent trip to the Galápagos Islands.

_____ 17. a. The new president is tall and fit and with a carefully trimmed beard.
  b. The new president is tall and fit, and he has a carefully trimmed beard.

_____ 18. a. Bill's major in college is mathematics. A challenging course of study but which offers many opportunities in education and in industry.
  b. Bill's major in college is mathematics; it is a challenging course of study, but it offers many opportunities in education and in industry.

_____ 19. a. The price of our new house in that small town is much lower than our old one in the city.
  b. The price of our new house in that small town is much lower than the price of our old one in the city.

_____ 20. a. Mary throws a terrific fastball, but, of the two, Roberta has a better curve ball.
  b. Mary throws a terrific fastball, but, of the two, Roberta has the best curve ball.

_____ 21. a. The trip down that quiet river was much more pleasanter than yesterday's trip through all those rapids.
        b. The trip down that quiet river was much more pleasant than yesterday's trip through all those rapids.

_____ 22. a. We fished for several hours in that quiet cove and finally caught two huge bass about sunset.
        b. We fished for several hours in that quiet cove. Finally catching two huge bass about sunset.

_____ 23. a. We decided to climb the higher of the three peaks. The one that seemed to offer the greater challenge to our climbing abilities.
        b. We decided to climb the highest of the three peaks, the one that seemed to offer the greatest challenge to our climbing abilities.

_____ 24. a. That trail down the mountain is more straighter than the other one. Which seems to have the most twists and turns.
        b. That trail down the mountain is straighter than the other one, which seems to have more twists and turns.

_____ 25. a. My father likes to once in a while take a long, leisurely bike ride, but which seems to make him more tireder than it should.
        b. Once in a while, my father likes to take a long, leisurely bike ride, but the ride seems to make him more tired than it should.

NAME _____ SCORE _____

Directions: The following passage contains no internal punctuation, no punctuation at all except what is proper at the end of a sentence. Supply internal punctuation where it is needed, and correct any errors that you find in the passage. Make your corrections on this page.

Eli Whitney

Eli Whitney born on December 8 1765 in Westborough Massachusetts was the son of a prosporous farmer. Very early in his life his father let him develop his mechenical and busines skills by manufacturing and selling nales during the revolutionary war. Whitney graduated from Yale University and moved to the South to seek his fortune.

He made two major contributions to American industrail progress. His first invention by far the best known of his two contributions was the cotton gin. Recognizing that getting the seeds out of cotton was a labor-intensive and time consuming process Whitney set out to mechanise the work. He developed a wooden drum with hooks on it that pulled cotton fibers through a screen and left the cotton seeds behind. Whereas one man working by hand could clean 1 pound of cotton a day Whitney's machine could clean 55 pounds of cotton a day. This revolutionized cotton farming and made it immensely profitable.

His second invention or rather innovation was an application of the priciple of interchangable parts to the manufacture of guns and machinaery. Others before him had used this principle, but Whitney made it commercially workable for the first time. His first work was in the manufacutre of muskets for the US government. He reasoned that if the parts of a musket were al made to precise specifications guns could be manufactured in large numbers on an assembly line by semi skilled workers. Prior to this gun making had been the work of gunsmiths skilled artisans who built each gun individually.

Eli Whitney's assembly line for manufacturing muskets probobly influnced Henry Ford when he began to construct automobiles on an assemly line.

Appendix C   ANSWER KEY TO PRACTICE SHEETS

Practice Sheet 1, Page 5

1. drove	6. were	11. lay	16. ripped
2. parked	7. arrived	12. opened	17. made
3. was	8. created	13. featured	18. copied
4. matched	9. came	14. played	19. became
5. filled	10. packaged	15. is	20. enjoys

Practice Sheet 1, Page 6

1. One	6. people	11. All	16. team
2. lives	7. wealth	12. detectives	17. work
3. Some	8. Two	13. No one	18. occurrence
4. books	9. women	14. painter	19. man
5. deal	10. I	15. crew	20. speaker

Practice Sheet 2, Pages 15 and 16

1. 3, 6	6. 1, 1	11. 6, 4	16. 3, 5	21. 5, 4	26. 4, 1	31. 6, 3	36. 6, 4
2. 4, 2	7. 4, 1	12. 5, 5	17. 3, 4	22. 1, 6	27. 3, 6	32. 3, 5	37. 4, 4
3. 4, 1	8. 5, 6	13. 1, 3	18. 1, 2	23. 1, 4	28. 1, 6	33. 4, 4	38. 6, 4
4. 5, 1	9. 6, 4	14. 5, 4	19. 1, 4	24. 1, 3	29. 2, 4	34. 1, 5	39. 4, 1
5. 4, 3	10. 6, 4	15. 5, 4	20. 4, 5	25. 3, 5	30. 5, 1	35. 6, 5	40. 3, 1

Practice Sheet 3, Page 27

1. 1	5. EMT	9. product	13. 1	17. members
2. 1	6. 1	10. student	14. 1	18. pilot
3. technicians	7. 1	11. friend	15. 1	19. 1
4. player	8. supporters	12. support	16. hitter	20. representatives

Practice Sheet 3, Page 28

1. calm	5. firm	9. inventor	13. brown	17. rested
2. restless	6. delicious	10. good	14. 1	18. cheerful
3. sad	7. tired & dirty	11. 1	15. sight	19. student
4. exhausted	8. 1	12. sweet	16. 1	20. fan

Practice Sheet 4, Page 35

1. students opened books	11. John maintains cars
2. Senators tabled motion	12. Yolanda helps roommate
3. movie dates itself	13. roommate made grades
4. boss has cleared schedule	14. workers graded roads
5. I scheduled classes	15. they will pave roads
6. I will meet class	16. workers graveled driveways
7. Biologists have classified plants and animals	17. costs exceed capabilities
8. Johnny owns cars	18. Johann will finance car
9. he will have sold one	19. company has credited amount
10. Ownership creates work	20. company provides statement

Practice Sheet 4, Page 36

1. O.C.	6. I.O.	11. I.O.	16. O.C.
2. D.O.	7. D.O.	12. D.O.	17. D.O.
3. I.O.	8. O.C.	13. I.O.	18. D.O.
4. D.O.	9. O.C.	14. D.O.	19. D.O.
5. D.O.	10. O.C.	15. I.O.	20. D.O.

Practice Sheet 5, Pages 43 and 44

1. will have 1	21. might have 3
2. will have been 1	22. should 1
3. have 3	23. need 3
4. will be 3	24. might 5
5. will have 4	25. should 4
6. should 5	26. have been 1
7. did 3	27. has 3
8. should have 2	28. be 2
9. catch 3	29. is 1
10. made 5	30. could 3
11. should have 4	31. might 4
12. did 2	32. ought 3
13. consider 5	33. would 4
14. has been 1	34. should 1
15. has 1	35. are 2
16. has 2	36. used 4
17. have 2	37. are 1
18. give 4	38. is 5
19. has 4	39. has been 3
20. make 5	40. had 3

Practice Sheet 6, Page 53

1. 5, was named	6. 5, were colored
2. 4, was told	7. 3, has been discovered
3. 3, should have been started	8. 4, will be given
4. 3, must be filled	9. 5, has been called
5. 5, are kept	10. 4, had been read

Practice Sheet 6, Page 54

1. J. Jenkins	4. What	7. Who	10. comptroller	13. What
2. charges	5. you	8. director	11. captain	14. people
3. qualified	6. whom	9. job	12. Who	15. What color

Practice Sheet 7, Pages 65 and 66

1. 0	6. S	11. C	16. 0	21. C
2. S	7. C	12. S	17. C	22. S
3. C	8. 0	13. 0	18. 0	23. C
4. S	9. C	14. C	19. C	24. S
5. C	10. C	15. S	20. C	25. C

Practice Sheet 8, Pages 77 and 78

1. 1	6. 8	11. ·10	16. 8	21. 5	26. 3	31. 1	36. 5
2. 10	7. 4	12. 9	17. 7	22. 5	27. 2	32. 6	37. 7
3. 2	8. 7	13. 9	18. 7	23. 4	28. 2	33. 2	38. 3
4. 9	9. 5	14. 9	19. 6	24. 4	29. 1	34. 3	39. 8
5. 3	10. 6	15. 8	20. 6	25. 3	30. 1	35. 4	40. 1

Practice Sheet 9, Page 87

1. man
2. storm
3. Jim Roberts
4. Mary Allen
5. textbook
6. puppy
7. person
8. book
9. person
10. place
11. Gray's Repair Shop
12. time
13. man
14. Senator Schmidt
15. bill
16. bill
17. anyone
18. Jill Crockett
19. someone
20. tutor

Practice Sheet 9, Page 88

1. someone we can usually depend on for a ride
2. forecasters that I listen to
3. information that is inaccurate
4. sport in which failure is fairly common
5. batter who is successful
6. job in which several mistakes are allowed without any penalty
7. people for whom accuracy is very important
8. Accounting, which is not the same as bookkeeping,
9. job that requires great attention to detail
10. expression that successful accountants can use
11. balance that is reasonably close to correct
12. uncle, who is quite wealthy,
13. mistakes that he makes
14. People who don't have an extra large balance
15. money that seems to be extra
16. people with whom I graduated from high school
17. people who have left town
18. places where they can find interesting activities for recreation
19. Hawaii, where they can pursue surfing as a hobby
20. skiing, which is an exciting sport

Practice Sheet 10, Page 99

1. Ap.
2. S
3. S.
4. S.C.
5. D.O.
6. O.P.
7. D.O.
8. S.
9. Ap.
10. S.
11. O.P.
12. S.
13. D.O.
14. S.
15. O.P.
16. D.O.
17. S.
18. D.O.
19. Ap
20. D.O.

Practice Sheet 10, Page 100

1. Ap. that she had studied accounting in college
2. D.O. that Alexis had studied accounting in college
3. S.C that the candidate hold a degree in accounting
4. D.O. whose dog is sleeping in my driveway
5. D.O. when that new movie will be in town
6. S. that this movie will open before the end of the month
7. D.O. whether it will play in our small town or not
8. D.O. if you will be joining us for dinner
9. O.P. what the speaker said in his opening remarks
10. D.O. that he was misunderstood
11. D.O. who that woman in the blue suit over by that table is
12. D.O. why they were asked to attend this meeting
13. D.O. what we are expected to do at this meeting
14. S. That there is a representative here from each of our branch offices
15. D.O. if you see anyone here from the main office
16. Ap. who actually called this meeting in the first place
17. D.O. who holds the record for the most homeruns in a single season
18. D.O. where you found the recipe for this delicious chocolate cake
19. S. that such recipes are usually passed down from grandmother to mother to daughter
20. S.C. that your brother found the recipe and baked the cake.

Practice Sheet 11, Page 113

1. S.	5. S.	9. O.P.	13. S.	17. D.O.
2. O.P.	6. O.P.	10. O.P.	14. S.C.	18. O.P.
3. D.O.	7. S.C.	11. O.P.	15. D.O.	19. S.
4. S.C.	8. S.	12. D.O.	16. S.	20. D.O.

Practice Sheet 11, Page 114

1. N	5. N.	9. N	13. N	17. Adv.
2. Adv.	6. Adv.	10. N	14. N	18. N
3. N	7. N.	11. N	15. N	19. Adv.
4. Adj.	8. N.	12. N	16. N	20. N

Practice Sheet 12, Pages 123 and 124

1. _____	11. _____	21. car	31. Jorge
2. people	12. _____	22. _____	32. _____
3. _____	13. _____	23. _____	33. _____
4. people	14. woman	24. _____	34. Jorge
5. _____	15. _____	25. car	35. he
6. people	16. person	26. Jorge	36. Jorge
7. workers	17. _____	27. Jorge	37. Jorge
8. car	18. family	28. cell phone	38. _____
9. car	19. _____	29. Jorge	39. client
10. ramp	20. _____	30. Jorge	40. cell phone

Practice Sheet 13, Pages 141 and 142

1. F	9. S	17. S	25. F	33. S
2. S	10. F	18. S	26. S	34. F
3. F	11. S	19. S	27. S	35. S
4. S	12. F	20. F	28. S	36. F
5. F	13. S	21. S	29. S	37. S
6. S	14. S	22. S	30. F	38. F
7. F	15. F	23. F	31. S	39. S
8. S	16. F	24. S	32. S	40. F

Practice Sheet 14, Page 151

1. b	4. b	7. b	10. b	13. a
2. a	5. a	8. b	11. a	14. b
3. b	6. a	9. a	12. a	15. a

Practice Sheet 14, Page 152

1. b	4. b	7. a	10. a	13. b
2. b	5. a	8. a	11. a	14. b
3. a	6. a	9. b	12. a	15. b

Practice Sheet 14A, Pages 155 and 156

1. b	6. a	11. a	16. a
2. a	7. b	12. b	17. b
3. b	8. b	13. b	18. a
4. b	9. b	14. a	19. a
5. b	10. a	15. b	20. b

Practice Sheet 15, Pages 163 and 164

1. 5	6. 7	11. 3	16. 4
2. 1	7. 6	12. 6	17. 5
3. 2	8. 2	13. 2	18. 2
4. 3	9. 1	14. 7	19. 6
5. 4	10. 5	15. 1	20. 1

Practice Sheet 16, Page 171

1. a	3. a	5. b	7. a	9. a
2. b	4. a	6. b	8. b	10. b

Practice Sheet 16, Page 172

1. a	3. b	5. a	7. b	9. b
2. b	4. b	6. b	8. b	10. b

Practice Sheet 17, Pages 183 and 184

1. history, 2; math, 1
2. long, 3; report, 4
3. handsome, 3; throat, 2
4. runners, 4; long, 3
5. titles, 2; slides, 1
6. afternoon, 1; noisy, 3
7. away, 4; pasture, 2
8. up, 5; leisurely, 3
9. that, 5; immediate, 3
10. meeting, 4; short, 3
11. car, 1; sleepy, 3
12. graphics, 4; programming, 2
13. big, 3; tomatoes, 1
14. choices, 4; simplest, 3
15. chairs, 2; umbrellas, 1
16. left, 5; quickly, 1
17. office, 4; table, 1
18. short, 3; woodpile, 1
19. arrived, 4; house, 2
20. Yes, 4 o'clock, 1
21. old, 1; farmers, 2
22. project, 4; old, 3
23. inside, 5; table, 2
24. hour, 4; do, 1
25. room, 2; high-tech, 3
26. fence, 4; street, 2
27. fact, 4; people, 1
28. new, 3; jacket, 4
29. Karen, 4/5; library, 2
30. river, 2; water, 4

Practice Sheet 18, Page 193

1. us, 6
2. James, year, 1
3. wish, Karen, 5
4. Johnson, photographer, 2
5. hope, John, 3
6. was, least, 4
7. Smith, jacket, 1
8. weekend, rain, 2
9. Richard, 3
10. morning, know, 4
11. said, 5
12. room, 6
13. Williams, 1
14. Williams, 2
15. Williams, moment, 1

Practice Sheet 18, Page 194

1. R where Mr. Roberts has his office
2. R that has such good Italian food
3. R who wrote this report
4. N who wrote this report,
5. R that appear on the cover of the report
6. R whose names appear on the cover
7. R whom the company president names CFO
8. N which runs north and south at this end of town,
9. R striding purposefully into the room
10. N who is striding purposefully into the room,
11. N which are both quite impressive,
12. R who took a class from Mr. Black last term
13. who took this class from him last term,
14. N whom you met at my house last week,
15. R when my history paper is due
16. N when my history paper is due,
17. R whose pleasing personality wins many friends
18. N whose pleasing personality impresses many people,
19. N shielded from the north winds by a hill,
20. R when you have about an hour to spare

Practice Sheet 19, Page 207

1. W o'clock, oven's
2. W days, car's, rough, its
3. W 9:30
4. W it's, paper's, hours
5. W well kept
6. W "Only taxes,"
7. W Let's, we're
8. W BTU's, room's
9. W C's, D's, I'll
10. W it's
11. W impressive: deans
12. W he's, she's, hers
13. I'm, one's, it's
14. W 'Your assignment's on page 252?'"
15. C

Practice Sheet 19, Page 208

1. Jane said, "I left my tennis racquet on the hall table."
2. The shop foreman observed, "I will need to hire two new mechanics if we take. . . ."
3. My brother has often told me, "You need to lose some weight before. . . ."
4. Mrs. Carlson asked us, "Can you help me with the work in my garden tomorrow?"
5. Did she say, "The buses will be late today"?
6. The officer told me that it would be almost an hour before the road opens for traffic.
7. My inspector said that my car would need some work before it can pass the emissions test.
8. The baseball scout responded that my swing is good, but I need to improve my speed on the bases.
9. The tourists asked if we could tell them where the Chamber of Commerce is located.
10. Carl asked the service manager if his car would be ready by late afternoon today.

Practice Sheet 20, Page 215

1. W inside, robbery; finished,
2. W run?" Jaime.
3. W Jim's directions, confused and
4. W football, catch,"
5. W GPS Allison. works?"
6. C
7. C
8. W Street, it," Ray.
9. W nouns, "his" "its."
10. W dinner," Brett. "If it's, I'll, home."
11. C
12. W "AL", Alabama, "AL"
13. W Mrs. Garden; beautiful and tomatoes, green beans,
14. W "gift", "I immediately."
15. C
16. W Ph.D. chemistry and
17. W "AK" Alaska?" George. I'm
18. C
19. W me?" Martha. "My
20. W for gross domestic product'; 'gross

Practice Sheet 20, Page 216

1. Crawford, job, can't
2. There's reason, there, yours out-of-town gas?
3. trip, Barbara, who's experienced, Rosa, Kelli, rivers but
4. office, bring a laptop pens,
5. huge, dog, threateningly, would-be alleyway,
6. Drs. Jameson, right, discussion after experts' mixed-fuel
7. impressed, didn't think, players' program, didn't
8. we're face, you've changes that
9. anticipate, or . . . guess, arrive, classrooms
10. It's, now, they'd trouble. You don't suppose, do you, they're longer?

Practice Sheet 21, Pages 229 and 230

1. set, are
2. lay, woke
3. taken, spent
4. stung, swung
5. become, rode
6. written, said
7. blew, had
8. drowned, begun
9. worn, climbed
10. tore, flung
11. bought, made
12. laid, showed
13. built, sought
14. hung, found
15. knew, seen
16. shined, shone
17. burst, drew
18. broken, dragged
19. frozen, sunk
20. thrown, dealt
21. eaten, spoken
22. flown, driven
23. run, spoken
24. rang, went
25. rose, raised
26. were, was paying/paid
27. lent, repaid
28. clung, hung
29. lain, set
30. slain, given
31. caught, fell
32. chosen, chose
33. swum, been
34. dug, brought
35. gave, given
36. done, did
37. crept, spent
38. come, stole
39. brought, taught
40. close, left

Practice Sheet 21, Pages 231 and 232

1. C came
2. have been have seen
3. C C
4. C chosen
5. to admit C
6. became C
7. C broken
8. began is
9. blown C
10. lying came
11. C C
12. laid announced
13. taken have been sitting
14. sworn saw
15. said C
16. worn paid
17. C C
18. have been stolen
19. C C
20. C C
21. C sprung
22. laid sit
23. to see left
24. rose crept
25. be found
26. were gone
27. were try out
28. C was
29. take registers
30. C found
31. had showed
32. rang C
33. had to go
34. sets C
35. C glowed
36. hung sat
37. set scratched
38. raised shown
39. given dropped
40. shaken blown

Practice Sheet 22, Page 239

1. need	5. seems	9. have	13. are	17. do
2. is	6. do	10. come	14. are	18. was
3. seem	7. hang	11. fills	15. repeats	19. were
4. were	8. is	12. is	16. doesn't	20. sit

Practice Sheet 22, Page 240

1. C	5. C	9. stand	13. C	17. have
2. plays	6. have	10. line	14. thinks	18. are
3. is planning	7. C	11. is	15. enjoy	19. were
4. Is	8. were	12. C	16. has	20. C

Practice Sheet 23, Pages 249 and 250

1. b, it	5. b, it	9. b, she, her, she	13. b, you	17. b, their
2. a, they	6. b, which	10. a, their, you	14. a, it	18. b, their, their, their
3. b, they	7. b, which	11. b, their, their	15. a, they it	19. b, which
4. b, you, you	8. b, she, her, she	12. a, their, their	16. a, it	20. b, this

Practice Sheet 24, Page 259

1. 4	5. 6	9. 5	13. 1	17. 4
2. 5	6. 4	10. 1	14. 4	18. 1
3. 2	7. 6	11. 7	15. 5	19. 2
4. 3	8. 1	12. 4	16. 6	20. 4

Practice Sheet 24, Page 260

1. whoever	5. its	9. me	13. her	17. her
2. your	6. I	10. she	14. she	18. us
3. Who	7. she	11. Whoever	15. Your	19. We
4. yours	8. me	12. Whomever	16. them	20. she

Practice Sheet 25, Page 269

1. unbelievable, Adv.	6. high, Adv.	11. colt, Adj.
2. horse, Adj.	7. I, Adj.	12. respected, Adv.
3. flying, Adv.	8. all, Adv.	13. is known, Adv.
4. tall, Adv.	9. has been falling, Adv.	14. was broadcast, Adv.
5. grade, Adj.	10. rain, Adj.	15. played, Adv.

Practice Sheet 25, Page 270

1. wonderfully	6. faster	11. Apparently	16. rough
2. quiet	7. closely	12. well	17. roughly
3. bad	8. repeated	13. calm	18. sure
4. almost	9. readily	14. carefully	19. some
5. really	10. badly	15. clearest	20. highest

Practice Sheet 26, Pages 285 and 286

1. Unless, annoyed	11. teach, think	21. suspect, besides	31. sense, should have
2. great, really	12. assent, affect	22. any way, invitation	32. Since, right
3. as far as, a great many	13. advice, very	23. inferred, course	33. extremely, those
4. Almost, somewhat	14. way, distance	24. that, incredibly	34. disinterested, among
5. farther, very	15. sorts, used	25. should, take	35. am not, all right
6. not very, enthusiastic	16. bare, breath	26. adopted, adapted	36. anywhere, desserts
7. number, might have	17. rein, patience	27. past, already	37. personal, stationery
8. altered, accept	18. principal, whole	28. later, proceed	38. two, too
9. All together, altogether	19. It's, quiet	29. heard, incidents	39. criteria, extremely
10. nature, angry	20. led, as if	30. dyed, seen	40. that, off

Practice Sheet 27, Page 299

1. analyses	6. commandos, oes	11. fungi, funguses	16. octopuses, octopi	21. spies
2. aquariums, a	7. Dutchmen	12. handfuls	17. plateaus, plateaux	22. theses
3. archipelagoes, os	8. fathers-in-law	13. infernos	18. podia	23. turkeys
4. assemblies	9. flamingos, oes	14. lilies	19. scarves, scarfs	24. vortices, vortexes
5. Charleses	10. folios	15. mice	20. sheriffs	25. wives

Practice Sheet 27, Page 300

1. C	11. C	21. W	31. W	41. C
2. C	12. C	22. W	32. C	42. W
3. W	13. C	23. C	33. C	43. C
4. C	14. C	24. W	34. C	44. C
5. C	15. W	25. W	35. W	45. W
6. C	16. W	26. C	36. W	46. W
7. W	17. W	27. C	37. W	47. C
8. C	18. C	28. C	38. W	48. C
9. C	19. W	29. C	39. C	49. C
10. W	20. C	30. C	40. C	50. C

Practice Sheet 28 has no key

There is no key for the practice sheets for this lesson as there are many possibilities for constructing the sentences.

INDEX